STUDIES IN MODERN BRITISH RELIGIOUS HISTORY

Volume 26

CONSCIENCE, CONSCIOUSNESS AND ETHICS IN JOSEPH BUTLER'S PHILOSOPHY AND MINISTRY

STUDIES IN MODERN BRITISH RELIGIOUS HISTORY

ISSN 1464–6625

General editors
Stephen Taylor
Arthur Burns
Kenneth Fincham

This series aims to differentiate 'religious history' from the narrow confines of church history, investigating not only the social and cultural history of religion, but also theological, political and institutional themes, while remaining sensitive to the wider historical context; it thus advances an understanding of the importance of religion for the history of modern Britain, covering all periods of British history since the Reformation.

Previously published volumes in this series are listed at the back of this volume.

CONSCIENCE, CONSCIOUSNESS AND ETHICS IN JOSEPH BUTLER'S PHILOSOPHY AND MINISTRY

BOB TENNANT

THE BOYDELL PRESS

First published 2011
The Boydell Press, Woodbridge

ISBN 978–1–84383–612–4

The Boydell Press is an imprint of Boydell & Brewer Ltd
PO Box 9, Woodbridge, Suffolk IP12 3DF, UK
and of Boydell & Brewer Inc.
668 Mt Hope Avenue, Rochester, NY 14620, USA
website: www.boydellandbrewer.com

A CIP catalogue record for this book is available
from the British Library

The publisher has no responsibility for the continued existence or accuracy of
URLs for external or third-party internet websites referred to in this book,
and does not guarantee that any content on such websites is,
or will remain, accurate or appropriate.

Papers used by Boydell & Brewer are natural, recyclable products
made from wood grown in sustainable forests.

Printed in Great Britain by
CPI Antony Rowe, Chippenham and Eastbourne

Contents

Acknowledgements

I am grateful to a number of people for their kindness and support during this project: all at the Boydell Press; Stephen Prickett, who gave his early encouragement; Nicky Trott and John Coyle, successive heads of Glasgow's Department of English Literature; Jeremy Gregory, for organizing the Wesley tercentenary conference, my paper for which provided some material for Chapter 4; Robert Ellison, William Gibson, Michael Houlden, John Morgan-Guy, Peter Rowlands, Laura Stevens and Anne Tennant, who read parts of the draft – in some cases large parts. As mathematical physicists Michael and Peter were invaluable in commenting on Chapter 3. John Hendy QC helped refresh my knowledge of the master–servant relationship in English law.

The staff of many libraries supplied their usual assistance with their usual courtesy and warmth – for what other group of people could that adjective constitute such high praise? I am especially grateful to staff at the Bodleian and Worcester and Oriel Colleges; the British Library; Cambridge UL; Durham UL (especially Margaret McCullom) and Durham Cathedral Library; the Scottish National Library; John Rylands; and the Glasgow UL (especially Archie and Linda in the Research Annexe).

Special thanks should be recorded to all at Eighteenth-Century Collections Online and Early English Books Online. How did we ever manage without you?

Thanks above all to Sandy Brewer, for comprehensive support and criticism and for sharing her knowledge of the history of the British Sunday School movement and of the twenty-first century. And to Jackson, most beautiful of cats, and Brother, his brother, who for the common good labours tirelessly among the local wildlife and who typed much of the first draft.

'Happy the man ...'

Abbreviations

Short title used	Work
Fifteen Sermons (1726)	*Fifteen Sermons Preached at the Rolls Chapel*, London, James and John Knapton, 1726
Fifteen Sermons (1729)	*Fifteen Sermons Preached at the Rolls Chapel. The Second Edition, corrected: To which is added a Preface*, London, James and John Knapton, 1729
The Analogy	*The Analogy of Religion, Natural and Revealed, to the Constitution and Course of Nature. To which are added Two brief Dissertations ...*, London, James, John and Paul Knapton, 1736
Six Sermons	[a term used sometimes, for convenience and without bibliographical propriety, for the six sermons below, when discussed as a group]
SPG 1739	*A Sermon Preached before the Incorporated Society for the Propagation of the Gospel in Foreign Parts; ... on Friday, February 16, 1738–9*, London, J. and P. Knapton, 1739[1]
Spital 1740	*A Sermon Preached before the Right Honourable the Lord-Mayor ... on Monday in Easter-Week, 1740*, London, John and Paul Knapton, 1740
Martyrdom 1741	*A Sermon Preached before the House of Lords ... Jan. 30, 1740–41*, London, J. and P. Knapton, 1741
Charity Schools 1745	*A Sermon Preached ... on Thursday May the 9th, 1745*, London, B. Dod, 1745
Accession 1747	*A Sermon Preached before the House of Lords ... on Thursday, June 11, 1747*, London, John and Paul Knapton, 1747
Infirmary 1748	*A Sermon Preached ... for the Relief of Sick and Diseased Persons ... on Thursday, March 31*, London, H. Woodfall, 1748

---

[1] The SPG minutes record the first three months of the year as, for example, '1738' instead of '1738–39'. The researcher needs to be aware that allowance for this was not made when the SPG archives in Lambeth Palace were bound, so that chronological order is not preserved.

Other abbreviations

CCEd   *Clergy of the Church of England Database*
EEBO   *Early English Books Online*
EECO   *Eighteenth-Century Collections Online*
DNB   *Dictionary of National Biography*
OED   *Oxford English Dictionary*
ODNB   *Oxford Dictionary of National Biography*
SPCK   *Society for Promoting Christian Knowledge*
SPG   *Incorporated Society for the Propagation of the Gospel in Foreign Parts*

Note

Throughout, except in quotations, the calendar has been treated as if the year began on 1 January.

Introduction

Joseph Butler (1692–1752) is a major figure in the history of the anglophone world. In terms of influence and the sales of his works he was perhaps the most successful British theologian and moral philosopher of the eighteenth century. Later, in the nineteenth century, his influence grew further, in the British Empire and the USA, because of the rapid increase in university-level education. The question was asked seriously and frequently, whether he or Newton were the greater thinker.[1] It is probable that more copies of his works were produced in the nineteenth century than of all other eighteenth-century British theological and philosophical writers combined. He is also generally agreed to be of continuing relevance, and arguably the greatest moral philosopher whom Britain has yet produced, deploying a methodology of the most extraordinarily fruitful suggestiveness. He provides, more than almost any other early modern writer, shocks of recognition: the things he says, and the way he formulates them, simply seem right – they have been taken into the common stock of our thinking – and yet remain exciting and persuasive. However, it has often been forgotten, and sometimes even doubted, that he was committed to the supreme and sufficient moral authority of the Bible; to the spiritual economy of the Church of England's liturgy; and to the systematic theology of Protestant Christianity. His works are the product of his profession: teaching and guiding his congregations and junior clergy and helping set out the mission of the Church in the language and priorities of his day. Reading Butler with this in mind is a core strategy of the present book.

His works are best considered in three groups. The first is his prentice work: the correspondence with Samuel Clarke (1713–17), about metaphysics, and *Fifteen Sermons* (1726), about Christian ethics and human nature. The second, his main achievement, is a corpus comprising the second edition of *Fifteen Sermons* (1729), *The Analogy* (1736) and the two dissertations appended to it. Taken together, these offer a more integrated approach to those same subjects, but in an apologetic context and with a reconsidered methodology. The third group, from his years as a bishop, is the six occasional sermons (1739–1748),

---

[1] For example, 'this immortal work' (J. H. Overton, *The Church in England*, 1897, vol. II, p. 223); 'shall we place higher the name of [Isaac] Newton or of Butler?' (Archibald Campbell, Bishop of London, *Harmony of Revelation and the Sciences. Address delivered to the Members of the Edinburgh Philosophical Institution, November 4, 1864*, Edinburgh, 1864, p. 5); 'not inferior in profound thought to [Locke or Newton] … and [with] a more permanent effect on the destinies of men than both …' (Albert Barnes, *Butler's Analogy: A Review*, London [1860], p. 11).

which we will sometimes refer to collectively as *Six Sermons*. These applied his doctrine and extended his thought into various social issues. Associated with them is a clutch of minor publications, letters and fragments.

Butler's intellectual trajectory was of a common type: adolescent agonizing (his protracted student years, with a long-delayed move from Presbyterianism to the Church of England); youthful research (as a lecturer and parish priest); mature administration (as a bishop). In his late fifties he showed signs of decreasing intellectual vitality and died at the age of sixty. Living in times when the established church carried an unusually heavy political burden he was committed to the Whig cause through his background in Dissent as well as philosophically. However, although he gave his loyalty unreservedly – in a conscious act of will – he was politically passive, abstaining from politics (career requirements and public duties always excepted) even to the point of straining his close and lifelong friendship with Thomas Secker, the future Primate. Despite the testimony of a few close friends he was probably a lonely, disturbed and not very likeable man, consciously regulating his life in society according to his status and his theory of ethics. Under the terms of his will his secretary destroyed his private papers.[2] In the glimpses which remain to us he did not impose himself socially. He is remembered riding around his parish on a black pony, very fast; turning up to a late-night supper in London, saying little and saying it not well; walking in his garden late at night, worrying about whether society collectively could go mad. He subordinated his personality to the requirements of his duty, a word which for him had no negative emotional colouring but, indeed, denoted a healthy mentality.

After his death his works' already high standing rose: his moral philosophy in Oxford, and later in Cambridge, Dublin, Glasgow and beyond; his practical theology in the SPG and SPCK; and then, in the nineteenth century, across academic and public life in Britain and the anglophone world in general. Indeed, they continue to be influential to the present day in academic disciplines far beyond his home base of moral philosophy. At no point, however, has there been a consensus in presenting his achievements in a fully integrated way.

> [Though] his system is incomplete, it does seem to contain the prolegomena to any system of ethics that can claim to do justice to the facts of moral experience.[3] [*The Analogy*] was perhaps the one hammer-

---

[2] 'Lastly, 'tis my positive and Express will that all my Sermons Letters and papers whatever which are in a Deal Box lock'd directed to Dr. Forster and now standing in the little Room within my Library at Hampstead be burnt without being read by anyone as soon as may be after my decease' (codicil to Butler's will, quoted from the working copy in Durham University Library, MS SGD 35/12). The Durham copy, with annotations by a diocesan official, contains information not available from the British Library original.

[3] C. D. Broad, *Five Types of Ethical Theory*, London, 1930, p. 83.

blow which, more than any other, caused the rapid and almost complete demise of Deism.[4]

Such claims seem still to represent the fragmented received opinion about Butler. The first acknowledges his power of analysis and exposition – his departure from both scholastic and Cartesian tradition to a direct appeal to common experience. For Broad, at least, he stands with Spinoza as virtually a fresh start for moral philosophy. The second comment, about his contemporary impact, is historically more questionable and records less a tribute than a general agreement to set aside a work whose moment was felt to be long passed. It fails to engage with the fact that in the nineteenth century *The Analogy* was to go through at least eighty-six editions. Taken together, these quotations hold in place the wedge driven between Butler's two main works in the late nineteenth century.

The present book seeks to reintegrate Butler and offer a fresh, close reading of his work. It advances a number of suggestions: that his apologetic strategy was not to defeat deism (whatever that term means) but to build a consensus by demonstrating that all human knowledge and activity rested on the same probabilistic basis; that, in his account, human consciousness is intrinsically an ethical faculty (or perhaps function) created by the conscience; that human society and morale are fundamentally dynamic rather than institutional; that inclusiveness – the containing of the entire population in networks and circles – was the basis of a politically and ethically healthy society; and, that, so as to resist destructive forces proceeding from the deep structures of political and human nature, social policy should tend towards equality and be impelled by personal and community activity, supported, but not driven, by legislation.

Butler was conscious that his adaptation of mathematical theories of probability entailed that he could not achieve conclusiveness of demonstration or finality of victory. His acceptance of this point is a central component of his method and aims.

Besides this he was a pastoral minister. He did not seek to destroy given tendencies of thought and humiliate their practitioners but to persuade that things were not as simple as the enthusiasts supposed and that some of their claims were unwarrantable affronts to the facts of nature as accepted and negotiated by the practical activities of generation after generation.

This comes close to home. The rampancy of enthusiasm is something which the present day has in common with Butler's. If, as is widely claimed, the modern 'globalized' world is becoming multi-polar, a congeries of jostling parochialisms creating anxiety in the status quo, the science of human nature may seem the more important as a unifier and medium of dialogue. It is thinkers in non-philosophical disciplines who have most boldly addressed this. Evolu-

---

[4] Kenneth Hylson-Smith, *The Churches in England from Elizabeth I to Elizabeth II, vol. II: 1689–1833,* London, 1997, p. 33.

tionary biologists like Antonio Damasio;[5] geneticists like Richard Dawkins, with his curiously medieval 'memes';[6] mathematicians like Eric B. Baum, with his computer-derived model of the mind;[7] evolutionary zoologists like Stephen Jay Gould;[8] Einar Haugen and the ecolinguists;[9] Manuel Castells, the sociologist:[10] these, selected somewhat at random, are representatives of new disciplines producing a flood of work – so high and wide that it defies the bibliographer – which appropriates the metaphysical speculations which were largely rejected by twentieth-century philosophy. That their ideas are usually vulnerable to logical and philosophical critique matters less than that they are obviously about questions felt to be important within self-confident and rapidly developing disciplines. Above all, they are vivacious – 'enthusiastic', to recycle the eighteenth-century term. In the 1720s and 1730s Butler engaged with their contemporary equivalents, the speculative works of natural philosophy and deism, applying to them a new bundle of concepts to create a synthesis which disciplined their vivacity without oppressing it. He did not kill theologically unorthodox thinking; he offered it rehabilitation. Thus he was welcomed by 'atheists' like Hume and mathematicians like Bayes as well as by both evangelical and orthodox churchmen. If it were done critically and accurately, it might be interesting to identify Butler's methods and bring them together with the works of the deists' modern equivalents. In his deployment of the young discipline of probability theory, Butler virtually called for a programme of research into the human psychological and sociological condition; indeed, in effect he launched it with his *Six Sermons*. In Chapter 6 we will look at the nineteenth-century failure to engage with this, symbolized by the 'Whewell project', which was proposed for that specific purpose.

Butler contrasts with the confident and elegant Berkeley and Hume in being sharply aware of the culture-bound nature of his ethics and of the prime importance of dynamic social cohesion and consensus, a word which did not exist in English until more than a century after his death; his brilliance in improvising terms which supplied its hitherto unacknowledged absence deserves recognition. Butler was a Whig nation-builder, but he was also not only widely-read both in contemporary European and classical theology and philosophy but was also unusually aware of humankind's animality, the unstable and contingent status of our civilization and the at least partial validity of cultures other than his own.

---

5 Antonio R. Damasio, *Descartes' Error: Emotion, Reason, and the Human Brain*, New York, 1994.
6 Richard Dawkins, *The Selfish Gene*, Oxford, 1976.
7 Eric B. Baum, *What is Thought?*, Cambridge, MA, 2004. 'The Mind is a Computer Program' is the title of his second chapter.
8 For example, Stephen Jay Gould, *Rocks of Ages: Science and Religion in the Fullness of Life*, London, 2001.
9 Einar Haugen, *The Ecology of Language*, Stanford, CA, 1972.
10 Manuel Castells, *The Information Age: Economy, Society and Culture*, Oxford, 1996–2000.

He was also the most practically-oriented of contemporary philosophers; his range is immense. He originated strategies ultimately adopted for emancipating slaves and evangelizing colonial peoples. He saw that the capitalist mode of production deskilled workers and that there must be compensatory public policy and infrastructure. He theorized about the relationship between personal and public charity, about extended families and the need for workers to maintain their rights. He contributed to what in essence became the constitution of the Episcopalian Church of the USA. As a moral and political philosopher, a case can be made for his being a basis of the Scottish Enlightenment – Hume, Kames, Reid and Adam Smith all acknowledged their debt – as well as 'one nation' Toryism and Liberalism: his works were edited by Gladstone himself.

Striking coincidences between Butler and some moderns are the observation that the mind is a survival mechanism, with a degree of functional redundancy, and the belief, to use Baum's rather incautious words (*What Is Thought?*, p. 3), that there is a possible 'analogy' between the 'short list of [simple] laws [of physics]' and a similar set which shows that 'the mind is a complex but still compact program that captures and exploits the underlying compact structure of the world'.

The doctrine which Butler synthesized from his critiques of Hobbes and Shaftesbury was that our healthy, vigorous and unashamed self-interest must combine with a consistent devotion to the duty of loving our neighbours and engaging our interests with theirs. Humankind, he says explicitly, is an animal species, part of and totally involved in the natural world and able to function as any other animal. It is also, however, a specially-equipped moral species, with a faculty or function (the conscience) which is fed data by the affective cognitive faculties, so that the mind necessarily interprets such data in an ethical way. The individual person's engagement with the social and natural worlds is characterized by a process of development, the education of the conscience and the growth of consciousness. To improvise a metaphor from computer technology, he believes that we process data through an 'ethics programme'. If we disable the programme, or use only a narrow range of its capabilities (by wilfully corrupting our conscience), our consciousness etiolates and we degenerate towards a merely animal status. Thus he emphasized the 'steady state' aspect of society as against the Social Contract-style 'big bang' foundation myth; schematically flat power-relationships as against hierarchical; the generation-on-generation redevelopment, through education, of the ethically human, rather than its once-for-all institution.

Alan G. Padgett has remarked that 'theology, done properly, is a form of worship'[11] and this seems to apply to Butler, his work painfully shaping subjective experience into forms appropriate to the public sphere. Thus he is a quin-

---

[11] Alan G. Padgett, *Science and the Study of God: A Mutuality Model for Theology and Science*, Grand Rapids, MO, 2003, p. xiii.

tessentially practical philosopher: his ethics and his anti-deist work are closely allied theoretically to his social philosophy. The connection can be stated briefly.

Broadly, for a Christian apologist there are three types of response to the proposition that an analysis of the natural world is all that is necessary as the basis for a good and happy life, which is roughly what the deists claimed.

One is to reinforce the doctrine that Christianity is a religion of the Book. This requires the development on the one hand of critical methods to investigate textual authority and on the other of an account of the modes of reception of the Book. Unlike pioneering contemporaries such as Richard Bentley,[12] Robert Lowth,[13] Thomas Newton[14] and his own follower, John Heylyn,[15] Butler mentioned this only in passing.

Another type of response is the juridical: to maintain that a culturally dominant phenomenon is not required to defend itself strategically but is entitled to unpick attacks on it in detail. It is obvious that Butler did pursue this strategy.

The third type of response is to develop propositions that the Christian revelation is empirically effective, for example, that it effects changes in human understanding and conduct. It seems, equally, that Butler also pursued this. His theory of a developing human psychological nature, which could be presented in secularized form, is set in a framework of ritual and ceremony (so that he was attacked as a closet Roman Catholic): democratic constitutional forms, educational institutions, liturgical practices, organized civic charity. His account of ecclesiastical toleration provides safeguards against the elitism implicit in a communion from which some, chiefly from lower social classes, dissented.

The juridical context and the forensic nature of much of his argument entails that his thought is connected to his use of language with an intimacy unusual in a philosopher, even in a period which produced Berkeley's and Hume's dialogues. Butler's works remain pulpit rhetoric, addressed to congregations whose members were assumed to have differing degrees of sophistication, commitment and ability to concentrate. His writing is semantically dense, but his syntax often goes round the houses, sometimes to avoid ambiguity, sometimes to distinguish between what he is saying and what he might carelessly be supposed to mean, and sometimes to occupy positions which he wishes to avoid defining too precisely according to contemporary expectations. He thinks somewhat at an angle to his contemporaries and immediate predecessors, particularly Locke. He is so conscious of the fundamentally metaphorical and messy nature of language that lengthy stretches of *The Analogy* are devoted to discus-

---

12 Richard Bentley, *Proposals for Printing a New Edition of the Greek Testament and St. Hierom's Latin Version*, London, 1721.
13 Robert Lowth, *De sacra poesi Hebraeorum*, Oxford, 1753.
14 Thomas Newton, *Dissertations on the Prophecies*, London, J. & R. Tonson, 1754, an anti-deist work.
15 *Theological Lectures at Westminster-Abbey*, London, J. & R. Tonson and S. Draper, 1749. See pp. 128–9.

sions of it.[16] However, even allowing for the presumed excision of many of the perorations,[17] his sermons are shorter than the contemporary average and there is evidence that he reworked in order to compress: some of the later occasional sermons, written quickly to deadlines and published as delivered, are notably longer and more discursive. It is therefore a matter for consideration, why *The Analogy*, whose advertised thesis could be discussed adequately in fifty pages, bulks so large. As a Victorian critic observed,

> [*The Analogy*] bears plenary evidence that it must have been written by ... a condensing and epitomizing process. Any man may be satisfied of this who attempts to express the thoughts in other language than that employed in the Analogy. Instinctively the sentences and paragraphs will swell out to a much greater size, and defy all the powers we possess to reduce them to their primitive dimensions ...[18]

The Analogy is indeed an extremely concentrated work; simply, its anti-deist apologetics is less its main subject than its spine.

His works' origin in a rhetorical genre and their lack of scholarly apparatus creates an immediacy which has shaped Butler literature curiously. The most striking thing about reviewing this is the frequency with which he is cited ahistorically. A modern psychologist writes as if he were occupying a chair in a sister university. A lawyer reports his contribution to present-day law. A philosopher cites two dozen living colleagues, and in among them appears Joseph Butler, unadorned by his episcopal title, and without even the observation that he has not published much lately. Not even Hume is treated thus. This is the result of his intense concentration on clearing away difficulties and supporting commonsense positions by penetrating insight and a general goodwill.

> [His] article [about] toleration contains excellent doctrine, and shews him to be endowed with good-nature and humanity.... He thinks that ... virtue consists only in doing good to our neighbour; that neither the Greeks nor Romans were idolaters; opinions, which, however erroneous, are an indication of his benevolent disposition.

---

[16] In this he was not unique. Monboddo's sprawling *Essay on the Origin and Progress of Language* (Edinburgh, A. Kincaid and W. Creech, 1773–1792), is an extreme example of the Enlightenment's growing awareness of the special nature of language. The first chapter of Jay F. Rosenberg's *Accessing Kant* (Oxford, 2005) is devoted to 'Intelligibility' (e.g. p. 27), in part because modern philosophical language has departed so far from even Kant's 'categorical' style of expression that Kant is on the verge of needing the support of literary criticism to recover his full meaning. With Locke we have also seen such a project: William Walker's *Locke, Literary Criticism, and Philosophy* (Cambridge, 1994).

[17] Sermons traditionally contain four consecutive sections: the introductory *exordium*; the *exegesis* (expounding the doctrine so as to explain how it flows from scripture); the *application* (of doctrine to the congregation's circumstances); and the culminating *peroration*.

[18] Albert Barnes, *Butler's Analogy: A Review*, p. 9.

Matters of faith apart, and making allowance for the one's dogged commitment and the other's addiction to irony, Butler and Voltaire seem not so very dissimilar.[19]

Modern Butler studies

Since the present work attempts a refreshed reading of Butler it seems useful to survey the present state of affairs. Beside a handful of journal articles, a small body of really excellent work about Butler has been produced in the last generation. Terence Penelhum's *Butler* came first (London, 1985). Where analysis and interpretation are concerned, to seek disagreement is to find, but Penelhum's book is a masterly account in the conventional manner. Here and in other publications he provided the standard Butler for the late twentieth century. The collection we will refer to as *Tercentenary Essays*, edited by Christopher Cunliffe,[20] is also of very high quality and some contributions are outstanding, most notably Jane Garnett's 'Bishop Butler and the *Zeitgeist*: Butler and the Development of Christian Moral Philosophy in Victorian Britain' and Basil Mitchell's 'Butler as a Christian Apologist'. Present disagreements with some of its contents are mostly left tacit. Cunliffe's article in the *Oxford Dictionary of National Biography* (2004) is an effective short biography and overview of his work, while Lori Branch's essay 'Bishop Butler' (2007)[21] is a sensitive and balanced account which pays due regard to his priesthood.

This corpus, however, accepts a pre-existing account of the context and presents again a familiar Butler. By contrast, the present work, while asking to rest on their achievement, delivers an account of the development and exercise of Butler's praxis – his ethics, pastoral record, social policy and relations with the Church – by applying a variety of critical tools, rather than offering a systematized account of his doctrine.

In general, there has been a lack of development in dedicated Butler studies. E. C. Mossner's *Bishop Butler and the Age of Reason* (New York, 1936), which assembled an account of his ideational context, was still considered sufficiently useful to be reprinted ahead of the tercentenary (Bristol, 1990). As the twentieth century wore on *The Analogy* dropped out of print in Britain, for the first time since the original publication, but *Fifteen Sermons* remained a textbook, often with the dissertation *Upon the Nature of Virtue* included: W. R. Matthews's British edition (London, 1914) was reprinted frequently, despite its textual inaccuracies, and several new teaching editions appeared in America.

---

[19] The quoted passage was, in fact, written of Voltaire. Advertisement to *The Philosophical Dictionary for the Pocket*, London, Thomas Brown, 1765, the first, anonymous, English translation of Voltaire's *Lettres philosophiques* (1764).

[20] *Joseph Butler's Moral and Religious Thought: Tercentenary Essays*, London, 1992.

[21] In the *Oxford Handbook of English Literature and Theology*, ed. Andrew Hass, David Jasper and Elisabeth Jay, Oxford, 2007, pp. 590–606.

Butler's oblivion as a theologian was mentioned earlier. The cases of Ian Ramsey and David Jenkins, both successors of his as Bishops of Durham, are enlightening. While drawing on Butler, but in seeking to make positive apologetic statements, both misrepresented him. It would be premature to suggest that Butler's demise as a theologian was due to sloppy reading, but it certainly cannot have helped.

Ramsey, in his 1957 book, *Religious Language* (London, 1957)[22] was prompted by the thought that the reductionist linguistic analysis of the logical positivists could help strengthen discourse about religion. He found a boldness in Butler's formulation of the mind–body distinction, a 'discernment without which no distinctive theology will ever be possible'; a 'self-awareness' that is more than 'body awareness' (p. 15). He argued persuasively that a question about personal motive quickly develops into a series which can only be ended by the protest, or affirmation, that 'I'm I' (pp. 40–3) but attempted to support it with the observation that, for Butler, the conscience is obeyed 'because it is conscience' (p. 43). This is simply not true; as we will see, Butler accepted, and made this fact central to his analysis of the human condition, that the conscience could be undeveloped, become diseased, be cured and educated and therefore be overruled.

Jenkins, in his foreword to *Tercentenary Essays*, remarked (p. ix) that Butler remains a 'quarry for ideas', likening his approach to faith to Hans Küng's 'reasoned trust'. Jenkins, however, thinks that Butler separates from Küng in his belief that God's existence is a matter of rational demonstration. None of Butler's works, however, argues such a thesis, the central point of *The Analogy*, indeed, being the contrary: that all human propositions are probabilistic, liable to the same set of objections and tested by their usefulness. Actually, 'reasoned trust' is a rather good description of Butler's faith. He took many things for granted and was very interested in the bigger proposition that it is useful that people can and do take things for granted. He was more interested in faith than belief. If theologians read Butler more closely they might find him more interesting.[23]

Turning to philosophical literature, the shortcomings in historicity and the aggressive secularism of much twentieth century writing has meant that most modern philosophical work around or stimulated by Butler is vulnerable to challenge in detail and is sometimes seriously misconceived. Indeed, one recently active area of discussion is based on a misunderstanding of the single word, 'cool'. Too many scholars have been acquainted with Butler at second-hand or from selections of texts made by third parties whose interested motives they do not appreciate.

[22] He was later to deliver a lecture about Butler to the Friends of Dr Williams's Library: *Joseph Butler ... Some Features of his Life and Thought*, London, 1969.
[23] The present work, indeed, may be considered a rebuff to Jenkins' doubt that 'Butler [produces] ... a method [useful for] the late twentieth century' (pp. viii–ix).

Nevertheless, in the twentieth century, and in their different ways in both Britain and America, Butler was reinvented as a secular, mainstream philosopher. The *Fifteen Sermons'* Preface, the sermons *On Humane Nature* (the modernized spelling, 'human', unwittingly disturbing his aim)[24] and the dissertation *Of the Nature of Virtue* serving as exemplars and provoking a body of high-quality work. Because this corpus embodied only a restricted range of his thought, Butler studies inevitably lacked the richness and diversity of those around Hobbes, Locke, Berkeley and Hume. G. E. Moore placed Butler's dictum, 'Everything is what it is, and not another thing' at the head of his *Principia Ethica* (Cambridge, 1903), appropriating him for the new, analytical philosophy, and based on it the argument that while material qualities are 'perfectly worthless in themselves [i.e., without intrinsic values], [they] are yet essential constituents of what is far from worthless'. In plain English, values, including ethical values, exist only because they attach to real objects and transactions in the real world. C. D. Broad[25] discussed Spinoza, Butler, Kant, Hume and Sidgwick and rated Butler very highly, as providing the definitive critique of theories of moral egoism. We have already noted his view that '[Though] his system is incomplete, it does seem to contain the prolegomena to any system of ethics that can claim to do justice to the facts of moral experience'. Broad's great reputation in America[26] perhaps ensured Butler's continued prominence there. One of Broad's achievements was to develop the suggestion that Butler's robust and commonsense thinking could survive a supposed lack of systematic analysis and terminological accuracy, whose deficiencies could be supplied by modern philosophers. Thus, the twentieth century recast him in a manner directly opposed to the nineteenth century 'proto-Kant' reading. Austin Duncan-Jones's *Butler's Moral Philosophy* (Harmondsworth, 1951), Alan White's 'Conscience and Self-Love in Butler's Sermons', an especially accurate analysis,[27] and, a decade or two later, P. Allan Carlsson, Anders Jeffner and T. A. Roberts produced dedicated studies within this narrative.[28] Oddly, and rather against the prevailing temper of at least some philosophical strains – perhaps because of the oblivion into which *The Analogy* and *Six Sermons* had fallen – twentieth-century philosophers and theologians alike ignored the centrality of doubt and uncertainty in Butler's method and ideology.

---

24 Butler's works use both 'humane' and 'human'. While some of this is due to the compositor, 'human' tends towards a biological sense ('the Structure of the human Body', *The Analogy*, 1736, p. v), while 'humane' tends to acknowledge the ethical nature of humankind.

25 *Five Types of Ethical Theory*, 1930.

26 As an example, the contributors to Paul Arthur Schilpp's *The Philosophy of C. D. Broad*, New York, 1959, a dialogue with Broad about his work, were largely American. In this work, Broad couples Butler with Plato and Sidgwick as 'very eminent moral philosophers' (p. 820).

27 *Philosophy*, vol. 27, no. 103 (October 1952), pp. 329–44.

28 P. Allan Carlsson, *Butler's Ethics*, The Hague, 1964; Anders Jeffner, *Butler and Hume on Religion: a Comparative Analysis*, trans. Keith Bradfiel, Stockholm, 1966; T. A. Roberts, *The Concept of Benevolence: Aspects of Eighteenth-Century Moral Philosophy*, London, 1973.

So much for background. Recently, Butler has been largely set aside by historians of philosophy. He features abundantly in Isabel Rivers's two volumes,[29] which plot the development of a stream of philosophical and religious ideas in eighteenth-century Britain, but its subject inevitably relegates him to the supporting cast. The contributors to the *Cambridge Companion to Thomas Reid*[30] neglect him, despite Reid's large and acknowledged debt, and, more understandably, he is entirely ignored by the *Cambridge Companion to Berkeley*,[31] where he features not once in the index to this volume about his friend. In the Reid Companion, Terence Cuneo's essay on 'Reid's Moral Philosophy' provides an inaccurate account of Butler. To say, for example, that 'Reid, like Butler, takes it to be clear that the basic principles of morality are … "immediately perceived without reasoning, by all men come to years of understanding" …' may be true of Reid but most certainly not of Butler, who expends much effort on the Christian revelation's morally educative effect on the conscience and the social being. We will see, moreover, that Butler thought it quite possible for a person to live adequately, at least in a society buttressed by Christianity, with a corrupt conscience and an ethically undeveloped mind – indeed, he cites the moral philosopher Shaftesbury as an example.[32] However, several scholars, notably John P. Wright,[33] have contributed to this mapping process and, in possibly the best single article of recent years dedicated to Butler, Paul A. Newberry provided that rarity, an accurate reading of an aspect of his work,[34] while Donald Baxter has written convincingly on Butler's account of identity.[35] The question of the relationship between Berkeley's and Butler's thinking awaits assessment.

In America theorizing about moral education continues to be an active area of scholarship and Butler remains important, at least in some streams. The school of Lawrence Kohlberg has resorted to Butler's combination of created nature and socialization and maintained it as a living area of enquiry.[36] Butler's extreme position on the mind–body problem continues to attract philosophers who tend from ethics towards accounts of the mind. Thus, Sydney Shoemaker[37] has sought

---

[29] *Reason, Grace, and Sentiment*, Cambridge, 1991 and 2000.

[30] Ed. Terence Cuneo and René van Woudenberg, Cambridge, 2004.

[31] Ed. Kenneth P. Winkler, Cambridge, 2005.

[32] The belief that 'Butler exalts conscience' is of long standing: these words are quoted from G. E. M. Anscombe's essay 'Modern Moral Philosophy', reprinted in *Collected Papers, volume iii: Ethics, Politics and Religion*, Oxford, 1981. To make this claim without qualification can only be the result of a careless reading of too few texts.

[33] 'Butler and Hume on Habit and Moral Character', in *Hume and Hume's Connections*, ed. M. A. Stewart and John P. Wright, University Park, PA, 1995, pp. 105–18.

[34] 'Joseph Butler on Forgiveness: A Presupposed Theory of Emotion', *Journal of the History of Ideas*, vol. 62, no. 2 (April 2001), pp. 233–44.

[35] 'Identity in the Loose and Popular Sense', *Mind*, NS, vol. 97, no. 388 (October 1988), pp. 575–82.

[36] For example, Lawrence Kohlberg, *The Philosophy of Moral Development: Moral Stages and the Idea of Justice*, San Francisco, CA, 1981. See also Kenneth E. Goodpaster, 'Kohlbergian Theory: A Philosophical Counterinvitation', *Ethics*, vol. 92, no. 3 (April 1982), pp. 491–98.

[37] Sydney Shoemaker, 'Self and Substance', *Noûs*, vol. 31, Supplement: Philosophical Perspectives, 11, Mind, Causation, and World (1997), pp. 283–304.

to uphold Butler's and Reid's 'immaterial substance' theory of the self against Locke and Hume and to introduce practical and *ad hominem* arguments which suggest that there remains life in Butler's strategy of suggesting that philosophical debate is nothing unless a component of practical social living. Philosophers like Henson, Sober, Phillips, Estlund and Nelson have presented theories about selfishness, self-love, happiness and mutual benevolence grounded in readings of Butler.[38] There was an exchange between Millar and Brinton about what Butler meant by 'following nature'.[39] A distinct philosophical stream (for example, Novitz and Dillon) has developed, from critiques of Butler, thinking about respect, self-respect and forgiveness.[40]

On a wider stage, Butler continues to be of importance to the American school of liberal philosophers who place ethics at the centre of their accounts of polity and society. We will glance at these at the end of Chapter 6.

Turning from the philosophers, more specialized recent work about Butler has emerged from a wide variety of disciplines. It may surprise that Butler is a significant figure in the historiography and theory of the law. In a later chapter, for example, we will notice Alexander Welsh's demonstration of his influence on nineteenth-century jurisprudence in Britain and India.[41] Several other scholars have resorted to him when working on modern-day practical questions. Most interestingly, J. P. Day used him as an authority when building a case against the American social policy of discriminatory compensation, principally by applying his thinking on 'resentment' as a corrective to the implications of modern legislation and legal practice. Butler is quoted, decontextualized and almost as if he were a contemporary, his thought nevertheless being sufficiently robust to serve Day's purpose.[42]

He has also emerged as a political theorist. Although his opposition to Locke is not widely or sufficiently recognized – David Nicholls, *God and Government in an 'Age of Reason'* (London, 1995) is an exception – so that he is still routinely cited as a follower rather than critic of Locke, he is increasingly

---

[38] Richard G. Henson, 'Butler on Selfishness and Self-Love', *Philosophy and Phenomenological Research*, vol. 49, no. 1 (September 1988), pp. 31–57; Elliott Sober, 'Hedonism and Butler's Stone', *Ethics*, vol. 103, no. 1 (October 1992), pp. 97–103 (a hedonistic reply to Henson); David Phillips, 'Butler and the Nature of Self-Interest', *Philosophy and Phenomenological Research*, vol. 60, no. 2 (March 2000), pp. 421–38; David M. Estlund, 'Mutual Benevolence and the Theory of Happiness', *The Journal of Philosophy*, vol. 87, no. 4 (April 1990), pp. 187–204; William N. Nelson, 'Mutual Benevolence and Happiness', *The Journal of Philosophy*, vol. 91, no. 1 (January 1994), pp. 50–1.

[39] Alan Millar, 'Following Nature', *Philosophical Quarterly*, vol. 38, no. 151 (April 1988), pp. 165–85; Alan Brinton, '"Following Nature" in Butler's Sermons', *Philosophical Quarterly*, vol. 41, no. 164 (July 1991), pp. 325–32; Alan Millar, 'Reply to Brinton', *Philosophical Quarterly*, vol. 42, no. 169 (October 1992), pp. 486–91.

[40] David Novitz, 'Forgiveness and Self-Respect', *Philosophy and Phenomenological Research*, vol. 58, no. 2 (June 1998), pp. 299–315; Robin S. Dillon, 'Self-Forgiveness and Self-Respect', *Ethics*, vol. 112, no. 1 (October 2001), pp. 53–83.

[41] 'The Evidence of Things Not Seen: Justice Stephen and Bishop Butler', *Representations*, no. 22 (spring 1988), pp. 60–88; 'Burke and Bentham on the Narrative Potential of Circumstantial Evidence', *New Literary History*, vol. 21, no. 3 (spring 1990), pp. 607–27.

[42] 'Compensatory Discrimination', *Philosophy*, vol. 56, no. 215 (January 1981), pp. 52–72.

claimed as a source of American liberalism. Edward W. James made claims about Butler's contribution to the foundations of American political liberalism[43] which, although there is no acknowledged continuity, seems to have been extended by James Duban, who documents Butler's political influence in nineteenth-century America and hints that the Butlerian conscience is a source of the USA's sense of moral authority and, presumably, the interventionist instincts of its liberal tradition of foreign policy.[44] Daniel Walter Howe makes a related point, that a reading of Butler changed the balance of the American tradition of Cambridge Platonism.[45] The present work avoids this potentially enormous but largely unexploited field of research into the American cultural and political assimilation of Butler.[46] A study of Butler's influence in America would be most interesting and might test theories about fundamental differences between the British and American liberal traditions and even the development of policy, for example, the different traditions of foreign policy and healthcare provision, which surely have ethical as well as political origins.

In discussions of public policy as an intersection of politics and religion, Stephen Darwall[47] shows excitingly (e.g., p. 156) that notions of personal dignity and (self-)worth arise from the ethics of the Hume–Adam Smith axis. Butler avoids these concepts, whose prevalence has become a social problem in our own narcissistic times, but when Darwall writes (p. 157) that 'Smith's political theory amounts to institutionalizing a neo-stoic ethic of self-command', he perhaps identifies a rift between two neo-Stoic traditions, or between Butler's doctrine of social benevolence and Smith's conscious alternative to it, a system from which a doctrine of command politics was to develop. Butler's anxiety-tinged social thinking, in which consensus generates authority, provided the nineteenth century with a robust and practical model, but we await a critical study of the social policy implications.

Where recent accounts of religion in the context of political culture are concerned, material has been generated by several studies as groundwork for a correction of the secularist and so-called 'progressive' historiography of the mid-twentieth-century British school. The present author sketched a movement among theologians, philosophers and poets who sought to create an ideological stream distinct from Locke's.[48] David Nicholls (*God and Government in an 'Age of Reason'*) described the tradition, in words taken from the moral philosopher

[43] 'Butler, Fanaticism and Conscience', *Philosophy*, vol. 56, no. 218 (October 1981), pp. 517–32.
[44] 'Consciousness and Conscience: The Liberal Christian Context of Thoreau's Political Ethics', *The New England Quarterly*, vol. 60, no. 2 (June 1987), pp. 208–22.
[45] 'The Cambridge Platonists of Old England and the Cambridge Platonists of New England', *Church History*, vol. 57, no. 4 (December 1988), p. 482.
[46] Mossner, a member of this tradition, is culturally so disabled from recognizing irony in Butler that in his 1936 monograph he calls the SPG sermon 'a travesty of all practical morality' (p. 172).
[47] Stephen Darwall, 'Sympathetic Liberalism: Recent Work on Adam Smith', *Philosophy and Public Affairs*, vol. 28, no. 2 (spring 1999), p. 150 n23.
[48] 'The Anglican Response to Locke's Theory of Personal Identity', *Journal of the History of Ideas*, vol. 43, no. 1 (January 1982), pp. 73–90.

Richard Price ('I reckon it happy for me that this book [i.e., *The Analogy*] was one of the first that fell into my hands', p. 46) and recorded the main influences on Price as the Cambridge Platonists, Newton, Samuel Clark and Butler. David Brown found the possibility of continuing relevance to modern Christian apologists in Butler's account of doubt.[49] C. D. A. Leighton positioned the nonjuring mystic William Law as a significant mainstream Counter-Enlightenment thinker, and linked him, Butler and Hutchinson.[50]

Concluding a survey of treatments of Butler beyond the confines of academic moral philosophy, there has been James Downey's study of Butler as preacher[51] but only the occasional article from a literary critical direction seeking to demonstrate Butler's influence, for example on Alexander Pope and Jane Austen,[52] although there also exists a thin stream of critical analysis of the nineteenth-century novel which asserts an origin in Butler of certain characteristics of fictional narrative.[53]

More serious, of course, is his present non-existence as a theologian and his active 'derecognition' as a founder of modern psychology.[54] As we will see, even those most eminent modern moral philosophers who cite him with respect seem not to have read beyond a small selection of his works and their frequent confessions of ignorance are too lacking in contrition to merit absolution. Perhaps theologians are the most curious case. If any one British Christian secured in the mainstream the primacy of trust and faith, and the validity and creativity of doubt, it was Butler. He not only wrote a book about it but, proportionately to the contemporary market, it was probably the biggest-selling 'heavy' book of the nineteenth century. So why, rather than being sensitively revisited, has he been ignored?

---

[49] 'Butler and Deism', in *Tercentenary Essays*. See his remarks about 'a declining confidence in the power of reason. Not only does Butler retreat from proof to probability ...' (p. 8). The implications of the words 'confidence' and 'retreat' do scant justice either to Butler or to the modern communities of scientists and theologians.

[50] 'William Law, Behmenism, and Counter Enlightenment', *The Harvard Theological Review*, vol. 91, no. 3 (July 1998), pp. 301–20.

[51] *The Eighteenth Century Pulpit*, Oxford, 1969.

[52] Philip Drew, 'Jane Austen and Bishop Butler', *Nineteenth-Century Fiction*, vol. 35, no. 2 (September 1980), pp. 127–49; James McLaverty, 'Warburton's False Comma: Reason and Virtue in Pope's "Essay on Man"', *Modern Philology*, vol. 99, no. 3 (February 2002), pp. 379–92.

[53] For example, Jan-Melissa Schramm, *Testimony and Advocacy in Victorian Law, Literature and Theology*, Cambridge, 2000.

[54] Contrast the generosity of a mid-twentieth-century working psychologist's tribute to Butler (Joan Wynn Reeves, *Body and Mind in Western Thought*, Harmondsworth, 1958) with his complete absence from Graham Richards, *Mental Machinery: The Origins and Consequences of Psychological Ideas. Part 1 1600–1850*, London, 1992, and Suzanne R. Kirschner, *The Religious and Romantic Origins of Psychoanalysis*, Cambridge, 1996.

The present work

This book is intended as a refreshed reading of Butler's works, starting from the obvious and incontrovertible facts that today his work is linguistically and ideationally exotic and that he was professionally obliged (and willing) to put his philosophical activities to the service of his ministry. In any case, there is no point in flattering modern sensibilities with the pretence that he was secretly an atheist or a career-conscious conformist.

Because a close reading, rather than a history, is offered, the book avoids the somewhat speculative distinction between 'deist' and 'Christian'. It is suggested that Butler saw the self-proclaimed deists somewhat sympathetically, as contemporaries with much ground in common but with inadequately developed analyses and narratives based on an etiolated account of the human condition. Butler's works are more or less orthodox in their sincere adherence to Protestant doctrine – clearly, he does not provide classic formulations and expressions of the doctrines of redemption or the Trinity (apologetics tend by their nature to be unbalanced and unsystematic) – but, especially in the case of *The Analogy*, they are grounded in contemporary casts of thought and seek to rehabilitate deistic contemporaries within the broad Church.

Butler's terminological fuzziness has been accepted and welcomed. Butler thought that it did not blur necessary distinctions but pointed out that human nature and the world itself are theoretically not amenable to systematic treatment. For example, if he draws back from stating definitely whether the 'affections' are either, on the one hand, externally stimulated emotions or, on the other, a faculty within the structure of the mind, it is because he thinks such an enquiry is not worthwhile, and possibly worse than that. Idle speculation is morally and philosophically dangerous. It encourages reification, which he avoids rigorously, although his nominalism is qualified by the supposition that the set of words about ethics comes from somewhere and resonates in our common humanity. A study of his thinking about language is needed, but in the confines of the present book it was possible to provide a chapter about this or one about his reception in the nineteenth century, but not both. The latter was chosen, as tending to appeal to a broader selection of the likely readership.

The absence of a correct and complete edition was a great hindrance. David E. White's excellent 2006 edition is for the general reader, not the scholar.[55] It at last offers a textually improved alternative to the abundant but increasingly fragile supply of the nineteenth-century Bohn's Standard Library and Gladstone editions. The philosopher and theologian, however, need to be aware that White does not present the latest editions prepared by Butler; that he modernizes aspects of the orthography and typesetting in the interest of accessibility; and that his editorial apparatus is minimal. He offers the best texts yet published of

---

[55] *The Works of Joseph Butler*, ed. David E. White, Rochester, NY and Woodbridge, 2006.

a selection of the fragments and minor works, including some corrections of previous errors of transcription, but the presentation of accessible, clean texts necessarily conceals evidence important to the scholar. The 'standard' editions, Gladstone (1897) and Bernard (1900), are atrociously inaccurate. Bernard's is much the better, but contains bad mistakes and presents an orthographically inauthentic, and therefore misleading, text, especially in its transcriptions and arbitrary divisions of the surviving manuscript fragments. Gladstone's contains hundreds of non-orthographical errors and arbitrary editorial decisions, and, one fears, is sometimes wilfully misleading. Gathering and organizing materials for what amounts to new editions was therefore a necessary preliminary for Chapters 1 and 2, and parts of 4. It is hoped that the text does not advertise this labour over-ostentatiously.

Chapter 1 gives an account of the surviving correspondence between Butler and Samuel Clarke. It is based on two theses: that the issues discussed in it were fundamental to his future work; and that Butler's professed satisfaction with Clarke's replies was sincere, although possibly a matter less of conviction than of disciplined submission. This chapter appears to be the first published discussion of this correspondence and corrects some crucial editorial and interpretive errors.

Chapter 2 discusses *Fifteen Sermons*. Based on materials for a variorum edition, it analyses the changes introduced into the second, 1729, edition (after which Butler introduced few significant changes). It demonstrates that the revisions constituted a comprehensive review of the first edition and a strengthening of its account of the centrality of love. It shows that *Fifteen Sermons'* critiques of Hobbes and Shaftesbury were of fundamental importance to his life's work. This chapter has no methodological precedent.

Chapter 3 considers certain aspects of *The Analogy* (1736). It makes the novel claim that the book originated in now-lost Rolls sermons, and perhaps others from the 1730s, reworked, supplemented by new material and organized into an apologetic. It continues by analysing Butler's key tools: the terms 'analogy', 'probability', 'tendency' and 'doubt' and their relation to contemporary mathematics. This is used, together with a discussion of the term 'personal identity', to describe how Butler revisited his ethical theories and their underlying metaphysics.

Chapter 4 analyses Butler's application of his thinking to his conduct as Bishop of Bristol. It offers the first published discussions of his consecration and his relations with John Wesley[56] and argues the consistency of his ministry to his philosophical method.

Chapter 5 is the first detailed published discussion of the *Six Sermons* (1739–48). It suggests that they present a fairly coherent political and social platform based on his ethics and his account of the human condition. It gives an account

---

[56] Apart from Frank Baker's affectionate hagiography, *John Wesley and the Church of England*, 2nd edn, London, 2000.

of his concept of 'charity', its practical institutional applications, its relationship with contemporary employment law and its application to theories of citizenship and slavery.

Chapter 6 concerns some narrowly limited aspects of the posthumous use of Butler's work in the period to the end of the nineteenth century: one hundred and fifty years for when it is almost impossible to overstate his importance. A statistical analysis of the SPG anniversary sermons, 1751–1800, provides material for a preliminary account of his ethics' absorption into Church of England missionary theology. Five case studies then demonstrate his suggestiveness for Romanticism and early nineteenth-century Christology; the attempts to present him as a systematic moral philosopher of a proto-Kant variety, as a proto-Utilitarian and a theoretical stabilizer of Victorian religiosity.

This book is not a biography (although it presents some new facts and interpretations and most chapters include biographical narrative), nor a church history, nor a history of ideas. It is a critical reading. A decision was taken to minimize the account of influences on Butler and his ideational place among his contemporaries, who are used, if at all, mainly to help clarify his meaning. The network of acknowledged influences by Butler on contemporaries and successors has been set aside, except in Chapter 6's specific case studies. Claims of influence are suppositious, even those supported by documentation. Statistical investigations seem more useful: in the long run, language cannot lie. With regard to Hutcheson, whose main work was published posthumously, and long after Butler's own works, I do not think assumptions about Butler's knowledge of the early *Essay on the Nature and Conduct of the Passions and Affections* (1728) add to an understanding of his critique of Shaftesbury.[57] In the case of Epictetus, a treatment of Butler's undoubted debt seems unnecessary to make intelligible what he actually wrote. The temptation to discuss Butler's debt to Pascal, some of whose works he certainly knew, has been resisted. There is no evidence that Butler knew directly his work on probability theory.[58]

---

[57] This point is discussed briefly in Chapter 1, p. 27, n. 32.
[58] Albino Babolin summarized the case and relevant scholarship up to 1992 in his contribution to *Tercentenary Essays*.

1

Student

Main texts: the Butler-Clarke letters

Introduction

This chapter discusses the correspondence between the youthful Butler and Samuel Clarke, who, although prevented by his suspected Trinitarian heterodoxy from high office in the Church,[1] was the friend and translator of Isaac Newton[2] and was at this time considered Britain's leading metaphysician. Clarke had given the Boyle lectures for 1704 and 1705 and published them under the titles, *A Demonstration of the Being and Attributes of God: more particularly in answer to Mr. Hobbs, Spinoza, and their Followers. Wherein the Notion of Liberty is Stated, and the Possibility and Certainty of it Proved, in Opposition to Necessity and Fate* (1705) and *A Discourse concerning the Unchangeable Obligations of Natural Religion, and the Truth and Certainty of the Christian Revelation* (1706). Butler read at least the 1705 volume.

The correspondence, which extends from 1713 to 1717, may best be examined in three groups. The first consists of five letters by Butler about two points arising from the lectures, together with Clarke's five replies. These ten letters date from 4 November 1713 to 8 April 1714. Clarke published them, together with a reply to another anonymous critic, as *Several Letters to the Reverend Dr. Clarke, from a Gentleman in Glocestershire, relating to the first Volume of the Sermons preached at Mr. Boyle's Lecture; with the Dr's Answers thereunto*.[3] They appeared both as an addendum to the fourth edition of the

---

[1]   The traditional Arian reading of Clarke (and Newton) has been corrected by Thomas C. Pfizenmaier (*The Trinitarian Theology of Dr. Samuel Clarke (1675–1729): Context, Sources, and Controversy*, Leiden, 1997) and 'Why the Third Fell Out: Trinitarian Dissent', *Religion, Politics and Dissent, 1660–1832*, ed. Robert D. Cornwall and William Gibson, 2009, pp. 17–34. It nevertheless remains the case that Clarke was so suspected, and treated, by his contemporaries.
[2]   Isaac Newton, *Optice: ... Latine reddidit S. Clarke*, London, S. Smith & B. Walford, 1706.
[3]   London, James Knapton, 1716. Quotations are from this edition. Because the letters are quite short, and to facilitate cross-checking between editions, references are given to the relevant letters rather than to page numbers.

lectures[4] and in the volume of correspondence between Clarke and Leibniz.[5] Clarke was probably all the more happy to publish the exchange because, in the light of concerns raised in Convocation by his *Scripture Doctrine of the Trinity* (1712), he had complied with the suggestion that he desist from writing about Trinitarian doctrine.[6]

Only a single item of the second group of letters survives, sent by Butler from London and dated April 1714. The third group, of three letters from Butler and two replies by Clarke, were written in a burst between 30 September and 10 October 1717, when Butler, having at last conformed, was a commoner at Oriel College, Oxford. The second and third groups were not published until the nineteenth century, although the third group, expunged of the more personal passages, was projected for publication by Clarke with the 'next edition' of the Leibniz correspondence, from which we can surmise that there were no further relevant letters by Butler.[7]

The complete surviving correspondence, although well-known, has never been published in an accurate edition. Nor has it previously been the subject of a published analysis, not even in Penelhum's *Butler* or the *Tercentenary Essays*, where one might have hoped for it, since it connects not only with the debates around English deism but also with Descartes, Locke and Leibniz. Unfortunately, since the correspondence belongs as much to Clarke as to Butler, a full discussion is not appropriate here.

The letters do, however, give insights into the development of Butler's thinking and, at one point, show the genesis, on an identifiable day and in rough-hewn form, of an idea which has come to be of fundamental importance to Western thinking about the mind. In what follows, for convenience and ease of identification, Butler's letters are numbered consecutively and suffixed with his initial (1B to 9B). Clarke's replies are given the same numeral as the Butler letters to which they respond, with the suffix C. Thus 1B is answered by 1C.[8]

---

4 Samuel Clarke, *A Demonstration of the Being and Attributes of God ... The Fourth Edition, Corrected. There are added in this Edition, Several Letters to Dr. Clarke from a Gentleman in Glocestershire*, London, James Knapton, 1716.

5 *A Collection of Papers, which Passed between the Late Learned Mr. Leibnitz, and Dr. Clarke, in the Years 1715 and 1716. Relating to the Principles of Natural Philosophy and Religion*, London, James Knapton, 1717.

6 ODNB, 'Samuel Clarke'.

7 Clarke marked Letter 9B, 'These to be added to Leibnitz's Letters next Edition' and struck through all but the first paragraph. British Library Add. Mss. 12, 101 (13).

8 The best available texts are as follows:

First group (source: Butler-Clarke, *Several Letters*, 1716): Letter 1B: Anon to Clarke, 4 November 1713; Letter 1C: Clarke to [JB], 10 November 1713; Letter 2B: Anon to Clarke, 23 November 1713; Letter 2C: Clarke to [JB], London, 28 November 1713; Letter 3B: Anon to Samuel Clarke, 5 December 1713; Letter 3C: Clarke to [JB], 10 December 1713; Letter 4B: Anon to Clarke, 16 December 1713; Letter 4C: Clarke to [JB], 29 January 1714; Letter 5B: Anon to Clarke, 3 February 1714; Letter 5C: Clarke to [JB], 8 April 1714.

Second group (source: British Library Add. Mss. 4370): Letter 6B: J Butler to S Clarke, Hamlin's Coffee House (London), Tuesday morning [11 or (more likely) 18 April 1714]; [no reply by Clarke is extant].

Butler was born in Wantage, Hertfordshire, on 18 May 1692, of a Presbyterian father, Thomas.[9] He was to become 'the first conformist of this family',[10] which was sufficiently well-off that money was not to be a great limiting factor in his life; indeed, he was later to provide financial support to relatives and others.[11] At the age of about nineteen, he was sent to an academy run by Samuel Jones in Gloucester (it moved to Tewkesbury soon after Butler joined). Since Butler recorded that he never wanted any but a ministerial career, it may be presumed that he wished to prepare for the Presbyterian ministry. Despite Jones's youth (he was barely thirty) he was successful in assisting the development of a large number of ministerial and civic careers.[12]

Jones had been born in Pennsylvania and educated in Wales and at the University of Leiden. His curriculum, based on his Leiden notes, was exceptionally wide and the new academy acquired a correspondingly high reputation. It comprised sixteen students, including the man who was to become Butler's closest friend, Thomas Secker (later Archbishop of Canterbury), as well as Isaac Maddox (later Bishop of Worcester) and John Bowes (later Lord Chancellor of Ireland). There were also several students who became prominent in the world of Dissent: Samuel Chandler; Jeremiah Jones, author of the posthumous *A New and Full Method of Settling the Canonical Authority of the New Testament* (1726), which was reprinted by the Clarendon Press as late as 1827; and Daniel Scott, the theologian and lexicographer, who dedicated the two volumes of his *magnum opus*, a Greek lexicon, to Secker and Butler in 1745–6.[13] By Secker's account, the members rose at five and were obliged always to speak Latin, except when below stairs amongst the family.[14] Students were required to translate the Hebrew Bible into Greek, read Isocrates and Terence and, a clear reminder of Jones's Leiden days, study the logic of Heereboord as well as mathematics and Locke's *Essay Concerning Human Understanding*. Jones's library was 'composed for the most part of foreign books ... very well

---

Third group: Letter 7B (source: *European Magazine*, London, J. Sewell, vol. 41, January 1802, pp. 9–10): J Butler to S Clarke, Oriel College, 30 September [1717]; Letter 7C (source: *ibid.*; said to have been written on the reverse of 7B, as a draft reply): [SC] to [JB], 6 October 1717; Letter 8B (source: Oriel College; MS presented in 1852 by J. H. Newman): J Butler to S Clarke, Oriel, 6 October 1717; Letter 8C (source: *ibid.*, drafted by Clarke on reverse of 8B): [SC] to [JB], 9 October 1717; Letter 9B (source: British Library, Add. Mss. 12101 (13)): J Butler to S Clarke, Oriel College, 10 October 1717; [no reply by Clarke is extant].

[9] Except where indicated, the details of Butler's biography are taken from Thomas Bartlett's *Memoirs of the Life, Character and Writings of Joseph Butler*, London, 1839, still the standard biography, and cross-checked with Christopher Cunliffe's ODNB article. Durham University, Lambeth Palace and the Bodleian (in this case Rawl. J. 4° 5 (221)) contain some source material.

[10] Bodleian: Rawl. J. 4° 6 (63).

[11] Butler's account books in Oriel College record payments to his brother.

[12] For a detailed account of Jones's academy and its curriculum, see Robert G. Ingram, *Religion, Reform and Modernity in the Eighteenth Century*, Woodbridge, 2007, pp. 29–32.

[13] Scott also published *An Essay towards a Demonstration of the Scripture-Trinity*, London, J. Noon, 1725, in which was included a *Letter to ... Dr. Clarke ... concerning the Difficulty of Reconciling Prescience and Free-Will*, by another hand.

[14] DNB, 'Samuel Jones', quoting Secker, letter to Isaac Watts, 18 November 1711.

chosen'.[15] Perhaps on his own account, Butler read other contemporary publications, including Clarke's Boyle lectures and Shaftesbury's ethical works. His letters to Clarke suggest, what would otherwise seem unlikely, that he may have read some of the early works of his future friend George Berkeley. The list of students emphasizes how porous were the walls between Old Dissent and the Church of England,[16] how small the theological, as opposed to cultural, differences and how generally comradely the relationships.[17] However, to move out of the intimate family of Old Dissent into the Anglican mainstream was a profound social change which required detailed justification. Thus Maddox, who, like Butler, became noted for his charitable benevolence and kept on good terms with dissenters, was to become best known for his *Vindication of the Government, Doctrine, and Worship of the Church of England, established in the Reign of Queen Elizabeth* (1733).

The Tewkesbury correspondence

When Butler first wrote to Clarke he was four months from the end of his time with Jones. His letters constituted a definite, but not yet decisive, step towards a profound change in his life. The first letter, like all of this group, was sent anonymously and dated 4 November 1713, initiating a master–disciple relationship which ultimately was to result in Clarke's successful sponsorship of Butler's first official appointment, the Rolls Chapel lectureship, and a thirty-year association with the Knapton publishing house. It was posted in Gloucester, ten miles away, by Secker, despite Butler's love of riding.[18] 'Here Mr Butler wrote his Letters to Dr Clarke: which I used to carry to Glocester, & put into the Post-Office there; and then to fetch the Answers; that the Correspondence might be kept secret.'[19] Secker's role was certainly to preserve anonymity, as the sender's name was transmitted with the mail (the postal charge was paid by the recipient).

Butler's first letter (1B) is by far the longest of the series. It starts in an enigmatic way, noting that he is 'one who is to you a perfect Stranger, tho' you are not so to him; but I hope the Occasion will excuse my Boldness'.[20] Whether

---

[15] Secker, quoted by Ingram, p. 32.

[16] Despite being Presbyterians, the Butler family rented their house from the dean and chapter of Windsor, next to the parish churchyard (Bartlett, p. 2).

[17] W. M. Jacob, *The Clerical Profession in the Long Eighteenth Century*, Oxford, 2007, documents both the positive and negative, revealing (Chapter 8, 'Pastoral Care') the frequent non-competitiveness at local level as well as the complexities in Anglican ministers' sense of identity as clergy (e.g. p. 209).

[18] An anecdote from Henry Phillpotts, bishop of Exeter, dating from 25 January 1835, records him 'riding a black pony, and riding always very fast' in his Stanhope days (Bartlett, p. 77).

[19] *The Autobiography of Thomas Secker, Archbishop of Canterbury*, ed. John S. Macauley and R. W. Greaves, Lawrence, KS, 1988, p. 4.

[20] Since this is our first quotation of Butler it will be recorded that Gladstone changed the word order of this passage. Orthography apart, Gladstone's, and even Bernard's, major and minor departures from the best available texts (whether printed or holograph) are numbered in the hundreds.

Butler knew Clarke through his writings, or had actually been in his presence but not introduced – for example, in a church when Clarke was fulfilling his ministerial duties – must have been as unclear to Clarke as to us. The nature of the 'Occasion' was never made explicit but as the exchange progressed it would have become fairly obvious to Clarke, a working priest, that some sort of crisis of faith underlay the questions of metaphysics.

Following a tradition of physico-theological defenders of the faith which stretched from Walter Charleton's *The Darknes of Atheism Dispelled by the Light of Nature. A Physico-Theologicall Treatise* (1652), the first Boyle lectures (*The Folly and Unreasonableness of Atheism*)[21] had been given by Richard Bentley in 1692, with sermons on the 'Faculties of Humane Souls', the 'Structure of Animate Bodies' and the 'Origin and Frame of the World'. His successors had pursued similar methods, arguing that the evidence of design in the universe could be used as the basis for analogical arguments about the existence and nature of God: the scientific, empirical replacement for one stream of the Aristotelian scholastic theology of the pre-Reformation era. Indeed, 1713 had already seen the publication of William Derham's reworking of his Boyle lectures, *Physico-Theology: Or, a Demonstration of the Being and Attributes of God, from his Works of Creation.*[22] Clarke had sought to change direction by introducing *a priori* metaphysics into his account of the divine nature and its expression in the created universe. Butler's first letter signals solidarity with that aim by raising two points in Clarke's argument which, if successfully met, would greatly strengthen his position and go some way towards defending Clarke's theology as Trinitarian.

This served both religious and career purposes for Butler. He signals the former by writing that his reading of Clarke 'has failed me', so that 'I almost despair' (Letter 1B). Butler, who appeals to Clarke as 'one who seems to aim at nothing more than that good Work of instructing others', thus puts him under the responsibility of recovering a situation which his publications' allegedly defective presentation of doctrine had actually exacerbated. Whether Butler intended to be as sharp as this is unclear, but thus to address the phrase 'good Work', a theological and pastoral term, to a minister of religion was to strain civility. Butler's approach is at the permissible extreme of urgency and shows that he is not merely a bright young student hoping to break a lance with an established master but someone in search of spiritual guidance. The irony of a young Dissenter finding his way into the Church of England through dialogue with a priest officially suspected of heresy should not be far from our mind, particularly given that while no-one ever claimed that Butler's work presented

---

[21] Until several decades into the nineteenth century the terms 'sermon', 'lecture' and 'discourse' were virtually synonymous. 'Lecture' does not imply a more secular approach than 'sermon'.

[22] London, W. Innys, 1713, much reprinted and translated. Derham's 1715 work, *Astro-Theology: Or, a Demonstration of the Being and Attributes of God, from a Survey of the Heavens*, London, W. Innys, was further to explore the questions of time and space which Butler and Clarke discuss.

a rounded theology, he was too important a figure in the next two centuries not to be upheld as a bastion of orthodoxy.

In 1B Butler raises two questions. We will consider each in turn, ranging across all the group's ten letters. The first question concerns necessity and self-existence. He begins by ascribing the following argument to Clarke:

> To suppose a Finite Being to be Self-Existent, is to say that it is a Contradiction for That Being not to exist, the absence of which may yet be conceived without a Contradiction; which is the greatest absurdity in the World.

Butler observes that Clarke has limited the phrase 'the absence of which' by the observation that absence from one place entails the possibility of absence from all places.[23] He argues that Clarke has demonstrated merely that a being may only be in one place at one time. Butler's claims are essentially two. The first (and we are here collapsing a sequence of arguments into a single statement) is the apparently commonsensical one that ubiquity is not a necessary quality of existence, whether of a created or a self-existent being. The second claim is methodological: that a human analysis of something is not necessarily structured in the same way as the structure of the object being described – in other words, ironically, in view of his later career, that the analogical method is virtually useless, whether in metaphysics, epistemology or natural science. His actual words are these: '… there is a great difference between the order in which *things* exist, and the order in which I *prove* to my self that *they exist*' (3B). At this point, lacking an explicit commitment to the trust in God which analogical argument reveals, Butler stands on the brink of never becoming the philosopher he did actually become, since a belief in the reality of the generic kinship of created and creator, and of humankind and the entire creation, comes to underpin his entire work.

Clarke has two lines of reply to Butler (and, again, this is not an account of the order of the points made in his sequence of letters). He argues that for something to exist necessarily is to entail that it exists in every point of space and time, but he adds that space and time themselves exist necessarily (as viewed, of course, by creatures within the created, contingent universe), because the objects of the universe could not exist without them. This is a point which is expounded in his correspondence with Leibniz. Clarke thus rejects an implication of Butler's second, methodological claim, which is that, as Leibniz argues, space and time are analytic concepts. For Clarke they are really existing substances. But as Clarke acknowledges, the word 'substance' is ambiguous,

---

23 This derives from Newton's definition of space: 'Absolute space, in its own nature, without relation to anything external, remains always similar and immoveable …' (Scholium to the Definitions of the *Principia*, 1687). For a mathematician's perspective on the philosophical influences of Newton's conception of space, including its influence on Kant, see Joan L. Richards, 'The Philosophy of Geometry to 1900', in *Companion Encyclopedia of the History and Philosophy of the Mathematical Sciences*, ed. I. Grattan-Guinness, Baltimore, MD, 1994, pp. 913–19.

for, viewed from within the created universe, such substances in the divine being function somewhat as natural laws or conditions of existence, parts of the '*Cause* or *Ground*' of all created objects' existence (2C). Clarke pulls his rejoinders together by reminding Butler that self-existence is necessary, not contingent, and that necessity must '*operate … every where* and *at all times* alike' (3C). Self-existence (that is, existence which is not the result of an act of creation) entails necessary existence, because the created universe comprises only and all contingently existing things and is a condition of the created universe. His second line of reply is a statement of the First Mover argument, in terms of Newtonian physics and Cartesian philosophy.[24] '*Motion* cannot be *necessarily-existing*' (3C).[25] Another example, Clarke says, is the amount of matter in the universe. '*Determination* of a *particular Quantity*, or particular *Time* or *Place* of Existence of any thing, cannot arise but from somewhat *external* to the thing itself … [the quantity of matter in the universe could have been determined] only [by] the *Will* of an *Intelligent* and *free Agent*' (3C). There is an existential hierarchy of space and time over motion and matter and this hierarchy actually governs the human analysis of the universe. It will become apparent in a later chapter that Butler took this proposition into his own philosophy.

Pushing Newtonian physics this hard in this direction – 'GOD said, *Let Newton be!* and all was Light'[26] – now seems unreasonable, but its extraordinary and revolutionary predictive and explanatory power made it inevitable that metaphysicians would seek to map the penetration of the empirical and contingent by the rational and *a priori*. Butler was genuinely reassured and convinced by Clarke's explanations – the lighter tone and more fluent style of his later letters witness this – but it is greatly to his credit that in his mature works he never made the mistake of over-emphasizing the importance of metaphysical speculation. This self-restraint is possibly Butler's greatest asset as a philosopher. It is seldom that thinkers are driven passionately towards moderation.

The second strand in the Tewkesbury correspondence concerns the unity of the divine nature. In his Boyle lectures Clarke had argued that the proposition that two self-existent beings could exist was self-contradictory: they might either of them be supposed to exist alone (Butler calls this Clarke's first proposition), so that (second proposition) it will be no contradiction to imagine the other not to exist. Butler thinks (1B) that these two propositions are of different logical types and need a third proposition to make it possible to discuss them

---

[24] Clarke's primary source is Newton's laws of thermodynamics, but see also Descartes, *Les principes de la philosophie, deuxième partie, Œuvres philosophiques et morales*, Paris, 1948. For a discussion of the conceptual distinctions about teleology and necessity between Cartesians and Aristotelians, see Dennis Des Chene, *Physiologia: Natural Philosophy in Late Aristotelian and Cartesian Thought*, Ithaca, NY, 1996, especially Chapters 6.4 and 7.2.

[25] Bernard prints 'necessarily existing' as two words, which changes the meaning somewhat. From here on, throughout this book, editorial transgressions will be passed over in silence, except when a note is essential.

[26] Alexander Pope, 'Epitaph, Intended for Sir Isaac Newton', *Poetical Works*, 1966, p. 651.

together, in a similar way that a formal proof of the equality of the angles at the base of an isosceles triangle is needed (we intuit easily enough that they are always equal but cannot immediately say why).

Clarke is content to state, in a manner reminiscent of Newton (see note 36 below), that 'self-existence' is both independent of relations and able to exist without other beings, whereas created beings cannot exist 'without *presupposing* and *including* antecedently the existence of *that which is necessary* ... [which] includes necessarily a *Presupposition* of the existence of *Space* and *Time*' (1C). The discussion turns toward the question, whether necessary things are causes or, on the contrary, '*Affections which belong, and in the order of our Thoughts are antecedently necessary, to the Existence of all Things*' (2B). 'Affection' is a term which Butler uses as an alternative to Clarke's 'property or mode' (2C) and which is fundamental to his mature works. It means sometimes a property or mode of another person or object which humans know about because it exerts 'affects' on them and at other times the mechanism by which it is known.[27] We will discuss later Butler's concern to avoid reification as a means to schematic neatness, even at the cost of conceptual fuzziness.

'Affection' is presumed to have been borrowed, during his period of student reading at Tewkesbury, from Shaftesbury's *Inquiry concerning Virtue or Merit* (1711).[28] Butler's intellectual development is striking because, in a dialectical fashion reminiscent of scholasticism (as opposed to the contemporary controversial fashion), he was to base his ethics on critiques of his three most prominent British predecessors, Hobbes, Locke and Shaftesbury.[29] Shaftesbury uses the term 'affection' to mean 'a human impulse towards something': he writes of 'an affection towards self-good' and of 'excesses' of affections. He thus supposes that affections may be good (or bad) and proposes that a sense of right is as natural as natural affection itself. His opinion is that to seek salvation is not selfish (selfishness is intrinsically a bad thing) and that there is a distinction between the religious and the moral conscience.[30] All of these propositions are rejected, or even reversed, by Butler, who in his mature works holds that self-love (rather than self-good) is an affection, not the target of affections; that there is no such thing as 'excessive' affections, only ones which, to the person's or society's harm, may not be checked by contrary affections; that it is the Christian's duty to be selfish, in the sense that one's own salvation is one's first duty;

[27] John Habgood recently restated this theologically in his Bampton Lectures, *Varieties of Unbelief*, London, 2000, p. 55: 'The religious aspiration after goodness is a thirst for God himself, God as the ultimate fulfilment of all hopes and desires, and God as the summation of all values.'
[28] See also Shaftesbury's 'Philosophical Regimen': 'To have natural affection is to affect according to nature or the design and will of nature' *The Life, Unpublished Letters, and Philosophical Regimen*, ed. Benjamin Rand, London and New York, 1900, p. 3.
[29] Shaftesbury was educated, indeed, almost raised as a son, by Locke. Charles Taylor, *The Sources of the Self: The Making of the Modern Identity*, Cambridge, MA, 1989, traces his intellectual debt and his partial filial rebellion, pp. 248–55.
[30] *Characteristics*, Treatise IV, *Inquiry concerning Virtue or Merit*, Bristol, 1999, volume 1, pp. 249, 250, 253, 260, 273.

and that there is such a thing as a conscience (but not two different types). Whatever his merits, Shaftesbury's terminology has an improvisatory feel to it, redundancies being multiplied to justify conclusions which he wishes to reach. By contrast, as we will see in Chapter 2, Butler's conceptual apparatus is spare and his analysis austere. If Shaftesbury is intellectually sloppier, however, he must take credit for two big Butlerian ideas: grounding ethics in an account of human nature (through the affections and conscience) and recognizing the significance of the human ability to form habits.[31] It was not Butler but another follower of Clarke, the philosopher-priest John Balguy, who defended Clarke against Shaftesbury, in his 1726 *Letter to a Deist*, and aimed his *Foundation of Moral Goodness* (1728) against Shaftesbury's follower, Francis Hutcheson.[32] Balguy's principal arguments, however, were directly contrary to Butler's: that morality is not grounded in the instincts or affections, but in the 'unalterable reason of things' and that rectitude, not benevolence, is the prime divine attribute.[33] His *Divine Rectitude: or, a Brief Inquiry Concerning the Moral Perfections of the Deity; Particularly in respect of Creation and Providence* was published in 1730, in time for its core doctrine to be controverted, at least by implication, in *The Analogy*. Balguy's core assumption, as displayed in his title, was that God was a moral being:

> It is not to be doubted but the *Intention* of the Deity, in creating the World, was the *Production of Happiness*, or the Communication of Good ... [and the] *Motive* ... by which he was determined to execute this great Design, was the *Rectitude* of the Thing itself.[34]

This is crude metaphysics and Butler was actually rather closer to Thomas Bayes, a mathematician and Presbyterian minister, of whose ideas the title of

---

[31] Shaftesbury, *Characteristics*, p. 302. John P. Wright extends this account forward to Hume in 'Butler and Hume on habit and moral character', *Hume and Hume's Connections* but does not notice Shaftesbury's priority or, more crucially to his account, the importance of 'habits' in the Butler–Clarke correspondence (see below). Isabel Rivers (*Reason, Grace, and Sentiment: A Study of the Language of Religion and Ethics in England 1660–1780, vol. II, Shaftesbury to Hume*, pp. 334–5) mentions Edmund Law's and Paley's late-century discussion of habit with regard to Locke's epistemology but not its earlier absorption into Shaftesbury's and Butler's ethics.
[32] It may well be that Butler knew Francis Hutcheson's Shaftesburian *Essay on the Nature and Conduct of the Passions and Affections* (1728). That Butler, notoriously reticent about his sources and targets, does not name him is not evidence against this. However, Shaftesbury himself is his acknowledged target; his knowledge of Shaftesbury can be seen in the Clarke correspondence; Hutcheson's book postdates *Fifteen Sermons'* first edition; and Butler's practice, in both *Fifteen Sermons* and *The Analogy*, is to attack the source rather than followers. The temptation to divert into intellectual history has therefore been resisted. The two volumes of Isabel Rivers's *Reason, Grace, and Sentiment* (1991 and 2000) are an essential resource in this respect.
[33] *Letter to a Deist, Concerning the Beauty and Excellency of Moral Virtue*, 1726; *The Foundation of Moral Goodness*, 1728 and 1729; *Divine Rectitude: or, a Brief Inquiry Concerning the Moral Perfections of the Deity; Particularly in respect of Creation and Providence*, 1730; all published in London by John Pemberton.
[34] *Divine Rectitude*, pp. 8–9. Note ('... determined ...') the supposition that God was compelled to actions by the inner logic of their 'rectitude' – a compound of 'situationally appropriate' and 'morally right'.

his *Divine Benevolence* (1731) gives a hint sufficient for present purposes and who, after Butler's death, was to make a fundamental contribution to probability theory with his eponymous Theorem.[35]

The apparent fuzziness of the term 'affection' has often troubled philosophers and students of Butler, who have consistently overlooked this early use and his unsuccessful attempt, long predating Balguy's work, to introduce it into Clarke's own vocabulary, a failure which would confirm Butler in his theological and philosophical independence. The phrase Clarke uses to characterize this ontological status, and which, Butler adopts, both here and in the later Oxford correspondence, is 'a *sine qua non*' (for example, 2C), but it is clear, both from the Butler–Clarke correspondence and that between Clarke and Leibniz, that Clarke is carrying forward the Newtonian conception of space as a substance,[36] closely connected with the necessary, self-existent, being of the Creator. In letter 2C Clarke says explicitly, 'I apprehend [space] to be a *Property* of the Self-existent Substance,' that is, of God, who is aware of his existence as (necessary) space; humans must, by analogy, be aware of their existence as (contingent) relationship 'penetrated' (3C) by the substance, space. The mechanism of this awareness is that of like recognizing like – an affection, in Butler's terms.

The treatment of the question of the unity of the divine substance returns to its starting point by a route which could not have been anticipated. Clarke attempts (4C) to settle the question by developing the argument that the necessity of the various things they have discussed is recognized by humankind because of the nature and role of its cognitive and reasoning faculties. Previously he had said, 'All *Other Substances* are *IN Space*, and are *penetrated by it*; but the Self-existent Substance is not *IN Space*, nor *penetrated by it*, but is it self ... the *Substratum* of *Space*, the *Ground* of the Existence of *Space*, and *Duration it self*' (3C): a God in whom, literally, we move and have our being. Now, in an analogy with a blind man's perception of objects by touch alone (he perceives only the quality of 'hardness') Clarke observes that 'those Properties necessarily *infer* [i.e., carry into our minds] the Being of a *Substance*, of which *Substance itself* the Persons have *no Idea*', a Lockean argument which George Berkeley had recently refuted.[37] It is at this point (5B) that Butler shows real acuteness. In the most fluent passage of his five Tewkesbury letters, he observes that ideas – sense data – cannot survive the removal of their stimuli. Clarke's blind man, says Butler, supposes there is:

> *Somewhat external*, to give him the Idea of *Hardness*[;] ... he supposes it impossible for him to be thus affected, unless there were some Cause

35 See Chapter 3, p. 90.
36 See Isaac Newton, *Principia*, definition 8, scholium; also John Locke, *Essay Concerning Human Understanding*, II.xxiii.2.
37 *New Theory of Vision* (1707); *Human Understanding* (1710). Berkeley and Butler were to become friends, but the biographical and critical basis of an account of their intellectual relationship is at present entirely lacking.

of it; … [but] should this Cause … be taken away, his Ideas would be so too: Therefore, if *what is supposed to be the Cause* be removed, and yet the *Idea* remains, *That Supposed Cause* cannot be the *Real one.*

But, in point of fact, we do remember. Since, according to Clarke (Butler observes), the self-existent substance (God) is the 'substratum' of the material world, it sustains our memories of the objects of sense perception.[38] He defeats Clarke's proposal that the identification of necessity is a function of human-kind's faculties by proposing that the only test would be to enquire what would happen if the self-existent substratum ceased to be – and then describes his own proposal as 'absurd'. While the modern reader notes his implication that Clarke's solution is not capable of demonstration, Butler, by contrast, notes the corollary: that he cannot mount a credible objection. The difference is between modern disbelief and contemporary trust in God. Neither is definitely incontro-vertible.

In Butler's account the blind man's experience is 'immediate' and 'affective' – as opposed to 'effective'. This latter word is in Butler's active vocabulary, so that the two concepts were distinct for him and we can be sure that for Butler a 'cause' influences rather than compels human reaction to the affect (incidentally safeguarding free will).[39] It was impossible for Butler to envisage that in the real world God would indeed remove the cause. To do so would reduce him from God to dæmon. He must believe that God guarantees the continuity of his crea-tion and we recognize this as a version of Berkeley's argument, developed in publications which were then very recent. The affective relationship is between affective mechanisms in the human and in the objects of the created world (and, indeed, in God). This is so obvious to Butler that he does not distinguish between such affections and the emotions as usually understood, nor consider whether the emotions are symptoms of the affective relationship or mechanisms through which affective influences become motives to action.[40]

In his closing reply (letter 5C) Clarke says, '[Y]our granting the *Absurdity* of [your] *Supposition* … is consequently granting the *necessary Truth* of *my Argument* …' It was not for three years that, in a different context and evidently with sincerity, Butler wrote (letter 9B), '… tho' I did not see ye forces of your Argument for ye *Unity of ye Divine Nature* when I had done writing to you upon that Subject, yet by frequently considering what you have offered upon it,

---

[38] Something similar had recently been said by Joseph Addison in *Spectator* 413 (24 June 1712), about the 'disconsolate knight', bereft of the God-given pleasures of the imagination.

[39] James A. Harris (*Of Liberty and Necessity: The Free Will Debate in Eighteenth-Century British Philosophy*, Oxford, 2005, pp. 133–4) quotes *The Analogy* on necessity and notes Butler's distrust of speculation, but does not consider this point.

[40] His later remarks about resentment, however, suggest that, if pressed, he would suppose that emotions were symptoms, or by-products: he takes pains to justify the practical usefulness, indeed, the indispen-sability, of anger, while regretting its unsettling quality. See Chapter 2.

I am now *fully satisfied* that it is conclusive'. We will see in a later chapter that Butler did indeed take a version of Clarke's metaphysics into his mature work.

The London correspondence

Butler left Jones's academy in February 1714 at the age of almost twenty-two (Secker was to follow him in June)[41] and was not admitted at Oriel College (as a Commoner) until 17 March 1715, matriculating on 15 December 1715.[42] He apparently spent the intervening year in London and probably introduced himself to Clarke soon after his receipt of Clarke's letter 5C. This, dated 8 April 1714, had been sent to Gloucester and forwarded to Butler at Hamlin's coffee-house. Butler replied (6B) in mid-April. Letter 6B shows that his decision not to enter the Presbyterian ministry must have been taken during the course of the correspondence: further evidence that the Tewkesbury exchange was motivated by spiritual as well as philosophical concerns.

Letter 6B is an acknowledgement of Clarke's letter 5C; its only real purpose is to reveal Butler as the 'Gentleman in Glocestershire', now resident in London and available to meet: Clarke too was in the city, as rector of St James's, Picca-dilly, and it may be presumed that a personal relationship began at this time. Butler writes that he has been 'obliged to quit those studys, that had a direct tendency to Divinity, that being what I should chuse for the business of my Life, it being, I think, of all other studys the most suitable to a reasonable nature' (6B). Since he had been intended by his father for the Presbyterian ministry his giving up divinity is proof that he now felt definitely unable to enter it. Conse-quently, he is now being guided by his father towards the law, like his academy colleague John Bowes. Secker chose medicine and went to study first in Paris and then Leiden.[43] Neither profession required, in all dioceses, formal subscrip-tion to the Thirty-Nine Articles, not even, in the case of medicine, 'occasional conformity'. 6B continues:

> I say, my being obliged; for there is [e]very encouragement (whether one regards interest or usefulness) now a days for any to enter that profes-sion [i.e., the Anglican ministry]; who has not got a way of commanding his assent to received opinions without Examination.[44]

[41] Ingram, p. 32.
[42] *Registrum Orielense: An Account of the Members of Oriel College, Oxford*, two volumes, Oxford, 1902, vol. II, *The Commensales, Commoners and Batellers admitted during the years 1701–1900*, p. 43.
[43] There was no medical school in Britain until 1726 (W. M. Jacob, p. 4). In his narrative Ingram points out (pp. 40–3) the high intellectual status of medicine elsewhere. D. K. Money, *The English Horace*, Oxford, 1998, p. 46, recounts that in seventeenth-century Padua the professor of theoretical medicine ranked top in precedence, with philosophy second.
[44] Gladstone transcribed 'very encouragement' as 'every encouragement', thus, in the present author's opinion, providing a tactful (if, unfortunately, silent) editorial emendation in the interest of meaning. Bernard unwarrantedly amends this phrase to 'very little encouragement' in the interest of what he sees as plausibility. Butler would still be tactless, even if Bernard's emendation were accepted. Ian Ramsey (*Joseph Butler ... Some Features of his Life and Thought*, p. 6f) records the same opinion about Bernard's

Certainly, following the 1688 Revolution, which, although grounded in the popular will, was narrowly based in its execution,[45] the Church was actively promulgating toleration and generally welcoming the conforming of dissenters, but it was hardly adroit or tactful to suggest that even a somewhat heterodox Anglican clergyman and potential sponsor had taken up the priestly vocation out of considerations of 'interest or usefulness'. Again we suppose that Butler was acutely distressed.

In the five months between letters 6B and 7B (30 September 1717) there were several developments. Butler conformed to the Church of England, entering Oriel College as a commoner (17 March 1715).[46] He kept close contact with Secker, who visited him several times at Oxford ('[we] talked our own Talk without controul') and maintained a correspondence (now lost), which extended past his own ordination,[47] about Trinitarian doctrine (Secker was studying under Thomas Hardy, a once and future Anglican clergyman, currently a dissenter, and was inclining towards Clarke),[48] the 'inspiration of the Scripture', where he followed the Frenchman Richard Simon (who was therefore known to Butler, at least at second hand) and the Thirty-nine Articles, to which Secker was also inclined.[49] Butler met Edward Talbot at Oriel, who, with Clarke, was the foundation of the Butler circle's entire patronage.[50] In 1717, according to Bartlett, Butler occasionally officiated at Edward Talbot's parish church in East Hendred, near Wantage, and while service as a deacon is implausible, we may accept that his presence assisted Talbot in some form or other.[51] This was in the diocese of Salisbury, so that Talbot's father, who was the bishop and was later to ordain Butler, was responsible for licensing, or tacitly sanctioning, any formal service which was undertaken and, since patronage of Butler was to be transferred from son to father, may be presumed to know about any informal service. Most impor-

emendation as the present author. David E. White ('very encouragement') is the first to print this accurately, at the cost, of course, of intelligibility.

[45] John Miller's analysis (*James II: A Study in Kingship*, London, 1978, especially Chapter 13 – his concluding view of James's 'extreme political incompetence and sheer bad luck', p. 241) – is supported by Robert Beddard, 'The Unexpected Whig Revolution', in *The Revolutions of 1688*, ed. R. Beddard, Oxford, 1991. Recent studies are more nuanced: William Gibson's account (*James II and the Trial of the Seven Bishops*, London, 2009) of the leading bishops' actions in defence of the constitution (pp. 152–61) and (Chapter 7) of James's contribution to his own defeat and Steven Pincus's *1688: The First Modern Revolution*, New Haven, CT, 2009. The present author ('John Tillotson and the Voice of Anglicanism'), describes how Tillotson synthesized a new pulpit rhetoric to stabilize the situation.

[46] Oriel College Records.

[47] Porteus, p. 6.

[48] Ingram, p. 32.

[49] Ingram, p. 32.

[50] Edward Talbot's father, William, had been Bishop of Oxford until 1715, when he was translated to Salisbury. See CCEd.

[51] Thomas Bartlett, *Memoirs of the Life, Character and Writings of Joseph Butler*, London, 1839, p. 14. A much earlier account, however, records that Butler 'assisted the Rev. Edward Talbot in the divine service ... soon after his admission at Oxford', which suggests a start to Butler's informal deaconry as early as 1714 or 1715 (William Hutchinson, *The History and Antiquities of the County Palatine of Durham*, Newcastle, S. Hodgson & Robinson, 1785, vol. 1, p. 576).

tant to posterity, if not to contemporaries, was the publication in 1716 of the Tewkesbury correspondence by Clarke's publisher, James Knapton.[52] Butler's letters were soon (1717) to be translated into French and would ultimately be bound in with Leibniz's as well as Clarke's and reprinted twice by Knapton in the 1720s. A knowledge of Leibniz's work is revealed in Butler's letter (7B).[53]

The Oxford correspondence

The third group of letters, the Oxford correspondence, came in a rush: three by Butler (7B–9B) and two by Clarke (7C and 8C) in the remarkably compressed space of eleven days from 30 September 1717.[54] Even more than the first group they appear, from their context and contents, to have been stimulated by a sense of personal crisis. Typically, his response to a crisis was to use thinking about theology and philosophy to prepare him for spiritual and career decisions – a practice that he was to make central to his account of the conscience. At this time Butler vented his frustrations by expressing discontent with the alleged low level of Oxford collegiate life: '[we] are obliged to mis-spend so much time here in attending frivolous lectures and unintelligible disputations, that I am quite tired out with such a disagreeable way of trifling' (7B). He was still under pressure from his father to take up the law and Clarke was engaged in exploring the possibility of his moving to Cambridge: in 7B Butler reminds Clarke that they have discussed face to face the possibility of such a move. Clarke had offered an introduction to Richard Laughton (this is confirmed in Butler's postscript to letter 9B), who in 1717 was in the process of seeking (unsuccessfully) election as Master of Clare College at Cambridge: if his removal there was to be a contribution to Laughton's future power base, Butler is thus seen moving in a highly politicized environment. By September 1717 Butler's father had agreed to his moving to Cambridge, but only in order to take his degree in laws. It is notable proof of the strength of Butler's sense of ministerial vocation and his complete intellectual absorption in metaphysics and ethics that despite such frustrations he continued rigidly to resist his father's wish that he finally commit to the law.[55] In its passages about 'frivolous lectures and unintelligible disputations'

---

52 See Chapter 2 for a discussion of the Knaptons' importance.

53 A comparison of the Butler–Clarke correspondence with the surviving Newton side of the Bentley–Newton exchange in 1692 (about Bentley's 1692 Boyle lectures) is revealing of the close kinship of Newton's and Clarke's metaphysics and cosmology and of the currency of the sort of speculation engaged in by Butler (Clarke also published his exchanges with a number of other correspondents). The Newton letters were not published until 1756 but it is difficult to believe that Clarke did not know them. See Richard Bentley's *Works*, London, 1838, vol. III, pp. 201–15.

54 The date of letter 8B is misread as 3 October [1717] by Bernard. Gladstone correctly reads it as 6 October [1717].

55 Secker seems to have considered medicine as an alternative to a conforming ministry; during the period of his theological correspondence with Butler he was already 'possibly one of the best-trained [English doctors] of his day' (Ingram, p. 39, quoting a 1982 essay by John Guy). That he followed Butler into the Anglican priesthood after five years' medical studies in three countries may suggest Butler's

at Oxford and about the virtue of practical relief for the poor letter 7B provides proof of a sense of pastoral vocation as well as intellectual interest.

The Oxford correspondence contains the third, and most personally urgent, of the questions put to Clarke by Butler: it concerns freedom of action and virtue. Letter 7B is one of the most important things that he wrote – a critique of Clarke's correspondence with Leibniz in which we see him feeling his way towards identifying the main subjects of his mature work. He starts by observing that Clarke has said that freedom and action are identical ideas and expresses his understanding and agreement with this:

> I see great reason to be satisfied that *Freedom* and *Action* are *identical ideas*, and that Man is, properly speaking, an *Agent* or a *Free Being* ... I am satisfied that it is in our power to *act or not to act* in any given case, yet I do not see that it follows from thence that it is in our power *to act virtuously*; because the *physical* and the *moral* nature of an action comes [*sic*] under quite two different considerations. Virtue does not consist *barely in acting*, but *in acting upon such* [and such] *motives*, and to *such* [and such] *ends; and acting upon such motives*, &c. evidently supposes *a disposition in our nature to be influenced by those motives*, which disposition not being an *action*, does not depend upon *us*, but, like the rest of our affections, seems to proceed from our *original frame and constitution*.

Butler makes three propositions in this passage. The first (P1), adopted from Clarke, is that 'Freedom and Action are identical'. The second (P2) is that a moral action, being motivated, differs from a merely physical action. The third (P3) appears to follow in some way from P2: that a moral action consequently has its origin not in our will but deep in our created nature, and, in consequence, is an affective expression of a certain likeness to the Creator's mind: something which led directly to Butler's interest in analogy.

P2 runs directly counter to Descartes' analysis of action as an automatic response to external stimuli. Shaftesbury-like, Butler here sees an action, when considered ethically, as being validated not by any moral quality pertaining to the will but by the appropriateness of its flowing from our human nature. His logic appears weak. We have seen that in letter 1B he had objected to what he considered was Clarke's yoking together logically different sorts of propositions. Yet it is obvious that P1 and P2 are incongruous, P1 resulting from some sort of *a priori* definition of ontological categories and P2 being at least partly amenable to empirical enquiry. P3 has behind it some sort of contact with propositions about beauty or grace in relation to ethics, but Butler does not explain it.

We should also consider his resort to the term 'affections' in this passage. Humankind (Clarke and Butler agree) cannot conceive of anything without its existing in space and time, which, seen from the contingent universe, are thus

---

influence. With some restraint, Ingram (p. 44) restricts himself to describing the lack of evidence at this stage as 'maddening'.

necessary components of the 'substratum' which supports all created objects and beings. Butler now seems to transfer to human nature the idea that the affections reveal a necessarily moral dimension within its 'original frame and constitution'. It would seem to follow that if this is the case, acting immorally would cause some form of existential unease. Let us, perhaps prematurely, provisionally call this unease 'conscience'. In securing his meaning to Clarke's metaphysics, Butler summons to his aid from the Tewkesbury correspondence (and presumably from subsequent face-to-face discussions) Clarke's term *sine quâ non*. He then advances another radical idea:

> Now that we have not this disposition when we neglect our duty is evident from this, that if we always had it, we should always *certainly, though not necessarily*, do our duty. How then can we be accountable for neglecting the practice of any virtue, when at what time soever we did neglect it we wanted [i.e. lacked] that which was a *sine quâ non*, or absolutely necessary to the performance of it, viz. a disposition to be influenced by the proper motive?

Here Butler envisages that people may exist in whom God has withheld, destroyed or damaged the relevant properties or affections, which, we have seen, are a necessary part of the human substratum – literally, of that creativity which has made us human. Such experiences of disengagement from the Holy Spirit, similar to that of Addison's 'disconsolate knight', were actually reported at the time.[56] In the practice of religion is revived the elements of propitiation and anxiety about God's promises – a harbinger of the Great Awakening's assurances.[57] Indeed, as we will see in Chapter 5,[58] he discussed this explicitly at an especially low point later in life, but in a more secure conceptual environment. Meanwhile, we cannot avoid the likelihood that Butler had very strong personal experiences of despair and desolation, and even fears of insanity, during the years leading up to his ordination.

Butler was to develop a psychology and an account of the relationship between the person's private nature and public actions involving what we might call socio-ethical training, but for the moment he is interestingly placed: he does not yet have an account of how we may freely indulge in vice and his account of how we may always avoid vice is purely and confessedly superficial: avoid the actions, even if we are 'indifferent to that which is the only proper motive why

---

[56] The contemporary Congregationalist minister and hymn-writer, Simon Browne, became insane, convinced that God had 'annihilated in him the thinking Substance, and utterly divested him of Consciousness ... He looked upon himself as no longer a moral agent', as Anthony Atkey put it in his sermon at Browne's funeral, *The Rectitude of Providence under the Severest Dispensations*, London, J. Roberts, 1733, p. 22f. 'I am doing nothing that requires a reasonable soul. I am making a dictionary: but you know thanks should be returned to God for everything, and therefore for dictionary makers' (DNB, 'Simon Browne').

[57] Chapter 4 gives an account of Butler's examination of Wesley on a closely related point. Work on this phenomenon is in preparation.

[58] See pp. 143–4.

we should avoid it'. When he thus speculates that people cannot be blamed for their vicious actions, or praised for their morally good actions, we are reminded quite forcibly of his background in Dissent and of the ethics and theologies of some of the mid-seventeenth-century antinomian sects. It is not surprising that he records that 'our people here [in Oxford] never had any doubt in their lives concerning a received opinion; so that I cannot mention [this] difficulty to them'.

In replying, Clarke states positions without arguing them. He flatly contradicts the immature (in Butlerian terms) P2, noting (8C) that men are rational and that consequently there cannot be:

> a Dispos[ition] to be infl[uenced] by wrong Motives. This can be noth[ing] but mere Perverseness o[f] Will … Men [have] by nature strong inclinations to certain Objects. None o[f] these inclinations [are] vitious. But Vice c[on]sists in pursuing [the] inclination towards any Object in certain Circumstances, [notwithstanding] [that] Reason or ye natural Dispos[ition] to be infl[uenced] by right Motives declares to ye mans Conscience … [that] ye Object ought n[o]t to be pursued in those Circumstances.[59]

He provides some hints which may have been extraordinarily fruitful. Thus he claims, that 'wh[ere] ye Man commits ye Crime, ye natural Dispositio[n] was only towards the Object, n[o]t formally towards ye doing it upo[n] wrong Motives; & generally ye very essence of ye crime c[on]sists in ye Liberty o[f] ye Will forcibly overruling ye actual Disposition towards being infl[uenced] by right motives …' (8C). Butler (9B) replies, that 'I did not at all design to say that ye Essence of any Crime consisted in ye man's having a natural Disposition to be influenced by wrong Motives.' The intellectual reasons for Butler's capitulation may be obscure – Clarke asserts without arguing – but Butler's retreat was permanent and became a feature of his philosophy.

Another hint thrown out by Clarke is the identification of the 'disposition' raised by Butler with 'the faculty of reason, which makes [us] capable of rewards or punishments'. He says that it is '[not] in our power any further than as 'tis affected by habits'. This is seized on by Butler in his last letter, 9B: '[I] hope in time to get a thorough Insight into this Subject by means of those Helps you have been pleased to afford me.'

Butler's interim solution (letter 8B) has two elements. One is the 'Capacity to discern Right Motives … [This is] our Understanding or Faculty of seeing Truth' – an unButlerian use of 'truth'. His second element is the familiar 'Disposition in our Natures to be influenced by Right Motives' and once again he attaches to it the 'affective' sine quâ non tag – and, a new addition, says that

---

[59] Letters in square brackets supply abbreviations or left-margin lacunae, except that '[that]' is an editorial interpolation, for the sake of clarity. In all these transcriptions, italics replace the originals' underlinings. As far as is convenient without pedantry, Clarke's orthography is preserved because in producing cleaned-up text the published transcriptions have all misread and mispunctuated.

it is 'a Desire inseparable from a Conscious Being of its own Happiness'. It is a reminder of Butler's pre-modern environment that he uses the opaque term 'Conscious Being', rather than the then more technically philosophical term 'consciousness'. By it he means something like 'conscious happy state', not wishing to suggest a reified functional separation between happiness and the consciousness of it – an example of Butler's conceptual austerity and a reproach to the modern tendency to postulate faculties which are functionally redundant. Since everyone commits a *'first Vicious Action'* he must originally have had, *'antecedent* to ye commission of it, a *Stronger Disposition* to be influenced by ye *Vitious* than ye *Virtuous* Motive'. In other words, humankind is originally sinful, a diagnosis later to become involved with the doctrine of ethical personal development.[60] He continues worrying away at this and, although the issue is unresolved, as far as he is concerned – letter 8B is surely a record of new, improvised and undigested thoughts – comes to an unstable position which can lead in only one direction: a human disposition towards the vicious, which neutralizes that towards the good and 'incapacitates man from being a moral agent'. With that illogicality – the ontological difference between moral and immoral being merely verbal, a matter of positive and negative – the matter rests.

There has been a consensus among students of Butler from the early nineteenth century to the present that he mounted an effective and even sufficient critique of Clarke's work.[61] This view rises from an analysis of the correspondence as an intrinsically conflictual philosophical debate. It is presumably strengthened by the decline of Clarke's reputation as a philosopher. It is alleged both that Butler's questions are not answered satisfactorily and that Butler was not fully convinced by the answers. Two pieces of evidence contradict this view. The first is Butler's own, explicit, confession that Clarke had met his objections. We must, I think, take this at face value; Butler was neither a twentieth-century philosopher nor a liar or hypocrite. The second is that while in letter 1B he rejects analogical thinking, he eventually builds his intellectual career on a use of it which is at once limited, cautious and eclectic. When moving away from using (but without rejecting) *a priori* metaphysics like Clarke's and opting for a method which inductively pieces together evidences of what we nowadays see as of different types (and we have seen that Butler himself, in 1B, had the ability to diagnose such differences) he does not become Clarke's mouthpiece but does acknowledge his arguments as important items in the pool of evidence. He is thus led to perhaps his most important thought: that all inputs from all epistemological systems and associated physical apparatus are essentially of one type. Moreover, he subsequently based his professional life on Clarke's patronage

---

[60] Butler's references to original sin are few but some are noted in later chapters.
[61] For example, Bartlett, p. 10: 'It was of these letters to Dr. Clarke that Sir James Mackintosh, in his *Dissertation on the Foundations of a more just Theory of Ethics*, remarked, "He suggested objections to the celebrated Demonstration, which were really insuperable, and which are marked by an acuteness which neither himself nor any other ever surpassed".'

and on a cautious use of one of his ideas as a corrective to Shaftesbury. He submitted, cautiously but definitely, to Clarke's authority.

In this chapter we have tried to live with, and find understanding in, Butler's conceptual fuzziness and not to force in logic a correspondence which is informal and not originally intended for publication. It is necessary, however, to argue for a relaxed approach to the distinctions between terms like 'empirical', 'contingent', 'necessary', '*a priori*' and 'rationalist'. Michael Ayers[62] has most usefully discussed the question whether George Berkeley was an empiricist or rationalist and has identified the origin of the distinction in medical theory, which Butler is likely to have discussed with Secker after the latter's study of medicine in Paris. Butler, guided by and accommodating himself to Clarke's metaphysics, is an even sharper case in point. J. L. Mackie observed that 'The rationalist Samuel Clarke holds that these eternal and necessary differences of things make it fit and reasonable for creatures so to act ... even separate from [all religious considerations]' and wrote of 'Clarke's necessary relations of fitness between situations and actions'.[63] It should be borne in mind that while we readily and usefully attach the term 'empiricism' to Berkeley and Butler, not only were they, as ordained clergymen, professionally committed to revealed and therefore, in a sense, 'necessary' accounts of the nature of things but that their very methods were based on them. The glimpses of Butler being introduced to the tool of analogy are especially a caution. The twentieth-century analytic and secular tradition imposes enormous anachronisms on the thinking of the early Enlightenment, and whether Berkeley and Butler may finally be considered mainstream Enlightenment thinkers is, perhaps, debatable. In these letters Butler is frankly muddling through, intellectually and emotionally, and is clearly not combating Clarke but working towards an acceptance of his metaphysics. This appears in the gap that opened up in letter 8B, under Clarke's pastoral care, between affective causes (influence) and effective causes (determination), between the divinely necessary and the humanly contingent, increasingly seen in the context of the relationship between ethical choice and mental health, between sanity and the great unmentionable, original sin. Using as groundwork the most celebrated contemporary metaphysical thinking, Butler was to turn from logic and epistemology to propose an intuitively plausible system of affective mechanisms. He thus developed an account of the human ethical condition for richer and more powerful than the existing Cartesian and Lockean models.

---

[62] Michael Ayers, 'Was Berkeley an Empiricist or a Rationalist?', in *Cambridge Companion to Berkeley*, ed. Kenneth P. Winkler, Cambridge, 2005, pp. 34–62.
[63] J. L. Mackie, *Ethics: Inventing Right and Wrong*, Harmondsworth, 1977, pp. 31, 40.

2

Fifteen Sermons

Main texts: *Fifteen Sermons* (first edition, 1726; second edition, 1729)

Introduction and biography

It is noteworthy that Butler's entry to the clerical profession did not take the usual route of a college fellowship followed by preferment: it continued the hesitant and improvised nature of his life since Tewkesbury. To remember that it was John Wesley, not he, who was 'ordained as a Fellow of a College' and launched his career by publishing a university sermon preached in St Mary's[1] is to identify the curiously lumbering quality of his life. He graduated B.A. on 11 October 1718. He was ordained by William Talbot (Bishop of Salisbury and the father of his close friend Edward): deacon on 26 October and priest, in Clarke's church, St James's, Piccadilly, on 21 December 1718.[2] Thus, he bypassed the full year's service as deacon prescribed by the Church of England ('except for reasonable causes it shall otherwise seem good unto the Bishop'),[3] perhaps because on the excuse of his occasional service, formal or informal, in Edward's parish. On 27 March 1721 Talbot also presented him with the prebendal stall of Yetminster Prima in Salisbury Cathedral.[4] Butler did not end his studies, taking bachelor's[5] and doctor's degrees in the law, which, together with his interest in mathematics and economics, was to colour his works. His first

[1] See p. 133.
[2] In 1718 Talbot ordained a total of nine candidates on four occasions in Clarke's church, St James, Piccadilly. Butler was priested at St James on the last of these, 21 December (four other candidates were ordained deacon on the same occasion). The circumstances of his ordination as deacon were more unusual. On 21 September Talbot had ordained eight candidates in Salisbury Cathedral – apparently his only ordinations there in 1718 – but appears to have held a special service to ordain Butler as deacon in the Bishop's Palace chapel in Salisbury on 26 October, Butler travelling to Salisbury for the occasion, even though Talbot was to hold another ordination at St James on 30 November. It seems likely that the prospect of the Rolls appointment had been raised too late for Butler to join Talbot in Salisbury on 21 September and that it was necessary to move things along. Source: CCEd.
[3] Final rubric to the *Ordering of Deacons*.
[4] CCEd.
[5] 10 June 1721. See *Members of Oriel College*, vol. II, p. 43.

significant appointment had come at the age of twenty-seven: through Clarke's influence he became lecturer at the Rolls Chapel in Chancery Lane.[6]

Weinreb and Hibbert[7] note that the chapel was 'not only a place of worship for the Master of the Rolls and his family, but for the masters, clerks, and registrars of the Court of Chancery ... The preacher was practically a domestic chaplain, though occasionally special sermons were preached to large congregations.' Cunliffe adds that, 'The Rolls Chapel ... became a chapel for the legal profession as well as a record repository' (ODNB, Joseph Butler). In a guidebook contemporary with Butler's tenure, William Stow records that the chapel was 'a Repository now of Charters, Patents, Commissions, and other Matters, made up in Rolls of Parchment, from the beginning of King *Richard* the Third, in 1484' and that services were held 'every Sunday in term time at 10am [this service including a sermon] and 3pm', the Sacrament being given 'every second *Sunday* of the 4 Terms, [and] on *Christmas day, Easter Sunday*, and *Whitsunday*'.[8] Its listing in Stow implies that services were open to the public, even if the core congregation was drawn from the barristers and clerical personnel of London's legal community: we will see below Butler's references to the character of his congregation in the *Fifteen Sermons*. In accepting the lectureship and proceeding to his two law degrees he may have seen himself as offering a compromise between his father's and his personal wishes for his career. More importantly, as an appointment to a private chapel, the position was both political in nature, with a high profile in the legal profession, and not subject to diocesan administration or visitation.

In 1716 Butler's predecessor, Thomas Bisse, had published *The Beauty of Holiness in the Common-Prayer*, a much-reprinted series of four sermons on church music – actually, a single lecture sub-divided rather arbitrarily – which pioneered the reform and revival of Anglican liturgical music. Bisse was not politically active, staying within the orbit of his elder brother, Philip, then Bishop of Hereford, but an interest at that time in ritual and liturgy places him fairly reliably towards the Tory end of the contemporary spectrum. Bisse's own predecessor, from 1709, had been Francis Atterbury, who, by 1718 was in contact with the Jacobites and bound soon for prison and exile. While the titles and doctrine of Atterbury's published Rolls sermons (*The Duty of External*

---

[6] The date of July 1719 is usually given (for example, it is accepted by Cunliffe in his ODNB biography and in his 1729 Preface, p. xxxiv, Butler writes of preaching at the Rolls over 'a Course of Eight Years', which seems to suggest 1719–26). William Hutchinson, *The History and Antiquities of the County Palatine of Durham*, records that 'it was in 1718, that, at the recommendation of Mr Talbot, in conjunction with that of Dr Clarke, he was appointed by Sir Joseph Jekyll to be preacher at the Rolls' (vol. 1, p. 576). This must mean that an indication that the appointment was available was prior to and thus occasioned Butler's ordination. Bodleian MS Rawl.J.4⁰ 5 (221) gives a date of July 1721 for the Rolls lectureship, which was immediately after his acquiring his first law degree from Oxford (B.C.L., 10 June 1721) – a temptingly plausible suggestion, but against the evidence. It is likely that Butler proceeded to B.A. in order to raise his status ahead of ordination and the Rolls position.

[7] Ben Weinreb, Christopher Hibbert, *et al.*, *The London Encyclopaedia*, London, 2008, p. 653.

[8] William Stow, *Remarks on London*, London, T. Norris & H. Tracy, 1722, pp. 121–2.

Worship excepted) were not as provocative to his enemies as those of some of his other sermons, the Rolls Chapel might have been seen as overdue for a loyal Whig in support of a new Master of the Rolls. Butler, former Presbyterian and protégé of Clarke, a victim to Atterbury's enmity in Convocation, was seen to fit the bill, the appointment locking him into the Whig circle, even if we can detect no great enthusiasm on his part,[9] and securing for it the most powerful mind of his generation.

At this time, atypically, Butler exerted his influence on behalf of a third party: he apparently wrote to Secker in about May 1720 that he had persuaded Edward Talbot to recommend Secker to his father if he accepted ordination.[10] This seems to mark the high point of Butler's leadership in their relationship: Secker was the more political and sociable, and was soon to claim credit for arranging Talbot's appointments of Butler, in his new diocese of Durham, first to the rectory of Haughton-le-Skerne (in 1722), next to Houghton-le-Spring (in 1724) and then (in 1725) to Stanhope, in the Darlington deanery – the 'golden rectory', so-called because of the size of its rector's income but also, with conscious irony, because that gold was derived, in alchemical fashion, from tithes of the local lead mines.[11]

Thus were Butler's years of study unusually protracted and his settlement into a competent living delayed, compared with others enjoying a similar quality of patronage. The indirect evidence – the alleged correspondence with Secker from, presumably, as early as their separation when leaving Jones' academy until Secker's ordination in 1722[12] – suggests a laborious discussion of Christian doctrine. As Presbyterians the key points are likely to have been about the relation between Church and State and, given that Secker records that they discussed Trinitarian doctrine, the balance between the Calvinistic and Arminian accounts of humankind's relationship with God. It may be – and this is purely speculation – that the reinterpretation of Clarke through the critique of Shaftesbury which was described in Chapter 1 was elaborated in these early London years into the Butlerian account of the relationship. It is plausible that the lost Butler–Secker correspondence in effect duplicated and extended what survives of the Butler–Clarke correspondence, but enriched by their studies of medicine and the law and by Secker's access to recent continental works as well as British ones.

From now until his translation to Durham Butler lived in an intensely politicized, hard-line Whig, environment.[13] The Master of the Rolls was Sir Joseph

9 See p. 127.
10 Porteus, *op. cit*, p. 6; Ingram, p. 42.
11 William Morley Egglestone, *Stanhope Memorials of Bishop Butler*, London, 1878, p. 8.
12 Ingram, p. 43.
13 William Gibson, 'William Talbot and Church Parties 1688–1730', *Journal of Ecclesiastical History*, Vol. 58, No. 1, January 2007, pp. 26–48, has shown that ecclesiastical politics were less consistent and factional than parliamentary, which under Walpole were rigorously organized. The Church was less interested in controlling publications than were the politicians, and the Whig clergy was not uniform in

Jekyll, a protégé of Gilbert Burnet[14] and patron of the Arian William Whiston and the deist Thomas Chubb.[15] He had been appointed Master of the Rolls in 1717 and Butler's appointment as preacher at the Rolls was, we may infer, an appointment building on his political success, as was the simultaneous rebuilding of the chapel itself, in part with a grant from George I.[16]

Incidentally, Butler later became associated with a love of building work, at his Hampstead home,[17] in Bristol and at Durham, where the work he ordered on remodelling the castle is still visible.[18] It is therefore notable that one of the reasons alleged for his move to Stanhope was the intimidating dilapidation of the Houghton-le-Spring rectory. From parish financial accounts published by Egglestone Butler showed inexperience, and even incompetence,[19] in his efforts to keep the Stanhope church in good repair, which speaks poorly of his ability to manage contractors and churchwardens[20] and perhaps a high level of anxiety to be seen to do the right thing and to please his superiors.[21]

In 1726, presumably at the end of term, Butler moved permanently to Stanhope, not resigning his Rolls lectureship until the autumn, possibly in case he changed his mind about his voluntary rustication.[22] Between 1726 and 1733

---

its evaluation of theology and liturgy, but the bishops were the junior partners in the relationship with the government. See Chapter 5, pp. 169–70.

[14] *DNB*, Joseph Jekyll.

[15] *ODNB*, Joseph Butler.

[16] *DNB*, Joseph Jekyll.

[17] Egglestone, *Stanhope Memorials of Bishop Butler*, p. 76n, gives details. The Hampstead house was the property of Lionel Vane, who had been baptised at Stanhope – another example of Butler's curious passivity in allowing others to organize his life for him. He even had some Stanhope stained glass copied for the Hampstead house.

[18] See Sharp MS 94, Durham Cathedral Library for Butler's alterations and projections at Durham Castle and Bishop Auckland (which were completed posthumously by his successor, Richard Trevor). The account of his Durham and Castle Auckland works is somewhat amplified by William Hutchinson (vol. 1, pp. 578–9).

[19] Ingram, p. 50, quotes Secker on Butler's lack of talent in this direction.

[20] Egglestone (pp. 38–9) records that as late as October 1733 George Sayer, the Archdeacon of Durham, was still constrained to require a detailed inventory of the church, as well as repairs to many dilapidations and even the provision of a new prayer book; this despite years of effort in committee by Butler. The need for frequent external whitewashing suggests chronically sub-standard work, which at one point needed Butler to indemnify a churchwarden against legal threats by the contractor. He did, however, use the parish's committee to effect an equitable distribution of the lead tithe (Egglestone, p. 18). If Butler's building talents flourished as a bishop it was very likely because of support from his diocesan officials.

[21] In an undated letter of 1732, when 'Mr Blacket's People' (miners and tenants of the Bishop of Durham) were opening a pit in some woodland, he wrote to the bishop that he had interviewed them in vain ('I am not able to get any Account at all what … they design') but 'upon further Inquiry [with a third party] I am fully assured … concerning ye good Condition of ye Grove' (Durham University Library MS CCB Box 182 File 34457A, item 10). In a second letter, dated 11 August 1732, he remarked, somewhat conspiratorially, to the bishop that, 'having lived some time among Miners, [I] may be supposed to have Reasons wch yr Lordship may not thoroughly enter into' (*ibid.*, item 11). 'Reasons' here probably means something like monetary interests: he is offering to put his involvement in local business at the bishop's service.

[22] During his tenure of Haughton-le-Skerne and Houghton-le-Spring he alternated between the Rolls Chapel and the parishes but he was to demonstrate a readiness to resign offices when they became financially unnecessary. Stanhope's large endowment was very likely the key factor in his decision to resign the Rolls position.

Butler was 'buried' in his Stanhope parish,[23] visited by friends, including Benson and at least one Talbot (the late Edward's sister, Caroline). Since Secker claims to have been deeply involved in his intellectual work[24] it is unlikely that they did not meet; a work like *Fifteen Sermons 1729* is not produced in exile, physical or psychological. Besides his parochial work he first revised *Fifteen Sermons* for a second edition and then composed, or compiled, *The Analogy*. From internal evidence presented in the next chapter it seems that the two tasks were methodologically similar: the editing, supplementing and reorganizing of largely existing material to suit his mature position. In 1733 he proceeded to his D.C.L.[25] and became Charles Talbot's chaplain when he was appointed Lord Chancellor. This seems to have been facilitated by Secker[26] and if it is true that Secker helped edit *The Analogy*, which must have been done at this time and could hardly have been effected by post, this may suggest that Butler resumed visits to London or, as William Hutchinson narrates, even reverted to residence split between Stanhope and London; Butler had always maintained a curate in Stanhope.[27] In any case, on publication of *The Analogy*, and despite retaining Stanhope, he resumed his metropolitan career, more or less full-time, as Clerk of the Closet to Queen Caroline.[28]

Fifteen Sermons 1726

Just after Butler moved to Stanhope, James and John Knapton published *Fifteen Sermons Preached at the Rolls Chapel, by Joseph Butler, L.L.B. Preacher at the*

---

[23] A quip to Queen Caroline ascribed to Laurence Blackburne, Archbishop of York. Hallifax, *The Works of Butler*, 1849, vol. 1, p. xliv. See also William Hutchinson, *The History and Antiquities of the County Palatine of Durham*, vol. 1, p. 577, who implies that the period of exclusive residence in Stanhope was between his leaving the Rolls and assuming the Talbot chaplaincy. 'This retirement, however, was too solitary for his disposition, which had in it a natural cast of gloominess … [He] felt at times, very painfully, the want of that select society of friends … which could inspire him with the greatest chearfulness' (p. 577).

[24] For Secker's claims of input into the production of *Fifteen Sermons* and *The Analogy*, and Butler's lack of gratitude and public acknowledgement, see Ingram, p. 52: 'I was somewhat serviceable to him in the Method & Thoughts of this Book; but very much in making the Language of it more accurate & intelligible, which cost me a great deal of time & pains.' A study of the 1729 changes to *Fifteen Sermons*, however, suggests that Secker, in perhaps justifiable irritation, exaggerated the philosophical importance, if not the extent, of his editorial contribution. As we will see below, the substantive changes at least to *Fifteen Sermons 1729* were conceived by Butler as a whole and represent a stage of development towards the positions taken in *The Analogy*.

[25] Bodleian: Rawl. J. 4° (221); *Members of Oriel College*, vol. II, p. 43.

[26] William Coxe, *Memoirs of the Life and Administration of Sir Robert Walpole*, London, 1798, vol. I, p. 551.

[27] Egglestone (pp. 62–3) records that James Wannup, who was inherited by Butler, died in December 1734 and was promptly replaced by Joseph Dover, who was also the curate of the neighbouring St John's in Wardales (Durham UL MS DDR/EV/VIS/4/2 (1736, p. 6). Dover was still in post when Butler held his primary visitation in 1751 (DDR/EV/VIS/4/2, 1751, p. 13).

[28] Bodleian: Rawl. J. 4° (221). Butler's association with Queen Caroline is dealt with by Stephen Taylor, 'Queen Caroline and the Church', in *Hanoverian Britain and Empire: Essays in Memory of Philip Lawson*, ed. Stephen Taylor, Richard Connors and Clyve Jones, Woodbridge, 1998.

Rolls, and Rector of Stanhope in the Bishoprick of Durham, a work featuring rebuttals of Thomas Hobbes, whose solidly established Europe-wide reputation and predominance as a political theorist, and even epistemologist, was still relatively unchallenged by the Whig John Locke.[29]

The Knaptons were the leading publishers of Whig churchmen in the earlier eighteenth century. Their long list of authors included Samuel Clarke; his brother John, a Newtonian and a Boyle lecturer; the leading Latitudinarian Benjamin Hoadly;[30] the Arian controversialist John Jackson (who wrote in support of both Clarke and Hoadly and against the Trinitarian Daniel Waterland); John Conybeare, later Butler's successor as Bishop of Bristol; and White 'Weathercock' Kennett, an early convert to the Whig cause and a defender of Hoadly. Other Knapton authors included Edward Stillingfleet, one of the greatest of the Glorious Revolution generation; John Sharp, of the family which predominated in the Durham diocese for much of the century; William Warburton, the Church and State theorist; and Edward Chandler, Butler's bishop in the Durham diocese. The Knaptons also published translations of Leibniz, Grotius and Jacques Rohault and – another touch of the Whiggish Enlightenment – a dictionary of all the religions. Their list, which also included non-Whig items, is remarkable for high quality and historical significance.

Fifteen Sermons 1726 is unusual in being published without a preface and with only the most formal and perfunctory of dedications:

> To the Right Honourable Sir Joseph Jekyll, Master of the Rolls, &c. The following SERMONS, preached in his Chapel, are with all Humility Dedicated, by his most dutiful, and most obedient Servant, Joseph Butler.

The occasion of its publication was obviously his resignation from the lectureship. Perhaps the book was assembled hurriedly once the decision to resign had been taken. Sermon collections were not at this time particularly numerous – about half a dozen a year were published,[31] but most of these were collec-

---

[29] Howard Williams, *Kant's Critique of Hobbes: Sovereignty and Cosmopolitanism*, Cardiff, 2003, by characterizing Hobbes as the theoretician of eighteenth-century national state and international relations, by implication reinforces his appeal to the 1688 Whigs. Jeffrey R. Collins, *The Allegiance of Thomas Hobbes*, Oxford, 2005, has detached him from interregnum Royalism and made a start to assessing his theological appeal. The philosophical difficulties experienced by Whig theologians in separating themselves from Hobbes's powerful work are described in Bob Tennant, 'John Tillotson and the Voice of Anglicanism', in *Religion in the Age of Reason: A Transatlantic Study of the Long Eighteenth Century*, ed. Kathryn Duncan, New York, 2009, pp. 97–119.

[30] Hoadly was Talbot's successor-but-one as Bishop of Salisbury. It was Hoadly who had made the quintessentially Whig claim that '[one's] Title to God's favour cannot depend upon his actual being, or continuing, in any particular method; but upon his *Real Sincerity* in the conduct of his Conscience, and of His own Actions under it' (*Preservative against the Principles and Practices of the Nonjurors both in Church and State*, London, James Knapton, 1716, p. 90). As we will see, Butler, who was to adopt the position that sincerity is not enough (see Chapter 4, pp. 140–1), was intellectually semi-detached but politically loyal.

[31] Bob Tennant, 'John Tillotson and the Voice of Anglicanism', presents some preliminary statistics of the publication patterns of single and collected sermons in this period. Because of the present undeveloped state of sermon studies, Tony Claydon's groundbreaking 'The Sermon, the "Public Sphere" and the

tions (often posthumous) of a life's work. Unlike later in the century there was no *de facto* requirement to publish sermons as a qualification for promotion. Moreover, *Fifteen Sermons'* neutral title and lack of a preface were unusual for a book which made an original contribution to philosophy. A title something like *Sermons on Human Nature, preached at the Rolls Chapel* and a suitable preface would have been more usual.

Whether publication was at the initiative of the author, the publisher, his ecclesiastical patrons or Sir Joseph Jekyll cannot be determined. Recently, in 1724, the Knaptons had published William Wollaston's deistic *Religion of Nature Delineated*. This was a work heavily influenced by Clarke's doctrine and method. Proceeding ostentatiously from axioms and disputations on objections to them via a theory of nature to ethical doctrine – truth, in its various senses (they are not clearly distinguished), being proposed as the basis of all the virtues – the work, which was commercially very successful, clearly influenced Butler, so that the *Fifteen Sermons* must have seemed a natural, albeit more orthodox, successor: a work of moral philosophy less systematic than Wollaston's, but using a similar method, cutting much deeper in its account of human nature and, unlike Wollaston's, able to serve as an assistant to clergy. If Wollaston was seen as the member of the Knaptons' list who had reworked Clarke's metaphysics into moral philosophy, it might explain why Butler provided no prefatory material to his first edition: he was seen as working within the space which Wollaston had created, his sermons being examples of practical theology protected and validated by Wollaston's definition and creation of that space. Another publication in 1726 was the book worked up from his 1724–25 Boyle lectures by Thomas Burnet (the son of Gilbert). As befitted a salaried member of the diocese of Canterbury Burnet was published not by the Knaptons but by Arthur Bettesworth. Delivered in sixteen sermons but recast in non-sermon form as the two-volume *Demonstration of True Religion, in a Chain of Consequences from Certain and Undeniable Principles*, it is an extension of Clarke's *a priori* method, attempting to present, across 823 pages, a chain of deductions from a set of premises. Like Butler's sermons it adopts an anti-Hobbes strategic positioning.[32] Much of Burnet's life's work was devoted to an attempt to minimize the differences between orthodoxy and Arianism.

This perhaps explains an otherwise puzzling feature of Butler's career. It would have been most natural to publish a controversial work first and a positive work of ethical doctrine second. It is possible that Wollaston and Burnet were seen as having, for the time being, set out definitively the Clarke-Whig position – it is always bad politics to issue too many policy statements at one time, risking differences to be exploited by opponents. Instead, and rather missing its

---

Political Culture of Late Seventeenth-century England', in *The English Sermon Revised*, ed. L. A. Ferrell and P. McCullough, Manchester, 2000, lacks a statistical assessment of the genre.

[32] For example, 'By Right is meant by every one, ev'n by Mr. *Hobbs* himself, a Power or Privilege of acting, or enjoying, any thing granted by a [natural] law', vol. 1, p. 209.

moment, Butler's *Analogy* waited until after 1729, when *Fifteen Sermons* was definitely off his hands, and had its greatest impact in the next century, when an intellectual revolution in Europe and America had revived forms of deism, and when, ironically, he superseded Paley, who may have supposed himself actually to have superseded Butler. Thus, it is possible that the very tightness of the political unity of the Whigs diverted their intellectually most powerful, and least partisan, controversialist away from the intellectual services which he might have rendered.

At the Rolls chapel Butler had two functions: he preached as a member of Jekyll's household and, in term-time, gave more formal lectures ('sermon' and 'lecture' were overlapping terms) to the wider group around the Rolls. The *Fifteen Sermons* are not domestic preaching but from the more public occasions.

> [The] Reader ... is not to look for any particular Reason for the Choice of the greatest part of these Discourses; their being taken from amongst many Others, preached in the same Place, through a Course of Eight Years, being in great Measure accidental. Neither is he to expect to find any other Connection between them, than that Uniformity of Thought and Design, which will always be found in the Writings of the same Person, when he writes with Simplicity and in Earnest. (*1729*, p. xxxiv)

Thus we should emphasize the not-quite-obvious, that despite their nearly three centuries of use as a set book of moral philosophy, these sermons are performance texts to be delivered in a liturgical context. He did not overwrite their pulpit style, as Thomas Burnet had done with his Boyle lectures, in which the chapter divisions obviously do not even coincide with the original sermons. Moreover, they were not recast, like John Wesley's, to suit them for domestic use, nor were they revised to polish their literary style, nor did they acquire scholarly appendices which, in other authors' cases, bulked as large, and sometimes even larger, than the main text.

On the contrary, when revising *Fifteen Sermons* for its second edition, Butler actually added features which strengthened oral delivery. It will not be laboured beyond this point, but the 1729 edition retains many colloquial figures.[33] The interjection, '... I say ...' or 'really ..., I say really' is found in Sermon IV, p. 69; Sermon VIII, p. 153; Sermon IX, p. 174; Sermon XII, p. 249; and Sermon XV, p. 303. The phrase '... you see ...' is found in Sermon X, p. 188; and Sermon XI, p. 208. Sermon X, p. 189, actually introduces the gestural 'then' into the text and, p. 198, retains the purely gestural 'Well, ...'. Sermon XIV, p. 293, retains 'Goodness. I say Goodness.' In Sermon VII, p. 127, there is even a mild oath: 'Good God, what Inconsistency, what Perplexity is here!' Contrary to his reputation, there is plenty of humour and irony in *Fifteen Sermons*, of the heavier sort which best suits public performance: 'This surely looks suspicious of having somewhat in it', he remarks at the end of a passage arguing (against Hobbes)

---

[33] All the examples are from the 1729 edition.

for the existence of disinterested love of one's neighbour (Sermon XI, p. 222). Note also the remarkably colloquial first sentence of Sermon XIII (p. 261): 'Every Body knows, you therefore need only just be put in Mind, that ...'. These retentions and additions show that the *Fifteen Sermons* remained in his repertoire of texts to preach. While the 1729 Preface pulled the fifteen together as a group it was not an attempt to disguise their heterogeneity: it advertised it. The sermons are exegetical, their thinking based on Butler's understanding of the Scriptures and their extrusion into ethical doctrine. Some of them are exegetical in a narrow sense: they set themselves to explicate and apply to the present day the doctrine of their assigned biblical texts. They are intended to teach and encourage good personal conduct rather than to offer instruction in a philosophical method. Even the first three sermons, which are commonly considered the most 'philosophical', are grounded in exegesis – Sermon II, for example, refers emphatically to the Pauline text on which it is based (*1726*, p. 32; *1729*, p. 32).

Three sermons are attached to occasions in the church calendar (Sermon VI on the first Sunday in Lent, Sermon VII on the second Sunday after Easter, Sermon XI on Advent Sunday). The fifteen include four pairs,[34] which would have been preached at the beginning and end of the working week-day.[35] It should be noted that the famous three sermons *Upon Humane Nature* are in fact a pair (two halves of one long text) and a singleton unconnected with them. In most cases the preliminary exordia and the concluding perorations are so perfunctory as to suggest that they have been subjected to cuts, although the fourth sermon begins with a discussion of the English translation of its text and the twelfth ends with a special prayer – not an invariable contemporary practice. Butler's resort to the books of Revelation and Ecclesiasticus, of which some chapters were used in the Prayer Book despite it being uncanonical, points to a commitment to the entire liturgy and the full scope of doctrine and experience.[36] Although delivered in a liturgical context – routinely during morning prayer[37] – and having a simple version of the traditional exordium-exegesis-application structure[38] their strategy of supplementing biblical doctrine rather than expounding it may have led subsequent students to mistake sophistication

---

[34] Sermons II and III; V and VI; XI and XII; and XIII and XIV. Each pair is a long sermon divided in two, as can be seen from examining their internal structures.

[35] Modern scholars seem especially insensitive to the liturgical dimension. Even Brian Hebblethwaite, attempting to draw a philosophical point from their sharing a Biblical text, seems unaware that Sermons II and III were two halves of a single 'lecture', preached in the morning and evening of the same day (*Tercentenary Essays*, p. 204).

[36] Ecclesiasticus is quoted at the end of both Sermons IV and V. Sermon VII ends with Revelation 21.4 and Sermon XV with Revelation 15.4–5.

[37] Sermon VII refers to 'the first Lesson for the Day', 'which you have [just] heard' (*1729*, p. 118).

[38] In Sermon VII, for example, the transition from exegesis to application is signalled by the phrase, 'To bring these Observations home to ourselves ...' (*1729*, p. 131).

for secularism.[39] Indeed, the three sermons *Upon Humane Nature* were revised only relatively lightly for *1729*, where the bulk of the new writing – the major efforts to integrate more tightly the volume's contents – came in the completely new Preface and in the sermons on love (XI–XIV). Thus, contrary to received opinion, the Butler of 1729 was more concerned with developing his theology and philosophy of love (both for God and for humankind) than his account of the characteristics and structures of the human mind and nature.

We also need to remember that in preaching against the deists, who were within the Whig circle, as well as against Hobbes, who was increasingly appropriated by the Tories, Butler, as tactfully as was consistent with the duties of his ministry, sought to engage with and transform tendencies in his master's household and in the circles in which he moved.

Fifteen Sermons 1729

We will accept Butler's view that *Fifteen Sermons 1729* superseded *Fifteen Sermons 1726* and treat the earlier publication as prentice work, a transition between the Clarke (and Secker) correspondence, and as a comparator for *1729*. The remainder of this chapter is based on the materials for a variorum edition of the work, a physical marking-up of the *1729* changes on a copy of *1726*, but ignoring the few changes introduced after 1729.[40] For reasons of space we use less than half of *1729*'s new material, but the omissions do not affect the account of Butler's second and better thoughts. They represent the mature Butler's conscious legacy from the Rolls Chapel period. From their distribution it appears that *1726* was minutely scrutinized, corrected, supplemented and harmonized, wherever possible without damaging the contents as working sermons. Butler's (and presumably Secker's)[41] marking-up required changes to be kept as closely as possible equivalent in length to the original: there are very few insertions or deletions which affect pagination and many of the verbal changes would have benefited from being granted a few more words. A copy of *1726* was undoubtedly delivered to the Knaptons overwritten and interleaved, the typesetter following standard practice in respecting the original's line by line layout (to minimize the risk of mistakes), and sometimes introducing paragraph breaks to achieve this.

Every passage quoted below was edited or added to *1729*, unless otherwise stated.[42] That *1726* is referred to so seldom is evidence of the comprehensiveness of the rethinking, applied in a unified way throughout the volume. The

---

[39] For example, Sydney E. Ahlstrom, *A Religious History of the American People*, New Haven, CT, 1972, p. 354, refers to 'his [impressive] essays on ethics'.

[40] The third (1736) edition adds a substantial footnote: a claim that a passage of Sermon XIII, *Upon the Love of God*, was supported by Augustine in *The City of God*.

[41] The challenge of assigning some changes specifically to Secker has been resisted. Butler, after all, literally authorized all the changes.

[42] Where use is made of material unchanged from *1726*, both locations are given.

Butler of 1729 appears as a more mature and powerful thinker and a more accurate writer than the Butler of 1726. His basic doctrine and strategy changed little, although there were to be distinct changes in priority and emphasis in *The Analogy*.

An account of *Fifteen Sermons* is avoided. The texts, and the questions raised by modern analyses are well-known: all too many arise from misunderstanding eighteenth-century mind-sets and language, while others arise from seeking in Butler the categorical or logical approaches which have been developed since he wrote. W. R. Matthews's 1914 edition, with its analyses of each sermon, has done service for generations of students of moral philosophy and remains available, as do several late twentieth-century American editions, also prepared for students. Penelhum's modern account is exceptionally accomplished and altogether invaluable, although the fact that he contributed to a series called *The Arguments of the Philosophers* imposed upon even him the seemingly perennial duty of saying what Butler should have said, somewhat at the expense of identifying what he actually did say. The reader may notice fundamental differences between the present account and Penelhum's, but to discuss these would deflect from the present book's primary aim.

1729 differs from *1726* in possessing a 34-page Preface, signed off 'Stanhope, *Sept.* the 16th, 1729'. It sees the addition or comprehensive reworking of nine substantial passages (some are more than a page long), ten sentences, and twenty-four clauses and phrases. Much other material is redistributed. There are twelve minor changes introduced to clarify the meaning, three to correct the syntax and many scores of changes to the punctuation, orthography and paragraphing (some of the latter may have been introduced by the compositor). There are six significant deletions. The least changed sermon is the last, *Upon the Ignorance of Man*. The most changed is Sermon XI, the first part of *On the Love of our Neighbour*, which is virtually a new text.

Some editing changes are pettifogging or obscure. Perhaps the most remarkable is in Sermon VI, where 'every Observation' is changed to 'all Observations' (*1729*, p. 109), with a consequent series of changes from singular to plural in a string of verbs but for no apparent semantic gain. Elsewhere the clause 'But so far as he is good' is changed, gratuitously, to 'But, so far as he is a good Man' (Sermon IV, *1729*, p. 77), again without any obvious improvement of sense or style. Either Butler felt that they sounded better in pulpit delivery or he passively accepted Secker's suggestions: it is natural enough to suggest minor revisions simply to establish co-ownership of the process. Other revisions occasionally build up rhetorical episodes, enhancing their clarity and power in oral delivery. Thus, in Sermon XI, *Upon the Love of our Neighbour*, which draws on resources of irony to unite his congregation against Hobbes, his particular target, Butler redrafts to create a passionate appeal: 'Is Benevolence less the Temper of Tranquillity and Freedom than Ambition and Covetousness?' (*1729*, p. 219). Some of the small changes, however, are actually quite important doctrinally. In Sermon XIII (*1726*, p. 267; *1729*, p. 274), 'indeed' becomes 'then'. The change has the effect of removing an implied criticism of the Bible for suggesting that Job felt that God was far off. In another place (a footnote) 'There are secondary Uses of our Faculties which administer to Delight, as the primary administer to Necessity ...' becomes 'There are secondary Uses of our Faculties: They administer to Delight, as well as to Necessity ...' (Sermon IV, *1729*, p. 67). The revision shows Butler removing a piece of terminology (primary-secondary ideas) which is reminiscent of Locke but is applied improperly.

Contrary to readings which present the sermons as disguised philosophical tracts, Butler's rhetorical tactics are intimately connected with his pastoral motives. Two examples from Sermon VI may be enlightening. At *1729*, p. 102 he changes 'Humane Nature' to 'we'. The effect is to note that it is 'we' who feel things, not human nature, or even 'our' human nature. Simultaneously Butler draws his audience to himself and eliminates the reification which easily insinuates itself into narratives based on axioms. Similarly (Sermon VI, *1729*, p. 110), he redrafts 'there is also manifestly much more Good done by the former ...' as 'we also manifestly discern much more Good done by the former ...', making the observation person-centred and empirical in appeal, rather suggesting that 'we' have privileged access to objective truth.

The sermons were thus subject to a thorough critical reanalysis. Butler did not feel the need to add or delete sermons, although others, from his own testimony, certainly existed. *Fifteen Sermons 1729* offers three changes of emphasis. First, by the addition of a prefatory essay Butler announced both the unity and the intellectual importance of the second edition. Second, by elaborating some of its contents, and thereby placing the volume in a controversial context, he made a statement about the relation of ethics to the nature and role of the Church and society. In this respect *Fifteen Sermons 1729* is a stage in the continuum of Butler's life-work. Third, while preserving their status as discrete liturgical texts, the revised contents presented a fairly coherent view of human nature and the ethical aspect of the human condition. The following account will correct received opinion, which originated as early as 1738,[43] that *Fifteen Sermons* consists of the Preface and the three sermons *Upon Humane Nature*, to which were added another dozen sermons only loosely connected with them.

Butler never deviates from his self-imposed limitations. In Sermon VIII, *Upon Resentment*, he describes his aim as to look at human nature and its circumstances as they are, not as they might be, and to consider their relations. God enables us to do this, whereas he does not encourage us into speculations, 'these being Questions which we have not, that I know of, any thing at all to do with' (*1726*, p. 138 and *1729*, p. 138). But Butler explicitly does not eschew metaphysics: he wishes to ask '*Why or for what End such a Passion was given us:* And this chiefly in order to shew, what are the Abuses of it' (*1726*, p. 139 and *1729*, p. 139). The final clause here is typical of his mature restraint.

---

[43] Vincent Perronet, *A Second Vindication of Mr. Locke*, London, 1738. See Chapter 3 for a discussion of this work.

Butler did not leave Clarke's sphere of influence but produced formulations of much greater delicacy and tact, bringing him closer to common subjective experience. We see this in Sermon XII, *Upon the Love of our Neighbour*. In *1729* a passage is edited and displaced, in which he draws attention to his sermon's text (Romans 13.9) and remarks that '[a] Comparison [is] also being made in the Text between Self-love and the Love of our Neighbour' (*1726*, p. 239; *1729*, p. 244). A change from the *1726* passage signals a typical mature Butlerian caution about intruding schematic metaphysics into an account of human psychology, as these words are entirely deleted: '… and it being evident, that the Love of Others, which includes in it all Virtues, must necessarily be in due Proportion to the Love of ourselves …' (*1726*, p. 239). This deletion, of an assertion which does not, and presumably could not, have empirical grounding, removes a barrier to persuasion and thereby, incidentally, strengthens his sermon's exegetical power.

The metaphysical basis of Butler's ethics

Since the example set by Henry Sidgwick,[44] Butler's grounding in Clarke's metaphysics has received virtually no attention. Admittedly, Butler himself plays a double game. In the Preface he claims to use empirical and inductive methodology rather than the deductive method of Clarke, 'chiefly … [and in] The first three [discourses] wholly' (p. vii). This is not, however, altogether true: he advances arguments based on what looks like empirical evidence (and most certainly on experiential insights into human nature) but it is secured by a reassertion of the metaphysical system in which they are grounded. Indeed, he claims that his apparent divergence of method from Clarke is for reasons of clarity:

> In the former [deductive] Method the Conclusion is express'd thus, that Vice is contrary to the Nature and Reasons of things: in the latter [inductive], that 'tis a Violation or Breaking in upon our own Nature …; and thus they exceedingly strengthen and enforce each other. The first seems the most direct formal Proof, and in some Respects the least liable to Cavil and Dispute: The latter is in a peculiar Manner adapted to satisfie a fair Mind; and is more easily applicable to the several particular Relations and Circumstances in Life. (pp. vi–vii)[45]

It is notable that *Fifteen Sermons'* late Victorian editors – Gladstone, Bernard and Matthews – all, at this point, compare Butler to the Stoics and cite Cicero.[46] The Preface is certainly the place where the density of appeals to authorities reaches a peak in his works, with references, explicit or implicit, to Clarke, Hobbes, Shaftesbury, Locke, Wollaston, Fénelon (and possibly Guyon), Bossuet,

---

[44] See Chapter 6.

[45] This passage provides an example of especially infuriating errors in transcription by subsequent 'standard' editors, in this case W. R. Matthews's London 1914 edition of *Fifteen Sermons*.

[46] Butler's use of Cicero is discussed in Chapter 3.

the Epicureans, Rochefoucauld ('and this whole set of writers'), Cicero and the Stoics. The presence of others can be inferred. Indeed, the Preface seems above all to 'place' Butler's work in a network of authorities and critiques – hence the otherwise redundant reference to the Clarke circle's William Wollaston as a successful practitioner of the deductive method who 'says, that to place Virtue in following Nature, is at best a loose Way of Talk' (pp. viii–ix).

The Preface, therefore, takes on the appearance of a manifesto. Indeed, by claiming that ''Tis true indeed, that few Persons [i.e. authors] have a Right to demand Attention ...', and by remarking on the distinction between the obscurity which arises from complexity of thought and the disorder due to intellectual laziness (pp. iv–v), Butler also implicitly makes a fairly large claim for himself, in marked contrast to his diffidence in the Clarke correspondence.

The argument that the deductive and inductive reinforce each other – and that they reach the same end by different routes – is the germ of the proposition which was to dominate *The Analogy* through its discussion of probability theory: a denial of their theoretical distinction.

But, more immediately, the Preface, while emphasizing the empirical, explicitly locates Butler's ethical doctrines within the Clarke orbit. He introduces into it his famous statement, 'Every thing is what it is, and not another thing' (Preface, p. xxix). This statement is not at all what G. E. Moore was to take it to be, for, in context, it asserts the functional integrity of the bundle of affections in the mind, which is itself essentially a functionally ethical thing. What Butler actually says is 'Self-love and Benevolence, Virtue and Interest are not to be opposed ... Every thing is what it is, and not another thing.' The inclusion of 'Virtue and Interest', which seems a different sort of pairing from that of the two chief affections, might seem to obfuscate matters and has caused difficulties to some analysts. Butler is not, however, suggesting that the two pairs are like, ontologically or functionally, but, rather, denies that any such pair functions dialectically. On the contrary, he asserts that existence is a unity and not a categorical or dialectical system of 'things'. This thought is not supported by groundwork in *Fifteen Sermons* and is not adequately explored until *The Analogy*. The widespread ignorance of the later work causes incomprehension of the earlier.

The Butler–Clarke correspondence, and the authorities cited in the Preface, indicate that when Butler calls affections 'things' he is mindful that, in Clarke's terminology, they are immaterial substances, not Lockean properties of objects, whether primary, like shape, or secondary, like colour. We saw above that a patch of Lockean language was removed from *1729*. Immaterial substances cannot be perceived through the senses. We saw in Chapter 1 that space and time are immaterial substances within the Godhead, but, in the created world, are the framework of our existence. '*Sine quâ non*' was Clarke's term, 'affections' was Butler's. They can be known only by their effects (or, more accurately, 'affects'). As we have seen, Butler generally thinks that emotions are only their symptoms. This is emphasized in a 1729 revision to Sermon XI, *Upon the Love of our Neighbour* (*1729*, p. 216), where a parenthesis is added – '(for these will presently appear to be the same as to this Question)' – to clarify that while in the case instanced, affections and actions are practically indistinguishable, they are different sorts of things theoretically.

The dynamics of the affections – we will see below that their interactions with wider reality are infinitely rich – would produce a highly individualized and unsocial apprehension of the rest of the creation and of the Godhead: the person would be at the mercy of the arbitrary reception of affects by affections: 'And ... from this Uncertainty, it cannot but be, that there will be different Opinions concerning Mankind, as more or less governed by Interest' (p. xxvii). An integrated personality requires a dedicated faculty. Hence arises Butler's belief (Preface, pp. xxvii–xxviii) that the most fundamental of affections, self-love, is a 'general affection' and that without the 'particular Affections' this general affection[47] is left with 'absolutely nothing at all to employ itself about; no End or Object for it to pursue, excepting only that of avoiding Pain', as in the Epicurean philosophy. Thus the account of the affections and their interaction with other objects and beings guarantees the social and ethical dimensions of life. So also, '[the] Goodness or Badness of Actions does not arise from hence, that the Epithet, interested or disinterested, may be applied to them; ... but *from their being what they are*; Namely, what becomes [i.e. is appropriate to] such Creatures as we are, what the state of the Case requires, or the contrary' (Preface, p. xxix, italics supplied). The ethical import of the affections exists without consideration of its relation to their function as survival mechanisms (the 'interested'). It also has nothing to do with the supposed 'interested (= bad)/disinterested (= good)' model. In *1729* he draws, more sharply than before, the distinction between, on the one hand, the animal sensations and survival mechanisms and, on the other, the ethical (deletions from *1726* struck through; additions italicized):

> Every one of our ~~Faculties~~ *Passions and Affections* hath its *natural* Stint and Bound, *which may be easily exceeded; whereas* our Enjoyments can *possibly* be but in a determinate Measure or Degree. *Therefore such Excess of the Affection, since it cannot procure any Enjoyment, must in all Cases be useless; but is generally attended with Inconvenience, and often downright Pain and Misery. This holds as much with regard to Self-love as to all other Affections.* (*1729*, p. 212)

Sensuous pleasure ('Enjoyments') is limited by the capacities of our 'natural' physiological equipment. The drives of the affections – and note how Butler moves back towards Clarke in his technical substitutions for the term 'Facul-ties' – can exceed nature and cause extremes of psychological discomfort. Such discomfort is 'useless' – it does not serve as a survival mechanism – and incon-

---

[47] Butler thinks that there are two main or general affections, self-love and benevolence, but in this passage he considers only self-love. The term 'general Self-love' is introduced in Preface, p. xxvi.

venient. It is not merely an unpleasant sensation but a psychologically disabling condition, which we may as well call, in a modern phrase, a mental illness: the automatic, non-ethical consequence of the contingent interplay of the unmediated affections, which harms the being who possesses them. However, it is a consequence of Butler's theory that such conflicts will be perceived through the experience of emotions.

Two of the great strengths of Butler's theory of the affections are, first, its denial of Shaftesbury's urbane and aristocratic doctrine that everything in the human ethical being is in balance, and second, through an appeal to his congregation's experience, its ability to build on the existence of contradictory impulses and conflicting emotions. In any given individual, and given situation, the mix of affections may be different, so that human subjective experience is theoretically unlimited in variety. No philosopher or psychologist before Butler – not even Aristotle – was able to achieve such an insight. This gives his work apparently permanent appeal and value. It is also one of the areas in which he seems to anticipate David Hume. Locke's account of the human individual is that each is a substance, uniquely overwritten as memory onto the substratum of matter.[48] Hume's critique rejects the putative substratum and instead is formulated in terms of the individual as a unique and integrated 'bundle ... of different perceptions'.[49] Butler's account of the human individual seems to be of an immaterial substance – again we wonder about the actual influence of Berkeley's writings or conversation on him – and a unique bundle of affections, whose functions are experienced as emotions. John P. Wright[50] has most usefully discussed the likeness of Butler and Hume on the emotions and thoughts in relation to the nature of habit and reminds us that habit eventually supplants thought and feeling. Butler uses the term 'cool' and Hume 'calm'. In his poem 'Resolution and Independence', Wordsworth was to use the term 'mild'. All three (and Hobbes makes a fourth) are acutely aware of the constant barrage of threats to the individual's social and economic viability and the resentment (anger, rage, etc.) which is a perpetual factor in the emotional mix of an insecure humanity. For Butler, if not for all the others, the ethical person gradually becomes a unified personality, conscious of social relations ('benevolence') as an aspect of worship and imbedded in the culture of Christian society.[51]

Although we should be extremely cautious about alleging influences, it is a matter of record that Hume sought introductions to Butler over a period of several years from 1737 and was rebuffed,[52] suggesting that he had already

---

[48] John Locke, *Essay* II.xxvii §26.

[49] Hume, *Treatise of Human Nature*, I.IV.vi. Terence Penelhum's 'Butler and Hume', *Hume Studies*, 14 (1988), pp. 251–76, is an effective account.

[50] John P. Wright, 'Butler and Hume on Habit and Moral Character', in *Hume and Hume's Connexions*, ed. M. A. Stewart and John P. Wright, University Park, PA, pp. 105–18.

[51] This is echoed in W. H. Auden's ironic lines 'Let us honour if we can/The vertical man,/Though we value none/But the horizontal one' ('Shorts, 1927–1932').

[52] Bartlett, pp. 80–1.

read Butler and felt that their philosophies were in some ways akin. In his brief analysis of their theories of knowledge J. R. Lucas[53] sought to advance Butler's philosophy at the expense of Hume's, reminding us of some of the shortcomings of Hume's doctrine and arguing plausibly for notionally non-pejorative terms like 'thin' and 'flat' to describe them, in contrast to terms like 'rich' and 'creative' to describe Butler's. Positioning himself, it would seem, with Popper and John Macmurray[54] he pointed to various difficulties in Hume's doctrine, such as the circularity of his implied argument that acts of inductive reasoning could be used to rule out non-inductive reasoning, and reminded us that there are types of argument that are neither deductive nor inductive, including some commonly used in interpreting the results of experiments in the natural sciences. Butler, whose richly intuitive writing is based on a simple, Clarkean, metaphysical scheme, avoids some of these objections. We will discuss this in the next chapter.

Be that as it may, we might ask of Butler, as we can of no philosopher before and of few after him, an account of the infinite variety of human personalities, even within the same culture and with overwhelmingly the same genetic make-up. Why is the mix of the affections unlimited in variety, why do the affections have different relative strengths in different individuals? Butler acknowledges that different individuals have different sensitivities in feeling the effects of their affections. To go beyond that would be to speculate. Such a complex of questions, however, leads into a discussion of Butler's theory of the conscience and consciousness, which seems to be its product.

Through anger to benevolence

It is remarkable that although Butler attaches the term 'useless' to over-active affections he does this solely with regard to those relating to, or subordinate to, self-love. He also says that self-love, the chief of these introvert affections, even if interpreted as the purely selfish, Epicurean variety,[55] is a better guide than passion (the lesser affections): 'it would manifestly prevent numberless Follies and Vices' (Preface, pp. xxxi–xxxii). Thus, whatever its merely prudential role in practical affairs, self-love opens up the ethical analysis of situations, through its mediation, for the person's greater good, of otherwise unregulated and automatic affections. In combination with the extrovert affections (led by benevolence) and the conscience there is the possibility of a good life. To Butler it seems to follow, from the actually unsatisfactory state of affairs, that people are deficient in self-love, and consequently cause harm to themselves. This greatly

---

[53] J. R. Lucas, *Butler's Philosophy of Religion Vindicated*, Durham, 1978, pp. 10–12.

[54] Lucas's argument appears to be a version of that advanced by John Macmurray in *The Self as Agent*, London, 1957, chapter I.

[55] Because Butler puts so much emphasis on the role of the will and habit-forming he is able to accommodate the belief that following a specific philosophy may change, somewhat, personal reactions and behaviour.

interests him. He devotes much time to discussing what appear to be the negative, harmful, anti-social affections, such as anger.

It is probable that Butler himself thought that his treatment of anger was a major philosophical innovation, a Christian rebuttal of both Hobbes and Shaftesbury, taking the full horrors of the emotion head on and rehabilitating it. He arrived early at a definitive position: Sermon VIII, *Upon Resentment*, is one of the least edited of the fifteen in *1729* and our account, uniquely in this chapter, must therefore be mainly from material carried over unchanged from *1726*.[56] Butler first recognized 'instinctive Anger' as a natural phenomenon and beyond the ethical sphere (*1729*, p. 141). This sort of anger is a protective mechanism:

> Sudden Anger upon certain Occasions is meer Instinct: As merely so, as the Disposition to close our Eyes upon the Apprehension of somewhat falling into them; and no more necessarily implies any Degree of reason. ... The Reason and End, for which Man was made thus liable to this Passion, is, that he might be better qualified to prevent, and likewise (or perhaps chiefly) to resist and defeat, sudden Force, Violence and Opposition, considered meerly as such, and without Regard to the Fault or Demerit of him who is the Author of them. (*1729*, pp. 141–2)

Thus, the moral philosopher finds it acceptable for one to lash out in an adrenalin rush when under threat, even if the person threatening one's security is in the right. It follows that one should be thoughtful and careful in asserting one's right, or that of society, when the offender might feel threatened. Translated from the political to the personal level, this is a kind of concession to Hobbes's theory of sovereignty.[57] It has obvious social and juridical implications, which indeed were to appear in the *Six Sermons*. Butler is acutely aware of human anger but, as a theologian, is not afraid of it: 'Hatred, Malice and Revenge, are directly contrary to the Religion we profess, and to the Nature and Reason of the thing itself. Therefore, since no Passion God hath endued us with can be in itself evil ...' (*1729*, p. 144). This reinforces his position, that the affections are, as it were, 'animal' – not intrinsically within an ethical sphere, even though from God: a strong statement against the sufficiency of natural religion and against the ideological superstructures which the deists raised upon it:

> [It] is by no means Malice. No, it is Resentment against Vice and Wickedness: It is one of the common Bonds, by which Society is held together; a Fellow-feeling which each Individual has in behalf of the whole Species, as well as of himself. (*1729*, p. 144)

---

56 Text quoted from *1729*, to avoid the implication that the second edition's text is not under discussion. The pagination of *1726* is identical.

57 See *De corpore politico* (*The Elements of Law*, ed. J. C. A. Gaskin, Oxford, 1994), Chapter XXVIII, 'Of the Duty of them that have Sovereign Power'; and G. A. J. Rogers and K. Schuhmann, *Thomas Hobbes: Leviathan, a Critical Edition*, London, 2003, vol. 2, for Hobbes's functional and objective definitions of personal 'worth' and 'honour' (Chapter 10, pp. 70–1) and for the self-restraints essential for a successful sovereign (Chapter 30, pp. 276–9).

We are naturally friends with our fellows, on whose behalf we feel anger analogous to that which we feel when our personal interests are threatened.

That anger which is not instinctive but amenable to the control of the will is termed 'resentment' and 'deliberate anger' (e.g. *1729*, pp. 143–4): an affection which responds to human anger at threats to one's rights and security. Here Butler runs up against the lack of a ready-made vocabulary. 'Deliberate' anger is an awkward term and should probably not be taken too seriously: it means something like 'anger which dissipates when the case has been considered'. This is one of Butler's fundamental and radical insights into the human social condition, an economical expression of the type of protest represented by exclamations like 'That's not fair!' This resentment is socially self-validating: society, as a construct on top of the given of human nature, is simply like that because, unless it is a Hobbesian tyranny, it consists of people getting along together – in fact, being friends – in a way which is natural but unstable and so mediated ethically. He continues by extending this insight, claiming (*1729*, p. 145) 'From hence it appears, that it is not natural, but moral Evil; it is not Suffering, but Injury, which raises that Anger or Resentment, which is of any Continuance.' Moreover, the whole judicial process is possible only because the resentment which the population feels collectively is of a low intensity.[58] In Sermon VIII itself (*1729*, p. 153) a sentence is added about the social and juridical good effects of (hot) resentment: 'This however is to be considered as a good Effect, notwithstanding it were much to be wished that Men would act from a better Principle, Reason and cool Reflection.' Given enough personal and collective self-discipline society could be regulated wholly by deliberation – but not yet. While such insights were expressed negatively in *1726*,[59] in *1729* positive statements appear, as his social doctrines are clarified and sharpened. In the good (Christian) man resentment is a tool used ('in the strictest way of Moral Consideration') to direct compassion against poverty and suffering (*1729*, p. 152), to the extent that the rich may justly forfeit all respect (*1729*, p. 51).

Thus Butler accounts for anger as self-defence and as aid to deliberation. When he considers the third possible category – anger which persists even when found to be unreasonable (to invent an example, anger felt at fairly losing a game) he follows the logic of his metaphysics and produces something original, simple and profound:

> As to the Abuses of Anger, which it is to be observed may be in all different Degrees, the first which occurs is what is commonly called *Passion*; to which some Men are liable, in the same Way as others are to the *Epilepsie*, or any sudden particular Disorder. (*1729*, p. 148)

---

58 From here the account returns to the analysis of the *1729* changes.

59 '*Why or for what End such a Passion* [= resentment] *was given us:* And this chiefly in order to shew, what are the Abuses of it' (*1726*, p. 139). In *1726* he does not choose to ask 'what are the right uses of it'.

Lacking an inherited or consensual vocabulary[60] he calls them 'abuses of anger' even though they are temperamental and not under voluntary control: they are illnesses, with all that this implies for social action. Some forms of anger cannot be drawn into the ethical sphere: hatred, malice and revenge. They are 'directly contrary to the Religion we profess, and to the Nature and Reason of the thing itself' (*1729*, p. 139). Hatred is unchristian and consequently anti-social and unethical, but it certainly exists and must be accounted for.

> [Since] no Passion God hath endued us with can be in itself Evil; and yet since Men frequently indulge a Passion in such Ways and Degrees, that at length it becomes quite another thing from what it was originally in our Nature. (*1729*, p. 140)

Thus he several times inserts into *1729* formulae which avoid alleging the existence of evil as an objective force and suggest its location in mental ill-health. Yet this (to modern ears) secularist viewpoint is where he relies most heavily on his religion. In the Preface (p. xvii) he attacks Shaftesbury's analysis of virtue for neglecting to '[take] into Consideration … the Idea of reflex Approbation or Disapprobation'. 'Reflex' means 'derived from, consisting in, the conversion of the mind or thought upon itself'.[61] That this is a comment on Shaftesbury's poor theology is evident from one of Butler's fragments, not published by him:

> What a wonderful Incongruity it is for a Man to see the Doubtfulness in which things are involved, & yet be impatient out of Action or vehement in it. Say a Man is a Sceptick, & add, what was said of *Brutus quicquid vult valde vult* [i.e., whatever Brutus willed, he willed intensely], and you say, there is the greatest Contrariety between his Understanding & his Temper that can be express'd in words.[62]

Immoderate emotions are bred by scepticism because the sufferer lacks the discipline and procedures to control them. For Butler, the practice of faith – literally, the daily offices of the Prayer Book – are a buttress of good mental health.[63] Humanity, however, is surrounded and penetrated by immoderation, so that the good life is one of continuous struggle and self-examination. This is intrinsic to the human condition in this life and no escape is possible from:

> Fear, Resentment, Compassion and others; of which there could be no Occasion or Use in a perfect State: But in the present we should be exposed to greater Inconveniences without them…. They are Incumbrances indeed, but such as we are obliged to carry about with us, through this various Journey of Life. (*1729*, pp. 155–6)

---

[60] 'Let this be called Anger, Indignation, Resentment, or by whatever Name any one shall chuse; the thing itself is understood, and is plainly natural' (*1729*, p. 156).

[61] OED, reflex a (3b).

[62] BM Add. MS 9815 (26).

[63] There is no direct evidence to support the speculation that the curative disciplines of the Prayer Book were a personal factor in Butler's decision to join the Church of England. It is, to put it at its most cautious, not incompatible with a reading of the late *Fragments*. See Chapter 4, pp. 140, 144.

Whether or not this was suggested by the 'great burden' on the back of Bunyan's Christian, it reminds us of Butler's intellectual roots in an older, less urbane culture, in which, Hobbes-like, humankind cannot hope for the luxury of contemplating the ultimate beauty, coherence or utility of a morally good life. The human condition is a state of chronic stress. Indeed, so stressed is Butler's own thinking around this that *1729* follows *1726* in noting that 'the Precepts to *forgive*, and to *love our Enemies*, do not relate to that general Indignation against Injury and the Authors of it, but to this Feeling ... when raised by private or personal Injury' (*1726*, p. 157; *1729*, p. 157). Behind the practice of the revealed way of Christianity are the Clarkean affective structures of human nature. The conflict between the natural humankind and revealed religion is not to be resolved in this life. We recall Butler's speculation recorded by his chaplain Josiah Tucker in the garden of the episcopal palace in Bristol about whether nations may go mad – in other words, feel as incompetently about injuries as individuals may.[64] In practice, forgiveness involves the setting aside of resentment against specific persons in specific situations, not the application of a general principle – because, one supposes, there cannot be an affection which works to cancel the result of a class of external stimuli but only one which works to neutralize instances by counteraction.[65]

Before leaving the congeries of anger which Butler, like Hobbes, recognizes in humankind it will be well here to settle a point which has been discussed, to little profit, by many recent moral philosophers: the question of Butler's alleged principle of 'cool' self-love, which is in essence taken to mean a cold and calculating approach to self-interest.[66] It will appear in Chapter 5 that Butler was in no way personally sentimental or professionally Sentimental, but neither did he hold positions such as that described. In modern English, 'hot' is opposed by 'cold' and 'warm' by 'cool'. 'Cool' can be moved towards 'hot' or 'cold': 'it was a wonderfully cool day' means that it was still warm enough for comfort; 'he received the suggestion coolly' means coldly. It can also mean 'dégagé': 'the king of cool'. Things were very different in Early Modern English, where 'warm' was usually quite 'hot' (OED 'warm', a, 9, 10a, 10b, 11) – 'you grow warm, sir', as Shakespeare has it in *Hamlet* – and 'cool', when applied to emotions (OED 'cool', a 4a), is fairly 'warm'. 'Hot' is associated with 'red' and with anger. In Dryden's translation of the *Aeneid*, 10.380, we find: 'Thus threatening comets, when by night they rise,/ Shoot sanguine streams, and sadden all the skies ...' and in Pope's *Iliad*, 'Like the red star that fires the autumnal skies' (5.8). Comets simply are not red in colour: this is obvious and was known to all these poets, but they were definitely associated with divine anger and portents

---

[64] This is discussed in Chapter 4.

[65] A point made, in slightly different terms and without reference to the affections, by Paul A. Newberry, 'Joseph Butler on Forgiveness: A Presupposed Theory of Emotion', 2001, p. 233.

[66] These philosophers are not named, although some of the relevant works are cited in the Introduction. This is a principled decision: if editors and historians of language and of ideas fail to deliver accurate texts and contexts for philosophers to work on it is not surprising if the latter make interpretative errors.

of violence. In Homer, Sirius, the dog star, is redder in metaphor (the hot 'dog days' bred pestilence) than it is in fact. 'Hot' was, and is, associated with anger and we have already seen Butler's doctrine in this regard. When he wishes to emphasize that self-love is not hot and angry, he naturally calls it cool – like Handel's blissfully 'cool airs' in 'Where'er you walk', it is not cold, but reassuringly cooled from hot to something comfortable. If he were constructing a metaphor today he would move towards the word 'warm' – neither hot nor cold but comforting and certainly not calculating and detached. In *1729* 'cool' is actually introduced at one point. Having discussed the social and juridical good effect of (hot) resentment he inserts, 'This however is to be considered as a good Effect, notwithstanding it were much to be wished that Men would act from a better Principle, Reason and cool Reflection' (*Upon the Forgiveness of Injuries, 1729*, p. 153), which in turn is glossed by another inserted passage:

> Anger also or Hatred may be considered as another false Medium of viewing things, which always represents Characters and Actions much worse than they really are. Ill-will not only never speaks, but never thinks well, of the Person towards whom it is exercised. Thus in Cases of Offence and Enmity, the whole Character and Behaviour is considered with an Eye to that particular Part which has offended us, and the whole Man appears monstrous, without any thing right or human in him: Whereas the Resentment should surely at least be confined to that particular Part of the Behaviour which gave Offence; since the other Parts of a Man's Life and Character stand just the same as they did before. (*1729*, p. 171)

Thus anger holds a key place in Butler's psychology and ethics: the introverted personal insecurity felt by a humanity richly churning with conflicting affections and mediated by self-love meets the extrovert world through feelings of anger and affective diagnoses of unfairness which are mediated by benevolence: in Butler's account, as we saw above, people feel angry (have 'Fellow-feelings', *1729*, p. 144) about the dangers and frustrations in their friends' situations, 'friends' being located in a fluid system of concentric and overlapping circles, a dynamic which the extrovert, social affections use to build society.[67]

Typically, *1729* is more positive about this than *1726* and its formulation constitutes a truly original, and historically important, theological development in theorizing the relationship of humankind with God. In the following passage deletions from 1726 are scored through, insertions are italicized and an editorial comment added in square brackets.

> We … feel the same Kind of Satisfaction and Enjoyment (whatever would be the Degree of it) from this higher Acquaintance *and Friendship*, as we feel from common ~~Friendships~~ *ones*; the Intercourse being

---

[67] The circles of friends are analysed in Chapter 3, as the main locus of Butler's exposition is in *The Analogy*.

real, and the Persons equally present, in both Cases. We should have a more ardent Desire to be approved by his better Judgment, and a ~~higher~~ Satisfaction in that Approbation, ~~than any thing of this Sort which could~~ *of the same Sort with what would* be felt in respect to common Persons, or be wrought in us by their Presence ... remembring still that he [= God] is perfectly Good, *and our Friend as well as our Governour.*

(*1726*, pp. 264–5; *1729*, pp. 270–1)

Whereas in *1726* friendship was an earthly analogue *1729* locates it in the relationship with God – 'in the same sort'. God is our friend, as well as governor; the two changes, in the second and last lines, recall the language of contemporary Dissent[68] and anticipate, and perhaps prompt, the slogans of the later Sunday school movement, such as 'What a friend we have in Jesus',[69] and for a similar reason: Butler wishes to emphasize both that God is our friend (the New Testament provides little support for this claim)[70] and that the psychological mechanism of the affections is the same. God is the friend of people in the same way as the master of a household is a friend of the domestic servants in the household.[71] This theme will reappear in John Heylyn's sermon at Butler's consecration (Chapter 4) and in the social policy of his own *Six Sermons* (Chapter 5). On the one hand, God is a constant presence in our lives and, on the other, our human friendships are of the same type as our mutually loving relationship with God. Thus Butler revisits and strengthens his insight. This is a metaphysical doctrine but it is also likely that it expresses Butler's own religious experience. God and a human friend are both 'equally present' and in both cases 'the Intercourse is real'. There is a further point, located in the words, 'whatever would

---

[68] For example, James Wood, *Readiness to good Works, and Largeness of Mind in them [1 Timothy 6.17–19]*, London, R. Hett, 1732: 'He [i.e. God] that has given you Hearts to love, fear, and choose him, is a Friend that will never forsake you.' This was a sermon in the annual series for the benefit of the Gravel Lane charity school. Research into the relationship between Butler's ethics and educational theory is in progress.

[69] Sandy Brewer, 'From Darkest England to *The Hope of the World*: Protestant Pedagogy and the Visual Culture of the London Missionary Society', *Material Religion*, vol. 1, no. 1 (2005), pp. 98–124. Research into the omnipresence of Butler's works and popularised versions of them in the nineteenth century might illuminate the particular complex of ethics, psychology and pedagogy which Brewer finds in the Sunday School movement, whose pioneers were heavily influenced by Butler. See Chapter 5, pp. 173–4.

[70] Most of the AV's uses of 'friend' are OT. In the NT the most plausible cases which might support Butler's characterization of God as a personal 'friend' of individuals are in Luke 11.6 and John 3.29. But Luke's parable is considered, both by modern scholars and in the great commentary by Butler's older contemporary, Matthew Henry, to be focused solely on the rewards of importunate prayer, and John's to define the role of John the Baptist. See Ian Randall, *What a Friend We Have in Jesus: The Evangelical Tradition*, London, 2005, passim.

[71] Making allowances for cultural differences (and especially the primacy in Butler of epistemology and the property analogy), Butler's thoughts are reminiscent of Aquinas, for whom ethics follows from friendship, of both humankind and God. See P. J. Wadell, 'Growing Together in the Divine Love: The Role of Charity in the Moral Theology of Thomas Aquinas', in *Aquinas and Empowerment*, ed. G. S. Harak, Washington, DC, 1996, pp. 148–63; and Celia E. Deane-Drummond, *Creation Through Wisdom: Theology and the New Biology*, Edinburgh, 2000, pp. 99–107. A reading of such works emphasizes the fact that Butler's strategy was to move towards orthodoxy from a basis in contemporary peri-deist 'natural philosophy'.

be the Degree of it'. Some people have stronger and some weaker 'affections'. The point, however, is, as it were, the plot of the contours charted by each individual's affections, not their absolute intensity. Religious and social paternalism aside, this is an egalitarian Christianity and ethics. In the same sermon (*1726*, p. 269; *1729*, p. 276) he notes that 'Religion does not demand new Affections, but only claims the Direction of those you already have, those Affections you daily feel; though unhappily confined to Objects, not altogether unsuitable, but altogether unequal to them.'[72] The practice of the loving relationship with God is a pair with the practice of social friendship: the complex is what makes us distinctively human, in our approach to each unique moral problem.[73]

Butler, as we have remarked, is not a Sentimental 'Man of Feeling',[74] let alone a Victorian sentimentalist. The unwary reader may be shocked and repelled by some aspects of the charitable policy of the *Six Sermons* discussed in Chapter 5. But he here introduces the concept of 'friend' into Anglican theology and thereby opens the way to the theology and practice of charity which grew so quickly and immensely in English society in succeeding generations.

If, in his metaphysical scheme,[75] people have affections of love – which seems empirically undeniable – do they experience hatred? This might seem equally undeniable. However, Butler does not deal in emotions but affections. If we consider that an affection is an automatic response to (almost, a movement towards) something in a second party, and originally in the divine nature, it would seem as theoretically difficult to postulate an affective hatred, as it would be heretical to ascribe hatred to God. Thus, we find that Butler, in his most counter-intuitive doctrine, denies the reality of hatred and on this denial founds the sketch of a whole theory of psychology and society, which becomes a key component of his philosophy as it matures, where it is signalled by words like 'resentment',[76] 'hot' and 'cool'.

In Sermon I, *Upon the Social Nature of Man*, Butler discusses the evil that men do to themselves and the sources of that evil. Into *1729* he inserts the following observation (the words in italics being reworked from *1726*):

---

[72] Note 'you': addressed to his congregation of lawyers and administrators.
[73] Gordon Kendal, 'A God Most Peculiar' (*passim*), in *Tercentenary Essays*, presents very well the 'particularity' of Butler's approach to ethics and the unique integration of religious ethics and ethical religion.
[74] The title of a best-selling Sentimental novel by Henry MacKenzie, London, 1771.
[75] When Kendal (*op. cit.*) draws comparisons between Butler and Leibniz on this point, however, it must be remembered that although Butler had heard of, and very likely read, Leibniz through Clarke, the origin of his doctrine of the affections must pre-date such knowledge. Moreover, to denominate Butler's doctrine of affections as 'hedonism' is to forget that they are the point of contact between God and the human mind – the 'God in us' component – and that emotions such as pleasure are not, for Butler, ends but symptoms.
[76] 'Resentment' is a late entrant into English, according to the OED first recorded from the Italian by John Florio in 1611. Butler uses it more or less in its main sense (2.a. 'A strong feeling of ill-will or anger against the author or authors of a wrong or affront; the manifestation of such feeling against the cause of it').

> ... that Mankind have ungoverned Passions which they will gratifie at
> any Rate, as well to the Injury of Others, as in Contradiction to known
> private Interest: But that as there is no such thing as Self-hatred, *so
> neither is there any such thing as Ill-will in one Man towards another.*
> (*1729*, pp. 18–19)

Living in a less narcissistic society than ours, he feels able to appeal to a
social consensus that self-hatred does not exist (we will see that, in his terms,
what we might call self-hatred comes within the scope of resentment). He postulates a theoretical identity of 'hatred of oneself' and 'hatred of others' – a single
'affection' which does not, in fact, actually exist and, moreover, cannot exist,
although it can be formulated: a point which featured in Clarke's anti-nomi-
nalist metaphysics. There are other affections – 'ungoverned Passions' – which
are sociopathic and self-harming, but this is precisely because of their being
ungoverned, not because they are intrinsically evil. Evil has no reality: it is a
conceptual self-deception – indeed, in Sermon X, *Upon Self-Deceit*, Butler characterizes it as a 'counterfeit' (*1729*, p. 194),[77] in resorting to which, in the pursuit
of unrestrained self-gratification, the individual causes spiritual self-harm:

> Truth, and real good Sense, and thorough Integrity, carry along with
> them a peculiar Consciousness of their own Genuineness: There is a
> Feeling belonging to them, which does not accompany their Counter-
> feits, [examples of which are] Error, Folly, Half-Honesty, partial and
> slight Regards to Virtue and Right, so far only as they are consistent
> with that Course of Gratification which Men happen to be set upon
> ... [It] is much the same, as if we should suppose a Man to have had
> a general View of some Scene, enough to satisfy him that it was very
> disagreeable, and then to shut his Eyes ... It is as easy to close the Eyes
> of the Mind, as those of the Body ... (*1729*, p. 194)[78]

The theory of resentment is built entirely on the proposition that it is socially
and ethically a beneficial affection, always supposing the validating presence of
the 'Consciousness of [its] own Genuineness'.

In theory, the same set of affections exists, more or less strongly, in everyone[79]
and their negatives do not exist, being merely logical constructs. Theology apart,
presumably Butler thought that if they did, the outright conflict, not liable to
mediation, would render the person fatally unstable. In this Butler seems to
anticipate the twentieth-century philosopher R. G. Collingwood and his theory
of the scale of forms.[80] The scale of the relevant emotions runs not from 'love'

---

[77] Also *1726*, p. 193, but *1729* sets this sentence in a reworked context, and should be the reader's first resort.
[78] The half-sentence 'Partial and slight Regards ... to be set upon' is an addition to *1729*. We have already suggested a reminiscence in Butler of Addison's *Spectator* papers on the imagination.
[79] *1729*, p. 244. This passage, relocated and heavily reworked, is from *1726*, p. 239. The concept of proportionality ('... as thyself ...') is new in *1729*.
[80] Collingwood has been thought worth reprinting. The reference is to *Philosophical Method*, 1933; republished Oxford, 2005, III.5.26, p. 82. He nowhere refers to Butler.

to 'hatred' but from 'greatest love' to 'least love', interacting with defensive anger. This requires Butler to consider the ethical nature of the various points on the scale (the metaphor is Collingwood's, not Butler's) and therefore also to consider concepts like (un-)reasonable and moderate, because on any scale there is a natural tendency to gravitate towards mean values: the extremes lack theoretical importance, as ('most … least') they are relative, not absolute, in value and are unstable. It will be anticipated, correctly, that this not only features in *Fifteen Sermons* but that there will also be found changes relevant to it in *1729*. In fact, this is an area of strength in *1726*: Butler had already provided sermons *Upon the Government of the Tongue*, two *Upon Compassion, Upon the Character of Balaam*, two *Upon Resentment, and the Forgiveness of Injuries* and two *Upon the Love of our Neighbour*. The most striking relevant amendment in *1729* is this (*1729* amendment italicized; editorial interpolations in square brackets):

> It cannot be imagined, that we are required to love [our enemies] with any peculiar Kind of Affection … [The injured party] ought to be affected towards the injurious Person in the same Way any good Men, uninterested in the Case, would be; if they had the same just Sense, which we have supposed the injured Person to have, of the Fault: *After which there will yet remain real Good-will towards the Offender.*
>
> (*1729*, p. 169)

In *1726* Butler says there is no affection dedicated to those who injure or threaten us. A victim who is good and good citizens in general share the same analytical understanding ('the same just sense') of the case, which implies a common moral nature and a social consensus. The effect of the *1729* addition is not only to reinforce the rhetorical appeal to the victim to apply benevolence to the aggressor (a strategy of forgiveness) but rather more: out of the pre-existing materials from *1726*, to propose that good-will naturally re-emerges once the defence mechanism, the resentment which has temporarily overlaid it, is removed. This obviously has implications for juridical theory, judicial practice and the assessment of strategies for approaching conflicts of all kinds. It is a reformulation of the biblical doctrine of forgiveness, using a post-Cartesian account of the nature of humankind as social beings: a more rounded account than hitherto presented from within the Church of England, or, indeed, in English moral philosophy.

Thus good ethics is not adherence to a system of maxims but a psychological praxis, a constant assessment of our actions, moderation in two senses: a tendency away from extremes and the presiding over formal, if internal, disputations. This is the quintessentially Butlerian doctrine, embodying what was evidently his own ethical practice.[81] It brings with it the conviction of the danger and instability of qualities like 'hot' and 'passionate' and the safety of qualities like 'cool', 'social' and 'thoughtful'. Thus, in Sermon I, *Upon the Social Nature*

---

[81] This sense of 'moderation' may be borne in mind in Chapter 4, with regard to Butler's examination, in his role as Bishop of Bristol, of John Wesley.

of Man, he changes the phrase 'wishing well to others' to 'wishing that Good to Another, which he knows himself unable to procure him; and rejoycing in it, though bestowed by a third Person[.] And can Love of Power any way possibly come in to account for this Desire or Delight?' (*1729*, pp. 6–7n). This opens the way for his account of benevolence.[82]

Any account of someone else's text necessarily involves selection and a degree of distortion. The reader is, nevertheless, invited to consider, whether approaching Butler's ethics through his account of anger clears away difficulties which have been raised by previous analysts.

If self-love dominates and moderates the introvert affections, and benevolence does the same with the extrovert ones, so that they constitute the two major drives in human nature, the relationship between the two must be a major component of the account of the integrated human being as well as of moral doctrine. It is a statistical fact, from the balance and pattern of the *1729* revisions, that Butler felt the need not to refine his doctrine of ethics but to develop his doctrine of love so as to be more coherent with it. Some changes merely give greater emphasis to the pair's primacy: one is a deletion (in Sermon XII, *Upon the Love of our Neighbour*) of the phrase 'as well as other passions' (*1726*, p. 237); another is the tweaking of a sentence so that it reads '[these moral qualities] are connected with Benevolence in Our Nature, and so may be considered [for this immediate purpose] as the same thing with it ...' (*1729*, p. 250n), a remark with which Butler glances at what he identifies as the impoverishment of Shaftesbury's theory of benevolence.

Other changes correct mistakes in setting out his theory. Formulations such as 'Self-love is not private Good ... [and] Interestedness is not Interest' (*1726*, p. 214) lacked clarity and did not flow naturally from the sermons' ethical axioms, while the proposal that he investigate whether the exercise of benevolence promotes the good of the agent is contrary to them (*ibid.*). Such formulations were deleted from *1729*.

Other, more important, revisions draw attention to the centrality of Christian doctrine and scriptural exegesis in his ethics. Hence in Sermon XII a paragraph is inserted (see note 79 above) whose purpose is to assert that what matters is not the strength of the affections but their proportions in any given individual. He derives not only the idea of the two principal affections from his sermon's text (Romans 13.9 – 'Thou shalt love thy Neighbour as thy self') but also the idea of their proportionality ('as thy self'), which he now introduces. He uses this as a new and more articulated basis, cautiously but firmly introduced,[83] to provide theoretical security for the argument displayed in *1726* that however

---

[82] John Macquarrie, deploying the concept of hope in the place of 'wishing well', was to describe the same relationship with a moral and social critique in his *Christian Hope*, London, 1978, e.g. pp. 9–10.

[83] '[It] should be questioned, whether it be the exact Meaning [of the text] ...' (*1729*, p. 244). This is one of the places where Butler acknowledges the need for a collegiate enterprise of Scriptural textual editing and exegesis.

much benevolence may be 'equal' to self-love in us, we cannot be 'equally' concerned for others' benefits, for while all affections which respond to the condition of others respond also to our own, there are other affections which respond only to our self-interest. The *1726* observation that we are especially 'entrusted' with ourselves (*1726*, p. 241; *1729*, p. 247) thus gains in resonance from a refreshed account of human nature which appears to follow from metaphysical axioms rather than empirical observation.

The appreciation that the selves with which we are entrusted are constantly under threat coheres with the theoretical imbalance between self-love and benevolence and leads to a revised account of the phenomenon that we feel greater sympathy for others in distress than pleasure in their good fortune (*1729*, p. 87). This observation takes its place in his anti-Hobbes strategy, the shared sense of fear's predominance being linked with the solidarity which he was to term the 'Cement of Society'.[84] People assist each other in bad times, rather than drawing together because of good times, even when this concerns our duty of thanking God for them.[85]

Perhaps the most fundamentally important revision is also in Sermon XI, where Butler preaches that it is not 'the Means and Materials of Enjoyment' but 'the Enjoyment of them' that constitutes 'Interest and Happiness' (*1726*, p. 222; revised and expanded into *1729*, pp. 226–8). This ('… Interest …') raises the question of ownership – and we note how in modern English the words 'enjoy', 'possess', 'property' and 'benefit', not to mention 'rights' and 'entitlement', remain entangled. The 1729 Butler, still addressing an elite audience – his examples of property are 'Riches, Houses, Lands, Gardens' (1729, p. 227) – now rejects the 'happiness-possession' nexus entirely:

> … the Object of every particular Affection is equally somewhat external to Ourselves; and whether it be the Good of another Person [i.e. benevolence], or whether it be any other external thing, makes no Alteration with Regard to its being one's own Affection; and the Gratification of it one's own private Enjoyment. (*1729*, p. 227)

This constitutes a radical, but logical and internally consistent, application of the concept of 'particular affections'. Self-love – immediate self-preservation – must be stronger than benevolence, so that the importance of the question of property does not simply go away, but the relative proportions of affections, be they general or particular, differ in each individual. It is the ethical practice which is important: the more that deficiencies in benevolence, or indeed self-love, are rectified by practice the closer will the individual approach the human

---

[84] Sermon V has a very long footnote against Hobbes – *1726*, p. 80ff.
[85] A study of the balance in the eighteenth century between sermons of thanksgiving and humiliation would be interesting in relation to this point but is at present frustrated by the lack of suitable bibliographical resources.

norm of good ethical choices.[86] To emphasize this, Butler adds at the end of this extended interpolation, that it is 'Religion, from whence arises our strongest Obligation to Benevolence' (*1729*, p. 228). The move away from virtue's, or the good man's, 'claiming' the world by his virtue is a further rejection of Hobbes's thesis that security is to be obtained by the possession of power and property, or submission to it. Typically, his crucial formulation is syntactically elaborate and ostentatiously cautious:

> There seems no other Reason to suspect that there is any such pecu-
> liar Contrariety, but only that the Courses of Action which Benevo-
> lence leads to, has [*sic*] a more direct Tendency to promote the Good of
> Others, than that Course of Action which Love of Reputation ... or any
> other particular Affection leads to. (*1729*, p. 217)

In Sermon XI (*1729*) Butler proceeds via a long rebuttal of Shaftesbury to discuss benevolence, advancing the proposition that self-love is a self-directed affection, corresponding to and, as it were, a mirror image of neighbour-directed benevolence, and thus entering the dynamics of practical ethics, of which, considered apart from benevolence, it is unaware.[87]

Hence although the ethically good is nothing but a social thing, it resists utilitarian analysis: it is simply recognized as such. It is the subject of much rewriting in Sermon XI.[88] Butler is not saying that the natural is good; he holds that good actions are the product of complex mechanisms of unconscious and conscious assessment ('what the state of the Case requires', *1729*, p. xxix). He clearly implies, however, that evil exists only as a product of a defective ethics[89] in a natural world which, unless mediated by the chief affections, is a Hobbesian state of conflict. This was to be elaborated in *The Analogy*.

The insight, that 'we may judge and determine, that an Action is morally Good or Evil, before we so much as consider, whether it be interested or disin-terested' (Preface, p. xxix), is, however, one of the fundamental building blocks

---

86 Here Butler enters the territory of modern 'normative' ethics. See Christine M. Korsgaard's Tanner lectures, *The Sources of Normativity*, Lecture 1. However, Korsgaard see ethics as normative, whereas Butler, with the contemporary restricted understanding of reason as merely combinative and mediatory of affections, sees human nature itself as tending towards norms. Butler seems more acutely aware of social realities and contingencies than the more purely philosophical Korsgaard.

87 Although an analysis is beyond the present work's scope, it seems that, personal acuity apart, Butler's superiority to Shaftesbury as a moral philosopher is due to the metaphysical basis of his theory of the affections. Shaftesbury, by contrast, argues *ad hominem* at all times: the aesthetic basis of his ethics is rather an extrusion from his aristocratic social affiliation than from a theory of human nature.

88 For example, a paragraph in *1729*, p. 214 becomes a much longer passage, *1729*, pp. 217–18, devoted to this question.

89 In this Butler differs from Malebranche. As Michael Ayers has noted of Malebranche, '"*Conscience*" is the mind's immediate reflexive apprehension of itself and its operations ...' ('Was Berkeley an empiri-cist or a rationalist', p. 42). Butler (who cites, in order to reject, Malebranche in at least one way in the *Fifteen Sermons*) sees conscience as an exclusively ethical faculty and as intimately connected with the will. For Butler human beings may lack a conscience – the ethical dialogue may atrophy to non-existence – whereas for Malebranche, for whom conscience is a faculty in the general human fund of epistemological tools, they can at worst possess a corrupted one.

of his thought. In making it he mounts an additional objection to Hobbes (whom he now, p. xxxi, links with the Epicureans and Rochefoucauld), accusing him of using tautologous terminology to conceal the fact that his doctrine of selfishness is empty of meaning.[90] While admitting (Preface, p. xxvi) the limitations of his own system's ability to analyse the complexities of motivation he seems to believe that the emotional currents washing around ethical actions are symptoms of the mutual engagement of the affections. His analysis of this is material for an account of an infinitely rich and complex ethically narrative of a race of societal individuals – and it is notable that Butler indeed features in modern theorizing about the development of the concept of narrative in both fiction and the law.[91]

Towards an account of conscience and consciousness

Thus, with his *a priori* account of the affections in some way lying behind the emotions which are facts of subjective experience, Butler draws the introvert and extrovert together. It remains to be seen, however, whether he can succeed in integrating them in an account of ethics, or social morale, because he thinks that ethics – judgements about right and wrong – is a system of values and reasoned decision-making, not of following nature, of which latter theory he has produced a telling critique.[92] The only model he has of reason is the contemporary, anti-rationalist, account of the comparison of percepts and concepts, a powerful but limited model, as Kant was to demonstrate.[93] He is, however, left in the same Cartesian trap of extreme individualism – indeed, extreme personal individuation – which he is later to criticize in Locke.[94] Thus Butler is always reaching towards the community of action and faith (that is, the Church) to which he is professionally committed. The means are there: the affections are common to all humans, even if in different strengths and proportions and capable of infinitely various combinations. As he points out in one of the conceptual climaxes of the Preface, this is true of animals:

> Brutes obey their Instincts or Principles of Action, according to certain Rules; suppose the Constitution of their Body, and the Objects around them ... [and in doing this act] according to the Rules before-mentioned, their bodily Constitution and Circumstances, act suitably to their whole Nature ... [and] there does not appear the least Ground to imagine them

---

[90] That Butler is capable of mounting such a critique of Hobbes's philosophical language should give pause to those who, perhaps prematurely, criticize what they suppose to be his ability to recognize his own terminological fuzziness.

[91] See, for example, Jan-Melissa Schramm, *Testimony and Advocacy in Victorian Law*, passim, but especially Chapters 1 and 2.

[92] Penelhum suggested (*Butler*, p. 101) that, compared to Aquinas, Butler has 'a more modest view of the epistemic status of the doctrines of natural religion'.

[93] Discussion of this point will be resumed in Chapter 3 in relation to the concept of analogy.

[94] Dennis Des Chene, *Physiologia*, pp. 370–77, gives an account of Late Aristotelian thinking about the physics of individuation as it was embraced by the Cartesians. See also Tad M. Schmaltz, *Malebranche's Theory of the Soul*, New York, 1996, esp. Chapter 5.2.2.

to have any thing else in their Nature, which requires a different Rule or Course of Action ... Mankind also in acting thus would act suitably to their whole Nature, if no more were to be said of Man's Nature, than what has been now said; if That, as it is a true, were also a compleat, adequate Account of our Nature. (Preface, pp. xiii–xv)

The human being has these animal resources, but others too, and Butler allows a semantic complexity to develop around the word 'nature' (for example, the twin definitions in Sermon II, *1729*, p. 33); there may be constituted a viable but amoral and somewhat less than fully human state – a state at which anyone could arrive by choosing to reject the most important part of their capabilities. In another glancing blow at Shaftesbury, he notes that the 'natural Authority of the Principle of Reflection or Conscience is ... in great Measure overlooked by many, who are by no Means the worst sort of Men' (*1729*, p. xvi).[95] Although Butler does not say so here, developing the thought only later, in the *Six Sermons*, it is evident that not everyone could enter this state without society ceasing to exist.

His solution is to develop a typically radical and powerful account of the conscience.[96] In Sermon XIII, *1726*, discussing humankind's love of God, he had written (the numbers in square brackets are added for the reader's ease in following the editing):

As the whole Attention of Life should be to obey his Commands; so the highest Enjoyment of it must arise from [1] a Consciousness of his Favour and Approbation; [2] from the Contemplation of this Character, and [3] our Relation to it. (*1726*, p. 266)

In *1729* this is edited into the following, with passage [4] added:

As the whole Attention of Life should be to obey his Commands; so the highest Enjoyment of it must arise from [2] the Contemplation of this Character, and [3] our Relation to it, from [1] a Consciousness of his Favour and Approbation, and [4] from the Exercise of those Affections towards Him which could not but be raised from his Presence.

(*1729*, p. 272)

The *1729* version is not only amplified but also is restructured to form a sequenced religious exercise.[97] The result is our feeling 'Joy, Gratitude, Reverence, Love, Trust, and Dependance' (*1729*, p. 272), these feelings being natural

---

95 The point of Sermon VII, *Upon the Character of Balaam*, to the text Numbers 23.10 ('Let me die the death of the righteous ...') is unexpressed because obvious to its hearers: that at a key moment Balaam and his ass exchange positions, the ass acquiring a human ethical insight lacking in its less-than-human(e) master.

96 This is not meant to suggest a chronology of Butler's development; his account of the conscience is more or less fully present in *1726*. *1729* elaborates the theological and pastoral implications.

97 The 'enthusiastic' Butlerian poet Christopher Smart also produces such structured sequences. This is the subject of Bob Tennant, 'Christopher Smart and *The Whole Duty of Man*', *Eighteenth-Century Studies*, vol. 13, no. 1 (1979), pp. 63–78.

consequences of the exercise of the complex of affections. The difference between the animal and the human is that the former is automatic. In the Preface Butler keeps circling around the concept of the watch as a metaphor for the mind (the 'System or Constitution of Humane Nature', p. x) but cautions against too great literalism.

> A Machine is inanimate and passive: but we are Agents. Our Constitu-
> tion is put in our own Power. We are charged with it: and therefore
> are accountable for any Disorder or Violation of it ... And ... this our
> Nature, *i.e.* Constitution is adapted to Virtue, as from the Idea of a
> Watch it appears, that its Nature, *i.e.* Constitution or System, is adapted
> to measure Time. (*1729*, p. x)[98]

Note the contrast between Butler and Paley. For Paley, who thought he was building on Butler, the analogy between human being and timepiece supports the argument that both are designed. Butler certainly did think that humankind was designed, but this is philosophically unimportant; such is his concentration on expressing exactly what he means about the human affections being God-given, and analogous to properties of the divine mind, that he uses the analogy in passing, and returns to the main idea: that people are adapted, 'Agents' and 'accountable'.

> [The] very Constitution of our Nature requires, that we bring our whole
> Conduct before this superior Faculty; wait its Determination; enforce
> upon ourselves its Authority, and make it the Business of our Lives, as it
> is absolutely the whole Business of a Moral Agent, to conform ourselves
> to it. This is the true Meaning of that ancient Precept, *Reverence thy*
> *Self.* (*1729*, pp. xvi–xvii)

'Reverence thy Self' recalls the various formulae quoted above about the source and the double direction of moral obligations and the obligation to develop ethical activity.[99] When people do not reverence their selves, they can fall outside the sphere of the ethical, and therefore beyond the reach of religion. Sermon X, *Upon Self-Deceit*, is based on 2 Samuel 12.7 – 'And Nathan said to David, Thou art the Man'. This is taken by Butler not to refer to people who 'are too far gone to have any thing said to them. The thing before us is indeed of this Kind, but in a lower Degree, and confined to the moral Character; somewhat of which we almost all of us [*sic*] have, without reflecting upon it' (*1726*, p. 183, *1729*, p. 183). Note the force of the phrase 'almost all of us': ethics is not a 'natural' thing, even though we all have the built-in, quasi-genetic, capability, the possession of which solely distinguishes humanity from the other animals. In Sermon II, *Upon Humane Nature* (*1726*, p. 43) Butler had already discussed

---

[98] These two sentences are here taken out of sequence, without, however, affecting their sense.

[99] Incidentally, the orthographical modernizations in the 'standard' editions suppress and distort Butler's meanings. 'Reverence thy Self' is very different from 'Reverence thyself' as printed by Gladstone, Bernard and Matthews. The word 'thyself' was available to, and used by, Butler in *1729*.

the conscience as mediating the exercise of interpersonal affective power. In *1729* he inserts a passage about 'prophane Swearing, and in general that Kind of Impiety' and characterizes it as contrary to our duty of 'Reverence and Dutiful Submission' (*1729*, pp. 43–4). In effect this is an early version of Wordsworth's 'natural piety' – behaviour which is reverent because of 'God in us' and which is a duty in that its required expression is ceremonial, in fact, liturgical.[100] Decisions to apply self-discipline in this regard are based on healthy self-love: twice in Sermon XI, *Upon the Love of our Neighbour* – and it is significant that self-love is not neglected in this account of benevolence – *1729* sees insertions about such actions being in 'their own Interest or Happiness, so as to have that Interest an Object to their Minds' (*1729*, p. 204) and 'reflecting upon his own Interest or Happiness' (*1729*, p. 206), even though all moral qualities may, on one level of analysis, be considered as 'the same thing' as benevolence (an insertion in Sermon XII, *1729*, p. 250n). It is ethics which guarantees the practical unity of self-love and benevolence and consequently the health and integrity of the individual, as well as the health of all social relations. In Aristotelian fashion, happiness may be defined as 'the well-being which consists in engaging in morally right actions'.[101]

Ethics and society

We have noted that those of the *Fifteen Sermons* which were most heavily reworked in *1729* were about love, and especially the pair *Upon the Love of our Neighbour*, which are preached about Christ's 'new commandment', Romans 13.9, '... Thou shalt love they neighbour as thyself'. It is significant that Butler chooses this text rather than the account in John 13.34: 'A new commandment I give unto you, That ye love one another; as I have loved you, that ye also love one another.' That is, he chooses Paul's broader doctrine of universal love, based on expanding circles of propinquity, rather than John's, where Jesus speaks in the context of the immanent establishment of the sacrament of communion, so that, as G. H. C. Macgregor put it, 'it is a question not of loving one's "neighbour," but of a special love of Christian to Christian, of *philadelphia* in distinction to universal *agape*'.[102]

We will therefore expect to find that a person living in isolation is literally beyond the ethical sphere, and Butler indeed holds this to be so.

In *1726* he had written, 'Benevolence, considered as a Principle of Virtue, is gratified by its own Consciousness, *i. e.* is in a Degree its own Reward' (*1726*,

---

[100] In Wordsworth this is evidenced by his descriptions of the measuring of space as ceremony. See, for example, stanza III of 'The Thorn' ('five yards ... on your left ... three yards beyond ...'), and the culminating, but notorious, lines, which, under critical pressure, Wordsworth bowdlerized: 'I've measured it [the pool] from side to side,/'Tis three feet long by two feet wide'.

[101] See the discussion of Sidgwick and Butler in Chapter 6, p. 204.

[102] G. H. C. Macgregor, *The Gospel of John* (in the *Moffat New Testament Commentary*), London, 1928, pp. 283–4.

p. 215). In *1729* this becomes, '... endeavouring to do Good considered as a Virtuous Pursuit, is gratified by its own Consciousness, *i.e.* is in a Degree its own Reward' (*1729*, p. 219). The amendment avoids the suggestion that one is right to feel gratified by the possession of faculties which are in-born. An awareness of benevolent affections is displaced by the practical activity of doing good and it is made clear that an action's goodness is determined by its motivation. It must be noted, however, that moral goodness still lies beyond the merely social and within the metaphysical, because these motivations flow from Butler's speculative account of the affections. On the one hand, society cannot certainly know what the agent's motivation is and, on the other, one's personal satisfaction is morally valid only if one feels assured about the meaning of 'virtuous'.[103]

To say, as he does, that 'the attempt to do good produces an awareness (consciousness) of itself and acquiring this awareness produces a pleasant feeling which is nature's way of rewarding us for the good endeavour', may seem laborious and unnatural but it must be remembered that Butler reread and revised the passage very carefully.

Moreover, in a passage typical of Butler's strategy of saying the most astonishing things in a manner which disguises and, to coin a word, habilitates[104] them, his new Preface has already coupled the love of God and the love of good morals in an explicitly mystical way: with reference to Fénelon he writes, '[both religion and morals] are, I think, fully determined by the same Observation, namely, that the very Nature of Affection, the Idea itself, necessarily implies resting in its Object as an End' (Preface, p. xxxiii). It is very easy to skate over what Butler is saying explicitly: he accepts the theology and religious practices of Fénelon and Madame de Guyon, which were widely criticized as 'Enthusiasm', 'as it [is called] every where by the Generality of the World' (*loc. cit.*), and which is therefore unacceptable in the Church of England. He then says that this 'Enthusiasm' is *necessarily* a consequence of the human mentality. Thus, Butler uses his formal rhetoric and rather convoluted syntax to set out his acceptance of mystical practices and asserts that a mystical apprehension and love of God is the product of the same affections that produce social benevolence. We will see this re-emerge, a decade later, in the sermon preached by Heylyn at his Bristol consecration in 1738 and in the cautious and qualified nature of his rejection of Whitefield's and Wesley's conceptions of their ministry.

This same revision clarifies and strengthens Butler's *1726* assumption about the awareness of personal gratification as, in some sense, a reward for virtuous behaviour. It follows from this refocusing that something intimately related to doing good is to wish other people well. Thus, in a footnote to the same sermon, in *1726* Butler had essayed a point against Hobbes:

---

[103] Butler is often accused of being an ethical intuitionist: of believing in the validity of our feelings that we have committed a good or bad action. This will be discussed in Chapter 3.

[104] Oddly, English doesn't have a word for an initial attempt to clothe a new idea in a socially acceptable guise.

> Is there not often the Appearance of Mens wishing well to others? and
> is this only the Desire of Power? (Sermon I, *1726, n.*, p. 6f)

This protest is feeble: it merely expresses a wish to deny Hobbes's theory that
self-interest is the sole motivation. In *1729* it is therefore rewritten thus:

> Is there not often the Appearance of one Man's wishing that Good to
> Another, which he knows himself unable to procure him; and rejoicing
> in it, though bestowed by a third Person? And can Love of Power any
> way possibly come in to account for this Desire or Delight?
>
> (*1729*, p. 6n)

The reformulation constructs a situation, not considered by Hobbes, which
empirically demolishes at least a part of his claim. It also appeals to his congregation's (and readers') experience – the 'shock of recognition' we noted in
the Introduction – thus reinforcing his doctrine by encouraging emulation and
repetition.

This introduction of the anti-Hobbes position is not merely local, however.
Our delight in a third person's bestowing good on the second person is reinforced
by a more general account of well-wishing and its corollary, of not wishing ill.
And here Butler delivers a subtle but robust piece of philosophical thinking,
which is a long-maturing product of his discussions with Clarke.

It is common, indeed virtually prevalent, to think in terms of opposites and,
in some form or another, mediations of opposites – a spectrum or scale, for
example, on which extreme good shades into extreme bad. As we have seen, the
1729 Butler not only flatly renounces such thinking but, in several interpolated
and amended passages, delivers an alternative analysis, which in later chapters
will be seen as central to his philosophy and his pastoral praxis. These passages
represent Butler's second and better thoughts about the human individual as a
constituent member of society and the relation of this social condition to the
ethical dimension of the more general human condition – we must remember
that although people are intrinsically social animals, for redemptive Christianity
the social does not entirely encompass the human condition.

In Sermon 1, the first of the three *Upon Humane Nature*, Butler had set out
at some length the ties that bind individuals together into social humanity. The
episode is worth quoting extensively:

> There is such a natural Principle of Attraction in Man towards Man,
> that having trod the same Tract of Land, having breathed in the same
> Climate ... becomes the Occasion of contracting Acquaintances and
> Familiarities many Years after; for any thing may serve the Purpose.
> Thus Relations merely nominal are sought and *invented*, not by Gover-
> nors, but by the *lowest of the People*, which are found sufficient to hold
> Mankind together in *little Fraternities and Copartnerships*: Weak Ties
> indeed, and what may afford Fund enough for Ridicule,[105] if they are

---

[105] Presumably a satirical reference to the South Sea Bubble: 'Fund enough for Ridicule' indeed.

absurdly considered as the real Principles of that Union; but they are in Truth merely the Occasions, as any thing may be of any thing, upon which our Nature carries us on according to *its own previous Bent and Bias* ... Men are so much one Body, that in a peculiar Manner they feel for each other, Shame, sudden Danger, Resentment, Honour, Prosperity, Distress ... from the social Nature in general, from Benevolence, upon the Occasion of natural Relation, Acquaintance, Protection, Dependance; each of these being distinct Cements of Society ... But ... [has] not Man Dispositions and Principles within, which lead him to do Evil as well as to do Good? ... These Questions ... may be answered by asking, Has not Man also Dispositions and Principles within, which lead him to do Evil to himself as well as good? ... But ... it may be proper to add, that there is not at all any such thing as Ill-will in one Man towards another, Emulation and Resentment being away, whereas there is plainly Benevolence or Good-will ... (*1726*, pp. 17–19; italics supplied)

'Cements of Society' is a striking phrase, and an anti-Hobbesian one: note that it is the 'lowest of the People', not the 'Governors', who invent and maintain the ties that bind – and, again, let us remember the elite nature of Butler's congregation, which he is drawing into a democratic ethics. Although the word 'cement' already had a history in English, applied to the binding love between two individuals (it is found in Shakespeare in this sense – *Anthony and Cleopatra*, III.2.29), Butler's application of it to principles unifying human society as a whole appears to be an original extension of the metaphor.[106] Furthermore, there is 'Copartnership': 'the possession of a joint share in any business, office, or interest'.[107] Social ties may be weak, but they are expressions and creations of 'our Nature' and will be invented wherever an excuse presents itself, to overcome the extreme individualism implicit in Cartesian and Lockean theories of the mind. Butler here is feeling his way towards a distinction between humankind as 'natural' individual beings and as social beings who are partly, and communally, self-developed. However, he then finds himself forced to acknowledge in our social nature the anti-social, unfraternal, elements which lead to social disruption, choosing to approach the phenomenon of the anti-social by asserting that it is exactly the same – he laboriously repeats his formula – as the phenomenon which leads people into self-harming courses: 'Dispositions and Principles within, which lead him to do Evil ... as well as good', but without ill-will or self-hatred.

Ill-will and self-hatred are terms as intelligible to Butler's contemporaries as to ourselves,[108] but Butler alleges that as an empirical fact they do not actually feature in the created world. This point is found in the quoted passage above; it was, indeed, discussed as what we identified as the second strand in

---

[106] See OED 'cement', n. 2c. A word search of ECCO, using its corpus and search engine in March 2009, does not challenge this suggestion.
[107] OED: copartnership, *n.*, 1 and 2 – this passage is one of the citations.
[108] Swift was a contemporary and we will see likenesses in Chapter 3.

the Butler–Clarke Tewkesbury correspondence. Ethics, consequently, is a matter for the created world and is not a part of that aspect of human nature which is analogous with the divine – the 'affections' – but an effect of their playing out in society.

This recalls a key exchange we noted in the Butler–Clarke correspondence, related to the question of crime. Butler was driven to deny that the essence of crime was man's having a natural disposition to be influenced by wrong motives; instead he appeared to accept Clarke's doctrine that crime, or by extension wrong-doing (Clarke merely accepted Butler's word in letter 8B), is the choice of an inappropriate object, not that choice's determination by a wrong motive. In Sermon I Butler advances a version of what he had accepted from Clarke. There is, however, a further consequence. If ill-will and self-hatred do not exist, then only good-will and self-love exist (and sufficient proof of these may be gathered empirically). The spectrum or scale, 'extreme good-will [or self-love] ... extreme ill-will [or self-hatred]' therefore must be reformulated as 'extremely great good-will [or self-love] ... extremely little good-will [or self-love]', as we previously noted with reference to Collingwood's scale of forms. As Butler says, in a passage inserted and edited into *1729*,

> Mankind have ungoverned Passions which they will gratifie at any Rate, as well to the Injury of Others, as in Contradiction to known private Interest: But that as there is no such thing as Self-hatred, so neither is there any such thing as Ill-will in one Man towards another, Emulation and Resentment being away. (*1729*, pp. 18–19)

If Butler is to maintain his thesis that the social and the psychological are structured identically, and that social harm and self-harm are formally equivalent, he now, in *1729*, realizes, what he did not in *1726*, that he must make two strategically and logically necessary admissions. One is a recognition of the full implications of the frequent intensity of human unreason and anger. The other is a denial that there is such a thing as 'Self-hatred'. To a twenty-first-century reader the existence of strong and seemingly irrational anger is as obvious as it must have been to Butler's congregation, whereas the second, perhaps, has become counter-intuitive: we have become accustomed to phenomena such as self-loathing, self-harming and the psychopathology of the physical and psychological abuse of children by their parents. Butler's rejection of the 'good ... bad (or evil)' scale in the human condition inevitably transforms the question from 'is this good, or evil?' to 'is this good or insufficiently good?' and in the case of the individual considered psychologically, replaces the observation, 'this person is evilly motivated' by 'this person is unsuccessful in being well-motivated'. A person on the 'bad' extreme of the scale is consequently socially maladjusted or mentally ill, rather than wicked.

These might seem large claims to make of a set of revisions on a single subject, however carefully they were pondered by their author. We can support them, however, by looking back at the extensive revisions concerning the basket of related subjects which have already been discussed: the phenomenon of anger ('resentment'), the concept of 'unreasonable', the ethics of discrimination by social class, the implications of the injunction to love others as ourselves, the question of the relative proportions of the affections in different individuals and the intrinsically ethical nature of the affection 'Benevolence'. While Butler is not always obviously consistent in his placing of 'Benevolence' as one of the two major 'affections' he does not have much to say about it in the revisions: that benevolence is the fundamental component which makes us social, ethical and fully human is a nexus of axioms which he never feels the need to revisit.

The treatment of benevolence returns to the subject of anger and 'resentment'. The 'good Influence [of resentment] … is obvious to every one's Notice' (*1729*, p. 152f) – fear of resentment restrains anti-social behaviour more than virtue, and the judicial expression of 'Resentment and Indignation' is more effective in bringing the offender to legal process than the victim's conscience. However much to be regretted, Butler concludes, in a sentence he feels constrained to add in *1729*, 'This however is to be considered as a good Effect, notwithstanding it were much to be wished that Men would act from a better Principle, Reason and cool Reflection' (*1729*, p. 153), that the conscience were more fully developed. This foreshadows his later interest in charitable education. Such additions to *1729* also suggest that there remained areas of formulation with which Butler was not yet entirely happy. These include the conscience, discussion of which has so far been avoided as far as possible.

Before we turn to *The Analogy*, it may be worth considering how very extraordinary it is that a reasonably balanced account of *Fifteen Sermons* may be attempted – how successfully is, of course, a matter for the reader's judgement – almost exclusively from a set of revisions. For this attempt to be anywhere near possible, Butler must have kept in mind a minute account of his moral philosophy and its relation to his science of humankind and applied it to every sentence in his book.

3

The Analogy

Main texts: *The Analogy* **(1736);** *Of Personal Identity* **(1736);**
Of the Nature of Virtue **(1736)**

Introduction

The Analogy was published in London and Dublin in 1736 (Butler signed the
work off with a short Advertisement dated May). A second, corrected, edition
appeared in the same year. The book was considered important enough for Edward
Bentham, a fellow and tutor at Oriel, immediately to set to work compiling
an index of the first edition, which Butler amended and supplemented.[1] Since
Butler did not publish the index, it was presumably used by Bentham in his
teaching then and (after Butler's death) when delivering an annual course of
lectures as Regius Professor of Divinity, for which post he was sponsored by
Secker.[2] This suggests that *The Analogy* almost immediately became important
in both systematic theology and apologetics.

    The Analogy was dedicated to Charles Talbot, the elder brother of his dead
friend Edward Talbot and the son of his patron William Talbot; Butler had been
his chaplain since 1733. Like the *Fifteen Sermons*, it was published by the
Knaptons, although by now the firm was diminishing as a force, deprived by
death of its leading author, Samuel Clarke, and with others of its 1720s list also
dead or inactive. Butler aside, its weightiest contribution in 1736 was Vincent
Perronet's first *Vindication of Mr. Locke*, which defended Locke's epistemology,
and its theological implications, from Peter Browne's *Procedure, Extent, and
Limits of Human Understanding* (1728).[3] Perronet demonstrates a knowledge

---

[1] An index would most naturally be made for the latest available edition. This perhaps suggests that
Bentham knew about the work and its potential importance in advance of publication. Bentham's index
was revised and published by Thomas Bartlett as *An Index to the Analogy of Bishop Butler* (1842).
The manuscript is in the Bodleian. Butler corrected and supplemented the manuscript, thus providing a
minimal commentary on Bentham's analysis, but this is not relevant for present purposes.
[2] DNB, 'Edward Bentham'.
[3] Vincent Perronet, *A Vindication of Mr. Locke*, London, James, John & Paul Knapton, 1736. Perronet
appears unaware both of the existence of Browne's *Analogy* (1733) and of his death, on 25 August 1735
(A. R. Winnett, *Peter Browne: Provost, Bishop, Metaphysician*, London, 1974, p. 189).

of Berkeley's *Alciphron* and its critique of Browne's use of analogy and was to review Butler's *Analogy* in his *Second Vindication of Mr. Locke* (1738). The other early notice of *The Analogy* was by Thomas Bott, who had been a friend of Clarke's but whose *Remarks upon Dr. Butler's Sixth Chapter of the Analogy of Religion, &c. Concerning Necessity; And also upon the Dissertation of the Nature of Virtue*, London, J. Noon, 1737) is scarcely worth noticing. Bott attacks Butler from an extreme libertarian position, denouncing the lack of aggression against atheism but making few substantial criticisms.[4]

Butler's full title is *The Analogy of Religion, Natural and Revealed, to the Constitution and Course of Nature.*[5] The book consists of a short Advertisement, a ten-page Introduction and two Parts, the first of seven chapters, the second of eight. Being a controversial and apologetic work, it starts at a different place from *Fifteen Sermons*, although its means are just as calculated rhetorically. The Advertisement claims that 'Christianity ... is ... discovered to be fictitious ... among all People of Discernment ... [and] set up as a principal Subject of Mirth and Ridicule, as it were, by Way of Reprisals, for its having so long interrupted the Pleasures of the World.' Having laboriously made its acknowledgement to Augustan irony, it proceeds with equally laborious deliberation. Appended to the work are two 'brief dissertations'. According to Butler (*1736*, p. 299), one, *Of Personal Identity*, was excised from Part I Chapter I, while the other, *Of the Nature of Virtue*, was excised from Part I Chapter III. Virtually every posthumous edition of the work provides a more or less elaborate analysis of its contents, presumably because it almost immediately became a standard teaching text. The prefatory material of Bishop Samuel Hallifax, the first 'standard' editor, runs to about 15 percent the length of *The Analogy* itself, and Daniel Wilson's (1825) to 30 percent. Since there is no technical language to explain, this phenomenon perhaps suggests that successive generations appropriated rather than explicated the book. By contrast, Butler himself, with something like genius, presents his entire argument in a single sentence. Although a very long one, it is a *tour de force* of simplicity: in essence a chain of relative clauses, each qualifying the substance of its predecessor. In miniature, it not only sums up the entire book but also exemplifies its method:

> That Mankind is appointed to live in a future State [Ch. i]; That There, every one shall be rewarded or punished [Ch. ii]; ... for all that Behaviour Here, which [signifies] Virtuous or Vitious, morally good or evil [Ch. iii]: That our present Life is ... a State of Trial [Ch. iv], and of Discipline [Ch. v], for that future one; Notwithstanding the objections ... against there being any such moral Plan as this at all [Ch. vi]; ... as it stands so imperfectly made known to us at present [Ch. vii]: That this World being in a State of Apostacy and Wickedness ... this gave occa-

4   He does, however, call Butler a Stoic and attempts to identify a consequential incoherence in his thinking, not by engagement with Butler's text but by the ascription of guilt by association.
5   *1736* indicates the first (London) edition; *1750* the last edition for which Butler was responsible.

sion for an additional Dispensation of Providence ... [Part II. Ch. i];
proved by Miracles [Ch. ii]; but containing in it many things ... not
to have been expected [Ch. iii]; a Dispensation of Providence, which
is a ... System of things [Ch. iv]; carried on by the Mediation of a
divine Person ... in order to the Recovery of the World [Ch. v]; yet not
revealed to all Men, nor proved with the strongest possible Evidence to
all those to whom it is revealed; but only to such a Part of Mankind, and
with such particular Evidence as the Wisdom of God thought fit
[Ch. vi, vii].[6]

The Analogy is one of the most densely and intensively written books in English:
Butler is everywhere thinking at full stretch, working to create unity of argument
from a range of different types of evidence. As Penelhum has pointed out,[7] he
steps back from the belief that human reason, working within the system of the
created world, can attain a comprehensive account of the world. Consequently,
there can be no systematic account of natural religion – a dagger in the heart
of the European Enlightenment. In opposition to a whole climate of intellectual
opinion, he wishes to demonstrate that the limits of human knowledge are to be
discussed not in terms of adequacy (approximation to truth) but sufficiency for
the purposes set out in the Christian revelation: an apparently drastic narrowing
of intellectual ambition. This is disguised by the sobriety of his language but
was evident to the many contemporary evangelicals who were drawn to him.[8]

Hence, although the book is tightly structured and methodically critical, it is
not systematic – in fact, it is intentionally anti-systematic. In their daily practical business, people give hostages to fortune at every point, but succeed in
muddling through. They are bad at speculating reliably about the reasons for
things; actually, Butler says, by their very nature they are incapable of doing
so. However, as *Fifteen Sermons* observed, they are capable of developing
their ethical consciousness. As we suggested in the last chapter, this democratic
approach – putting the street urchin, the privy councillor and the philosopher
on the same level – is based on the solid fact that very few people are moral
philosophers or natural scientists, yet they get by, building and sustaining social
relations. For Butler this fact is, literally, a saving grace.

Ethically, the conscience is fundamental to accounts of the human mind and
culture. It is, as it were, calibrated by social interactions and creates a healthy
consciousness and, in a virtuous circle, a better and healthier society. But societies will not inevitably develop sound ethical systems.[9] Although there will
always be interpersonal and social dynamics, they need not be populated by

6   *1736*, pp. ix–x.
7   *Butler*, p. 101.
8   For example, William Romaine, who emphasizes Butler's doctrine of conscience: *No Justification
by the Law of Nature [Romans 2.14]*, *The Whole Works*, vol. 6, London, 1821, pp. 82, 86. This sermon
was preached before the Lord Mayor and Aldermen, as early as 2 September 1741.
9   Butler did not take an 'all or nothing' approach to good ethics. In conversation with David Hartley
and John Byrom, shortly after *The Analogy*'s publication, he gave his opinion that humankind should

people endowed with consciousness in the sense that 'we' understand, 'we' being those who are the product of the process of culture- and nation-building with which Butler confirmed his association in the *Six Sermons*. The implication is that postlapsarian humankind's natural piety does not work very well but the culture of Christianity, the revealed religion, works a great deal better – in fact, sufficiently well to enable people to live a morally good life, given unremitting engagement.

Before examining this extension by *The Analogy* of *Fifteen Sermons'* account of our ethical nature and its environment, it will be helpful to consider the nature of the book itself.

Sources of *The Analogy*

Compositionally, *The Analogy* is *Fifteen Sermons 1729* writ large: a body of existing sermons, mostly from the Rolls period and amounting to at least half of the book, which was heavily reworked, supplemented by new material and directed towards a strategic aim which the original material served only implicitly. Because it will be argued that this explains certain features of Butler's new book, we will seek to persuade that it was indeed written in this way, supporting the general plausibility of this novel suggestion by examining four of many possible examples: Part II, Chapter VII, 'Of the particular Evidence for Christianity'; Part II Chapter I, 'Of the Importance of Christianity'; the dissertation *Of the Nature of Virtue*; and Part II, Chapter VIII, 'Of the Objections ... against arguing, from the Analogy of Nature, to Religion'. Their kinship with the *Fifteen Sermons* – a further presumption of their date – will emerge later and other chapters' origin in sermons will be noted later.

Sometimes it is obvious that a chapter is structured sermon-style. Part II, Chapter VII seems to begin with a specially composed link paragraph (*1736*, p. 236) but the first half (equivalent in length to the average Butler sermon) is then explicitly structured, with the classic 'outline' numbering system, popularized by John Tillotson, built into the text. The form (with *1736* page numbers supplied) is: Exordium (p. 236); Exegesis I.1 (p. 238), I.2 (p. 239), I.3 (p. 241), II.1 (p. 250), II.2 (p. 251), II.3 (p. 252); Application (p. 254). There is no Peroration. The 'outline' structure is especially appropriate for a sermon arguing about the nature of evidence and its application to the particular case. The second half of the chapter begins on p. 256 ('SECONDLY, I shall now endeavour ...').[10] From the density of Biblical references and footnoted citations of classics which

---

follow the good parts of Mahomet's teaching and reject the bad parts. John Byrom, *The Private Journal and Literary Remains*, ed. R Parkinson, Manchester, 1856, vol. ii, pt 1, pp. 96–7.

[10] Standard editions, based on Butler's lightly revised 1750 edition (*1750*, p. 375), read something like 'I shall now, *Secondly*, endeavour ...' (quoted from the widely available Bohn's Standard Library edition of 1889).

Butler would have read in his school and student days, it may be surmised that this second half too was originally a sermon, although of a less structured type.

Our second example is Part II Chapter I, a text which, with its prominent reference to Christianity being a 'Republication of natural Religion', might seem to originate in a relatively recent sermon aimed at Tindal.[11] It appears to consist of: Exordium (p. 141); Exegesis I (p. 144), II (p. 150), II.1 (p. 155), II.2 (p. 156), II.2.i (p. 158), II.2.ii (p. 158); Application (p. 160). Discussion of this text must wait, but here we may draw attention to the use of irony, duplicating that of *Fifteen Sermons* and turning the preacher–congregation linear axis (the line of sight from pulpit to nave) into a psychological unity ('we'), formed against sceptical third parties outside the church's walls ('they'):

> Those Persons appear to forget, that Revelation is to be considered, as informing us of somewhat New, in the State of Mankind, and in the Government of the World; as acquainting us with some Relations we stand in, which could not otherwise have been known ... And farther, as Mankind are for placing the Stress of their Religion any where rather than upon Virtue ... (*1736*, pp. 153, 158)

As our third example we will consider the dissertation *Of the Nature of Virtue*, of which Butler says, 'In the first Copy of these Papers, I had inserted [it] into the [chapter] ... *Of the Moral Government of God* with which [it is] closely connected' (*1736*, [p. 299]). Butler's words suggest both that it was a discrete composition and that *The Analogy* is in some sense a compilation. The dissertation repeats Butler's *1729* positions with regard to his selected antagonists, suggesting a common date of composition with the components of *Fifteen Sermons*.[12] It is about the length of a sermon and although there are signs of editorial revisions which address a readership rather than an audience,[13] there is a general feeling of orality, and an awareness of an audience typical of a Butler sermon (but which is lacking, for example, in the *Personal Identity* dissertation). Thus:

> *Again, suppose* one Man should, by Fraud or Violence, take from another the Fruit of his Labour ... *Nay farther*, were Treachery, Violence and Injustice, no otherwise vitious than as foreseen likely to produce an Overballance of Misery to Society ... *The Fact then appears to be* [such

---

[11] Matthew Tindal's *Christianity as Old as the Creation, or the Gospel a Republication of the Religion of Nature* was published in 1730. The last major production of eighteenth-century deism, it provoked at least thirty published replies.

[12] It refers to Epictetus, Hobbes, Marcus Aurelius, Cicero and (evidently) Shaftesbury (*1736*, pp. 309, 310, 316), whereas Hobbes does not feature in *The Analogy* itself. He is cited as an authority on the existence of the distinction between 'Injury and mere Harm' (*Of the Nature of Virtue*, *1736*, p. 310): an example of *The Analogy*'s method of building a case on the principles of Butler's opponents.

[13] For example, references to 'any author' and 'readers' are found in a short passage on p. 318. This provides a link between the fifth and final sub-topic and what looks like a fairly conventional sermon application. This passage immediately precedes the phrase, 'I speak thus', the inconsistency exposing careless editing.

and such] ... *But still*, since this is our Constitution ... (*1736*, p. 317;
italics and editorial insertion in square brackets supplied)

This orality is seen most clearly, perhaps, at the end of the dissertation, which
reads like a conventional Butlerian sermon 'application', turning from doctrine
to its reception by the listeners, with a final nod towards the Rolls Chapel's
congregation of professionals surrounded by the variety of citizenry with which
they must deal:

> *For this Reflection might easily be carried on, but I forbear* – The
> Happiness of the World is the Concern of Him, who is the Lord and
> the Proprietor of it ... *I speak thus* upon Supposition of Persons really
> endeavouring, in some sort, to do good ... But the Truth seems to be,
> that such supposed Endeavours, proceed, almost always, from Ambi-
> tion, [or] the Spirit of Party ... concealed perhaps in great Measure
> from Persons themselves. And though it is our Business and our Duty to
> endeavour ... to contribute to the Ease ... of our Fellow-creatures; yet
> from our short Views, it is greatly uncertain ... For it is impossible not
> to foresee, that the Words and Actions of Men in different Ranks and
> Employment, and of different Educations, will perpetually be mistaken
> by each other ... whilst they will judge with the utmost Carelessness ...
> (*1736*, pp. 319–20, italics supplied)

Language like this could only have been written for oral delivery. It is notable
that, unlike *Of Personal Identity*, which seems to have been written specifically
to contribute to *The Analogy*'s argument, *Of the Nature of Virtue* ends in a
specifically Christian way.

The origin of Butler's works in sermons goes a long way towards justifying
his apparently clumsy style. The fourth and last example we will consider is the
beginning of Part II, Chapter VIII:

> If every one would consider with such Attention, as they are bound,
> even in Point of Morality, to consider, what they judge and give Char-
> acters of; the Occasion of this Chapter would be, in some good Measure
> at least, superseded. But since this is not to be expected; for some we
> find do not concern themselves to understand even what they write
> against: Since this Treatise, in common with most others, lies open to
> Objections, which may appear very material to thoughtful Men at first
> sight ... (*1736*, p. 275)

The point is made better by lengthier quotation, but even in this short extract
can be seen discourse structured less by syntax than by the articulation of phrases
through the use of pauses and tonal dynamics. Note how the subject phrase, 'the
Occasion of this Chapter', recurs, semantically transformed, as 'this Treatise',
the whole passage feeling its way towards the string, 'to thoughtful Men at first
sight', which looks persuasive (we are surely all of us thoughtful) but is set
up to be immediately undermined. An orator could make this clotted string of
units come alive, its slowness and weight especially suiting public delivery. This

particular chapter, being the last in the book, was evidently subject to extensive revision towards its end.

The features we have identified in these passages can be found in both the *Fifteen* and the *Six Sermons*. While it would presumably be impossible to identify all the parts of *The Analogy* which are reworked from sermons, future developments in critical methods will surely increase the numbers which can be persuasively identified. At present we should be alert to the reinforcement of Butler's argument by local rhetorical strategies originating in the source sermons and to the work being so lightly provided with citations and critical apparatus.

Analogy, probability, tendency

The first sentence of *The Analogy*'s Introduction reads thus: 'Probable Evidence is essentially distinguished from demonstrative by this, that it admits of Degrees' (*1736*, p. i). So saturated is modern society with the concepts of statistics and probability – to a large extent absorbed into the mainstream via Butler's own work – that it is very difficult to appreciate how revolutionary this statement was in a theological and apologetic work of that time and how unusual in any work. In the early eighteenth century the meaning and use of the term 'probable' was still closely associated with its etymological root in 'provable', and not always distinguished very clearly from 'demonstrative'. By introducing 'Degrees' (a term which entails definitions and calculations) Butler signals his affiliation to the introduction of mathematical thinking and the emergence of 'probable' in its modern sense. The book thus enters what was then one of the newest of mathematical and logical worlds and, moreover, in its very title announces the appropriation by an Enlightenment theologian of a scholastic philosophical tool. That he assimilates mathematical probability into his analysis without technical ostentation is also remarkable. To put this in perspective we will discuss contemporary uses of 'analogy' and 'probability' which are by turns non-mathematical and clumsily mathematical.

An instructive contrast with Butler is Peter Browne's recent *Things Divine and Supernatural Conceived by Analogy with Things Natural and Human*,[14] the culmination of that aspect of his career which involved both metaphysics and theological controversies with thinkers as varied as John Toland, Archbishops William King and Edward Synge and George Berkeley. This book was a successor to his *The Procedure, Extent, and Limits of Human Understanding* (1728), in which he had attempted to restate and correct Locke's *Essay* in orthodox Christian terms. Theologically, Browne comes from a neo-Platonist direction, which is unfortunate, in that he also takes his definition of analogy from the less-defined Platonic rather than the Aristotelian model.[15] Analogy is

---

14 London, William Innys & Richard Manby, 1733.
15 The subject has been treated by G. E. R. Lloyd, *Polarity and Analogy: Two Types of Argumentation in Early Greek Thought* (1966), reprint Bristol, 1987, especially Chapter VI.

a term almost entirely unused by the seventeenth-century English Platonists, whose writings, from Henry More to John Norris, are almost glamorously meta-phorical, and often formally poetic.[16] Plato presents analogical arguments as dialectical and heuristic tools[17] but, as his extended comparison of men and animals shows[18] – he does not discuss the relation between subjective self-knowledge and the human observation of incommunicative animals – there is little distinction between metaphor and analogy.[19]

Thus Browne proposes that 'the Foundation of Analogy is an *Actual Simili-tude* and a *Real Correspondency* in the very *Nature* of Things; which lays a Foundation for a *Parity of Reason* even between Things different in *Nature* and *Kind*' (p. 3), but does not explain 'actual' and 'real'. He wishes to mount an alternative to Locke, by combining his epistemology with analogical reasoning, to correct the 'great and fundamental ... Error [of] our Modern Logicians, [which is] pernicious to human Understanding' (p. 28): that is, Locke's exclu-sive reliance on sensory ideas and reflection upon them, which, he argues, is unable to account for moral values and the human apprehension of God. He announces (p. 1) that he will write about '*Divine Analogy*, ... without which the Nature and Properties of God and supernatural Beings, and the Objects of another World, would be as utterly inconceivable to us as if they had no Exist-ence': a project which all too obviously depends upon circularity of reasoning. Berkeley, indeed, demonstrated that his speculations were atheistic in implica-tion.[20] Browne's scepticism about any form of non-reasoned knowledge extends widely: 'We cannot with our utmost Intention of Thought ... form ... any *Orig-inal* and *Purely Intellectual* Ideas of the Nature and workings of our own Mind ... because the most abstracted and exalted Operations of the Human Mind are Actions of both Matter and Spirit in *Essential Union*, and not peculiar to either *Alone* ...' (p. 23).[21] Thus he cannot even give an account of human nature without employing what he thinks of as analogical arguments. He thinks that 'tho' it be impossible in our present State totally to exclude *All* Mixture of sensitive [i.e. derived from sense data] Ideas from such Conceptions' (p. 29), 'the *Conscious Conceptions* we have of the Faculties and Operations of our Mind' may serve as an analogy of the divine mind (p. 29). That is to say, he sees 'mind' as the same reasoning faculty whether or not it is a synthesis of the 'intellectual' and the 'sensitive'. Whereas for Aristotle and Aquinas analogy concerns the rela-

[16] Examples range from Henry More's philosophical poem, *A Platonick Song of the Soul* (1647) to John Norris's prose *Metaphysical Essay toward the Demonstration of a God, from the Steddy and Immutable Nature of Truth* (*Miscellanies*, 1687).
[17] For example, *Statesman*, 285, speech by the Stranger, *Works*, ed. Benjamin Jowett, 3rd edn, Oxford, 1892, volume IV, pp. 485–6.
[18] *Republic* II, 374–6, *Works*, ed. Jowett, vol. III, pp. 55 ff.
[19] See Lloyd, p. 228 ff.
[20] George Berkeley, *Alciphron*, Dialogue 3. See *Works*, ed. A. A. Luce and T. E. Jessop, London, 1948–51, vol. 3, p. 5. Browne's reply, in his own *Analogy*, was answered neither by Berkeley nor Butler.
[21] Browne's reliance on Locke is indicated by his use as a technical term of the obsolete 'intention' (OED, 1), borrowed from the *Essay* II. xix §1.

tions between not the objects but the terms being compared,[22] Browne assumes that the word 'nature' identifies a large measure of overlap between human and divine. Although, he says, 'God is not wise in the same sense that a man is wise'[23] and 'is said to have *Knowledge, Power*, and *Goodness*',[24] implying the impropriety of ascribing human qualities to God,[25] and acknowledging a language-based definition of analogy, he generally uses it to compare objects, not relations. His thinking is obviously incoherent and inevitably he drifts into speculations about minds unattached to matter – devils and angels – even before the end of his second chapter.

Browne's is an interesting case because it exposes the radical change of nature in philosophical concerns which challenged even the Reformed Christianity which had grown up in tandem with it. The sophistications of medieval scholars like Catejan and Aquinas are beyond him: the line of tradition in categorical thinking has been definitely broken and the new orthodoxy was constituted by disbelief in rationalist, systematic metaphysics. For Aquinas analogies were relationships between predicates.[26] The likeness of these relationships was guaranteed by the categorical creativity of their subject[27] but the analogical method did not extend to discussing that subject or its creativity. If Aristotle's account was simpler he nevertheless held much the same view: analogical argument fell into two categories, the rhetorical ('enthymemes') where all premises might not be expressed, and the paradigmatic, which was involved with inductive evidence.[28] By these standards, Browne's project is not only an improper application of analogy but also misses the point that 'evidence' is not an absolute but a relative: it is what society agrees to receive as such, and in this philosophers and their inductive arguments are part of society. For example, what constitutes admissible evidence in an English court of law has changed over the centuries, subject to the developing practice of the common law and the decisions of statute law,[29] while any inductive argument falls apart if inspected with sufficient rigour, as Hume was shortly to demonstrate. Browne's work might have suggested to his contemporaries – indeed, it did to Berkeley – that attempts to graft together scholastic rationalism and modern post-Cartesian empiricism were self-defeating. In this context the appearance of the term 'analogy' in Butler's title seems a little like a manifesto.

This is even more the case because Butler's great seventeenth-century predecessor, Nicholas Malebranche, who reworked Descartes from a Christian

---

22 The subject is treated in James F. Ross, 'Analogy as a Rule of Meaning for Religious Language' (1961), reprinted in *Aquinas: A Collection of Critical Essays*, ed. A. Kenny, London, 1969.
23 Quoted in Winnett, pp. 131–2.
24 Browne, *Analogy*, p. 3.
25 Winnett (p. 152 ff) discussed this in greater detail in relation to Browne's understanding of Aquinas.
26 For example, Aquinas, *The Principles of Nature* §§36–9.
27 For example, Ross, p. 96 and *passim*.
28 See Lloyd, p. 405 f.
29 This is an important point for the present work and is discussed in Chapter 5.

perspective in publications known to Butler, avoided any acknowledged resort to analogical arguments. He did this by asserting that 'falsity or a relation that does not exist cannot be perceived; all that the mind directly perceives exists and exists as the mind perceives it',[30] a nominalism even more far-reaching than Butler's and congruous with Berkeley's. For Malebranche the human mind is in God; as we have seen, Butler takes the view that the human mind is, rather, a creation of God's, with affective faculties bearing a certain relationship to functions of the divine mind, but separated from it.

Malebranche's ethics grow directly from his account of humankind's epistemological condition and rationality, the conscience – a term which he does not use – being a general cognitive faculty which also has a narrowly ethical aspect:[31] 'We should never give complete consent except to propositions which seem so evidently true that we cannot refuse it of them without feeling an inward pain and the secret reproaches of reason.'[32] Thus, as Lennon observes (p. 20), Malebranche's argument is fundamentally about the filtering out of error and the receiving of pre-existing truth. In sharp contrast, in Sermon XIV, 'Upon the Love of God', Butler dismisses the core of Malebranche's work with a single phrase – '[his] fanciful Notion of seeing all Things in God' (*1729*, p. 292), thus revealing that he knew at least *De la recherche de la vérité*. Rejecting the Frenchman's speculations, he redefines Malebranche's 'inward pain' as the conscience, exclusively oriented to humankind's moral condition in its complex psychological and social environment. Remarkably, Butler also avoids discussion of the 'divine attributes' which were so central to theological, metaphysical, and deistical, discussions at the time.[33]

In announcing his use of analogical argument Butler contrasts with both the Cartesian Malebranche and the neo-Platonic Browne. Despite clear Aristotelian strains in his thinking, however, he adopts a rigorously minimalist position.

---

[30] Thomas M. Lennon, 'Malebranche and Method', in *The Cambridge Companion to Malebranche*, p. 20.

[31] Set beside each other, two essays in *The Cambridge Companion to Malebranche* (Nicholas Jolley, 'Malebranche on the Soul', pp. 31–58, and Tad M. Schmaltz, 'Malebranche on Ideas and the Vision of God', pp. 59–86) illustrate, by default, the adroitness with which Malebranche avoided discussions of ethics. In his earlier *Malebranche's Theory of the Soul*, New York, 1996, Schmaltz, *passim* but especially Chapter 3.1, provides the analytical groundwork for the discussion of good and evil to which Malebranche could have turned. In his 'Malebranche's Moral Philosophy: Divine and Human Justice' (*Companion*, pp. 220–61) Patrick Riley observes that 'the Treatise on Morality, for the most part, simply draws out the practical implications of Malebranche's metaphysics, theology, and epistemology' (p. 221), thus confirming that Malebranche's ethics are of the 'true to ...' (Platonic) variety and diametrically opposed to Butler's somewhat covert Aristotelianism.

[32] *De la recherché de la vérité*, I. 2. iv; quoted by Lennon, p. 17.

[33] The subjects of the first seven years of the contemporary Seatonian Prize poems in the University of Cambridge were, respectively, God's eternity, immensity, omniscience, power, justice, goodness and wisdom. All were approached by their authors through human and earthly analogies of those qualities rather than through metaphysical argument (*Cambridge Prize Poems ... 1750–1806*, 2 volumes, Cambridge, J. Deighton, 1817).

It is not my Design to enquire further into the Nature, the Foundation, and Measure of Probability; or whence it proceeds that *Likeness* should beget that Presumption, Opinion, and full Conviction, which the human Mind is formed to receive from it, and which it does necessarily produce in every one; or to guard against the Errors to which, Reasoning from Analogy is liable. This belongs to the Subject of Logick ... (*1736*, p. iv)

Thus Butler stands somewhat aside from the scholastics (as well as the Platonists); announces the deficiencies of the method advertised in his title; and disclaims the *a priori* disciplines of logic. When he adds the observation that 'Probable Evidence ... affords but an imperfect kind of Information; and is to be considered as relative only to Beings of limited Capacities' (*1736*, p. iii), he announces that probabilistic arguments are guides for action, not substitutes for knowledge.

He proceeds to the passage in Origen which may have been the basis of *The Analogy*:

Origen has with singular Sagacity observed, that *he who believes the Scripture to have proceeded from Him who is the Author of Nature, may well expect to find the same sort of Difficulties in it, as are found in the Constitution of Nature.* (*1736*, p. v)

Implied in Origen's thesis is the belief in a personal God, one, that is, who is not a system of Platonic ideas or *a priori* principles but one who, in however remote a way, resembles a creative human, all of whose works reveal peculiarities of character.

Butler produces a mirror-image of Origen, arguing that an account of the natural world does not evade the set of difficulties displayed in either natural or revealed religion. He thus throws the reader back onto faith and trust and, in the realm of ethics, minimizes his reliance on metaphysics to an irreducible core. Thus he continues by rejecting Cartesian rationalism, instead claiming that 'it is allowed just, to join abstract Reasonings with the observation of Facts, and argue from such Facts as are known, to others that are like them ...' (*1726*, p. v). By 'join[ing] abstract Reasonings [to] Facts' he must mean a process of comparison rather than speculation. This becomes an attack on the fundamentals of scientific method, as is clear from *The Analogy*'s Part II Chapter IV, 'Of Christianity, considered as a Scheme or Constitution, imperfectly comprehended', which is largely concerned with a discussion of inductive reasoning. In it Butler's general argument is that society has certain underlying assumptions, and that logical challenges or scientific correctives to them lack firm ground. As a conservative appeal to the proven practicability of the intellectual *status quo* this is a familiar line of argument, but it is extended into an frontal attack on Newtonian science – his own intellectual home base – which could hardly be mistaken by the contemporary reader:

It is ... but an exceeding little Way, and in but a very few Respects, that we can trace up the natural Course of things before us, to general Laws. And it is only from Analogy, that we conclude, the Whole of it to be capable of being reduced into them; only from our seeing, that Part is so. It is from our finding, that the Course of Nature, *in some Respects and so far*, goes on by general Laws, that we conclude this of the Whole.

(*1736*, p. 189; italics supplied)

Thus Butler anticipates Popper's idea that scientific thinking is fundamentally analogical in the Aristotelian sense. The Newtonian apple can strike your head, and we understand how because of the power and simplicity of the new physics. Being struck, however, by an earthquake or a famine (*1736*, p. 188) is to be the victim of an altogether more complex system – a thought which cannot but have attracted Hume, whose critique of causality is principally directed against the inadequacy of observed means to results.[34] In practice we trust analogy, but, outside the textbook, the real-life series of causal phenomena may be a long one and only at the beginning of the series may the items' context be sufficiently rich in informational content to be very convincing in an analogical argument. And we may note here that Butler's tacit definition of analogy – the extendibility of a series – is chosen to produce the weakest predictability. With an exception to be encountered later, he avoids the more powerful scholastic 'a:b::c:d' type, where a multiplicity of relationships is available for analysis, as well as equivocal series (for example, the series 1, 2, 4 ..., which might continue ... 8, 16, 32 or ... 7, 11, 16 but not, say, ... 5, 12, 25). As he says in the Introduction, 'Let us then, instead of that idle and not very innocent Employment of forming imaginary Models of a World, and Schemes of governing it, turn our Thoughts to what we experience to be the Conduct of Nature with respect to intelligent Creatures' (*1736*, p. viii). He proposes looking at the world not through a telescope or a microscope but at a normal, human level of magnification – what the modern army calls 'the Mark 1 eyeball'.[35] Reasonable doubt does not work against cautious support for weak assumptions but against conclusions against weak assumptions which every day turn out to be empirically useful: a method, as we will see in the next section, which might be described as forensic, insofar as weak assumptions are innocent until proven guilty.

---

[34] This thought, although not attributed to Butler, is developed by John Habgood (*Being a Person: Where Faith and Science Meet*, London, 1998, p. 144 ff) in his discussion of causation, in the context of the mind's multi-levelled evolutionary inheritance and his criticism of Daniel Dennett's genetics-driven materialist theory of mind.

[35] Butler's relationship with Berkeleian anti-abstractionist mathematics will be discussed in the section below about personal identity. '[The] truths of geometry [must] be judged by appeal to the senses' (Douglas M. Jesseph, 'Berkeley's Philosophy of Mathematics', in *Cambridge Companion to Berkeley*, p. 279). His theology may be seen in contrast to that of the previous generation, as exemplified by Thomas Traherne's poem 'Shadows in the Water', which makes theological play with the newly-developed microscope, and Robert Boyle's *Some Motives and Incentives to the Love of God* (1659), 4th edn, London, Henry Herringman, 1665, e.g. p. 59, where the telescope provides views of 'Seraphic Love' (the work's running title).

Butler thereupon sketches a programme of empirical experiment in ethics, along the lines of the collection and assessment of data by natural scientists. In other words, he regards such data from the natural world as a comparator (that is, not a standard but a determinable measure) to:

> the moral System of Nature; ... what Religion teaches us to believe and expect ... [The aim is to see whether] the known Constitution and Course of [natural] Things ... [and Religion] are not analogous and of a piece ... and resolved into the same Principles of divine Conduct ... [and the strategy is to test whether] the chief Objections against [the course of nature], are no other, than what may be alleged with like Justness against [the Christian revelation], (*1736*, pp. viii–x; editorial insertions in square brackets)

His claim to the availability of comparators in the natural sciences and his appeal to common belief in Christian revelation and the social practice which is founded on it make the commonsense point that the average person lives a social and moral life which is more soundly based than one reliant on extrapolations from the laws and predictions of the natural sciences. In doing so, of course, he is on firm ground: society obviously works, after a fashion, whereas even with Newton's laws on the scientific statute book, the natural world still looked problematic.

In arguing this Butler emerges from a context of discussions whose participants were already moving towards shaping ethical concepts through analogies with mathematics and its analogical relationship with metaphysics. In his recent tract, *The Analyst; or, a Discourse Addressed to an Infidel Mathematician*,[36] Berkeley had advertised his aim of '[examining] whether the Object, Principles, and Inferences of the modern Analysis are more distinctly conceived, or more evidently deduced, than Religious Mysteries and Points of Faith' and adopted as motto Matthew 7.5 on motes and beams.[37] Berkeley's basic argument was that Newtonian fluxions dealt with concepts which the mind finds next to impossible to conceive; that the intellectual mysteries underlying and involved with their formulation were analogous to religious mysteries; and that the socially accepted claims of mathematicians to be great masters of reason lent undue credibility to their own mysteries. Berkeley's critique of Newton's (and Leibniz's) 'fluxions' (the development of differential calculus for the analysis of motion) was thus the pioneering attempt to confront the metaphysical basis of many mathematical axioms.[38] Despite being mauled by the physician and

---

[36] London, J. Tonson, 1734.

[37] Taken from the title-page of the 1734 Dublin edition (published by S. Fuller & J. Leathly).

[38] An example from more popular literature is John Norris's *Metaphysical Essay*: '[If] two Circles touch one another inwardly ... [there must be] two ... distinct simple Essences as *Circle* and *Center* ...' (quoted from *Collection of Miscellanies*, second edition, London, 1692, p. 199).

mathematician James Jurin[39] these are arguments which have rarely gone away entirely but, of course, Berkeley's 'minute philosophers' and 'infidel mathematicians' have flourished greatly in recent years.[40]

Berkeley had concluded his tract with a series of sixty-seven queries, including such as these:

> *Qu.* 3. Whether the mistaking the object and end of geometry hath not created needless difficulties, and wrong pursuits in that science? ... *Qu.* 8. Whether the notions of absolute time, absolute place, and absolute motion be not most abstractedly metaphysical? ... *Qu.* 15. Whether to decline examining the principles, and unravelling the methods used in mathematics would not show a bigotry in mathematicians? ... *Qu.* 26. Whether mathematicians have sufficiently considered the analogy and use of signs? ... *Qu.* 63. Whether such mathematicians as cry out against mysteries have ever examined their own principles?[41]

As well as Jurin, Thomas Bayes replied to Berkeley. In the preface to his *Introduction to the Doctrine of Fluxions* (1736)[42] he wrote,

> If [people] are taught that it is inconsistent for a person to reject the mysteries of religion, and yet believe the mystery of Fluxions, will they not know how to draw the opposite conclusion themselves, that it is inconsistent to reject the doctrine of Fluxions because mysterious, and yet receive the mysteries of religion? And when they are taught to think that a person may be *justly* said to have faith, because they give into what they can neither demonstrate nor *conceive*; if this give them a mean opinion of the Mathematicians, 'tis odds if it don't give them a mean opinion of faith itself.[43]

Butler's *Analogy*, published virtually simultaneously, anticipates Bayes's argument and, in one of the boldest and most radical acts in British intellectual history, does not flinch from extrapolating its implications: belief in God was exactly equivalent to trust in God.

---

[39] Philalethes Cantabrigiensis [i.e. James Jurin], *Geometry No Friend to Infidelity: or, a Defence of Sir Isaac Newton and the British Mathematicians, in a Letter to the Author of the Analyst*, London, T. Cooper, 1734.

[40] Modern chaos theory appears to depend on the empirically unprovable claim that humankind's perception and mathematical diagnosis of patterns relate to some sort of objective reality in a non-nominalist way.

[41] *Works*, ed. Jessop and Luce, vol. 4, pp. 96–102.

[42] Published by John Noon, *An Introduction to the Doctrine of Fluxions* has sometimes been ascribed to James Hodgson. Noon never published another work ascribed to Hodgson, who was sixty-four in 1736 and by then publishing little (his book on fluxions was to be published posthumously in 1755). Noon was, however, Bayes's publisher at this time. The balance of probability is heavily in favour of Bayes's authorship.

[43] *Doctrine of Fluxions*, p. v. Note 'odds': probability theory was stimulated by a discussion in 1654 between Pascal and Fermat about gambling and remained close to games of chance (and calculations of actuarial risk) until Pierre Simon Laplace's *Théorie analytique des probabilités* (1812).

Bayes was a mathematician of originality, whose eponymous Theorem was a substantial contribution to the mathematics of probability; its implications, apparently, remain unexhausted.[44] His argument recognized the danger in the Christian revelation's being required to seek justification on a basis different from, and more rigorous than, mathematical metaphysics.[45] However, Bayes succeeds mainly in bolstering Berkeley's case, by deploying arguments like this: 'I am very well satisfied that [Berkeley] must have a notion both of a first and second Fluxion, if he at all understands himself, when he supposes *a line described by the motion of a point continually* accelerated ...' (p. 11). Berkeley's point is that a Clarkean metaphysics of religion may be spun as convincingly as one of Newtonian physics – he mentions, with irony, that Newtonians praise the latter while deriding Newton's own religion (Query 58).[46] Bayes had already produced a tract (*Divine Benevolence*, 1731) against Balguy's *Divine Rectitude* (1730): it is suggestive that, like Butler, and possibly influenced by *Fifteen Sermons*, whether *1726* or *1729*, he was moving towards a belief in benevolence as opposed to rectitude or principles of justice: towards, that is, an ethics based not on intellectual principles (whether held by God or humankind) but on personality and social relations.[47] It might be anticipated that Butler's ethics would be developed in parallel with theological developments in Christology.[48] However, Bayes still begins his 1731 tract with the traditional affirmation that a consideration of the divine attributes is 'the justest ground [of enquiry into moral perfection], because ... the clearer notion we have of God himself, the better we are furnished for arguing concerning him ...' (p. 5). He continues along these lines despite rejecting speculation by Clarke and Balguy about the fundamental importance of God's attributes of justice and rectitude. His main line of thought may be illustrated from these observations: 'The ideas of goodness and veracity are distinct[.] May not a person be veracious, and yet wicked?'

---

44 Bayes's Theorem was completed and published posthumously by the moral philosopher Richard Price, whose own major work was his *Review of the Principal Questions and Difficulties in Morals*, London, A. Millar, 1758, which also took its bearings from Clarke. It does not appear that there was any personal connection between Butler and Price, but the latter's central doctrine, 'the participation of the Human in the Divine Mind' (John Stephens, *Introduction* [p. vi] to *Four Dissertations*, 2nd edn, London, 1768, reprint Bristol, 1990) is, as we have seen, amply anticipated by Butler, whom he names as a prime influence. See also David Nicholls, *God and Government in an 'Age of Reason'*, p. 46. It appears that there are at least two streams of Bayesian thought current at present: synchronic and diachronic. See Stathis Psillos, 'Putting a Bridle on Irrationality', in *Images of Empiricism*, ed. Bradley Monton, Oxford, 2007, p. 135ff.
45 John Habgood (*Varieties of Unbelief*, Chapter 8, *e.g.* p. 124) observes that the twenty-first-century Christian is routinely held to higher standards than his scientific colleagues. In other words, Christianity has ceded the apologetic central ground to atheism.
46 Clarke himself would have regarded his metaphysics as closely supported by research in the natural sciences. His last publication was 'On the Proportion of Force to Velocity in Bodies in Motion', *Philosophical Transactions*, no. 401 (1728), addressed to Bishop Benjamin Hoadly.
47 The Whig party was continuing to diversify. Balguy, whose son was to be the dedicatee of Hallifax's edition of *The Analogy*, was a disciple of Clarke, an opponent of Shaftesbury (*A Letter to a Deist*, 1726) and a client of Charles Talbot.
48 See the discussion of Robert Morehead in Chapter 6, p. 187 ff.

(p. 9). 'I can't ... well understand ... persons puzzling themselves in searching for the boundaries between goodness and justice, ... between a communication of blessings, and infliction of judgments and calamities' (p. 10). In contrast to these criticisms of Balguy (and, by extension, Clarke), and setting out his own position, he writes, 'By the goodness of God we ought, I think, to understand *a disposition to communicate happiness to his creatures in general*; so that the end of goodness is answered by every action that produces more happiness than misery' (p. 10). Setting aside for now the fact that this expresses efficiently what came to be known as the version of utilitarianism called 'universal hedonism' (although, typically of the eighteenth century, in God-centred form), we note that Bayes mounts an argument about the relative descriptive economy ('convenience', p. 8) of different analytical schemes in metaphysics, rejecting those which, inelegantly, require additional internal levels of *a priori* argument. Thus he produces an exceptionally unified account of the personal God, the traditional 'attributes' being seen as humanly devised analogical and probabilistic tools rather than really existing components of the divine nature, which is overwhelmingly one of 'kindness'.[49]

Penelhum has remarked that 'Butler's thinking about probability is not at all systematic.'[50] It is certainly the case that Butler at all times avoids expounding systems. As we have seen, even *The Analogy*, his only mature non-sermon publication, was itself at least partly a redaction of sermons, in which such methods are inappropriate, so that all of Butler's works have a large *ad hominem* element.[51] We have also pointed to its theoretically anti-systematic nature. However, we may tease out his thinking and set it in its context.

Probability is a mode of mathematical calculation and while often attached to empirically framed phenomena is not theoretically tied to inductive reasoning. However, in eighteenth-century terms, if the universe is, axiomatically, the creation of an omniscient God, individual phenomena within the creation must appear to be contingent to beings inside it,[52] so that the distribution of their occurrence may even seem random.[53] In the Clarke correspondence Butler had observed that 'there is a great difference between the order in which things

---

[49] Bayes's elaboration of this point (pp. 11–19) seems of exceptional interest but is beyond the scope of the present discussion. It is couched entirely in non-mathematical language. Bayes's Section II (pp. 20–9) deals with the twin concepts of benevolence and kindness.

[50] Penelhum, *Butler*, p. 92.

[51] The only sermon sub-genre which was allowed to display scholarship and formal logic in its actual text (as opposed to footnotes) was the university sermon. Chapter 6 gives the example of William Whewell's sermons at Cambridge.

[52] While Gauss, in the next century, was to show that a three dimensional body – considered as a mathematical abstract – could be described from within, without the need for reference to space outside it, it has not been shown that this is possible of real objects and systems, so that the application of mathematical models to the natural sciences remains a matter of analogy and a stumbling block to a 'theory of everything'. See F. Waismann, 'Language Strata', *Language and Logic*, second series, ed. A. Flew, Oxford, 1966, p. 20.

[53] This was to be a point of discussion in the aftermath of the great Lisbon earthquake of 1755, which was felt to be a challenge to Enlightenment accounts of the providential in natural religion.

exist, and the order in which I prove to myself that they exist'.[54] We remarked that this constituted a rejection of a version of analogy, in fact, the Aristotelian model. The word 'order' implies both structures and sequences and should be borne in mind when considering Butler's thinking about probability. Butler discusses the assessment of probability as a function of reasoning from the natural phenomena which surround us, observing that probability is a matter of degrees, but capable of building to a 'moral Certainty' (pp. i–ii). In his *Calculation of the Credibility of Human Testimony*,[55] the bishop and mathematician George Hooper had defined '*moral Certitude Absolute*' as 'that in which the Mind of Man entirely acquiesces, requiring no further Assurance: As if one, in whom I absolutely confide [= have confidence], shall bring me word of 1200 *l* accruing to me by Gift ... and for which therefore I would not give the least valuable Consideration to be ensured' (*Works*, p. 129).[56] Hooper postulates a confluence of trust (in someone's moral probity), financial profit and payment for legal services ('Consideration').[57] Before Pascal the probabilities of games of chance were thought to be matters not of calculation but of justice, even litigation.[58] In advancing this assessment Butler is proposing a theory in which series, or accumulations, increase probability, which is how it has become commonly understood. When tossing a coin, after a sequence of ten 'heads' we feel that the probability of 'tails' is increasing, because a run of 'heads' must ultimately be balanced by a compensating predominance of 'tails'. On the other hand, somewhat counter-intuitively, the probability of 'heads' on the next throw remains 50 percent, without regard to the results of previous throws. This theoretical equivocation was already well recognized.[59]

For a limited humankind, probability is a non-empirical tool because an experiment (say, in tossing a coin and producing a given sequence) is not repeatable: how it is decided when an experimental sequence ends and a new one begins? Does one ask God? Or demand a ruling of a Supreme Court? Or physically perform some 'closure' ritual? To ask the 'repeatability' question is to discover that the empirical does not comprise all that is conceivable and useful. Probability is Butler's newly-adopted point of contact with *a priori* metaphysics, his

---

54 Letter 3B. See Chapter 1, p. 24.

55 *Works*, Oxford, James Fletcher, 1757, pp. 129–33; originally published in *Philosophical Transactions*, October 1699.

56 George Hooper (1640–1727), successively bishop of St Asaph and Bath and Wells. Hooper had been chaplain to the future Queen Mary during her period in the Netherlands, helping to reinforce her commitment to the Church of England. For a brief survey of Hooper's thought, see William M. Marshall, *George Hooper*, Sherborne, 1976, Chapter VIII.

57 OED 'Consideration 6': 'No promise is enforceable without consideration, unless made by deed'. The author has frequently encountered this sense of the term in industrial negotiations, as a relatively delicate way of demanding a financial return for a procedural concession, as an earnest of trust.

58 Glen Shafer, 'The Early Development of Mathematical Probability', in *Companion Encyclopedia of the History and Philosophy of the Mathematical Sciences*, ed. I. Grattan-Guinness, Baltimore, MD, 1994, p. 1295.

59 Reconciling these is Hooper's task in 'Calculation': however strongly one intuits that repetition reinforces a sequence, the probability of error builds in an accumulating deviation.

version of Berkeley's thinking about infinitesimals. In the practical application of his moral philosophy we will expect to find mechanisms of authority to tie the probabilistic into the societal.

Butler avoids probability models that emphasize the random nature of chance and choice. He chooses a model which is normative, tending towards the stability which people both desire and, intuitively, think is proper. He frequently uses the term 'tendency', to be discussed below, which implies a natural drive towards a norm. Because reliance on probability frequently delivers the 'wrong' result – and we can not predict how frequently, even if we can trust that in the long term medians and norms will be approximated – it entails the acceptance of doubt and, when practically necessary, of acting upon probabilities 'so low as to leave the mind in very great doubt which is the Truth' (*1736*, p. iii). In this respect Butler differs sharply from, say, Thomas Reid, whose acknowledged debts to Butler, and, more generally the areas of overlap between them, are concerned with matters of criticism, such as his dissection of Locke's accounts of personal identity and substance, rather than his metaphysical account of the human mind as the mediator between matter and divine immanence. When discussing probability in his Introduction, Butler's illustrations are textbook examples of the inductive method: reasoning from observations (of the ebb and flow of the tide) to natural laws which explain the observed phenomena. 'We cannot indeed say a thing is probably true upon one very slight Presumption for it; because, as there may be Probabilities on both sides of a *Question*, there may [in any given case] be some against it ...' (*loc. cit.*, italics supplied). Once again, as anticipated in the previous paragraph, we see the emergence of a pervasive juridical cast of thought. Since the admissibility or persuasiveness of testimony in many of the problems Butler sets would be a trivial contribution to their solution, we safely conclude, in opposition to Ramsey,[60] that the juridical approach which comes naturally to Butler (the possessor of two law degrees) coexists with a more metaphysical and mathematical system of concepts, even where it appears redundant: the probabilistic and the forensic are seen to be fundamentally one, united by the consideration that the acceptance of testimony in a court of law is based on a probabilistic calculation of reliability.

This approach is central to the thinking of one of the founders of the Royal Academy, John Wilkins, bishop of Chester (1614–72). In his *Principles and Duties of Natural Religion*[61] Wilkins discusses the existence of God by applying a forensic method to the evidence. He believes that such evidence has to be appropriate to the matter under discussion: 'When a thing is capable of a good proof in any kind, men ought to rest satisfy'd in the best evidence for it, which that kind of thing will bear, and beyond which better could not be expected, supposing it were true' (p. 26). In his essay on concepts of evidence in the

---

[60] Ian Ramsey, *Joseph Butler*, p. 14.
[61] London, T. Basset, 1675, and much reprinted. John Tillotson edited the volume and supplied the preface.

English common law and in the Indian legal code (a nineteenth-century creation of the British Empire), Alexander Welsh, who also quotes this passage from Wilkins,[62] comments of it that 'Lawyers may hear in these lines the cadences of the best evidence rule, as it was framed in the same era – though cherished by the common law as its own, the rule essentially goes back to Aristotle's *Ethics* (I.3).' Quoting a mid-eighteenth-century lawyer, Geoffrey Gilbert, Welsh remarks of the 'best evidence rule' that 'Gilbert means that the finding of a court of law, though based on less than certain demonstrations, must nevertheless be treated as certain and final' (pp. 71–2).[63] He notes that the doctrine was appropriated by Blackstone and cites instructions about circumstantial evidence, given by a chief justice to the jury in an 1849 murder trial, which closely resemble Butler's remarks on the force of probabilistic evidence. He asserts that '[this] standard of proof ... can still be said to be that of the common law today' (pp. 71–2, 73). Whereas the legal strategy of Thomas Sherlock's forensic apologetic, *The Tryal of the Witnesses of the Resurrection of Jesus*,[64] to which we will return, is to clear the accused apostles of the prosecution's charges of false testimony, Butler's approach in *The Analogy* is in effect altogether to waive the case for the defence and provide instead a massive summing-up (the defence having the last word in the trial), in which he does not defend his clients but destroys the integrity of the prosecuting counsel's case through an examination of the grounds of its accusations. This is logically sufficient and also accepts common ground with the other side, even if it rejects the opposing arguments: Butler's apologetics seek to be inclusive of even the most aggressive sceptics.

We are now positioned to understand Butler's theoretical radicalism as demonstrated by his location of a whole mass of problems within the scope of probability theory. His thesis is that probability 'is expressed in the Word Likely, *i.e.* like some Truth, or true Event ...' (*ibid.*, p. ii); the word 'Truth' is here supported by a single-word footnote: 'Verisimile'. This is a term, whose various forms, meaning 'probability, probable, likely', were used by Cicero in his *Academica* (*Academic Treatises*) and in *De natura deorum* (*Of the Nature of the Gods*).[65] Butler draws attention to its etymological components as support for his own definition of 'Likely': a supposition arising from 'the Mind's remarking ... a Likeness to some other Event, which we have observed has come to pass

[62] Alexander Welsh, 'The Evidence of Things not Seen: Justice Stephen and Bishop Butler', *Representations*, no. 22 (spring 1988), p. 71. Welsh, however, exaggerates the proximity to Locke of Wilkins and Butler's thinking. Both were actively in a critical engagement with Hobbes. Wilkins's publications predated Locke's and cannot be shown to have been indebted to him.

[63] Jan-Melissa Schramm has identified Butler as a key theological influence on Victorian reforms of the legal process's reception of testimony in her interdisciplinary study, *Testimony and Advocacy in Victorian Law*, Cambridge, 2000. See especially Chapter 1, 'Eye-witness Testimony and the Construction of Narrative'.

[64] London, J. Roberts, 1729.

[65] So many editions of Cicero, as well as commentaries, were current that this point seems to merit research beyond the scope of the present work.

... [building to] a Presumption, Opinion, or full Conviction' (*Analogy*, p. ii).[66] This second example which Butler gives differs from the first in describing the observation not of a series but a likeness or kinship of some sort. His examples include things like predictions that a child deprived of food will die (like other people who have been known to starve); that 'such[-and-such] Actions proceed from such[-and-such] Principles' (*ibid.*, p. iii); and that the King of Siam did not believe that water could become a solid (an example he takes from Locke's *Essay* and which Butler says is an example of analogical thinking by the King).[67]

This assemblage of examples does not at first appear to cohere. That of the starving child is curiously tendentious as an example of probability. Animals starve because their bodies require replacement energy and fabric. To reason about probabilities would seem to go round the long way, because belief in the consequences of starvation is trivial, but the phenomenon itself is socially important. Similarly, the King's disbelief in ice may be called probabilistic or inductive but seems more elegantly to relate to the already existing concept of experimental limits (the king's scepticism was justified – given the temperature range in his kingdom). Nevertheless, Butler wishes to insist on analysis by probability, because, for 'Beings of limited Capacities', all epistemological and inductive mental activity is probabilistic.

This sounds like a restatement of Locke's epistemology, but Locke's account of probability is vitiated from the start by the claim that we have 'an intuitive knowledge of the agreement or disagreement of the intermediate *ideas* in each step of the progress' of a demonstration of fact (the example relates to a geometrical axiom).[68] Locke refers merely to a visual appreciation of likeness, a narrowly limited ability which is distinguishable, on the one hand, from the emotion of assent felt when a proof is witnessed and, on the other hand, from a non-mathematically-minded person's assenting to the proposition on the grounds of the probability that experts know what they are talking about – what we call 'testimony' rather than 'evidence'.[69] He continues by observing that 'most of the propositions we ... reason [and] ... act upon are such as we cannot have undoubted knowledge of their truth; yet some of them border so near upon certainty' (*ibid.*, §2). Yet he cannot say why he thinks that such propositions border on certainty, except that truth, however extended the 'steps' within it, is recognized intuitively and immediately, while '*belief, assent*, or *opinion*' (of

---

[66] It will be noted that all three nouns may bear technical, legal meanings, relating, respectively, to the person bringing the action (who presumes likelihood of a given outcome), counsel (who expresses a view of the legal context) and judge (who, accepting the jury's verdict, decisively concludes the case).
[67] Locke derived the anecdote from F. T. de Choisy, *Journal du voyage de Siam fait en M.DC.LXXXV. et M.DC.XXXVI*, Paris, S. Mabre-Cramoisy, 1687, but Butler's own footnote (p. iii) cites Locke.
[68] Locke, *Essay*, IV. xv. 1.
[69] Thus Galileo, working before the development of probability theory: 'among the possible places [of the location of a nova], the actual place must be believed to be that in which there concur the greatest number of distances, calculated on the most exact observations'. Zeno G. Swijtink observes that this 'resembles a courtroom procedure in which credence is given to the opinion expressed by the largest group of concurring witnesses' ('Probability and Statistics in Mechanics', in Grattan-Guinness, p. 1378).

probabilities) are not and rely on something 'extraneous' and not 'manifestly showing the agreement or disagreement of ... those ideas that are under consideration' (§3). Within his self-imposed limits, Locke gives no theoretical anchor for this doctrine.

Butler's account of probability is not only grounded more securely than Locke's but is also more radical. In a famous passage, he gives a definitive, albeit implicit, answer to the question about his intentions:

> Probable Evidence, in its very Nature, affords but an imperfect kind of Information; and is to be considered as relative only to Beings of limited Capacities. For Nothing which is the possible object of Knowledge, whether past, present, or future, can be probable to an infinite Intelligence; since it cannot but be discerned absolutely as it is in itself, certainly true, or certainly false. But, to Us, Probability is the very Guide of Life. (*1736*, pp. iii–iv)

It is to be noted that Butler, like Malebranche, relates very rigidly argument to evidence (thus abolishing casuistry), and truth to knowledge (information). Knowledge is never probable but always certain: it is an item-by-item insight into the holistic structure of fact. In the examples from Butler just quoted, knowledge comprises the entire series (S^1, S^2, S^3... ∞): all the deaths from starvation, water in all its states, all actions proceeding from their principles. God possesses grounds of knowledge analogous to humankind's, but empirically comprehensive and therefore indistinguishable from reasoning from axioms. Thus, deductive and inductive reasoning are aspects of the same activity. Indeed, it is likely that Butler thought that axioms were statements whose human origin was intuitive but the empirical probability of whose truth was 100 percent. God shares the same type of mind as humankind, albeit one incomprehensibly more powerful and with infinite resources of information; this is the 'analogical' argument upon which the theory of the affections is based. This reinforces the point made in *Fifteen Sermons*, that God is a person, not a Platonic being, a concept contrary to Clarke's own conception of God and which, in retrospect, we can now see that the young Butler's correspondence, in a somewhat confused way, was working towards challenging.[70] Moreover, and contrary to Locke's thinking about innate ideas, Butler's suggestion is that the human affections are not only analogous to an aspect of the divine mind but also offer people knowledge not derived from sense perceptions and ideas but from an 'almost' intuitive apprehension of the relations between the divine and created minds. Butler's formulation is typically and deliberately fuzzy but has a theoretical grounding absent from Locke's use of the term 'intuitive'. Awareness of affections, through the feelings, provides self-knowledge and thus heads off the counter-intuitive implication of the British empirical philosophical tradition, that the self is a fortuitous and unstable association of the effects of an unknowable world. Thus, as we will

---

[70] See Chapter 1, pp. 25–6.

see, Butler is at pains to rebuff Locke's thesis that consciousness constitutes personal identity. To a greater extent than Locke, however, he assumes a unified theory of knowledge, and does so in conscious opposition to Descartes, who '[built] a world upon hypothesis' (*1736*, p. vii).

The key concept for understanding Butler's method in achieving this is 'tendency', a term which he deploys liberally. In brief, he believed that the laws governing the Creation, physical and spiritual, had a mutually reinforcing quality which naturally carried the person's (free) will in a certain direction, and that the effects of these laws, and their affective mechanisms, could be described probabilistically. At the same time he was strongly voluntarist: the immanent God, like the wilful human, was not a passive spectator of history.

The late seventeenth-century theologians generally used the term 'tendency' with a neo-Platonist connotation. Thus when John Tillotson emphasized the scriptural authority of the soul-body distinction, in his four sermons *Of the Immortality of the Soul, as Discovered by Nature, and by Revelation [2 Timothy 1.10]*,[71] he wrote of the 'tendency' of this doctrine of 'the immortality of the soul … to the happiness and perfection of mankind' (Second sermon, p. 347), but with no probabilistic implication. The philosophers and natural scientists, however, used 'tendency' in mathematical descriptions of Newtonian dynamics, even though behind it was still found older, neo-Platonist, ideas about animist natural forces seeking to fulfil their destiny. Thus John Clarke (translating Jacques Rohault's *System of Natural Philosophy* from his brother Samuel's Latin version) wrote, 'A Body in Motion has always a Tendency to describe that Line, which it would describe if it were at liberty':[72] he had exactly this in mind, offering a Newtonian (and empirical) correction of Cartesian rationalism and ('if it were at liberty') an acknowledgement of the countervailing forces in the infinitely complex system of the created universe. Butler's vocabulary resembles that of the Newton-Clarke school:

> And the known Course of human Things, the Scene we are now passing through, particularly the Shortness of Life, denies to Virtue its full Scope, in several other Respects. The natural Tendency, which we have been considering [= lack of human moral unity], though real, is *hindred* from being carried into Effect in the present State: But these Hindrances may be removed in a future one … For Virtue, from the very Nature of it, is a Principle and Bond of Union, in some Degree, amongst all who are endued with it. (*1736*, pp. 61–2)

The power of virtue, the unity of all good people across the world, would naturally be all-conquering but for such contingencies in the post-lapsarian world. The future life promises to be the fulfilment of the ethical template of the present

---

[71] The sermons, and their page references, are taken from the ninth volume of *Sermons on Several Subjects and Occasions, by the most Reverend Dr. John Tillotson*, 12 volumes, London, C. Hitch & L. Hawes *et al.*, 1757, in which they are numbered CLXXIV–CLXXVII.

[72] This passage is cited in the OED entry for 'tendency'.

life, but the improvement, almost but not quite the perfectibility, of the here and now offers in theory a 'universal Monarchy'.

Just as the moral has been shown to be part of the natural state of a healthy humankind so, Butler says, 'though natural Religion is the Foundation and principal Part of Christianity, it is not in any Sense the whole of it' (*1736*, Pt II Chapter I, p. 144). 'Christianity is a Republication of natural Religion' (p. 144):

> It instructs Mankind in the moral System of the World ... [and] it teaches [Christians] natural Religion, in its genuine Simplicity; free from those Superstitions, with which, it was totally corrupted ... Revelation is farther, an authoritative *Publication* of natural Religion, and so affords the Evidence of Testimony for the Truth of it. (p. 144, italics supplied)

An understanding of the world is less than convincingly to be derived from nature itself, because scientifically inductive evidence is accretional and probabilistic. We cannot tell if the miracles are no less the products of natural laws than anything else: being uncommon there is less empirical evidence for them, and therefore less inductive probability. This is Butler's argument in Part II Chapter IV ('Christianity a Scheme imperfectly comprehended', pp. 186–91):

> God's miraculous Interpositions may have been, all along in like manner, by *general* Laws of Wisdom ... [All exertions of miraculous powers] may have been by general Laws: Unknown indeed to us: but no more unknown, than the Laws from whence it is, that Some die as soon as they are born, and Others live to extream Old-age ... which ... we cannot reduce to any Laws or Rules at all, though it is taken for granted, that they are as much reduceable to general ones, as Gravitation. (p. 190)

Behind seemingly arbitrary events there is space for a probabilistic theory about the tendency of individuals to be fit for their socio-economic and ecological environment. Butler sees here, moreover, space for a theory of exponential growth in the ability to survive through exercise of an in-built ability to co-operate as a species – a growth process which accelerates towards very high degrees of probability. He observes the sceptic's objection that the Christian narrative of God's way with human redemption postulates 'a long Series of intricate Means ... round-about Ways ... [and] many perplext Contrivances' (p. 191) – in other words, that God fails the Occam's Razor test of economy of means and consequently of plausibility. He takes this objection sufficiently seriously to give its refutation a section of its own and his answer is perhaps unexpected:

> But the Mystery is as great in Nature, as in Christianity ... The Change of Seasons, the Ripening of the Fruits of the Earth, the very History of a Flower, is an instance of this: And so is human Life ... Men are impatient and for precipitating things: but the Author of Nature appears deliberate throughout his Operations; accomplishing his natural Ends, by slow successive Steps. And there is a Plan of things beforehand laid out, which, from the Nature of it, requires various Systems of Means,

as well as Length of Time, in order to the carrying on its several Parts into Execution. (pp. 191–2)

Thus the deists are accused of misunderstanding nature, the sole ground of their philosophy and ethics. God is a person, with a personality and a way of doing things. Even the great pagans of Classical Greece, lacking the 'positive Institutions' of Christianity, had less access to natural religion than we (pp. 147–8). Butler also suggests that baptism in the name of the Trinity binds more closely religion, psychology and access to reality (p. 150):

> By Reason is revealed the Relation, which God the Father stands in to us ... In Scripture are revealed the Relations, which the Son and Holy Spirit stand in to us ... And we are not now considering Baptism itself, as an external positive Institution ... but only the general Duty to be paid to the Son and holy Ghost ... [that is,] the religious Regards of Reverence, Honour, Love, Trust, Gratitude, Fear, Hope.
>
> (pp. 150–1, 152)

The 'Tendency' is towards orthodoxy and, in its social expression, benevolence and society-building. It can be exemplified by an episode in Part I Chapter III, 'Of the moral Government of God'. Despite being commonly identified as some sort of 'intuitionist' moralist, and one whom some, both Victorians and moderns, have laboured to show as compatible with the Utilitarians, Butler rejected the pleasure principle as the spring of moral choice and activity. The conscience becomes a reliable faculty of moral heuristics (this will be discussed below) but the whole question of ethics is separate from the gratification of the animal passions, while actions, as such, are not virtuous or vicious.

> The Gratification itself of every natural Passion, must be attended with Delight ... abstracted from all Consideration of the Morality of such Action. Consequently, the Pleasure or Advantage in this Case, is gained by the Action itself, not by the Morality, the Virtuousness or Vitiousness of it; though it be, perhaps, virtuous or vitious. (*1736*, pp. 50–1)

Human hopes are confirmed by 'a Tendency in Virtue and Vice to produce ... good and bad Effects ... in a greater Degree than they do in fact produce them' in a contingently messy and infinitely complex society (p. 58). This gives people collectively a motive to organize for good, working with the natural grain:

> Power in a *Society*, by being under the Direction of Virtue, naturally increases, and has a necessary Tendency to prevail over [any] opposite Power, [which is] not under the Direction of it; in like Manner as Power, by being under the Direction of Reason, increases, and has a Tendency to prevail over brute Force. (*1736*, p. 58; interpolations for clarity)[73]

---

[73] Butler did not edit for clarity in *1750*.

Then he produces one of the strangest passages in eighteenth-century literature. The comparison, or analogy, introduced about 'brute Force' takes him off in a new direction, with 'brute' being taken literally. Conjuring a bizarre, Swiftian, image[74] of hand-against-claw struggle for survival and dominance, he proposes, for sake of example, that the aggregate physical strength of the Earth's brutes is greater than humankind's aggregate physical strength but notes that 'Reason gives us the Advantage and Superiority over them; and thus Man is the acknowledged governing Animal [*sic*] upon the Earth' (p. 58). He then takes an even stranger turn, setting up a series of scenarios. The first is of two or three men desperately beset by 'ten times' the number of wild beasts. The second proposes that the men and the wild beasts ('irrational Creatures') are 'of like external Shape and Manner', so that initially the men do not know who is human friend and who animal foe. The third is of a group of men landing on an island 'inhabited only by wild Beasts' – whose very irrationality, including lack of prudential foresight, enhances the danger of their uninhibited, murderous rage. In all cases the men survive and dominate only if they stop behaving as individuals and unite for mutual benefit. 'So that rational Animals have not necessarily the Superiority over irrational ones; but, how improbable soever it may be, it is evidently possible, that, in some Globes, the latter [= wild beasts] may be superior', although there is a 'Tendency' for reason to prevail over brute force (pp. 59–60).[75] Butler observes that disunity is caused by 'false Self-interest and Envy, by Treachery and Injustice, and consequent Rage and Malice against each other', the brutes being united by 'Instinct' (p. 60). 'Self-interest', of course, is the sceptics' principle which has been subverted by Butler's 'self-love'. Unity is achieved by mechanisms with a high survival value and a sound ethical content, a rational and conscience-driven mediation between self-love and benevolence – ten men thus united may achieve what ten thousand otherwise may not, a virtuous circle of self-reinforcing power, increasing exponentially while unity is maintained, and which has an ethical dimension, because for Butler, as we have seen, an aspect of all human reasoning is ethical in nature, just as all power is 'under the Direction of Virtue', a fact which leads to its natural increase.[76]

While this episode is remarkable for its Swiftian power of conception, for imagining alternative worlds and for supposing that humanity is a moral, not a biological concept, its greatest interest for us here is that it conceives of power as accumulating not as the sum of each individual's power but as a product of these powers. This is an instance of 'combinatorial probability', a branch of mathematical thinking developed in the sixteenth century by Italian mathemati-

---

74 *Gulliver's Travels*, like *Fifteen Sermons*, was first published in 1726.

75 'Globe' can only mean 'world': Butler is here imagining parallel realities, including some populated by humans without ethics.

76 This strongly anticipates the neo-Darwinian doctrine of 'non-zero-sumness' in animal and human behaviour. See, for example, Robert Wright, *The Moral Animal* (1994), London, 1995, pp. 193–5.

cians such as Gerolamo Cardano (1501–76; *Liber de ludo aleae* (*On Casting the Die*), published only in 1663) and greatly developed in the famous correspondence between Pascal and Fermat.[77] Cardano provided the classic definition of probability as 'the number of favourable outcomes divided by the number of possible outcomes': that calculations of probability were products, not sums. We have seen that George Hooper had produced *A Calculation of the Credibility of Human Testimony* (1699) as a mathematical support for his earlier work against Roman Catholicism, *A Fair and Methodical Discussion of the First and Great Controversy between the Church of England and Church of Rome, Concerning the Infallible Guide*:[78] he sought to prove, against the tradition- (rather than Scripture-) bound Romanists, that testimony declines in accuracy and credibility as it is continued through a series of generations; his paper proposed a set of conditions and from them calculated a rate of decline. His thesis was adopted by Richard Bentley when proposing a new edition of the Greek Testament.[79] Hooper's thinking is mathematically probabilistic: he offers the suggestion that we may trust someone's testimony by, for example, a factor of five sixths (p. 130). This seemingly bizarre assumption is actually a restatement in arithmetical terms of calculations of the probability of given outcomes in scenarios adapted from Pascal and Fermat, using their 'method of expectations' or something derived from it,[80] assigning degrees of credibility between various testimonies and within sequential combinations of testimonies. Hooper's and Butler's thinking, although tending in opposite directions, is identical: they both think in terms of exponential rates of change in probabilities. Hooper does so negatively, his probability curve starting steeply from 0 and flattening as it approaches 1 (= certainty). Butler does so positively, his curve starting flat from the (very small) power of a single person and steepening as more people unite. In fact, hidden inside Butler's parables is a play on the ambiguity of the word 'power': human power is described by the series in which it is raised by successive arithmetical powers (x, x^2, x^3 ...), forming the exponential curve he has so vividly, even graphically, described. Perhaps he thinks that underlying the two senses is a single truth. It is as if Butler imagines Shaftesburian man, aristocratically disinclined to sink individuality into collective unity, being destroyed by Hobbesian nature. By contrast, power emerges from common social interests and the validity of the fundamental affection of self-love as against the delusory (and unchristian) Hobbesian concept of self-interest. Butler frames this with the concept of 'tendency', probabilistic but also amenable to empirical verification.

---

[77] Jan Gullberg, *Mathematics: From the Birth of Numbers*, New York, 1997, p. 963; Glen Shafer, 'The Early Development of Mathematical Probability', in Grattan-Guinness, p. 1293 ff.

[78] London, R. Chiswell & R. Bentley, 1689.

[79] See Richard Bentley, *Works*, volume III, ed. Alexander Dyce (1838), p. 478. First published (*Proposals for Printing a New Edition of the Greek Testament and St. Hierom's Latin Version*) by James Knapton in 1721.

[80] Shafer, *op. cit.*, p. 1295.

Since Hooper, a prominent and much-respected bishop, had died only in 1727 and, although not a Whig loyalist, had played a key part in securing the Crown for Reformed Christianity, it is likely that Butler knew of his work. Likenesses and affinities to Pascal have been observed in Butler by other scholars.[81] Since he certainly knew Malebranche he may well also have known Arnauld's *Port Royal Logic*, which was so important to recent and contemporary French philosophers.

If 'tendencies' meant causation viewed from a metaphysical concept of the natural, 'probability' was tendency observed from within a given system. We could adapt Kant and say that tendencies are a 'will to X', or we could adapt the language of Christian mysticism and say that some tendencies are the unconscious finding in God something which immediately answers to something in us. We could say with Locke that sensory ideas tend to trigger certain responses in us, or with Reid that we associate them with other things. Perhaps the nearest formulation of Butler's meaning of 'tendency' was a remark which S. T. Coleridge relayed to Hazlitt:

> A fisherman gave Coleridge an account of a boy that had been drowned the day before, and that they had tried to save him at the risk of their own lives. He said, 'he did not know how it was that they ventured, but Sir, we have a *nature* towards one another'. This expression, Coleridge remarked to me, was a fine illustration of that theory of disinterestedness which I (in common with Butler) had adopted.[82]

The substitution by Hazlitt of 'disinterestedness' for 'benevolence' shows his considered need to combat Paley's utilitarianism but the fisherman's observation could hardly be improved upon.[83]

Behind Butler's thinking about personal identity is an observation about knowledge which was left to Thomas Reid to elaborate.[84] Butler wrote that 'Consciousness of personal Identity presupposes, and therefore cannot constitute, personal Identity, ...', an observation which we will discuss in due course. The second half of the sentence is less familiar: '... any more than Knowledge in any other Case, can constitute Truth, which it presupposes'. Consequently,

---

[81] For example, Penelhum, *Butler*, Chapter IV and Albino Babolin, '*Deus absconditus*: Some Notes on the Bearing of the Hiddenness of God upon Butler's and Pascal's Criticism of Deism', *Tercentenary Essays*, pp. 29–36.

[82] William Hazlitt, *My First Acquaintance with Poets*, ed. Jonathan Wordsworth, Oxford, 1993, p. 45.

[83] In the same essay Hazlitt says of Coleridge that, 'He considered Butler ... a profound and conscientious thinker, a genuine reader of nature and of his own mind .... He mentioned Paley ... but condemned his sentiments, thought him a mere time-serving casuist, and said that "the fact of his work on Moral and Political Philosophy being made a text-book in our Universities was a disgrace to the national character"' (*ibid.*, pp. 33, 34).

[84] See René van Woudenberg: 'Reid on Memory and the Identity of Persons', in *Cambridge Companion to Thomas Reid*, Cambridge, 2004, p. 205, where Reid's theory of knowledge is contrasted with those of Descartes, Locke and Hume (Malebranche could have been added), but without reference to Butler's acknowledged influence.

knowledge is a category of belief and, in context, belief a matter of probability. Without doubt there can be no faith.

Personal identity

The Church of England navigated the post-1688 Whig project with care. The defence of European Protestantism demanded a policy of toleration and political inclusiveness, not only of English Dissent and Scottish Presbyterianism but of deist scepticism. This in turn required a modesty of ambition within the bench of bishops. Even for the fully committed leadership this could be painful. In the interest of political stability the government was to reject the Church's cautious proposals, strongly supported by Butler, to allow America-based episcopal oversight of the colonial clergy and even gave objective encouragement to the Presbyterian Church to intensify its persecution of Episcopalians by defeating calls to allow Scottish bishops to ordain their own clergy.[85] To defend the Whig settlement meant extending liberties far beyond the literal and metaphorical pale.

Butler exemplifies this by his beginning *The Analogy* with a defence 'Of a future Life' (Part I Chapter I), pointing out that 'a Proof ... of a future Life, would not be a Proof of Religion. For, that we are to live Hereafter, is just as reconcileable with the Scheme of Atheism ... as that we are now alive, is ... But ... any Presumption against such a State, is a Presumption against Religion' (p. 45). A more modest beginning for an apology could hardly be devised. Instead of alienating Whig supporters among the deists Butler instead proposes to put Christian and deist on the same basis, to offer corrections to the theory of the person presented in Locke's *Essay* and to leave the ideological power struggle about immortality for adjudication at the bar of the facts of life.

We will approach Butler's thinking about personal identity through a discussion of texts by Thomas Sherlock and Vincent Perronet, the first for its negative strategy and the second for its offering a contemporary critique of Butler's thought.

Sherlock published his seminal *The Tryal of the Witnesses of the Resurrection of Jesus* in 1729, the same year as the second edition of *Fifteen Sermons*. At this time he was the Bishop of Bangor, ironically in view of the part he had played, on the orthodox side, in the Bangorian controversy. Intellectually and stylistically *The Tryal* is one of the most successful of Anglican apologetics. It is presented as the transcript of a prosecution of Christ's disciples under English law for bearing allegedly false witness about the Resurrection. The trial starts with an invitation by the judge to the 'Council for Woolston' ('Mr. A') to begin.[86] Mr. A objects that he had nothing to object to and that Mr. B, 'the Council for

---

[85] These issues will be discussed in Chapter 5. In his ODNB article, Cunliffe adds the Mortmain Bill and the Quaker's Tithe Bill, which gave further consideration to groups within the Whig coalition.

[86] Thomas Woolston had recently been tried for blasphemy, this being the occasion for Sherlock's book. See ODNB, 'Woolston, Thomas'.

the other Side', should begin, by laying out the grounds in favour of Christ's resurrection. Mr. B in turn argues that 'the Evidence [for the resurrection] is old, and is a Matter of Record ... [and that] no Man is obliged to produce his Title to his Possession; it is sufficient if he maintains it when it is called in question' (p. 7). Mr. A replies that B is in effect calling in question A's sanity, by demanding that A 'admit Things incredible' (p. 8), so that it is for B to prove that A has no right to be called sane. The judge then gives his ruling:

> Sir [= A], you say right; upon Supposition that the Truth of the Christian Religion were the point in Judgment. In that Case it would be necessary to produce the Evidence for the Christian Religion; but the Matter now before the Court is, Whether the Objections produced by Mr. *Woolston*, are of weight to overthrow the Evidence of Christ's Resurrection ... [The] Objections ... therefore ... must be set forth. (p. 8)

This ruling goes to the heart of the English common law and the trial is conducted according to the current balance between testimony, based on the status and credibility of the witness, and circumstantial evidence.[87] It also makes a Whiggish point: a revolution is legitimate if it makes a sound critique of the *status quo*. Woolston, both in life and as portrayed in *The Tryal*, could claim to be continuing the Glorious Revolution, by exposing quasi-Papist superstition to the clear light of reason. In *The Tryal* he could only do this if his counsel could successfully take the initiative in the process. Procedure is everything.

> Defending counsel were only gradually permitted to advise 'the prisoner', as the defendant was invariably named, and only after 1760 were they allowed to cross-examine witnesses ... Circumstances typically told against the individual who was brought to trial ... Paley would state it flat out: 'Circumstances cannot lie.'[88]

Thus when Mr. B argues, successfully, for the right to speak second – in effect to be the defender rather than the prosecutor – he is taking the procedurally riskier way and relying on the strength of his two basic arguments: that the other side must challenge his right of possession; and that such arguments are likely to be vulnerable to the forensic strategy of defending witness testimony in the face of any plausible circumstantial evidence which might be adduced. These were bound to include the laws of nature, which Mr. A was sure to bring into evidence

---

[87] Alexander Welsh, 'The Evidence of Things Not Seen: Justice Stephen and Bishop Butler', pp. 60–88, gives such an account of eighteenth-century trial protocol and the relative weight of circumstantial evidence and witness testimony. His thesis is developed and extended in his *Strong Representations: Narrative and Circumstantial Evidence in England*, Baltimore, MD, 1992. Robert E. Rodes, Jr, *Law and Modernization in the Church of England: Charles II to the Welfare State*, Notre Dame, IN, 1991, chapter 1.I.C (Law and Administration) does not consider the testimony-circumstantial evidence dichotomy directly but gives several case histories which seem to suggest that contemporary church courts accorded greater weight to testimony than to evidence or its admissibility.
[88] Alexander Welsh, *ibid.*, p. 78.

to demonstrate the way things actually are. Sherlock relocates the orthodox case in probabilistic argument.

Mr. B's main strategy is to observe that the laws of nature (which the resurrection appears to contradict) are established *a posteriori* from observation and experience. A stone might be observed to roll uphill; if it does, our formulation of a law of nature will be changed (p. 61). If this, or a report of a resurrection, seems far-fetched, we are invited to consider reports of the freezing of water from the point of view of a resident of a hot country (p. 63), a hit at Locke, from whom Sherlock, like Butler, borrows it. In the event, Mr. B's defence strategy succeeds with the English jurors, who are not convinced by sceptical arguments.

Like Butler, Sherlock applies this argument to the question of personal immortality. In one of his sermons[89] he points to Plato, Aristotle and Cicero as proof that the pre-Christian belief in personal immortality was based not on 'philosophical Reasons ... [but on] a common Opinion ... which is received by the generality of Men', and which 'arose from the common Sense that Men have of the Difference of Good and Evil, and of every Man's being accountable for the Things done in this World'. Merely philosophical arguments for immortality are *a posteriori* rationalizations, seeking out 'physical Reasons to support the Cause'.[90] He also cites Cicero: 'Infidelity is of no older a Date than Philosophy' (p. 199). Sherlock here develops an argument close to Butler's. Since the 'natural Evidence [of intuition] ... supposes only that Man is a rational, accountable Creature' it follows that 'Man, as such, shall live to account for his Doings. The Question then, upon the Foot of Nature, is this, What constitutes the Man?' (p. 200).

In *The Analogy* Butler takes exactly the same line as Sherlock, bringing the weight of public opinion about the force of testimony up against the credibility of circumstantial evidence. His strategy is to reduce both to one level and to argue the essential unity of the multi-sourced human conversation about reality. Thus we find him writing:

> [Considering the miracles, readers should consider] the Importance of collateral things, and even of lesser Circumstances, in the Evidence of Probability, as distinguished, in Nature, from the Evidence of Demonstration. In many Cases indeed it seems to require the truest Judgment, to determine with Exactness the Weight of circumstantial Evidence ... [The] Proof of Religion is said to be involved in such inextricable Difficulties, as to render it doubtful ... [but] it is according to the Conduct and Character of the Author of Nature, to appoint we should act upon Evidence like to That, which this Argument presumes He cannot be supposed to appoint we should act upon. [*1736*, pp. 272, 279][91]

---

[89] Thomas Sherlock, *Discourse VI [2 Timothy 1.10]*, *Several Discourses Preached at the Temple Church* (1753), 4 vols, 6th edn, London, J. Whiston & B. White, 1772, vol. I, p. 187 ff.

[90] Sherlock, *ibid.*, pp. 193, 194, 198.

[91] The earlier passage in this quotation is also used by Alexander Welsh in his 'Burke and Bentham on the Narrative Potential of Circumstantial Evidence', *New Literary History*, vol. 21. no. 3 (spring 1990),

As we saw above, 'Revelation is ... an authoritative *Publication* of natural Religion, and so affords the Evidence of Testimony for the Truth of it' (p. 144). Circumstantial evidence is God's testimony, even if open to misinterpretation by fallible or interested juries (real or figurative).[92] We have already suggested that for Butler deductive arguments are only a special form of inductive, axioms replacing empirical examples. We now see that testimony and evidence are ultimately not distinguishable: humans have only one set of physical and intellectual apparatus, although they allow for a degree of intuition, the immediate recognition of likeness given by the affections.

The fundamental strategic importance of this question to *The Analogy* has become evident: without life after death our moral affections are redundant, even fraudulent, and there is no basis for a system of ethics. When considered by analogy with human society and its laws this does not entail intimidating extremes such as myths of hell-fire, which express the culture of absolutism and tyranny. Democratic myths of judicial reviews are more congruent with contemporary English culture. We find this position shared by Vincent Perronet in his critique of *The Analogy*, which forms the first twenty-four pages of his *Second Vindication of Mr. Locke* (London, Fletcher Gyles, 1738). Perronet is the first critic of Butler's formulation of the personal identity problem and identifies issues which were of salient contemporary interest. It is noteworthy that the *Second Vindication*, unlike his first *Vindication* of 1736, was not published by the Knaptons, possibly because it attacks an author from their stable and thus signals a political divergence.

For Perronet, as for Locke, the two types of identity (the human and the non-human) have common ground in the forensic. Perronet points out (p. 11) that Locke's forensic approach solves the 'same tree' problem: the human right to property, asserted in courts of law, settles in a commonsense way the question, is the tree identical across the years in which its constituent atoms are gradually replaced. The identity of self – judicially responsible identity – he restates by quoting Locke's thesis that personal identity 'consists in *Identity of Consciousness*, and in That alone' (p. 7): it is obviously unjust, however expedient, to punish someone for a crime which they cannot remember having committed. Judicial identity (a point Perronet does not make, but which Butler will in the *Six Sermons*), is involved with the idea that society seeks rehabilitation rather than revenge or deterrence. While Locke's consistency in applying this supports his greatness as a political philosopher it undermines his claim to be a Christian

---

p. 612. Because of the effect he demonstrates of Butler's philosophy on British and Indian law, Welsh's instinct is to assume that Butler tends towards weighting due process towards circumstantial evidence. While the latter is the new arrival in the courtroom, however, Butler accommodates it into his religious apologetics without supplanting the central position of testimony.

[92] It is on this ground that arguments against capital punishment began to emerge. A popular example is found in the tract, 'Cases of Circumstantial Evidence', in Chambers, *Miscellany of Useful and Entertaining Facts*, volume IV, Edinburgh, 1845, no. 32, p. 32.

philosopher.[93] As Perronet admits (it is 'plain Reason, if not plain Revelation', pp. 9–10), the implied limitation on God has no scriptural support.

Butler has a different, entirely ethical, perspective from Locke's. This is recognized explicitly by Perronet: '[Butler's] Objections have nothing to do with *Person* or *Personal Identity*, as understood by Mr. *Locke*' (p. 7). He asks, acutely (p. 17), '… if by *Person* be meant [by Butler] the same *Substance*, how will Consciousness prove to any Man, that he is the same *Person*, in this Sense; unless by *Person*, he understands the immaterial Spirit, and that Only?' Here Perronet is surely right, although it is less a point against Butler than an engagement with his account of 'person' as an immaterial substance[94] – the bundle of affections, conscience and will which was first identified in Chapter 1, and which is, 'almost intuitively', immediately recognized by others. In this Butler has the advantage of Locke. Persons can hardly be allowed to determine their own identity, because this would exalt interested testimony over circumstantial evidence in a court of law. Locke is thus forced to the brink of immaterialism and opens the way to Berkeley's even more radical theory, which exposes the incommensurability of the terms 'truth' and 'perceptual idea'.[95] Butler readily accepts property rights as an identifier but in denying the human consciousness a forensic status he reinforces his commitment to the 'immaterial substance' theory which he accepted in the Clarke correspondence. Perronet comments (p. 21), 'Tho' *He, Person*, or *Self* be certainly a *Substance*; yet Consciousness that *He* is the *same Person*, cannot, I think, be Consciousness that *He* is the *same Substance*, to any Man, who makes the Body one Part of his *Self* or *Person*'. This claim makes Perronet's situation worse, because the person is now a substratum of unknowable substance with a superstructure of consciousness – neither of which is easily defined.[96] Perronet is therefore reduced (p. 22) to stating explicitly what is implicit in Locke: that a 'thinking Substance' is 'best resolv'd into the Goodness of God' – he quotes a passage from Locke which echoes Descartes' 'trust in God' formula. The analysis ultimately fails; the circle cannot be squared. By contrast, and standing on public opinion, Butler

---

[93] In the Introduction to his *John Locke and Christianity: Contemporary Responses to the Reasonableness of Christianity* (1997), pp. xxiv–xxvi, Victor Nuovo discusses this in terms of Daniel Waterland's critique of Locke. He identifies Locke's 'covenantal' concept of the God–Christian relationship as the key area for consideration.

[94] John Tillotson had already made Butler's argument against the 'same numerical body' thesis of resurrection in one of his masterpieces, *The Possibility of the Resurrection Asserted and Proved [Acts 26.8]*, preached at Whitehall in 1682, presumably to King Charles II (*Sermons*, vol. 10, pp. 233–51).

[95] See, for example, George S. Pappas, *Berkeley's Thought*, Ithaca, NY, 2000, Chapter 9 ('Scepticism'), *passim*, but esp. pp. 238–47; Robert G. Muehlmann, *Berkeley's Ontology*, Indianapolis, IN, 1992, Chapter VI; and Kenneth P. Winkler, 'Berkeley and the Doctrine of Signs', in *Cambridge Companion to Berkeley*, pp. 125–65.

[96] The definition of 'consciousness' continues to evade a trans-disciplinary, and even intra-disciplinary consensus. Eric B. Baum (*What Is Thought?*, Cambridge, MA, 2004, Chapter 14) is reduced to 'very loose analogy' (p. 389) despite his strenuous affiliation to a single school of modern thought. Robert Audi, *The Good in the Right: A Theory of Intuition and Intrinsic Value*, Princeton, NJ, 2004, avoids using the term at all.

builds divine creativity and immanence into his theory of human identity. Thus a contemporary reviewer finds that Locke and Butler have diametrically opposed theologies and philosophies and fails to 'vindicate' Locke against Butler's critique.

This is the starting point of *The Analogy*'s first chapter ('Of a Future Life') and the dissertation *Of Personal Identity* which was excerpted from it. Chapter I argues for the likelihood of life after death from the preponderance of analogical evidence, while the dissertation argues against Locke's consciousness-based theory of personal identity and in favour of an immaterial substance theory.

In his essay 'Berkeley's philosophy of mathematics' Douglas M. Jesseph describes Berkeley's geometry as 'a science of approximations'.[97] 'The further the Mind analyseth and pursueth these fugitive Ideas, the more it is lost and bewildered; the Objects, at first fleeting and minute, soon vanishing out of sight.'[98] Butler was not a mathematician and it is unlikely that what he writes can be accounted an accurate exposition or critique of a mathematician's work, but he had clearly listened and pondered. 'When it is asked, wherein personal Identity consists, the Answer should be the same, as if it were asked, wherein consists Similitude or Equality; that all Attempts to define, would but perplex it' (*Of Personal Identity*, *1736*, p. 301). Butler's remark sounds akin to Berkeley's critique of the alleged misuse of infinitesimals in geometry: in practice we know that two objects are similar or equal, but to prove it may be theoretically impossible and be based on unacknowledged metaphysical assumptions. He continues by suggesting that the 'Similitude' of two triangles and the 'Equality' of two sums are the same sorts of concept as our view that our selves are the same at different times.

> But though Consciousness does thus ascertain our personal Identity to Ourselves, yet to say, that Consciousness makes personal Identity, or is necessary to our being the same Persons, is to say, that a Person has not existed a single Moment, nor done one Action, but what he can remember … Consciousness of personal Identity presupposes, and therefore cannot constitute, personal Identity, any more than Knowledge in any other Case, can constitute Truth, which it presupposes.
>
> (*Of Personal Identity*, *1736*, p. 302)

The last sentence here is forceful and elegant. In Chapter 1 we noticed the phrase, 'a Desire inseparable from a Conscious Being of its own Happiness' and its refusal, at some cost of elegance, to suggest that consciousness and happiness are separable (we cannot be happy without being conscious that we are happy). Hence, when he writes, that 'Consciousness of personal Identity presupposes, and therefore cannot constitute, personal Identity', he is separating

---

97 *Cambridge Companion to Berkeley*, p. 284.
98 Berkeley, *The Analyst*, quoted by Jesseph, p. 300.

personal identity decisively from mental states, even though he knows that it is not coextensive with the physical body either.

With the phrase, 'in any other Case' Butler departs from his normal serial account of analogy and commits himself to saying 'consciousness : personal identity :: knowledge : truth'. Thus consciousness identifies or acknowledges personal identity as knowledge identifies or acknowledges truth. Personal identity and truth are the objects of a heuristic process. Thus 'personal identity' is not a merely forensic term but an ontological one, with an irreducible reality.[99] This is a fundamental rejection of Locke's account of humankind and reminds us of a key passage in the 1729 Preface to the *Fifteen Sermons* (pp. xiii–xv)[100] describing the nature and actions of animals ('brutes'). Butler there commented, 'Mankind also in acting thus would act suitably to their whole Nature, if no more were to be said of Man's Nature, than what has been now said; if That, as it is a true, were also a compleat, adequate Account of our Nature.' Accounting people animals, in following their instincts, was inadequate not because they would be unhappy or dysfunctional but because such an account omits what is most fundamental about being human: the possession of the moral conscience. Butler continues to maintain a separation between animal nature (Locke's account of which he is not concerned to investigate too closely) and ethics, with the conscience developed through life by the practice of religion. Indeed, he formulates this in the most extreme way possible: when commenting that brutes too may be immortal he adds, 'And great Part of Mankind go out of the present World, before they come to the Exercise of these Capacities in any Degree at all' (p. 23). By these 'Capacities' Butler means 'great Attainments ... [which enable humans to become] rational and moral Agents' (p. 23). We have seen elsewhere Butler's hint that even Shaftesbury did not attain full flower as a person, while he also supposed that there may be 'Beings in the Universe, whose Capacities, and Knowledge, and Views, may be so extensive, as that the whole Christian Dispensation may to them appear ... as natural as the visible known Course of things appears to us' (p. 29). What we have called 'full humanity' is actually an ethical state potentially universal among suitably equipped created beings. The linking faculty is (self-)consciousness, which gives us access to our nature and the facility to analyse it, but, as we will see, is inseparably connected with the activity of conscience.

---

[99] A well-known problem of Descartes's theory of personal identity is the 'apparent gap': when Descartes is asleep he does not exist, according to his own theory. Peter Unger (*Consciousness and Value*, New York, 1990, p. 47) suggested that Butler and Reid had avoided this 'by requiring a less stringent, and less pure, relation between the self and conscious experience'. Whether this is true of Reid is not of present relevance, but Unger has misread Butler, who, as we show below, proposes that human beings are animals with the addition of a conscience (of which we are conscious) which works continuously to identify practical moral problems as they arise. Unger makes the all-too-common confession that 'I claim no scholarly expertise at all regarding [Butler and Reid]. Indeed, my sources are only the short selections in John Perry's anthology, *Personal Identity*.'

[100] See Chapter 2, pp. 67–8.

When setting down his dictum, 'Consciousness of personal Identity presupposes, and therefore cannot constitute, personal Identity', Butler calls the
contrary assumption a 'wonderful Mistake' (p. 302).

> [To] be endued with Consciousness, is inseparable from the Idea of a
> Person, or intelligent Being ... But though present Consciousness of
> what we at present do and feel, is necessary to our being the Persons we
> now are; Yet present Consciousness of past Actions or Feelings is not
> necessary to our being the same Persons who performed those Actions,
> or had those Feelings. (*1736*, p. 302)

As *Six Sermons* will show,[101] this entails a rejection of Locke's political theory,
which is grounded in his account of the individual. For Locke the 'same person'
argument exculpated an agent both legally and morally from responsibility for
actions which could no longer be remembered. Neither is the case for Butler,
because the substance, not the consciousness, constitutes the person.[102] Moreover, at this point in the *Dissertation* his doctrine of the affections re-emerges
for attention, with the observation that '... the same Property cannot be transferred from one Substance to another' (p. 303). Here the 'Property' (also termed
'Mode of Being', p. 303) of persons under review is a thing which does not
change through time and is unique to that person. Individuals are beings, not
complexes of ideas. 'And they are [the same living being, through "All these
successive Actions, Enjoyments, and Sufferings"], prior to all Consideration
of its remembring or forgetting; since remembring or forgetting can make no
Alteration in the Truth of past Matter of Fact' (p. 307). Indeed, as Butler elsewhere emphasizes, moral change happens only through practice in a course of
ethically guided life, so that a person without a long-term memory would remain
in ethical stasis, unable to cope with new challenges.

There remains Locke's idea that a whole system of metaphysics may be
cleared away by adopting a method of analysing the person purely through its
self-awareness. Butler raises several objections, directly and implicitly; we will
discuss only one.

This objection is logical in nature: self-consciousness is inextricably
connected with memory. Unless identity consists only of flashes of being,
consciousness of one's identity is guaranteed only by assuming that memory is
reliable. Butler points out that the reliability of memory cannot be challenged in
practice because the validity of all mental processes depends on it:

> But though we are thus certain, that we are the same Agents, living
> Beings, or Substances, Now, which we were as far back as our Remem-
> brance reaches, yet it is asked, Whether we may not possibly be deceived
> in it? And this Question may be asked at the End of any Demonstration

---

101 See Chapter 5, p. 159 ff.
102 To at least this extent, it is Butler, not Locke, who provides the theoretical basis in English law of
the question of legal responsibility.

whatever. Because it is a Question concerning the Truth of Perception by Memory: And he who can doubt, whether Perception by Memory can in this Case be depended on, may doubt also, whether Perception by Deduction and Reasoning, which also include Memory, or indeed whether intuitive Perception can. Here then we can go no further. For it is ridiculous to attempt to prove ... the Truth of our Faculties, which can no otherwise be proved, than by the Use or Means of those very suspected Faculties themselves.[103]

'Here then we can go no further': the reasoning on this subject is circular and we must choose to enter either a virtuous or a vicious circle.

It is memory alone which permits complexity in any act of mentation. 'The Person, of whose Existence the Consciousness is felt now, and was felt an Hour or a Year agoe, is discerned to be, not two Persons, but one and the same Person; and therefore is one and the same' (p. 304). Indeed, it appears impossible to be conscious of being conscious of being conscious, in an infinite regression, so that *esse est percipi*.

And this He, Person or Self, must either be a Substance, or the Property of some Substance. If He, if Person, be a Substance, then Consciousness that He is the same Person, is Consciousness that He is the same Substance. If the Person or He be the Property of a Substance, still Consciousness that He is the same (the same Property) is as certain a Proof that his Substance remains the same, as Consciousness that he remains the same Substance would be; since the same Property cannot be transferred from one Substance to another.[104]

In other words, to postulate that 'person' is a property, or something lying on top of a substance, is unnecessarily to multiply entities and explanations. The same is true of the specious argument that if we perceive ourselves there must be two distinct things signified by 'ourselves'.

If a person is a substance, whether material or (as Butler believed) immaterial, there is the question of whether it can be destroyed by death.

All Presumption of Death's being the Destruction of living Beings, must go upon supposition that they are compounded and so discerptible. But since Consciousness is a single and indivisible Power, it should seem that the Subject in which it resides, must be so too. (*1736*, p. 16)

'Discerptible' is a word which Butler may have coined. His source can only have been Cicero: '*animus nec dividi nec discerpi potest*' ('the soul cannot be

---

[103] *Of Personal Identity, 1736*, p. 308. This passage is quoted by Joan Wynn Reeves, *Body and Mind in Western Thought* (p. 136), a history of psychology which notes that 'Butler ... is curiously neglected in the psychological history books ... [His] theoretical structuring of personality ... finds its echoes in modern writers such as McDougall and Freud ... [and is an example of] investigating the relation of complex and organically integrated occurrences' (p. 137).
[104] *Of Personal Identity, 1736*, pp. 307–8.

divided or dismembered'),[105] a reminder of the fact that his work is built on classical material. Thus when arguing for an extreme dissociation of mind and body, holding that the eye is not a 'percipient' but merely an instrument, like spectacles ('glasses', *1736*, p. 20) he does not acknowledge Berkeley's thoughts about vision, which he must have known. He is content to suggest the passivity – in Cartesian language the determined nature – of matter, as his strategic aim is to develop the idea that all human activity is fundamentally ethical. Our sense of self is not primarily connected with our bodies – they change constantly and we can lose even major body parts and still be the same person, both objectively and subjectively.

> ... we have no way of determining by Experience, what is the certain Bulk of the living Being each man calls himself: and yet, till it be determined that it is larger in Bulk than the solid elementary Particles of Matter ... there is no sort of Reason to think Death to be the Dissolution of it, of the living Being, even though it should not be absolutely indiscerptible. (p. 18)[106]

The phrase, 'solid elementary Particles' is reminiscent both of classical atomic theory and of Berkeley's anti-fluxions theory about the illegitimacy of bringing conceptual infinity to the subdivision of atomic matter. On the other hand, if people are, for example, physically invaded – raped, shot or stabbed – or have their children killed or their home vandalized by burglars it is commonly reported that they feel that their identity has been undermined. Thus common experience supports Butler's suggestion that the person has a property relationship with the materials of body and society. This would not appear plausible if people were not mind as well as body.

From this it follows that everything distinctively human – society, religion, knowledge, language, and so on – is a system of what might be termed survival mechanisms in the material world for the immaterial personal substance. The term, 'survival mechanism', is an anachronism, but the evidence for Butler's having this sort of conception is abundant and strong: he thought in terms of negotiating ways through encounters, hence his emphasis on practical wisdom (his own term is 'prudence'), which is introduced as early as p. iv of *The Analogy*'s Introduction: 'an absolute and formal Obligation, in point of Prudence and of Interest, to act upon that Presumption or low Probability, though it be so low as to leave the Mind in very great Doubt which is the Truth'. Modern English was to shift 'prudence' towards 'praiseworthy caution'; Butler, in advocating a principle of action thus defined, recalls the etymological, and Biblical, meaning.

---

[105] The OED gives this passage of Butler as the word's earliest appearance. Johnson's *Dictionary* aside, all its other citations are of Butlerian or explicitly anti-Butlerian nineteenth-century writers.
[106] The words 'discerptible' and 'indiscerptible' both occur in this chapter but nowhere else in Butler – some slight evidence that the chapter may once have been a discrete (sermon) document.

Moral consciousness

We are now in a position to complete our discussion of Butler's ethical thinking in the Stanhope period. We have argued above that the dissertation *Of the Nature of Virtue* is an edited Rolls sermon. Here it may be added that it is aimed principally against doctrines of Hobbes and Shaftesbury and in that respect is fully congruent with *Fifteen Sermons*. During the preparation of the second, 1729, edition of *Fifteen Sermons* Butler made a sustained effort to clarify and integrate his thinking, especially with regard to the connection on the one hand between the relationship of God and the natural creation and on the other between the natural creation and ethics; we may take this as his version of the distinction between natural and revealed religion. We have seen that his approach to the Cartesian problem of trust was to suggest that an ethics-oriented mind was what distinguished humankind from the rest of the material creation and that the capacity for ethical thinking arose from the affections which were an analogue of certain modes of the divine being. We have also noted that *The Analogy* presents in its most extreme form Butler's account of the mind–body distinction and provides the context for the formulation, in *Of the Nature of Virtue*, which avoids the supposed conflict between self-interest and morality.

This is a subject which Butler discusses at length, but when Terence Cuneo[107] says that he was in a tradition which sought 'to reconcile the claims of morality with those of self-interest' this seems a very unnatural way of describing his doctrine, because for Butler ethics does not exist in the engagement of morality and self-interest but in the binary system of extrovert benevolence and introvert self-love, the product not of two distinct intellectual *motives* but two distinct affective *mechanisms*. As we have seen,[108] self-love protects the self with which the individual is entrusted, while benevolence builds society through care for the circles of family and friends and thence for the race in general.[109] Morality is the activity which effects transformation, not reconciliation.[110] Butler terms it 'active Behaviour', as opposed to a '*Perception* [whose object or occasion] is Satisfaction, Uneasiness or Loss'[111] and distinguishes between the latter's mere responsiveness – a desire for things which exist 'out there' to be chosen or rejected – and the creative nature of the process of 'Approbation and Disapprobation'. Whereas, for example, Shaftesbury thinks that people are enabled

---

[107] Terence Cuneo, 'Reid's Moral Philosophy', in *The Cambridge Companion to Thomas Reid*, p. 248.
[108] Chapter 2, p. 54f.
[109] See *Of the Nature of Virtue*, *1736*, p. 314 ('*Fourthly* ...'). Butler was heavily influenced by Stoicism, and readers will recall at this point Seneca's *On Tranquillity of Mind* (*Letters from a Stoic*, translated Robin Campbell, Harmondsworth, 1974, p. 70).
[110] When Cuneo observes (p. 259) that for Butler we 'immediately' know what we should do ethically he mistakes again, because, as well as the role of conscious judgement, he ignores the developmental process which is intrinsic to Butler's Christian and ethical psychology. We have discussed this as the dynamics between the various components of the individual's 'bundle' of affections.
[111] *1736*, p. 314 (italics supplied). There is some slight tautening of the text in *1750* but without affecting the sense.

by their moral sense to see things which are potentially good or ill in their effects, and that between individuals and worldly phenomena there is a one-to-one ethical correlation, Butler thinks that the human conscience interprets the world in ethical terms and moves to shape it. Thus it is legitimate, other things being equal, to favour a friend or benefactor, because 'Examples of Gratitude, and the Cultivation of Friendship, would be of general Good to the World' (*1736*, pp. 316–7). As a basis for a social policy this is perhaps more alien to modern theory than to modern practice, but it is certainly supportive of the patronage from which Butler himself benefited: we have previously noted his phrase 'Cements of Society'. The ethical is in the complex of the conscience and affections, not in the objective situation. The corollary is that, for Butler, an individual is not necessarily compelled to act ethically but, if insufficiently developed to be conscious of ethical 'Object[s] or Occasion[s]', may react in the same way that an animal does, ethics then being an inappropriate system for the analyst.[112]

Of the Nature of Virtue begins with the statement, 'That which renders Beings capable of moral Government, is their having a moral Nature, and moral Faculties of Perception and of Action' (*1736*, p. 309). The reader has only to delete 'moral' from this to see a problem, and, indeed, Bott describes the formulation as meaningless.[113] It is certainly unusual in evading Butler's (and Secker's) careful editing. Stripped of 'moral' the sentence appears less meaningless than trivial: without understanding and the power to act, people could respond neither to the conscience nor the instructions of competent authorities. However, it is sufficiently obvious that for Butler 'moral' is a different sort of adjective from, say, 'red' or even 'strong'. Thus he separates 'actions' from 'events' to emphasize this difference: events just happen; actions are inescapably ethical because human beings reflect on them in that sort of way.[114] This is a far-reaching proposition, entailing not only a distinction between a moral nature and a biological nature but between moral and biological faculties, so that a set of physical movements may in one context be sufficiently described as mere movements and in another as freely-willed moral action. This presses Cartesian theory to its extreme. It consciously identifies a potential in humans

---

112   Butler was not alone in seeing a dichotomy between 'natural' behaviour and that guided by revelation. John Conybeare (1692–1755), like Butler an anti-deist controversialist (*Defence of Revealed Religion against the Exceptions of [Tindal]*, 1732), a protégé of the Talbot family and Butler's successor as bishop of Bristol, argued that the natural law is discoverable by each person and therefore different for each, although still bringing with it the individual's duties. 'In consequence of this, we ought to distinguish between *a Rule of Fitness*, and *a Law of Duty*. The former will be the same to all Mankind; but the latter must vary in proportion to each particular Man's Attainments or Opportunities.' Revelation is needed by each person to supply their inadequacies (*The Needfulness of a Revelation, shewn from the Imperfection of the Law of Nature considered as a Rule of Duty [Luke 1:78–9]*, an undated sermon in *Sermons*, 2 vols, London, Samuel Richardson, 1757, volume II, p. 160f and *passim*).
113   Bott, p. 23.
114   *Of the Nature of Virtue*, *1736*, p. 311: 'It does not appear, that Brutes have the least reflex Sense of Actions as distinguished from Events.'

for a sort of schizophrenia, in that large majority of individuals who are not wholly without conscience but whose ethical 'algorithm' works imperfectly. We have seen hints of this in the *Fifteen Sermons*. Butler seems to have worked to a position where the integrity of the individual, its spiritual and mental good health, is a matter of a sort of continuous therapeutic process. We will expect to see explicit acknowledgements of the role of religion in the sustaining of the good life and in preventing mental breakdown.

Butler's reliance on the Roman Stoics emerges again in this account. His working model of the conscience is this:

> [our] Capacity of reflecting upon Actions and Characters, and making them an Object to our Thought: And on doing this, we *naturally and unavoidably* approve some Actions, under the peculiar View of their being virtuous and of Good-desert, and condemn Others, as vitious and of Ill-desert. (*1736*, p. 309, italics supplied)

In exercising it we become conscious of our special, moral, nature: 'the Principle of Reflection' as he had termed it in the *1729* Preface.[115] At this point, in a footnote, he cites the Graeco-Roman Stoic Epictetus about the self-referential character of the moral faculty. Epictetus says that intellectual faculties, or disciplines[116] (the examples he gives are grammar and music), extend only to the judging of their specialist subjects, whereas the 'reasoning faculty' is the one which 'alone is found to consider both itself, its powers, its values, and likewise all the rest'. '[This] most excellent and superior faculty alone ... the gods have placed in our own power.'[117] Although Butler may have been influenced by Epictetus, however, his own account is very different, because it is psychological and borders on a description of what would subsequently be called the unconscious; in effect, he demotes the ethical thought-processes from the intellectual summits of Epictetus' account to an automatic level, which then creates the higher awareness. 'It [= the conscience] appears from our exercising it *unavoidably* ...' (*1736*, p. 309, italics supplied) – a classic description of an inner monologue.[118] It also appears in the fact that we have a certain vocabulary, examples being *right, wrong, odious, amiable, base, worthy*: 'From our natural Sense of Gratitude, which implies a Distinction between, merely being the Instrument of Good, and intending it: From the like Distinction, every one makes between Injury and mere Harm, which, *Hobbs* says, is peculiar to Mankind ...' (*1736*, p. 310).[119] This constant processing, as in the *Fifteen Sermons*, is action-oriented

---

[115] *1729*, p. xvi; see Chapter 2, p. 68.
[116] *Discourses*, Book I Chapter I § 1, London, 1910, trans. Elizabeth Carter, p. 3. Carter's translation was published in 1758.
[117] *Discourses*, Book I Chapter 1 §2, p. 4.
[118] See also *1736*, p. 314.
[119] The tactical acceptance of Hobbes as an authority shows that even here Butler continues his strategy of accepting the enemy's ground.

and, although the term 'principle' replaces the earlier 'affection', the implications are the same:

> ... these Principles [are those] from which Men would act if Occasions and Circumstances gave them Power; and which, *when fixed and habitual in any Person*, we call, his Character ... It does not appear, that Brutes have the least reflex Sense of Actions as distinguished from Events, or that Will and Design, which constitute the very Nature of Actions as such, are at all an Object to their Perception ... Acting, Conduct, Behaviour, abstracted from all Regard to what is, in Fact and Event, the Consequence of it, is itself the natural Object of the moral Discernment; as speculative Truth and Falshood is, of speculative Reason. (*1736*, p. 311, italics supplied)

To paraphrase, the conscience, which through a lifetime creates mutually reinforcing habits, transforms seemingly random events into purposeful actions (which feel natural) and, by a process rather like feedback,[120] these actions are shaped into an ethical narrative by a continuous mental process which evaluates our conduct. Butler's genius for artful formulation avoids inventing faculties to 'explain' this process – the occupational hazard of the moral philosopher – but goes as far as to locate an element of feedback in two places: the 'habit' of response to external stimuli and the 'discernment' of self-evaluation. Moreover, there is a gap between a person's moral perception and consequent actions: thus an innocent person suffering from the plague is left to die in isolation, for the public good (*1736*, p. 312) – 'Innocence and Ill-desert are inconsistent Ideas',[121] that is, of different and incommensurable types. As we will see *Six Sermons* gives even more shocking examples. Ethics is the product of the action of conscience ('Reflection' on the emotional symptoms of the affections), in other words, it is a reaction to the natural world, somewhat at an angle to the animal or instinctual method of negotiating reality. But since the ethically good decision has only a contingent relationship with the messy societal world, natural behaviour, which, we might anachronistically say, is biologically determined and occupies a separate space, has some degree of adequacy too. The animal life, as Butler has described it in the 'brute Force' episode, may be nasty, brutish and short but it is in an important sense valid and of practical value.[122] As he remarks, with irony, Shaftesbury is not entirely a bad man (perhaps the most tactful way a writer has ever called an opponent sub-human). When he picks up on *Fifteen Sermons*' treatment of 'Resentment' this point is made with elegance and force:

---

120 We used the term 'virtuous circle' above. The change of metaphors is designed to avoid suggesting that quasi-Kantian schemata are here being imposed on Butler.

121 OED, 'inconsistent', II.2: '... not agreeing in substance, spirit, or form; ... not consonant or in accordance'.

122 The fact that Butler, like other Christian moral philosophers, is able to rely partly on the pagan classics, entails his belief that the Christian revelation is not necessary for at least a powerful insight into the nature of good.

> Men resent Injuries as implying Faultiness, and retaliate, not merely under the notion of having received Harm, but of having received Wrong; and they have this Resentment in Behalf of Others, as well as of Themselves. (*1736*, p. 78)

The word 'retaliate', used of conscious, ethical, decisions, is notable. Clearly non-pejorative, it indicates a mechanism of response and this is suggestive of Butler's overall view of moral behaviour as responsive rather than proactive. Hence comes what might be seen as his commonsensical approach to ethical priorities. 'Nature has not given [us] so sensible a Disapprobation of Imprudence and Folly, either in *Ourselves* or *Others*, as of Falshood Injustice and Cruelty ...' (*1736*, p. 314). This is not because 'Falshood Injustice and Cruelty' are necessarily ethically worse than 'Imprudence and Folly' but because they are more immediately injurious. Conversely, 'Imprudence and Folly, appearing to bring its [*sic*] own Punishment more immediately and constantly than injurious Behaviour, it less needs the additional Punishment, which would be inflicted upon it by Others, had they the same sensible Indignation against it, as against Injustice and Fraud and Cruelty' (*1736*, p. 315). Thus there is a mechanism which automatically seeks to impose a natural limitation on the practical damage done by bad ethics. He gives a greatly extended (to p. 317), proto-Darwinian, socio-biological account whose basis, significantly, is empirical and not analogical.[123] While our conscience is so constituted as to condemn various evil actions, it is 'abstracted from all Consideration, which Conduct is likeliest to produce an Overballance of Happiness or Misery. And therefore, were the Author of Nature to propose nothing as an End but the Production of Happiness, were His moral Character merely That of Benevolence; yet Ours is not so' (*1736*, p. 317). For Butler, benevolence is a tactical, social, mechanism, which works in the short range. Intention, conscience and the evaluation of their results are all. Ethics is a matter for all people, not for a specialist elite. Anticipating *Six Sermons*, Butler concludes his volume by considering problems of differences of social class and styles of discourse:

> ... the Use of common Forms of Speech generally understood, cannot be Falshood, and, in general, ... there can be no designed Falshood without designing to deceive.... For it is impossible not to foresee, that the Words and Actions of Men in different Ranks and Employments,

---

[123] J. L. Mackie, in his explicitly anti-theist *Ethics: Inventing Right and Wrong*, writes that 'Personal identity is not absolute ... [Our] concept of personal identity through time itself functions as a sort of institution ... Why we are like this in the first place a psychological question ... but more fundamentally it is a sociological and biological question to be answered ... by an evolutionary explanation ...' (pp. 191–2). Mackie's hopes of evolutionary biology's power to explain ethics remain unfulfilled (although theoretically the proposition is intriguing) but Butler is surely wiser. Where Mackie thinks that personal identity, which he admits to be an analytical construct, may be explained thus (so that research would be into theorists' theorizing), Butler believes that it is the individual's behaviour and evaluation of it which have a social and biological explanation. For Butler the person, as an immaterial substance, is not analysable.

and of different Educations, will perpetually be mistaken by each other: And it cannot but be so, whilst they will judge with the utmost Careless-ness ... of what they are not, perhaps, enough informed to be competent Judges of ... (*1736*, pp. 319–20)

The emphasis, rather than substance, of this treatment is certainly different from that in *Fifteen Sermons*. The anti-deist strategy plays up the personality of God. In the chapter *Of the Government of God by Rewards and Punishments* Butler speculates, 'Perhaps an infinitely perfect Mind may be pleased, with seeing his Creatures behave suitably to the Nature which he has given them; to the Relations which he has placed them in to each other' (*1736*, p. 49).[124] There is a human mode of activity which, when pursued consistently, fulfils potential and is pleasing, almost aesthetically so, to the Creator. There is a sense of the littleness of humankind and its simultaneous all-importance to itself, and to its Creator: 'the whole End, for which God made, and thus governs the World, may be utterly beyond the Reach of our Faculties: There may be somewhat in it as impossible for us to have any Conception of, as for a blind Man to have a Conception of Colours' (*1736*, p. 49). Indeed, he proceeds to show, what seems commonsensical but was hard for his contemporaries to accommodate, that 'natural' actions have their own pleasures, distinct from the pleasure of being virtuous. '[A vicious person has a] natural Faculty of Self-Government ... with all his Vices about him, like so many Harpies, craving for their accustomed Gratification ... Men can, to a great degree, get over their Sense of Shame, so as that ... they can support themselves against the Infamy of [their ill actions]' (pp. 69–70). This too is a form of survival mechanism. For Butler, then, the big question is not about the validity of the human feelings of right and wrong but about whether ethical judgements are arbitrary.

Faith, doubt and ethics

We have seen that the moral is a function of the response of the human affections to God, fellow humans and the objects of the world. The role of the conscience is to bring these responses to the awareness, an awareness which, in Butler, begins to be conceived as a faculty and to mediate between the internal conflicts inevitable amid the contingencies of life.[125] The natural affections ('religious

---

[124] A greatly extended treatment of this idea is found on pp. 49–51 ('Or the whole End, for which God made, and thus governs the World ...').

[125] In a purely secular and academic project, similar arguments about the intimacy of involvement of ethics and logic with the contingencies of life were advanced long ago by Stephen Toulmin when, in *The Uses of Argument*, Cambridge, 1958, he adopted a social model of philosophy, for example in his claims that logic may be a development of psychology or sociology (p. 3) and that it is 'generalised jurispru-dence' (p. 7). See also his comments about ethics and society in *Reason in Ethics*, Cambridge, 1950, Chapter 12 (although in Chapter 14.8 he flatly contradicted Butler's view of the relationship between religion and the conscience and ethical judgements). In neither case did he, however, engage with or acknowledge any debt to Butler.

Regards of Reverence, Honour, Love, Trust, Gratitude, Fear, Hope', pp. 150–2) are the means of drawing revealed religion into the ordinary practices of daily life: for Butler the City of God metaphor applied to the mind as well as to the Church:[126] 'In what external Manner, this inward Worship is to be expressed, is a Matter of pure revealed Command; ... But ... the internal Worship itself, to the Son and Holy Ghost, is no farther Matter of pure revealed Command, than as the Relations they stand in to us, are Matter of pure Revelation ... ' (p. 152). In Part II Chapter V ('Of the particular System of Christianity; the Appointment of a Mediator, and the Redemption of the World by him') this is developed in a very interesting and persuasive way. Butler here observes that innocent people frequently suffer for the faults of others and, specifically, that because men, 'by their Follies run themselves into extream [financial] Distress ... which would be absolutely fatal to them ... the Interposition and Assistance of Others' is necessary (p. 211). He has in mind the phenomenon that assistance to the indigent could, at least temporarily, cause real suffering to the donor. Such charitable behaviour, he notes, does not 'shock' people, but many nevertheless profess to be shocked at the claim that Christ voluntarily suffered for humanity's sins. Since this is a matter of historical record Butler can argue that since some or all of the punishment of sins is by natural means, to refuse to accept the probability of Christ's atonement is to deny the reality of the world. Again, it is the deists and sceptics who are insecure on empirical grounds:

> Let Reason be kept to: and if any Part of the Scripture-account of the Redemption of the World by Christ, can be shewn to be really contrary to it, let the Scripture, in the name of God, be given up: But let not such poor Creatures as we, go on objecting against an infinite Scheme, that we do not see the Necessity or Usefulness of all its Parts, and call this Reasoning. (p. 213)

This formula encapsulates a number of arguments already developed – the historical authenticity of Scripture; the anti-empirical incredulity of the deists; the irrational deist demand that human experience be a sufficient measure of the laws of nature – and combines them with a vigorous orality which may have originated in the pulpit.[127]

As always in *The Analogy*, Butler's concession to deist claims about the high standing of reason cuts both ways: he believes that revelation, the senior partner, strengthens the insights of reason; but by also accepting that any disjunction between them weakens the 'Scripture-account' he suggests that whatever its cultural distinctions or origins a 'reasonable' religion is sound, and that, ultimately, all religions are one which are not superstitious,[128] even if those separated from revelation are less adequate. This confirms the policy of toler-

---

126 See Chapter 5, p. 167.
127 Part II Chapter V is another chapter which, as indicated by its internal numbering system, seems to bear a reminiscence of a sermon's outline structure.
128 The importance of this for the Anglican missions of the nineteenth century is dealt with in the

ating denominational diversity.[129] In his suggestion that rituals of atonement, imitations of Christ, are virtually universal among the cultures of humankind he offers a method of binding together all religious practices (p. 213).[130] The analogical approach is radically conservative in its suggestion that the culturally bound beliefs and intuitions of the general mass of humankind through its history are unlikely to betray its survival interests – a proto-Darwinian thought of great power.[131]

There is no need for an account of Butler's arguments against deism: they are set out at length as *The Analogy*'s main theme and highlighted by the summaries which preface virtually every reprint, from Hallifax's to the present day. Two things, however, must be remembered about his ethics: that it is intimately engaged with doubt and faith; and is fundamentally anti-deist, or, more widely, oriented in opposition to theories of the 'natural' person.

Whereas Butler opposes Hobbes's doctrine, we have noted several times, seeping through the formality of his prose, a dislike of Shaftesbury which is more personal. Shaftesbury's influence was all-pervasive in the culture of the early eighteenth century. An example, from among the hundreds available, is the once-famous poem by Isaac Hawkins Browne, 'On Design and Beauty', which confessedly versifies Shaftesbury:

> The love of Order, sure from Nature springs,
> *Our taste adapted to the frame of things*:
>
> …
>
> True Poets are themselves a Poem, each
> A pattern of the lovely rules they teach;
> Those fair ideas that their fancy charm.
> Inspire their Lives, and every action warm;
> And when they chaunt the praise of high desert,
> *They but transcribe the dictates of their heart.*[132]

This exemplifies the corrosive effect of Shaftesbury's aristocratic and narcissistic thinking. The concept of doubt is not only alien to him and his followers

---

author's *Corporate Holiness: Pulpit Preaching and the Anglican Missionary Movement, 1760–1870* (in preparation).

[129] Butler's remarks about Islam suggests tolerance (if not yet constitutional toleration) of an even wider diversity. See Chapter 4, p. 125.

[130] One of the reasons for reading Lori Branch's *Rituals of Spontaneity: Sentiment and Secularism from Free Prayer to Wordsworth*, Waco, TX, 2006, is that it may be taken as an account of an Anglocentric approach to this proposition in the long eighteenth century.

[131] The American Presbyterian theologian Archibald A. Hodge (*The Atonement*, London, 1870, p. 118) used this observation of Butler's to argue that he '[usefully] reduces the question to a direct issue between the cultivated moral consciousness of a few "advanced thinkers," self-styled, of the nineteenth century, on the one hand, and on the other, the *natural moral instincts* of all races and nations' (italics supplied). The Butlerian Hodge sharply conflicts with Sidgwick; see Chapter 6, p. 204.

[132] Isaac Hawkins Browne, 'On Design and Beauty' (1734), quoted from the posthumous *Poems upon Various Subjects, Latin and English*, London, J. Nourse, 1768, pp. 96, 107, italics supplied.

but is theoretically impossible: doubt would be an ugly denial of the 'lovely rules'.

An apologetic strategy based on creating doubt about opposing arguments necessarily imports the same considerations into the grounds of faith and ethics. Just as Richard Hooker was 'judicious' in organizing his theological material so Butler is cautious and doubting. In his concluding chapter he sums up the case for using analogy and probability. Religion is a practical thing, 'a determinate Course of Life' (p. 278); the wish for certainty in religion conflicts with the fact of an incomprehensible deity. The core of Butler's answer to the question of commitment, affiliation and apologetics is the practice of doubt. This is not a version of Descartes' philosophical strategy, as Butler does not believe in, wish for or personally attain the finality of metaphysical or epistemological certainty. The important thing is the practice of good ethics through the exploitation of doubt.[133]

Butler deploys two strategies. The first, in accordance with the basic approach of the book as a whole, is to turn on its head the objection that arguments from analogy are weak. The second is to argue that to feel doubt is to display the humility essential to the Christian faith and practice.

The first strategy, set out particularly in Part II Chapter VI ('Of the Want [= lack] of Universality in Revelation'),[134] is already too familiar to detain us.

> Persons who speak of the Evidence of a Religion as doubtful, and of this supposed Doubtfulness as a positive Argument against it, should be put upon considering what That Evidence indeed is, which they act upon with regard to their temporal Interests. For, it is ... in many Cases, absolutely impossible, to ballance Pleasure and Pain, Satisfaction and Uneasiness, so as to be able to say, on which Side the Overplus is ...
>
> *(1736*, Part II Chapter VI, pp. 215–6)

Beyond the relatively unthinking conduct of day-to-day life the human condition is one of uncertainty and doubt, even about the basic amenities. Thus, *The Analogy* introduces a new factor into English cultural life: the permanence and spiritual fruitfulness of doubt in the faithful course of living. The corollary of Butler's doctrine is that his antagonists – and here are included those in the Cartesian tradition – are seeking certainties which simply are not available; are, in Habgood's phrase, 'requiring [religion] to pass evidential tests which would seem ludicrously excessive in most other areas of life',[135] including the natural sciences and mathematics, as Berkeley, for example, had demonstrated with

---

[133] The present account of Butler and doubt may, it is hoped, be contrasted fruitfully with Janet Broughton's thesis about Descartes in *Descartes's Method of Doubt*, Princeton, NJ, 2002, *passim*.

[134] This is one of the chapters that is pretty obviously an adapted sermon. It has a central, tripartite structure, discussing its subject from three different angles, in the classic manner, and at one point (pp. 218–19) a sentence lasting a whole page, and interspersed with oral figures ('... I say ...'), which, although elegant by no standard of taste, works fairly well when read aloud.

[135] *Varieties of Unbelief*, p. 124.

his paper on the differential calculus. In effect, deists and sceptics seek to deny religion the right to occupy space in civil society.

The second strategy is a more developed consideration of doubt as a religious and philosophical tool. Its primary locus is Part II Chapter VII ('Of the particular Evidence for Christianity'). Butler does not often write with broad gestures, but this chapter is an exception, and especially in the first half, which we have previously suggested to be an adapted sermon. What we have argued is the original 'application' section (pp. 254–6) begins with a spacious set of references to the historical record and Church fathers – Porphyry (and, in a footnote, Jerome), the Book of Daniel, the age of Antiochus Epiphanes – arguing that the prophecies present the coming dissolution of the Roman empire. The listener, now the reader, is here brought out of the previously closely argued and outline-structured Exegesis into the familiarities of the great sweep of history, set in unusually impassioned rhetoric. It sums up his purpose in publishing *The Analogy*:

> … [There] may be People who will not accept of such imperfect Information from Scripture. Some too have not Integrity and Regard enough to Truth, to attend to Evidence, which keeps the Mind in Doubt, perhaps Perplexity, and which is much of a different Sort from what they expected. And it plainly requires a Degree of Modesty and Fairness, beyond what every one has, for a Man to say, not to the World, but to Himself, that there is a real Appearance of somewhat of great Weight in this Matter, though he is not able thoroughly to satisfy himself about it … It is much more easy, and more falls in with the Negligence Presumption and Willfulness of the Generality, to determine at once, with a decisive Air, There is nothing in it. The Prejudices arising from that absolute Contempt and Scorn, with which this Evidence is treated in the World, I do not mention. For what indeed can be said to Persons, who are weak enough in their Understandings, to think This any Presumption against it; or, if they do not, are yet weak enough in their Temper to be influenced, by such Prejudices, upon such a Subject[?] (pp. 255–6)

The second half of this chapter appears to have been newly composed for the book and reintroduces a theoretical position with which we have become familiar: that actions which are in accordance with the general nature of things have an exponentially benign effect, 'For probable Proofs, by being added, not only increase the Evidence, but multiply it' (pp. 273–4). A mistake in proofs 'on one side [that is, evidence accepted by sceptics against miracles] may be, in its consequences, much more dangerous than a mistake on the other', which is a theologian's (and non-mathematician's) way of saying that estimates or calculations of probabilities may depend crucially on non-mathematical information about the circumstances.[136] Such mistakes arise from the weight of evidence and probability being misjudged, this being because of prejudice, which 'operates

136 Jan Gullberg, *Mathematics*, p. 966.

contrary Ways, in different Men. For some are inclined to believe, what they hope, and Others what they fear. And it is manifest Unreasonableness, to apply to Men's Passions in order to gain their Assent' (p. 273).

This temperamental difference was identified and accounted for in *Fifteen Sermons*, as a product of different balances and strengths of the individuals' affections. While the comment about the unreasonableness of appealing to passions in attempts to change opinions has a strongly ironic tinge, it is also a serious psychological point, while the final comment, about the difference between assent and actual behaviour, points towards a theory both of politics – the behaviour of people in an ordered society – and of religious discipline. If people obey commands to alter their actions because of the conviction of the importance of such change, and despite the impulses of their psychological make-up, what remains is to consider any tensions which may result and psychological (and consequently social) changes which such tensions may effect. At this point, emerging from *The Analogy*'s exploration of the intersection of religious experience with questions of probability and evidence, Butler is back on his home ground – ethics and the study of human behaviour. When we consider his observation of the uncertainty of a direct relationship between good ethical decisions and favourable outcomes, the full scope of his theory becomes evident. We have seen that Butler concentrates on ethical decisions arising in real, not hypothetical or schematically necessary, situations and that the relationship between the 'sincerity' of intention (the guide of conscience) and socially good effect is to be discussed probabilistically, so that he exempts outcomes from moral judgement. It also follows that the best ethical decisions of the conscience and reason are also to be considered only probably so. Sincerity is not enough, as Butler was to reflect in a late jotting. He cannot escape from the guidance of the Book, and of course does not wish to. In the next two chapters we will study his career as a bishop with this in mind.

4

Bishop

Introduction

This chapter will consider the practical application of Butler's thought to the conduct of his episcopal responsibilities, presenting readings of a selection of material which, for the most part, he did not publish.

From the first, *The Analogy* had a greater sale (judging by the number of editions) than *Fifteen Sermons*[1] and made Butler, perhaps reluctantly, a theological authority of first resort: he spent several years avoiding David Hume and Bartlett describes how he was approached by Henry Home (Lord Kames) in 1737,

> ... from an earnest desire ... to have some doubts removed ... [about] the Evidences of Natural and Revealed Religion. 'Dr. Butler [says Woodhouseless, in his *Life of Kaimes*] answered his letter with the utmost politeness, and endeavoured, as far as he could, by writing, to satisfy Mr. Home's inquiries, but modestly declined a personal meeting, on the score of his own natural diffidence and reserve, his being unaccustomed to oral controversy, and his fear that the cause of truth might thence suffer from the unskilfulness of its advocate.'[2]

This evasiveness and reticence in private matched his conduct in the House of Lords, where he cannot be shown to have made a speech. One of the few accounts we have of his social life is John Byrom's record of a conversation at David Hartley's home in March 1737. Butler played a minor part, although the oldest and most eminent person among those present, who besides David Hartley included John Lloyd MP, and Byrom himself.[3] Butler arrived at about 9

---

[1] Butler's publishing history is set out in Chapter 6, pp. 177–8.

[2] Bartlett, pp. 80–1. Home's best-remembered work is his *Elements of Criticism* (1788). Bartlett gives the dates of the letters about Butler from Hume to Home: 2 December 1737; 4 March 1738; 13 February 1738; and 13 June 1742. In the latter Hume reports that Butler has been recommending his *Political Essays* to acquaintances.

[3] John Byrom, *The Private Journal and Literary Remains*, vol. ii, pt 1, pp. 96–7; reprinted from Parkinson by Henri Talon, the student of William Law, in *Selections from the Journals and Papers of John Byrom*, London, 1950, pp. 169–72. All quotations in this paragraph are taken from the latter.

p.m., staying two hours, but leaving before supper and drinks. Byrom's account shows that Butler knew the theological works of Isaac Newton (Butler saying that Newton 'always thought that prophecy was the great proof of the Christian religion') as well as those of Pascal, Tertullian and Hobbes. Butler revealed that he had read Hobbes to Queen Caroline, with a listener, the Duke of Queensberry, delivering to the Queen the Butlerian dictum that 'there must be right and wrong before human laws, which supposed right and wrong; and besides, wherever was there that state of nature that [Hobbes] talked of? who ever lived in it?'[4] The conversation at Hartley's centred on the question, whether authority or reason had the priority. Butler took the side of reason. He 'hinted at a time when the whole Christian Church almost was in the wrong, and then what must become of authority? ... said that authority had brought the Roman Catholic to worship a piece of bread for the supreme God' and asked what Byrom would do if his father, speaking with parental authority, 'commanded what was contrary to the laws of God?' Besides being evidence that his published opposition to Roman Catholicism was not merely a formality for appearances' sake, this implies, as we have already noted, that one's circle of social and spiritual support can shrink drastically but remain functionally viable.

Butler's other recorded contribution to this discussion was about the influence of Mahomet. He suggested that people should follow him critically, in the right he taught, but not in the wrong, a unique expression in the surviving records of the theory of acculturation implied in his published works. Byrom felt that Butler, possibly demonstrating the reserve of the shy and the maladroitness of the insecure, was 'a little too little vigorous, which [the others] seemed to think too, for Mr. Lloyd said that he had wished that he would have spoken more earnestly'.

The three years after *The Analogy*'s publication were a height of public activity. Butler was appointed clerk of the closet by Queen Caroline (this lapsed with her death but he was appointed clerk of the closet to the king in 1746) and thus became one of those with whom Caroline discussed theological matters.[5] To bolster his income[6] there were several ecclesiastical preferments to add to his Talbot chaplaincy and Stanhope rectory, including a prebendal stall in Rochester Cathedral, but ultimately the award of the deanery of St Paul's enabled him to

---

4 Charles Douglas, third Duke of Queensberry, was a past and future member of the Privy Council but at this time a follower of the Prince of Wales, in opposition to George II. Butler's association with him constituted a misalignment in relation to the core of the leading Whig group and, in the person of the King, to the source of preferment to the higher levels of the clergy. It might explain why the King did not honour the full spirit of the Queen's dying wishes for Butler.
5 Bartlett, p. 40, alleges that there were meetings 'each evening' and links Butler's name with Berkeley, Sherlock and Secker, but there is no other evidence for this arrangement, nor for an association between Butler and Hoadly. On the latter point I would thank Hoadly's biographer, William Gibson (personal communication).
6 Service at Court was expensive. Butler paid out £49/1/6d per quarter as clerk of the closet. His lodging expenses were greater again: 'For lodgings at Kensington, 36*l*.; for lodgings at Hampton Court, 25*l*. &c. &c.' (Bartlett, p. 43).

resign from both Rochester and Stanhope. Queen Caroline had recommended him for a bishopric on her deathbed and within a year he succeeded Secker at Bristol. In these years he published only one work, his sermon for the SPG, which is unsurprising, given the large amounts of travelling and administration which had become necessary – he was never an idle sinecurist. He nevertheless continued to develop new thinking, finally publishing six occasional sermons, and extended his range into social, economic and legal questions, on all of which, if so minded, he could have produced substantial theoretical work. He did not, however, choose to publish his Bristol Infirmary sermon – a slight discourtesy to the City fathers – nor did he produce one, as the incoming Bishop of Durham, for the newly-founded Newcastle Infirmary, instead allowing his London Infirmary effort to be reprinted for its benefit. By refraining from publishing a sermon on the 1745 Rebellion he was in company with the majority of the bishops, but not with those associated with the Talbots – the astute Secker compensated by publishing a whole book of them. We do not yet know enough about this corpus to draw conclusions.[7] In general, he appeared reluctant to publish unless he felt that he had an original contribution to make and unless the occasion was of national or at least metropolitan status.

Because of his parliamentary duties, like most contemporary bishops he resided in his diocese only in the summer recess. He did, however, hold all four of his required triennial visitations and ordained clergy punctiliously, if not copiously.[8] He did not create a circle of clients, as many did. Cunliffe[9] notes that his diocese lay mostly in Dorset, administered by an archdeacon (Edward Hammond), with the Bristol deanery, essentially coterminous with Britain's second city, being administered by the bishop directly – an additional burden, caused by the see's poverty.

Butler supported the government loyally in the House of Lords, even against his better judgement, although his record of attendance declined over the years.[10] His closest friends, Benson and, especially, Secker, sometimes took positions independent of the government but he himself did not, to the extent that Secker

---

[7] The mapping and criticism of the vast corpus of eighteenth-century sermons – with at least ten times more pages than the century's output of fiction – is in its infancy. The British State Prayers Project is producing *The British Nations and Divine Providence: Public Worship and the State from the Reformation to the Twentieth Century*, Oxford, scheduled for 2012, and the *Oxford Handbook of the British Sermon 1689–1901*, scheduled for 2013, will give a critical overview, but the need remains paramount for an accurate and comprehensive catalogue to complete the pioneering work of J. Gordon Spaulding (*Pulpit Publications 1660–1782*, New York, 1995). See also Harry Caplan and Henry H. King, 'Pulpit Eloquence: A List of Doctrinal and Historical Studies in English', *Speech Monographs*, volume XXII, no. 4 (Special Issue, 1955).

[8] CCEd.

[9] Christopher Cunliffe, 'The "Spiritual Sovereign"', *Tercentenary Essays*, p. 39.

[10] This paragraph takes most of its material from Cunliffe's essay in *Tercentenary Essays*, which is not superseded by his ODNB article. The interpretation, however, is somewhat different. Clyve Jones ('The House of Lords and the Fall of Walpole', *Hanoverian Britain and Empire: Essays in Memory of Philip Lawson*, ed. Stephen Taylor, Richard Connors and Clyve Jones, Woodbridge, 1998) has published an analysis of House of Lords voting records which (p. 130) confirms Butler's loyalty.

increasingly cooled towards him. In this Butler was realistic: throughout, the government remained the senior partner. In 1748, for example, over the united opposition of the English bishops, the government disallowed all letters of orders to Episcopalian ministers in Scotland not issued by the bishop of an English or Irish see. This in effect made the Scottish bishops redundant for the next half-century, confirming their Church's decline to a sect and exposing it to further persecution from the Scottish establishment from which it never completely recovered.[11] Likewise, contrary to the considered position of Church leaders, and on a question where Butler himself had decided views, the government allowed the prospect of domestic instability and the growth of independently minded factions in the American colonies to frustrate the appointment even of suffragan bishops to oversee Anglican clergy in the North American colonies.[12] The only recorded issue on which Butler followed Secker in voting against the government related to the Spirituous Liquors Bill on 25 February 1743, which proposed to lower duties, a subject which clearly had an ethical dimension. Having decided on his political duty he carried it through as a matter of applied will and acquired habit, a living exemplar of his psychological and ethical theories.[13] Cunliffe quotes an extraordinarily embittered passage from Secker, which on internal evidence must refer to a conversation from June 1739:

> As my Favour with the Court & Ministry declined, [Butler's] friendship did. He said to me, at the End of the first Session, in which he sat in the House of Lords, that the ministers were both wicked Men & wicked Ministers. Yet he not only always voted with them, but expressed Contempt and Dislike of me for doing otherwise: & never, that I could hear, spoke a Word by way of Apology for me to any other Person.[14]

For Butler disloyalty was a moral crime. His notorious letter to Walpole about the Bristol appointment is a case in point.[15] It has been generally understood that he accepted Bristol under protest at its poverty being unfitting to his deserts. We have already noticed, however, the high cost of service at Court and he must have anticipated being asked to undertake a similar role in future. Other churchmen would simply have retained Stanhope; this would not have been against acceptable current practice. Moreover, although noting that 'the bishoprick of Bristol is not very suitable … to the condition of my fortune' most

---

[11] See Beilby Porteus, *Life of Archbishop Secker*, in *Tracts on Various Subjects*, London, Cadell & Davies, 1807, p. 37.

[12] See Stephen Taylor, 'Whigs, Bishops and America: The Politics of Church Reform in Mid-eighteenth-century England', *The Historical Journal*, vol. 36, no. 2 (1993), pp. 331–56.

[13] For Butler 'duty' did not imply unwillingness. One of the provisions in his will is phrased thus: '[My] under Secretary William Emm is altogether unprovided for and cannot now provide for himself in *the plain way he might easily have done had I not taken him into my family*. I give the said William Emm five hundred pounds' (italics supplied. Quoted from the Durham University copy, SGD 35/12, apparently made for use by Matthew Forster, his chaplain and executor in Durham).

[14] Cunliffe, p. 47, quoting Macauley and Greaves, p. 22.

[15] Bartlett, p. 73.

of his objection centres on whether the appointment was 'answerable to the recommendation with which I was honoured': his chief concern is that, while accepting that the King is circumscribed by the availability of dioceses, the offer fails to match the spirit of the Queen's deathbed wishes. Anther passage from Secker's *Autobiography* (pp. 15–16), narrating an incident from about 1734, alleges that Butler showed a lack of gratitude for Secker's assistance with Chancellor Charles Talbot's patronage. As we have seen, however (Chapter 1), it was Butler who had first obtained Talbot family patronage for Secker and this anecdote may say more about Secker's focused self-interest than Butler's ingratitude. The incident concerned Bishop Gibson's blocking Thomas Rundle's nomination to the Gloucester see. If Secker supported Gibson against Rundle, who was yet another Clarke/Talbot protégé, Butler would certainly have seen this as disloyalty. Such rigidities suggest that, unlike the future Primate, Butler was poorly fitted for politics.

The Bristol consecration

Butler was nominated to the see of Bristol on 19 October 1738 and consecrated at Lambeth on 3 December by John Potter, the Archbishop of Canterbury, Joseph Wilcocks, the Bishop of Rochester, and Robert Butts, the Bishop of Ely. Nicholas Clagett, the Bishop of St David's, was also in attendance.[16] A royal proclamation was issued to the Chancellor, Philip, Lord Hardwicke, apprising him of the election and confirming that he had been examined by Thomas Wilson, the ancient bishop of Sodor and Man,[17] 'at our Palace of Westminster the Twenty first Day of December in the Twelfth year of Our Reign'.[18] He was installed at Bristol 'by proxy, the Rev. Mr Fulton 6 January 1738[–39]'.[19]

The consecration sermon was preached by John Heylyn, the rector of St Mary-le-Strand and a chaplain in ordinary to the king. Selecting the preacher of a consecration sermon was the prerogative of the new bishop; the sermon was commonly in effect the bishop's manifesto. Heylyn was a choice significant for negative reasons: Butler could have been expected to choose a young, politically active preacher from the Whig core, whereas Heylyn was an outsider, over fifty years old and, at this point, the author of little besides sermons for the Societies for the Reformation of Manners (1729)[20] and the Charity Schools

[16] Lambeth Palace Library VB1/8, Act Book 1734–50, folio 120ʳ. See also Bodleian: Rawl. J fol. 2 (144). The Bodleian MSS are notes about Butler's career and, while not always accurate (for example, they omit the presence of Clagett – admittedly not officially involved – at his Bristol consecration), they contain some shreds of information not available elsewhere.
[17] At the time Wilson was 74; one of the century's greatest bishops, he served Sodor and Man for 57 years and outlived Butler, dying in 1755.
[18] Bodleian: Rawl A. 289 (51).
[19] Bodleian: Rawl. J. fol. 2 (144).
[20] John Heylyn, *A Sermon Preached to the Societies for the Reformation of Manners, at St. Mary-le-Bow, on Wednesday January the 18th, 1728 [Romans 13.4]*, London, Joseph Downing, 1729. The date is Old Style.

(1734).[21] He was also becoming increasingly mystical,[22] which is interesting, given that he may be called Butler's disciple.[23] He had moved far from his Reformation of Manners sermon, which taught that 'The Government is oblig'd, for its own Sake, to support Religion, because Religion is the best Support of Government' (p. 19) and that the Opposition manifested itself, the more disturbingly because with uncoordinated, spontaneous vigour, through a shared 'Licentiousness' among the deists, dramatists, pornographers and Jacobites.

Heylyn's 1734 Charity Schools sermon had been a marked development. First, the sermon, preached before the trustees and teachers of the schools, was not at all protective of their authority. The rich and poor 'were both of the *same nature*, equal in all the privileges of Humanity. They had the same appetites, the same affections, the same reason' (p. 5). 'Obedience does not barely consist in doing *what* we are commanded, but in doing it *because* we are commanded' (p. 16). Heylyn draws a distinction between charity and feelings: hospitals are unpleasing institutions, but it is charitable to support them, for the sake of the children (p. 19). A merely mechanical observance of charity, however, can 'gradually extinguish the Light of Conscience, and all sense of Real Christianity' (p. 22).

Things had developed further again by 1738. Heylyn's sermon[24] takes as its text 2 Timothy 2.15–16: 'Study to shew thyself approved unto God, a workman that needeth not to be ashamed, rightly dividing the world of truth. But shun profane and vain babblings: for they will increase unto more ungodliness.'[25] Paul is here saying something like this: 'In your ministry show that you are like a craftsman whose work has been tested and approved by God in an apprenticeship, one who can feel confident about the quality of his craftsmanship. In your preaching keep to the main thing or risk subverting your ministry.'

Heylyn's text is about the historical point at which the priesthood was emerging in the early Church, the priestly vocation developing by analogy with secular craft vocations – such as that followed by Christ himself, according to tradition.[26] He has two themes: preaching should be practical and relevant to the congregation; and 'Charity is the End of all Religion'. His method is that which he was to adopt in his Westminster Abbey lectures: textual analysis, assessing

[21] John Heylyn, *A Sermon Preached at St. Sepulchre's Church; April the 25th, 1734 [Luke 16.19–20]*, London, Joseph Downing, 1734.
[22] *Theological Lectures at Westminster-Abbey* (1749).
[23] In 1739 Heylyn also attended the SPG Board in Butler's absence, in effect as his deputy. See USPG Board minutes, Lambeth Palace Library.
[24] John Heylyn, *A Sermon Preached ... [at] the Consecration of ... Joseph, Lord Bishop of Bristol [2 Timothy 2.15–16]*, London, C. Rivington, 1738.
[25] Quoted from Heylyn's published sermon, not the AV.
[26] This was the great era of the expansion of Freemasonry. In the nature of things, no evidence is available to the present author. The Stanhope Church's eighteenth-century reredos, still preserved in the church, features a Masonic symbol.

the King James Bible in the light of alternative translations and readings in English, Greek and Latin.

The Analogy, through its anti-deist strategy, had distinguished more sharply than *Fifteen Sermons* between natural and revealed religion, emphasizing the inadequacy of the natural. In its ethical parts it gave an explanation of why revealed religion was spiritually and morally healthful. Thus Heylyn: 'When a devout regard to God is the motive of our actions, morality so practiced becomes the most improving exercise of Piety ... *The end of preaching is Charity*' (p. 13). He uses textual criticism to argue for retranslating the Authorized Version's I Timothy 1.5's phrase, 'the end of the commandment', as 'the end of preaching' and thinks that by 'preaching' Paul meant 'episcopal charge', thus putting charity at the heart of a bishop's transmission of doctrine to his clergy. Moreover, he uses Butler's terminology, revealing the grounding of Butler's ethics in Newtonian science as mediated by Clarke's metaphysics – 'Like Gravitation in the material world, it [= the affection of benevolence] is the great cause of motion ... Love is the master-spring in the human frame; and ... where that takes place, all other affections are regulated by it ... and thence the whole man will go true, as it were, mechanically, and by a happy necessity' (p. 17). This is a restatement of passages of *Fifteen Sermons*' 1729 Preface,[27] preserving the special priority of the affection of benevolence. The doctrinal and exegetical part of Heylyn's sermon concludes with another Butlerian point: that in preaching charity the minister should not encourage enthusiasm ('fond, passionate, or rapturous Sentiments', p. 21) but a course of doctrinally guided practice, what we may call a Christian praxis, 'explaining the other duties', keeping the Christian from 'ouvert acts of intemperance' (p. 22) and settling their 'unchristian disputes' with each other (p. 26). With (p. 15) a glance at Milton – perhaps a hint at Butler's dissenting origins – Heylyn describes the family, with its master and domestic servants, as an analogue of the family in God (pp. 11–2).[28] God 'endeavours to excite their [= people's] gratitude, engage their obedience, and work upon [i.e. dissipate, not increase] their hopes and fears' (p. 19), encouraging the growth and sanctity of the household on Earth and in heaven.

Whitefield and Wesley

A year into his Bristol career Butler met the necessity of negotiating the first manifestations of Methodism. The first incident, regarding George Whitefield, suggests that it took some time for him to impose leadership on his diocesan team.

---

[27] See Chapter 2, p. 65f.
[28] The family and the master–servant relationship is discussed in Chapter 5.

In early 1739 Whitefield, recently returned from America, was in the Bristol area, raising funds for his orphanage in Georgia[29] and preparing to embark on a new aspect of his ministry: preaching field sermons, to which he wryly attached the adjective 'mad'.[30] On Thursday 15 February, by coincidence the day before Butler preached his great sermon at the anniversary meeting of the SPG, Whitefield, needing the diocesan's permission to preach at St Mary Redcliffe, met the chancellor, Carew Reynell, a Secker appointment. Reynell was discouraging but promised to consult the Bishop,[31] which he failed to do. Whitefield, however, wrote to Butler direct and after a second and, it seems, considerably more conflictual meeting with Reynell, who quoted the Church's Canons and threatened excommunication,[32] received a letter from Butler which gave encouragement to preaching for the benefit of the orphanage. Indeed, he arranged a meeting with Whitefield in London on 30 May and made a donation of five guineas.[33] Whitefield took this as a signal to keep in touch, sending Butler on 5 December 1742 the published accounts, a report and a volume of his sermons.

Butler 'treated [Whitefield] with the utmost civility'.[34] He also read Whitefield's *Journals* when they were published, with sufficient care as to be able to quote them. In May 1739, he also showed his willingness to discount admitted breaches of canon law in the interest of charitable activity and did not act against Whitefield's preaching, which was not politically disloyal.

Butler's encounters with John Wesley were a different matter. We will discuss them with two questions in mind: the legal and administrative environment of Butler's actions and what the encounters reveal of his practical ethics. In both these regards, these meetings are of great importance, as they constitute records, however imperfect, between the Church of England's greatest moral philosopher and the founder of a worldwide communion.

Wesley had just emerged from his Oxford fellowship to start on his mission. His first 'field sermon' had been preached near Bristol on 2 April 1739 and although older than Whitefield he was seen as his protégé, and presented as such in the latest, 1739, volume of Whitefield's *Journal*. There are two documents, both written by Wesley, giving accounts of meetings with Butler and his

---

[29] This was the origin of what became known as the Bethesda project, controversy about which ran for three decades, raising questions about the role of the Church of England and the SPG in the North American colonies and bringing Whitefield into sharp conflict with Butler's friend, Thomas Secker. See Ingram, *Religion, Reform and Modernity*, pp. 222–6.

[30] For example, 'Yesterday I began to play the madman in Gloucestershire by preaching on a table in Thornbury Street' (letter to John Wesley, 3 April 1739, *Letters of George Whitefield for the Period 1734–1742*, Edinburgh, 1776, p. 405). According to his *Journal* it was only on 2 February that Whitefield first preached an extemporary sermon (*George Whitefield's Journals*, Edinburgh, 1960, p. 204).

[31] *George Whitefield's Journals*, p. 214.

[32] George Whitefield, *A Continuation [of the Journal]*, London, James Hatton, 1739, p. 25.

[33] Luke Tyerman, *The Life of the Rev. George Whitefield*, London, 1876, vol. 1, pp. 182–3, 233, 349.

[34] *George Whitefield's Journals*, p. 276.

diocesan officials. The first[35] records his interview by Butler in Bristol, at 11 a.m. on Thursday 16 August 1739, the second time they had met.[36] The second is Wesley's note of a further meeting, on Saturday 18 August 1739, in which Wesley was formally examined about his accusation on the intervening Friday that Butler's chaplain, Josiah Tucker, was doctrinally heterodox. This document remained unpublished until 1980.[37]

The 16 August meeting, at which only Butler and Wesley were present (to the exclusion of Reynell, despite his administrative interest) seems not to have been a formal examination. It lasted well over an hour, but is recorded in 814 words – less than ten minutes' worth of speech. Of these 71 percent are attributed to Wesley himself, but internal evidence suggests that this over-represents his contribution to the meeting. We must assume that Wesley's account may omit but does not grossly misrepresent. Wesley records the meeting as a succession of very short alternating speeches. The note falls naturally into two sections, the first concerned with the doctrinal and philosophical basis of their disagreement and the second with constitutional matters. We will discuss them in reverse order.

Butler was bound by the Prayer Book, the Articles of Religion, the Homilies, statute law and the Church's Canons and must have been aware that Reynell had wide-ranging concerns. Wesley attempts some defence: he declares his support for the Prayer Book. This appears when he denies that he administers the sacraments in his private meetings. He also accepts the doctrinal authority of the Homilies – indeed, he dares to quote them against Butler. At worst, therefore, he could be accused only of misinterpreting them, so that Butler is recorded as focusing on the canons, statute law and the articles.[38] If Butler had chosen to be pedantic or aggressive he could have examined Wesley over possible breaches of a large number of the most recent, 1640, canons:[39] numbers 1.1 and 1.2 A (the monarch's supremacy over the Church); 4 (doctrinal orthodoxy); 5.1 (schism and sectaries); 5.3 (conventicles); 6 (subscription); 8 (orthodox preaching). There were also grounds for suspecting breaches of the 1603 canons: 50 (preaching

---

35 The text used for this document is taken from John Wesley, *Works*, ed. Jackson, London, 1830, vol. 13, pp. 500–1. It is found in both Gladstone's and Bernard's editions. Since the document is short, page references are not given for quotations.

36 The document reveals that they had met on an unspecified previous occasion for 'a quarter of an hour'.

37 Frank Baker, 'John Wesley and Bishop Joseph Butler: A Fragment of John Wesley's Manuscript Journal 16th to 24th August 1739', *Proceedings of the Wesley Historical Society*, volume XLII (May 1980), pp. 93–100.

38 Butler's strategy constantly resurfaced in regions where Methodism was especially active and attractive to the established clergy. For example, in his primary visitation charge as Bishop of St Asaph in 1806, Samuel Horsley focused on the inherited neglect of proper licensing of preachers and comments, 'I need not tell you, my reverend brethren, that so much now are we under statute law, that the Common Prayer Book itself is nothing but a long Act of Parliament. All the Rubrics are clauses in that statute' (Samuel Horsley, *The Charges*, London, 1830, p. 138).

39 Throughout this chapter the text and numbering of the canons are taken from *The Anglican Canons 1529–1947*, ed. Gerald Bray, Woodbridge, 1998. The 1640 canons are found on pp. 558–78.

unlicensed); 71 (private preaching); 72 (casting out devils); 73 (private conventicles of ministers). There was ample ground for suspension and possibly for excommunication.[40]

Several of these canons, originally framed against those loosely called Anabaptists, appeared sharply relevant to the case of the Methodists and Butler raises questions of conduct which would breach them. Thus canon 72 (1603) forbad unlicensed ministers from 'hold[ing] any meetings for sermons, commonly termed by some prophecies[41] or exercises,[42] in market-towns, or other places ... nor, without such license, to attempt upon any pretence whatsoever, either of possession or obsession, by fasting and prayer, to cast out any devil or devils, under pain of the imputation of imposture or cosenage, and deposition from the ministry'. Wesley makes frank, if not full, admissions in this regard. He also in effect volunteers that he is in breach of canon 36 (1603):

> ... being ordained a Priest, by the commission I then received, I am a Priest of the Church universal; and being ordained as Fellow of a College, I was not limited to any particular cure, but have an indeterminate commission to preach the word of God, in any part of the Church of England. I do not therefore conceive, that, in preaching here by this commission, I break any human law.

This canon said, in part, that no person could preach, 'except he be licensed either by the archbishop, or by the bishop of the diocese, where he is to be placed, under their hands and seals, or by one of the two universities under their seal likewise'. Wesley does not consider that the reference to universities in this clause merely guarantees collegiate independence of the bishops. Unlicensed preachers are excluded from 'any ecclesiastical living, nor suffered to preach, to catechize, or to be a lecturer or reader in divinity in either university, or in any cathedral or collegiate church, city or market-town, parish church, chapel, or in any other place within this realm'. In other words, ordination into the ministerial vocation allowed the conduct of private worship (but not administering the sacrament) but, contrary to Wesley's claim (whether or not made ingenuously) did not create a mendicant friar-style 'indeterminate commission' separate from the diocesan and parochial structures of the Church. Moreover, canon 37 (1603) talks about priests, 'coming to reside in any diocese ... by what Authority soever he be thereunto admitted', being required to subscribe to three articles before being allowed to exercise any religious functions. Since the first of these articles makes the reigning monarch 'the only supreme governor ... in all spiritual or ecclesiastical things' one may wonder how Wesley could accommodate himself, since he declares himself ready to 'break any human law', a term including acts

---

[40] Bray, pp. 258–453. Wesley's then-unpublished *Journal* for this period in Bristol provides retrospectively enormous quantities of potential evidence against him. With regard to Canon 50, Butler himself had been licensed as a preacher by his then bishop, William Talbot, in 1724 (CCEd).
[41] See OED 'prophecy' 5.
[42] See OED 'exercise' 4 and 10a.

of both parliament and convocation, the proceedings of both being subject to royal assent.

In the examination Butler raised the question of Whitefield's *Journal* for 11 February 1738, which had just been published: 'Mr. Whitefield says in his Journal, "There are promises still to be fulfilled in me." Sir, the pretending to extraordinary revelations and gifts of the Holy Ghost is a horrid thing, a very horrid thing!' He had initially thought that Whitefield and Wesley were 'well-meaning' but such claims had revealed otherwise.

In his reply Wesley denies that this applies to himself but is uncharacter-istically defensive: 'A quarter of an hour I spent with your Lordship before, and about an hour now ... But how many with those who spake on the other side!' He does admit, however, that 'I do [pray over those who fall into fits] ... when any show, by strong cries and tears, that their soul is in deep anguish. I frequently pray to God to deliver them from it; and our prayer is often heard in that hour.' Unlicensed praying over people in fits was contrary to canon 72, adopted in 1603 to discipline antinomian conduct.[43]

What is notable, however, is that Butler has raised only questions which were covered by specific statute law as well as by canons. There were two key statutes in force. One, the 'Act for the Uniformity of Common Prayer and Service in the Church, and Administration of the Sacrament' was passed under Elizabeth I and made technically illegal most forms of dissenting worship. The other, the 'Act for the Uniformity of Public Prayers', was passed under Charles II and, in its twenty-first clause, rendered liable to three months' imprisonment any preacher who departed from the forms of the Prayer Book. It was thought necessary to have these two statutes debated and reaffirmed by parliament in 1750, when Butler, of course, was a member of the House of Lords.[44] This suggests that Butler approached the problem as primarily political[45] and that Wesley's words, as he records them ('... human law ...'), were intended to drive a wedge between Church and State, a disloyalty exacerbated by his admis-sion that he had been present in 'societies' (associations meeting under secular, or at least not formally ecclesiastical, constitutions and discouraged, although not yet proscribed by Combination Acts). The 1603 Canons had been passed by Convocation, but not Parliament, and given Royal Assent and while this effected a separation of the ecclesiastical from the civil it did not release the

---

43 The 1603 canons were actually adopted in 1604. In this regard, as late as 26 November 1762 Wesley is still having to deny the charge that he claims to possess 'miraculous powers', in his *Letter to the Right Reverend the Lord Bishop of Gloucester, Occasioned by his Tract "[The Doctrine of Grace:] On the Office and Operations of the Holy Spirit"*, Works, vol. 9, p. 122. The bishop in question was William Warburton.

44 The three Acts are, respectively, 1 Eliz. Cap. Ii; 14 Car. II Cap. Iv; and 23 Geo. II Cap. xxviii. See *The Clergyman's Assistant* (1806), 3rd edn, Oxford, 1807.

45 Wesley records (*Journal*, 5 June 1739) that he had been confronted by one Mr Nash with an accusa-tion of holding a conventicle in breach of the Act of Parliament, rather than the Canon. His response then had been to assert his political loyalty – revealing an interesting, and possibly well-judged, assumption about the courts' application of statute law.

clergy or laity from their sanctions.[46] Butler, his understanding sharpened by his protracted emergence from Old Dissent, is here faced with rebellion from within the Church itself. Elsewhere, Wesley proclaims his loyalty to the Prayer Book and its rubrics.[47] However, he claims here that there existed an authoritative guide to personal conduct independent of the framework and disciplines of convocation, parliament and the head of state – the system of 'human laws' which he thinks his peripatetic ministry has not broken but, rather, bypassed. Butler chooses not to acknowledge this tacit claim to an alternative locus of authority – it is not surprising that Wesley was suspected of recusancy – and concludes his examination ('I advise [sic] you to go hence [from this diocese]') by warning that Wesley was chiefly at risk from statute law.

Since this involved trial by lay jury he was raising the bar which any attempt at sanctions against Wesley must surmount. In other words, he was professionally disapproving but not intentionally punitive. His comment, 'a very horrid thing', does not express disapproval of mystical experience but of ecclesiastical presumption. We have already noted his choice of Heylyn and his acceptance of the mystical practice and experience of Fénelon and Madame Guyon, even at the likely cost of suspicion of enthusiasm.

If the constitutional part of the meeting showed a tolerance which transcended the disapproval which Butler was officially required to express, the theological part is interesting because it shows Butler's practical application of his ethics. It is short enough to print entire:

> *Butler*: Why, Sir, our faith itself is a good work; it is a virtuous temper of mind. *Wesley*: My Lord, whatever faith is, our Church asserts, we are justified by faith alone. But how it can be called a good work, I see not: It is the gift of God; and a gift that presupposes nothing in us, but sin and misery. *Butler*: How, Sir? Then you make God a tyrannical Being, if he justifies some without any goodness in them preceding, and does not justify all. If these are not justified on account of some moral goodness in them, why are not those justified too? *Wesley*: Because, my Lord, they "resist his Spirit;" because "they will not come to Him that they may have life;" because they suffer Him not to "work in them both to will and to do." They cannot be saved, because they will not believe. *Butler*: Sir, what do you mean by faith? *Wesley*: My Lord, by justifying faith I mean, a conviction wrought in a man by the Holy Ghost, that Christ hath loved him, and given himself for him; and that, through Christ, his sins

---

[46] Their legal status was that they were not binding on the laity '*proprio vigore*' – any further than they declared the law of the land. As acts of Convocation they were binding on all in holy orders. Wesley nevertheless called them into question, in his *A Farther Appeal to Men of Reason and Religion*, Part I, *Works*, vol. 8, p. 120.

[47] 'By the *Laws* of the church I mean the *rubrics*. Whether the *Canons* are laws of the Church of England is doubtful, seeing it is a question whether they were ever confirmed by any competent authority' (John Wesley, 'Ought we to separate from the Church of England?', MS 170 in the Methodist Archives, London). It was published by Frank Baker, *John Wesley and the Church of England* (1970), 2nd edn, London, 2000, pp. 326–40 and discussed on pp. 164–7.

are forgiven. *Butler*: I believe some good men have this, but not all. But how do you prove this to be the justifying faith taught by our Church? *Wesley*: My Lord, from her Homily on Salvation, where she describes it thus: "A sure trust and confidence which a man hath in God, that through the merits of Christ his sins are forgiven, and he reconciled to the favour of God." *Butler*: Why, Sir, this is quite another thing. *Wesley*: My Lord, I conceive it to be the very same.[48]

Butler starts by arguing for a psychological approach to the processes of faith ('virtuous temper of mind') and deploys an analogy between human and divine justice ('tyrannical Being'). And, having allowed Wesley to move the discussion from 'faith' to 'justifying faith', he carries his argument into Wesley's home territory ('this is quite another thing') and objects to his interpretation of the Homily on salvation.

If we accept that Butler did indeed say that 'our faith itself is a good work', the first comment must be that this is a natural and orthodox reading of the third sermon of the first book of Homilies, *Of the Salvation of all Mankind*, which discusses the spiritual, or psychological, context of 'sure trust and confidence in God's merciful promises ... whereof doth follow a loving heart to obey his commandments ... For how can a man have this true faith ...? Surely no such ungodly man can have this faith and trust in God.'[49] The 'sure trust and confidence in God', which constitutes 'godliness', produces faith, which is therefore in itself a good work. This is a central component of Butler's praxis as both individual Christian and minister, and we saw its theoretical basis laid out in *The Analogy*, in the relationship between faith and trust.[50]

Butler goes somewhat further than this. He is quoted as saying, 'Faith ... is a ... work; it is [also] a ... temper of mind'. This is problematic because 'work' (that is, in some sense, effective activity) and 'temper of mind' sound like different sorts of things, unless people are held partly responsible for creating their own mental and emotional characteristics. Yet this is what Butler does mean. We have already seen it discussed in *Of the Nature of Virtue*, where he wrote of the object of the conscience (that is, of the materials on which it works) as 'these Principles ... which, when *fixed and habitual* in any Person, we call, his Character'.[51] Butler did indeed believe that deliberate thought on ethical questions produced habits of behaviour and thus did indeed change both behaviour and the psychological processes which produced it.

We can be sure of the authenticity of the term 'temper of mind', which Butler uses in earlier works to identify bundles of affections which determine ethical relations: 'There is a Temper of Mind made up of, or which follows from all

---

48 Text taken from *Works*, vol. 13, ed. Thomas Jackson, London, 1831, pp. 499–501.
49 *Certain Sermons or Homilies [and] The Constitutions and Canons Ecclesiastical, to which are added the Thirty-nine Articles of the Church of England*, London, SPCK, 1890, p. 30.
50 Chapter 3, p. 86.
51 *Of the Nature of Virtue, 1736*, p. 311 (italics supplied).

three, Fear, Hope, Love; namely, Resignation to the Divine Will, which ought to be the habitual Frame of our Mind and Heart, and to be exercised at proper Seasons more distinctly, in Acts of Devotion' (*1729*, p. 280). We are most human when we pray – when we 'exercise' our temper of mind, thus strengthening and regulating it. And in Sermon XV, 'Upon the Ignorance of Man', Butler had argued that man is fitted for his purpose, although we do not know what exactly this purpose is. '[If] Somewhat else [than acquiring knowledge] be our Business and Duty, we may, notwithstanding our Ignorance, be well enough furnished for it; and the Observation of our Ignorance may be of Assistance to us in the Discharge of it' (*1729*, pp. 308–9). Butler does not regard this as an unprovable assumption; it is a product of a temper of mind which is empirically analysable, albeit by subjective means. The fact that a temper of mind exists is proof of metaphysical realities, even though our ignorance prevents us from exploring them (*1729*, p. 309).

The habit of thought which leads Butler to statements like 'our faith itself is a good work; it is a virtuous temper of mind' is a consequence of his meta-physics. In Sermon XI, 'Upon the Love of our Neighbour' (*1729*, pp. 213–17), Butler had felt his way around the distinction between self-love and selfishness, arguing that each is a valid basis of action, even if they lead (a thought developed in *The Analogy*) to Hobbesian, brutal, societies and monsters in human shape. In distinction to the uncertainties of pursuing unknowable self-interest, the fundamental concept of property arises with theoretical security from self-love (*1729*, p. 214) and is projected into society by mediation with benevolence. Given the difference in function between self-love and benevolence, between the inner and outer worlds, there cannot be a common system of affections which holds them together in a single system: each stands at the head of its own system.[52] Ethical coherence – in which Butler certainly believed – lies in the mediation of the private with the social relations of humankind: the creation, partly by the person's own efforts, of a temper of mind. It is because of this that Butler believes in the growth and atrophy of persons according to the intensity and sustention of their ethical practice. Butler had said, in the same passage, that 'All things which are distinct from each other are equally so'. In saying that distinctions between any two pairs are unqualified, that the determination of equality is a 'yes/no' switch, he means that all things have the same ontological value.[53] Since ethical mediation certainly exists, there is no hierarchy in creation, only the inner–outer dynamic. We experience shocks of recognition (be

---

[52] This represents a clarifying of his earlier uncertainty about the relative status of self-love and benevolence.

[53] It would seem that a version of this thought lies behind the concept of 'underdetermination' as developed by Bas van Fraassen – the theoretical propositions that all theories have empirically equivalent rivals and that because all such theories are equally supported by empirical evidence (in fact, that all are subject to Popperian verification and all will prove vulnerable), all are equally believable. See Bas C. van Fraassen, *The Scientific Image*, Oxford, 1980, *passim* and Maarten van Dyck's analysis of it, 'Empiricism and Underdetermination', in *Images of Empiricism*, ed. Bradley Morton, Oxford, 2007, p. 11ff.

they of the religious, epistemological or aesthetic experience), but attempts to analyse further necessarily end in perplexity.[54]

We have already seen that for Butler things (the world and humankind's sense of the world) are held together by faith, not reason.[55] Faith (which presupposes doubt) is the good work of a course of morally good conduct sustained by religious and moral exercise. Since these sustaining practices are both an engagement with the Church liturgy and subjective practice, the formulation may be considered to accommodate the Holy Spirit. Once again, Butler's metaphysics prove equal to meeting the test of doctrinal orthodoxy, even if, as apologetics, they are not classic formulations of it.

Certainly, in the document of the 16 August meeting there is visible a clash of cultures when Wesley defines faith. Wesley is emphatic that a one-off conversion experience constitutes a saving faith, while Butler, although prepared to accept the validity of such experiences, both denies any personal experience of it and takes a broader and more inclusive view, emphasizing process rather than event. This clash, however, disguises a point of contact between Butler's moral theology and the new evangelical movement. This can be illustrated by the analysis offered of Butler's thinking by Bettina von Eckardt,[56] who restated the extreme position that Butler, the 'proto-Kant', is the pioneer of systematic ethics based on an empirical and categorical account of human nature. Within a given system (in this case a 'temper of mind') the elements which comprise the system do so by bearing its functions. In this analysis, 'faith', functioning as some sort of procedure for building 'sure trust and confidence', allows the psychological system to become an integrated and dynamic whole. But since faith is a good work its quality is seen in the value and consistency of social relations, these being its location. In other words, people's faith bears such-and-such a relationship with their psychological feature 'sure trust and confidence' and also a relationship with society, the latter relationship being a function of the former. This analysis reveals the difference between Butler and Wesley as merely verbal. For Butler, faith is a psychological function, more or less well developed, development being seen as the degree of the completeness of integration between the various elements of the system of the mind. For Wesley, lack of faith is an act of resistance of the will to the work of the Spirit in what would otherwise become a healthy soul. Butler puts it positively, within a psychological framework, Wesley negatively, within a theological framework. They did not need to disagree – and the disagreement was not of Butler's seeking.

Two days after the meeting of 16 August another was held. Butler's chaplain, Josiah Tucker, had just written his *Life and Particular Proceedings of the Rev.*

54 *Of Personal Identity, 1736*, p. 301. See also Chapter 3, p. 108.
55 It is thus misconceived to characterize, with Baker (*op. cit.*, p. 95), Wesley's meeting with Butler as being between Wesley's 'newly-warmed heart' and Butler's 'cold logic'.
56 Bettina von Eckardt, *Ethik der Selbstliebe: Joseph Butlers Theorie der menschliche Natur*, Heidelberg, 1980, *passim*.

Mr. George Whitefield, and it may be in retaliation that Wesley accused Tucker of preaching heresy. Cunliffe goes too far in his ODNB article in assuming that Butler encouraged the writing of the *Life*. Another work on Methodism announced by Tucker never saw the light of day, nor was his sermon which had offended Wesley published. It is likely that Butler influenced publication rather than composition, particularly as he is nowhere, except in Wesley's account, recorded as actively hostile to Whitefield. Tucker's later work, *A Brief History of the Principles of Methodism, wherein the Rise and Progress, together with the Causes of the several Variations, Divisions, and present Inconsistencies of the Sect are attempted to be traced out, and accounted for* (1742), was commissioned not by Butler but by Hugh Boulter, the Archbishop of Armagh.[57]

In this final meeting there was discussion of whether Wesley's accusation constituted a formal complaint. In contrast to the informal arrangement of the first, which was not set up to produce an admissible judgement against Wesley, this one had a panel – Butler, as bishop, Reynell as chancellor and John Sutton, a long-established canon of Bristol Cathedral[58] – with Tucker attending. Wesley records Butler as saying,

> Nay, Mr. Wesley, you did bring it as a matter of complaint. For when I said, 'You have no right to make complaint against my clergy,' you said you 'thought everyone had a right to complain against those who taught false doctrine'.[59]

Butler's point ('… my clergy …') is that Wesley is not a colleague in the diocese and therefore cannot make informal and private criticisms but can only exercise constitutional rights. This being the occasion for loyalty to a member of his ecclesiastical household, Butler acts properly and unbendingly.

The debate concerned atonement for original sin, a revisiting of the previous discussion. Wesley was driven to admit that 'I can't be exact as to the [offending] words' in Tucker's sermon and that some passages of it merely 'seemed to me to carry [the offending] sense, although it was not advanced in express terms'. Butler observes that, '(to speak in the mildest terms) [Wesley] had been guilty of great want of candour and Christian charity', and delivers a typically Butlerian thought, '[taking] occasion … to offer several reasons why there must be something good in us, before God could justify us, some morally good temper, on account of which God justified some and not others'. Thus Butler repeats the 'faith = good temper' formula and hints that human good works have some connection with justification, albeit good works considered not as 'external

---

[57] Boulter, Bishop of Bristol (1719–24), had sought information about Methodism from 'an eminent Person, then resident in Bristol' (Tucker, *Brief History*, Preface [p. 6]). Since Tucker would not have described himself in those terms, we may assume that Boulter approached his successor, Butler, in his first summer of residence, and that Butler deputed his chaplain to reply, given his established interest in the subject.

[58] CCEd.

[59] This and the subsequent quotations in the main text from Baker, p. 99.

religion' but as constituting a rebuilding of the Christian's moral character. Although Wesley was driven to retract, however, Butler did not proceed against him. Since Wesley was clearly neither in the right nor a loyal Whig this shows some forbearance.

Internal religion

Resisting the growing trend, Butler published none of his Bristol visitation charges and the records of the corresponding visitations are not extant, so that we know very little about his conduct of the Bristol diocese. There does remain, however, a fragment of his fourth charge, which by its very existence confirms that he carried out scrupulously his duty of a triennial visitation. He also commented[60] that he spent the equivalent of his whole Bristol income on rebuilding the bishop's palace, or, alternatively, that 'the deanery of St. Paul's paid' for the Bristol building works.

There exist three holograph prayers and some fragments, printed by Steere from manuscripts in the British Museum. They are mostly undated but seem to belong to his later years.[61] They do, however, present a fairly coherent position. Fragment 1 distinguishes between endeavouring to please someone (he is thinking of God) and endeavouring to please him 'as a wise & good Man i.e. ... in ye particular way, of ~~doing~~ behaving towards him, as we think ye Relations we stand in to him ... require'. Most of Butler's surviving (non-Clarke) correspondence is to powerful public figures and upholds the prerogatives of a bishop against explicit or implicit claims on his conduct: ultimately, Walpole or the Duke of Newcastle (who both attempted to negotiate with Butler over favours or advantageous balances of relations in exchange for preferment) will be served better by ethically and constitutionally correct behaviour than by favours.[62] Fragment 2 implies the duty of worship in prescribed forms, departures constituting 'unspeakable Presumption'. Fragment 3 says that sincerity is

---

[60] Bartlett, p. 89.

[61] *Some Remains, hitherto Unpublished, of Joseph Butler*, 1853. In these paragraphs quotations are from new transcriptions. Because his edition is more accessible than Steere's I have noted Bernard's numbering of the fragments (vol. I, pp. 305–8), although in some cases it represents unwarranted editorial interference with undivided texts. The present work is the first to quote accurately from these documents. Steere's, Gladstone's and Bernard's errors are passed over in silence, while White, while generally accurate, is concerned with presenting a text accessible to the student.

[62] We have emphasized that for Butler charity was about the relationships between individuals and expanding circles of people. He did not apply these human standards to the legal relationships between institutions and did not tolerate suggestions that his official prerogatives be abridged. For example, a tenant of the bishop's in the Durham diocese complained, with regard to rents due to the bishop from Park Colliery that 'his Lordship ... fixes his Rule absolutely upon the Rental and makes no Deduction even for the Sesses and Taxes ... [If] strict Rule was to be observed we should be in the worst situation of any Tenant of the See of Durham' (Thomas Henry Carr, letter of September 1751, quoted in Edward Hughes, *North Country Life in the Eighteenth Century: the North-East, 1700–1750*, London, 1952, p. 319). During his overhaul of the Durham administration Butler had lists made of the visitation fees due (Durham University Library, MS DDR/EV/VIS/4/3).

not enough: 'such Indifference [as to whether our outward actions are good] is utterly inconsistent w[i]th Sincerity'. Fragment 4 presents the idea that 'No Person who has just notions of God can be afraid of His Displeasure any further than as he is afraid of his own Character' and this is reinforced by Fragment 16 ('Be more afraid of myself than of ye world') and by Fragment 18's dictum, 'Instead of deluding oneself in imagining one should not behave [w]ell in times & Circumstances other than those in wch one is placed, to take Care & be faithful & behave well in those one is placed in.' Fragments 5 and 6 suggest that sceptics cannot be good in their conduct. Fragment 7 merits quotation in full, as it is a salutary corrective to subsequent ideas of social benevolence which might, carelessly, seem to derive from Butler:

> In general a Man has no Right ought not to do other Peoples Duties Duty for them: for their Duty was appointed them for their Exercise. And besides, who will do it in Case of his Death. Nor has a Man any Right to raise in others such a Dependance upon him as that they must be miserable in Case of his Death, though whilst he lives he answers that Dependance.[63]

Thus Butler walks alone, trusting in God, negotiating each situation as it comes and distrusting himself. This colours, but does not, of course, limit, his ethical doctrine.

Of particular interest is a 'Letter to a Lady', resident in the Bristol diocese and evidently already known to Butler, dated 'London, December 22, 1747'.[64] She has raised a 'case of conscience': she evidently legally possesses lands which were formerly owned by the Church but feels uneasy about depriving the Church of income. Butler argues that 'Property in general is, and must be, regulated by the laws of the community ... and, therefore, we may with a good conscience retain any possessions, church lands, or tithes, which the laws of the State we live under give us a property in. And ... in England ... our ecclesiastical laws agree with our civil ones in this matter' (Bartlett, p. 99). He further denies that the Church has a divine right to a merely human gift. The Church, in other words, is the religious aspect of the English people's organization into a state. He then considers the ethical aspect of the question. The Reformation caused upheavals and the impoverishment of some parochial cures, so that:

> a man's possession of one of these impoverished cures is ... a providential admonition to do somewhat ... towards settling some competent maintenance upon it ... In like manner, as a person in distress, being my

---

[63] Transcribed from BL Add Mss 9815. In this fragment Butler first writes, 'Nor has a Man any Right to raise in others such a Dependance ...' and then replaces the deletion by 'And some Men ...'. The emendation has been ignored in the main text, as is syntactically incoherent, but clearly Butler had a second thought, that he did not want to exclude the possibility that there may be men who had such a right. Christ, of course, was a man.
[64] Text from Bartlett, pp. 98–101, reprinted by Gladstone, vol. II, pp. 369–70.

neighbour … is a providential admonition to me in particular, to assist him, over and above a general obligation to charity. (Bartlett, p. 101)

What is most striking is that Butler recognizes the lady's 'case of conscience', but as late as 1747 he continues to interpret the question according to the account of the human condition he had developed in the *1729* Preface, in a passage which we have already seen used in Heylyn's consecration sermon.[65] The conscience is an awareness of a relationship of otherwise conflicting affections and the nexus it creates requires benevolent resolution, if necessary through a deliberate judgement about a specific act of charity. His silence on the conscience, as opposed to the specific *case* of conscience, indicates that the conscience may alert but does not command. Thus, when faced with a problem, Butler continues to reach for his philosophical toolbox. This application of his philosophical analysis to a practical question feels fully assured, and leads to a statement which, for a bishop, was most radical: that his advice applies to tithes as well as land – a flat statement about one of the most contentious features of English law and one which would acquire great urgency in the nineteenth century.

Durham

Materials concerning Butler's brief reign in Durham are comparatively abundant, but they have very little relevance to the present work's subject. His ceremonial reception ('met at Fairwall-hall … by many of the gentry and clergy in about 18 or 19 coaches')[66] at the Cathedral and Castle (his Durham home),[67] was featured in the local press. His reply to the speech of welcome, allegedly printed in full, amounted to a terse 175 words:

> As for your kind Manner of expressing yourselves concerning my Character and Behaviour, This I shall make use of, to *remind myself of my Duty*: And you must give me Leave to consider it too as a Declaration, (of what however I had no doubt) that I shall have *your Concurrence and your Assistance* in any good Design, which may offer for the Benefit of the Diocese or Country.[68]

It was the speech of a shy and un-self-confident man, who relied on official structures and unofficial networks. He allowed his London Infirmary sermon to be reprinted in Newcastle in support of the proposed infirmary there.[69] He carried

---

[65] See p. 130.

[66] *The Diary of Thomas Gyll* (in *The Publications of the Surtees Society, vol. CXVIII*, Durham, 1910), p. 187.

[67] See *The Reverend Sir John Dolben's Speech to the Right Reverend Father in GOD Joseph … On his Lordship's First Arrival in his Diocese, on Friday June 28, 1751. With his Lordship's Answer*, Newcastle, J. White, n.d. The shelf-mark of the Durham University Library's copy is VI. G. 63 (1).

[68] *The Reverend Sir John Dolben's Speech*, p. 8. Italics supplied.

[69] *The Diary of Thomas Gyll* gives details; see pp. 182, 187, 188. Butler laid the foundation stone of the Newcastle Infirmary on 5 September 1751 (p. 189).

out a visitation and a thorough assessment of his diocese. His predecessor (or rather his friend Benson, the bishop of Gloucester, who during Edward Chandler's decline had managed Durham's affairs) had kept the deanery records in good order but the administrative changes for Butler's visitation may be ascribed to him, since the diocesan officials, including Ralph Trotter, the long-serving registrar, were the same.[70] In accordance with contemporary best practice he showed especial interest in the engagement of clergy with high educational qualifications, making a list of the twelve who held doctorates,[71] while, of his fourteen Durham ordinands, nine possessed degrees and another three had 'spent some time at university'.[72] In advance of his visitation he published a brief for the parochial officers and clergy.[73] He had also acquired a taste for building work and his residences in Hampstead, Bristol, Durham Castle and Bishop Auckland, were all subject to extensive rebuilding or planning – he even took a load of cedar wood to Durham with him, a gift from the Bristol burghers – while Bristol Cathedral received, controversially, a marble cross. There is a sense of intellectual decline as his final illness progresses, and the sole publication of his last years, the charge to the Durham clergy, shows this, by confirming his interest in 'external religion', or, rather, in an increasing separation between on the one hand the corporate responsibility for maintaining religious institutions and culture and on the other the private practice of faith. When his health collapsed (he died in the spa city of Bath on 16 July 1752)[74] it is said that he asked his chaplain, Nathaniel Foster, to reread John 3.16 ('For God so loved the world, that he gave his only begotten Son, that whosoever believeth in him should not perish, but have everlasting life'), because 'I never before felt those words to be so satisfactory and consoling.'[75] This seems of a piece with other anecdotes about the darkness and loneliness of Butler's inner life, such as the

[70] The archives of the Bishops of Durham are held by Durham University and include substantial, although imperfect, records of the eighteenth-century visitations and the parish clergy, listed by deanery. Jon Christopher Shuler ('The Pastoral and Ecclesiastical Administration of the Diocese of Durham 1721–1771; with Particular Reference to the Archdeaconry of Northumberland', unpublished PhD thesis, University of Durham, 1976) presents much valuable evidence. The relevant document is DDR/EV/VIS/4/3. The last visitation had been in 1746 by Benson, deputizing for Chandler, and Butler seems to have required the compilation of considerably more information about the clergy and other ordained staff than had been done for previous visitations: lists of livings in the bishop's gift, the clergy's educational qualifications, the diocesan officials and the livings in the gift of the dean and chapter. There was also a list of pluralists (p. 100ᵛ).

[71] Durham University Library MS DDR/EV/VIS/4/2, p. 109ʳ. The twelve included his friend Martin Benson (bishop of Gloucester) in his role as prebend of Durham.

[72] Shuler, p. 3. See also Butler's notes on the ordinands, Durham University Library MS DDR/EV/VIS/4/3, p. 26ᵛ.

[73] *Articles of Visitation and Enquiry, Concerning Matters Ecclesiastical Exhibited to the Ministers, Church-Wardens, and Sidesmen, of Every Parish with the Diocese of Durham, at the Primary Visitation of the Right Reverend Father in GOD, Joseph … In the Year 1751*, Durham, Isaac Lane, n.d., 8pp.

[74] 'The Bp of Durham dyed at Bath 16 June 1752 between the hours of 10 & 11 in the forenoon Aged 60 being born 18 May 1692' (added to the Durham copy of his will, Durham University Library MS SGD 35/12).

[75] Bartlett, p. 220. A hostile variant is given in J. E. Rattenbury, *Wesley's Legacy to the World*, Epworth, 1928, p. 89.

late-night incident in his Bristol garden when he held forth to Tucker about whether nations, as well as individuals, could go mad,[76] and Fragment 10, dated 'Sunday evening, June 13, 1742', in which he records a series of questions about faithfulness to God, which, despite their rhetorical form, suggest that, in this entirely private document, he continued to have crises of faith.

The Durham charge[77] is a fairly complete statement of the roles of the Church and its clergy, as Butler saw them in relation to the Christian community and wider society. They are conceived not in general terms but practically, from the viewpoint of the clergy to whom the charge was addressed. *Fifteen Sermons* had accepted the contemporary interest in empirical studies of the human mind and used an account of it as the basis of its ethical doctrine. Then *The Analogy* had accepted the fact of contemporary religious scepticism and had subverted it by demonstrating its theoretical insecurity and the advantage derived by Reformed Christianity from embracing social consensus. Now the charge seeks to establish a mode of professional clerical conduct in pursuit of the terms of ministerial ordination. We do not know to what extent the charge duplicates the lost Bristol charges; the fragment of the fourth, preserved by Secker, enjoins the visitation of the sick (a ministerial duty prescribed in the Prayer Book), but this is not mentioned in the Durham charge.

As always, Butler assumes a hostile social environment, where the tone is '*for* nothing, but *against* every thing that is good and sacred' (§1). Broadly, he has two aims: to guide his clergy in their relations with sceptics and with regard to practical apologetics (§§1–10); and to strengthen the practice of 'external religion' and the liturgy (§§11–28), while reminding them that these are 'subservient to promot[ing] the reality and power of [true religion]' (§12). The latter aim is to be achieved by organizing parish services and domestic worship in as full accordance as possible with the Prayer Book: the published charge caused offence by noting the success of Islam and Romanism in thus nurturing their 'superstitions' and the unfortunate consequences of the Protestant reformers' having reduced the liturgy to the bare essentials. It also enjoined helping parishioners to build a practical expression of their religious and spiritual duties into their daily lives. Butler advises his clergy of the need to inculcate reverence for religion in social groupings (§5–9) and warns (§7) of the dangers of engaging with sceptics' predilection for facile 'cavilling', in the light of the difficulty in casual conversation of adequately discussing the complexities of the faith (this recalls his letter to Home and his sermon on *Government of the Tongue*). He reminds them of the positive value of privately acknowledging and engaging with one's own doubt (§6) and, for parochial preaching, rejects *The Analogy*'s

---

[76] Tucker borrowed this thought for his *An Humble Address and Earnest Appeal*, Gloucester, T. Cadell, 1775, p. 20n, applying it, by inference, to the factional turmoil of the American Revolution. 'Why might not whole Communities and public Bodies be seized with *Fits of Insanity*, as well as Individuals? ... [This alone] can account for the major Part of those Transactions, which we read in History.'

[77] *A Charge Deliver'd to the Clergy, at the Primary Visitation of the Diocese of Durham*, Durham, J. Richardson, 1751.

negative strategy as inappropriate, church services being 'a time of devotion, when we are assembled to yield ourselves up to the full influence of the divine presence' (§§9–11). Butler's injunctions about 'external religion' are put forward in the context of his belief that the external forms of religion, which 'cannot [otherwise] be preserved amongst mankind', are means, not ends.

The Durham charge is in reality orthodox and unexceptionable in its position and of a piece with Butler's wider doctrine but together with the 'papist' Bristol cross it provoked a brief pamphlet war and accusations, from self-identified Protestants, of covert Romanism which dragged on for decades.[78] The shock thus professed indicates the extent to which Butler's works had attracted sympathetic attention from the dissenting and evangelical 'left' of English Protestantism.

---

[78] It is summarized by Hallifax in his edition of *The Works*, 2nd edn, London, 1841, pp. xiv–xx.

5

Six Sermons

Main texts: The six occasional sermons, 1739–48

Introduction

In *Fifteen Sermons* and *The Analogy* Butler was concerned with giving an account of the human mind, the introvert (self-love) and extrovert (benevolence), the dynamic relationship between them prompted by the conscience and the fundamentally ethical nature of the consciousness. In the last chapter we looked at several texts, mostly not intended for publication, which documented his personal application of his doctrine and the ministerial praxis founded on it. In the present chapter we turn to the six occasional sermons on questions of public policy. It is to be expected that such documents will be exemplars of the charitable application of benevolence and of the obligations and proper social relations of the Butlerian Christian.

The point will not be laboured below, but the continuity of method will also be noticed: in whatever Butler undertakes he always establishes his position or course of action in relation to ethical principles, doing new thinking where necessary, but always taking bearings from his moral philosophy. There is always, therefore, a doctrinaire strain in Butler's preaching and writing, which was entirely appropriate to his understanding of his office. The concept of duty should be borne in mind when considering his legacy to the nineteenth-century Church.

Although these six sermons are of great historical importance, and some of exceptional intellectual distinction, they have been little noticed and perhaps have been avoided as period pieces, which, of course, occasional sermons should partly be. Given that Butler is known as a religious apologist and moral philosopher, it may surprise the reader to encounter discussions of things like parliamentary legislation, such as the Truck Acts and the Master and Servant Acts; developments in economic theory; the east coast coal and shipping industries; the organization of the workhouse; the dangers of bureaucracy and institutionalization in charitable organizations; and the social implications of new technology. It reminds us that his chaplain, Josiah Tucker, moved from anti-Methodist polemic to political and economic questions (from internal evidence, very likely with Butler's encouragement) and that while it is true that 'the "long eighteenth century" was not … an age of major interventionist reforms'[1] the essential theoretical and cultural groundwork for the nineteenth-century reforms was done at that time. The shallow stream of proto-Utilitarian thinking (partly a product of the Reid interpretation of Butler) could not by itself have been sufficient to create the broad flow of Victorian social reform.

The six sermons are delivered with his authority as a Church leader and converge from the various perspectives and missions of the five institutions they served to provide a unified, extended consideration of the relationship between the inner and the outer – between the individual (self-love, property, religious experience, language as exploration) and society (benevolence, institution-building, religion as social love, language as social instrument). It has proved possible without distortion to treat the six as a single, complex statement of a gestating social theory. If Butler's health and intellectual vigour had lasted they could have been the basis of a coherent statement in the same way that his preaching in the Rolls chapel produced a moral philosophy and a science of social psychology.

The six sermons in context

The first of the six sermons (*SPG 1739*) was preached on Friday 16 February 1739 in St Mary-le-Bow parish church at the anniversary meeting of the Society for the Propagation of the Gospel in Foreign Parts. The SPG anniversary meeting was held in the church vestry immediately after the anniversary sermon in the church. Because of pressure of practical business the SPG's anniversary meeting more closely resembled the modern Annual General Meeting. The SPG was an Incorporated Society and because its official remit included arranging ministrations to the English communities overseas it was in some respects regarded as senior to the SPCK: its anniversary meeting was regularly attended by half a dozen or more bishops, together with other senior clergy and, increasingly, lay philanthropists. The preacher was almost without exception a bishop or about to become one; he was selected by the President, who was always the reigning Archbishop of Canterbury (by convention until 1882 and thereafter by rule) and while the President never preached the sermon, once past its infancy, with only one exception (Potter), every Primate preached the sermon in his years as a more junior bishop.[2] In Butler's time preachers were conventionally 'requested' to publish their sermons (at their own expense) and used their own publishers:

---

[1]   W. M. Jacob, *The Clerical Profession in the Long Eighteenth Century*, pp. 11–12.

[2]   The *locus classicus* is H. W. Tucker, *Classified Digest of the Records of the [SPG]*, London, 1893, pp. 833–5. See also Rowan Strong, *Anglicanism and the British Empire*, Oxford, 2007, *passim*, and Laura Stevens, *The Poor Indians*, Philadelphia, PA, 2004, chapter 4, *passim*. A comprehensive account of the annual SPG, SPCK and Church Missionary Society sermons after 1760, and a discussion of those of the earlier period is given in Bob Tennant, *Corporate Holiness: Pulpit Preaching and the Anglican Missionary Movement, 1760–1870* (in preparation). See also Chapter 6 of this book.

the Society had not yet adopted an official printer.[3] This implied a degree of ownership of the annual report, which was attached to the sermon as an appendix: there was an intimate sense of its being part of a continuing conversation within the Society, with a very high degree of consensus about theology and practicalities. In appointing successive anniversary speakers the President would inevitably have sought advice, so that within the overall consensus of the series there appeared patches of concentration on particular subjects.

Thus in the 1730s a succession of preachers focused on the viability of the anglophone communities in America – Hare (1735; Walpole's unsuccessful candidate as successor at Canterbury to the long-serving Wake), Lynch (1736; one of the small handful who did not become a bishop) and Clagett (1737). Hare especially, whose ethical theology is strikingly Butlerian, focused on the charitable duty of the 'good Men'[4] in the community of colonists and merchants to evangelize its members and the slaves and native Americans in and around it. There is, understandably, a strong element of anti-Catholicism and political expediency in this sequence. Clagett warns of the danger of the English adopting sectarian attitudes like the Jews of apostolic times.[5] Repentance, however, is available to all and Christ was sent to '*break down the partition wall*, that was betwixt *Jews* and *Gentiles*, and to *make both one*' (p. 10), an early example of church- and temple-building metaphors being applied to Anglican missionary work. In his footnotes Clagett cites many Spanish sources about missions and transmits the common Catholic observation that the Protestant Reformation had not tended in an evangelical direction. The basic strategy of the Hare–Clagett sequence may be described as nationalist but consciously non-sectarian. They were succeeded by a personally distinguished sequence nominated by Potter, the new Archbishop: Herring (1738), Butler (1739), Benson (1740) and Secker (1741), two of whom became Primates and three of whom were products of the Queen Caroline-Talbot-Clarke axis.

Butler's second occasional sermon (*Spital 1740*) was the annual charity sermon, preached at St. Bridget's 'on Monday in Easter-Week, 1740' before the Lord Mayor, the Court of Aldermen, the Sheriffs of London and the Governors of the hospitals in the City. At its next meeting, on 15 April, the Court 'desired' that Butler print his sermon.[6] A feature may be noted here which was typical of eighteenth-century sermons to charitable organizations: its function as an ideological framework for the annual financial and organizational report. Thus Butler's sermon breaks off in mid-flow so that these can be read to the assembly, and then resumes.

---

[3] This applied to all the bodies for which Butler preached in this period, except the House of Lords, and Butler duly took his to the Knaptons.
[4] Francis Hare, *Sermon preached before the [SPG] [Romans 10:13–15]*, London, S Buckley, 1735, p. 5.
[5] Nicholas Clagett, *A Sermon preached before the [SPG] [Acts 11:18]*, London, J. & J. Pemberton, 1737, p. 9.
[6] 'Spital sermon' is the contemporary designation, witness many title pages.

The third sermon (*Martyrdom 1741*) was preached on Friday 30 January 1741 at Westminster Abbey before his peers in the House of Lords, for the anniversary of the martyrdom of King Charles I, an occasion in the Church of England's liturgical calendar.

After a gap of four years the fourth sermon (*Charity Schools 1745*) was given on Thursday 9 May 1745, at Christ Church. It was the annual sermon preached under the auspices of the SPCK to the trustees and staff of the Cities of London and Westminster charity schools and 'Published at the Request of the Gentlemen concerned in the said Charity'. An historical and financial 'Account' of the SPCK was appended, reprinted and updated from previous years. It will be noticed that this was Butler's first publication outside the Knapton house: the SPCK, as befitted a publishing organization, had its own printer.

Like the third, the fifth sermon (*Accession 1747*) was preached before the House of Lords in Westminster Abbey on Thursday 11 June 1747 'being the Anniversary of his Majesty's Happy Accession to the Throne', a festival in the Church's calendar. This was his last Knapton publication.

The last of Butler's published sermons (*Infirmary 1748*) was another annual sermon, preached at St Lawrence-Jewry on Thursday 31 March 1748 before 'His Grace Charles Duke of Richmond, Lenox, and Aubigny, President; and the Governors of the London Infirmary, for the Relief of Sick and Diseased Persons, especially Manufacturers, and Seamen in Merchant-Service'. It was 'Published at the Request of the President and Governors' by Woodfall, their usual printer, which indicates the highly organized relationship between the Infirmary's function and its network of supporters. The facts that Butler suppressed his Bristol Infirmary sermon and that the London sermon was reprinted for the benefit of the Newcastle Infirmary in Butler's new Durham diocese suggests that the London Infirmary was regarded as an organizational model for the rest of the country.

Charity, liberty, class

We will begin by considering Butler's application of his theory of charity – the practical public expression of the affection of benevolence – to the organizations which he was asked to support. The six sermons are entirely built on an exposition of the political application of Butler's concepts of ethical identity and charity, which, in a new development, he sees as inseparable from ethical and political liberty. In *Martyrdom 1741* he defines liberty as an 'entire Coincidence of our Wills with the Will of God, [which creates] a State of the most absolute Freedom', and as 'that *perfect love*, which St. *John* speaks of': Scripture doctrine concerns mainly the social aspects of life, 'injoyed under civil Government' (pp. 3, 4). The sermon's subject, hypocrisy, is approached through an unusually extended exegetical exercise on its text (1 Peter 2.16: 'And not using your liberty for a cloke of maliciousness, but as the servants of God', p. 1). It includes a lengthy footnote (p. 2), carrying on, with many Scriptural citations, the exegetical examination of the Pharisees' and Sadducees' hypocrisy, which may be an offence against God and the conscience in the same way as it may be an offence against other people. Butler uses the example of the Jewish priestly class's alleged 'Pride, and Uncharitableness' (p. 2n), insinuated into their religion in the guise of zealousness for the external forms of religion. He sees this as an hypocrisy because humankind's conscience recognizes the existence of choices between right and wrong and can only be sustained in wrong by a chronic state of self-delusion. The fundamental instability of such self-delusion means that the State and the Church may be safely, and indeed necessarily, established on the basis of toleration, the lack of which is 'a general Tyranny; because it claims absolute Authority over Conscience: and would soon beget ... Tyranny over the Mind, and various Superstitions ... Now a reasonable Establishment provides Instruction for the Ignorant, withdraws them, not in the Way of Force, but of Guidance, from running after ... Conceits' (*Accession 1747*, pp. 13–4). In *Martyrdom 1741* Butler refers to Charles's parliament, in which 'the [ethically] better Part' of the rebels originated in a party with legitimate constitutional concerns (pp. 11–2) but, hypocritically, came to delude their conscience (pp. 7, 9–10) and cede leadership to the proponents of violence (*Martyrdom 1741*, p. 12). For Butler doctrinal differences are incidental to self-delusion and 'mere Wantonness of Imagination' (*Accession 1747*, p. 17).

> 'Let us transfer, each of us, the Equity of this our civil Constitution to our whole personal Character; and be sure to be as much afraid of Subjection to mere arbitrary Will and Pleasure in Ourselves, as to the arbitrary Will of Others. For the Tyranny of our own lawless Passions, is the nearest and most dangerous of all Tyrannies'.
>
> (*Accession 1747*, pp. 25–6)

It is interesting to set this argument against the mid-twentieth-century one that 'the personal is the political'. Conscience is not sufficient,[7] because the will can suppress it, but the will which engages with the conscience produces a healthy individual and a healthy polity. While in a state of self-delusion one cannot free oneself to respond to the natural conscience and therefore is also inhibited from access to the proper exercise of self-love and benevolence: people engage in 'a Multitude of superstitious Practices, which were [falsely] called Good Works' (*Accession 1747*, p. 27). There is no disjuncture between benevolence, charity and liberty.

Thus Butler continues to produce texts which may be termed doctrinaire – concerned to set out social programmes based on theory-driven analysis of the human condition. Charity, increasingly, comes close to being for him the only supremely important Christian activity. In *Infirmary 1748* he argues the 'Preheminence' of 'fervent Charity' ('this Grace or Virtue') as enabling the repair of failures of the moral affections and earning 'even Forgiveness of Men'

---

7   See Chapter 4, p. 136.

(p. 4). The unusual phrase, 'fervent Charity', which occurs twice in this passage and therefore acquires the force of a technical term, is particularly interesting because 'fervent' is a favourite word of John Wesley's, occurring some sixty-two times in his collected works.[8] The majority of Wesley's uses come in association with terms like 'prayer', 'gratitude' and 'love': it characterizes the intensity of his faith and personal relationship with God. Butler, who uses the word only in this construction, differs ostentatiously from Wesley in attaching it to a quintes-sentially social practice. In *Infirmary 1748*, Butler's last published sermon, this emphasis on charitable praxis reaches its full elaboration. While 'fervent' is a quality which might seem to submerge the person in religious experience – here, in a special intensity of the social in combination with the personal affections – Butler also sets close limits on its reception and influence on action.[9] The role of judgement is central: charity must offer long-term benefits to the recipient (*Infirmary 1748*, p. 5). Moreover, there must be strict limits on conduct and the role of feelings. The passage must be quoted at length, as it is the final and definitive statement of Butler's ministerial praxis.

> [This] Sort of benevolent Instinct left to itself, without the Direction of our Judgment ... [tho'] it be agreeable in Conversation, it is often most mischievous in every other Intercourse of Life; and always puts Men out of a Capacity of doing the Good they might, if they could withstand Importunity, and the Sight of Distress, when the Case requires it should be withstood.... Nor is it to be supposed, that we can any more promote the lasting Good of our Fellow-creatures by acting from mere kind Incli-nations, without *considering* what are the proper Means of promoting it, than that we can attain our own personal Good, by a *thoughtless* Pursuit of every thing which pleases us. For the Love of our Neighbour, as much as Self-love, the social Affections, as much as the private ones, from their very Nature, require to be under the Direction of our Judg-ment. Yet it is to be remembred, that it does in no sort become such a Creature as Man, to harden himself against the Distresses of his Neigh-bour, except where it is really necessary; and that even well-disposed Persons may run into great Perplexities ... by being over-sollicitous in distinguishing, what are the most proper Occasions for their Charity ... And therefore, as on the one Side, we are obliged to take some Care not to squander that which, one may say, belongs to the Poor ... so on the other side, when we are competently satisfied ... we ought by no means to neglect such present Opportunity of doing Good ...: for of these Delays there will be no End. (*Infirmary 1748*, pp. 5–7)

The application of reason and the doctrines of philosophy and religion are essential if the affective nature is to flourish with a developed social conscious-

---

[8] Word search on *The Works of John Wesley on Compact Disc*, Franklin, TN, Providence House Publishers, 1995.

[9] The Butler memorial in Durham Cathedral refers to Butler's 'fervid devotion'. 'Fervent' and 'fervid' had little difference in connotation in the eighteenth century.

ness – a term which is shorthand for Butler's proposal that the consciousness is intrinsically and entirely social and ethical and is based on an integration of the elements of human resources. The practice of charity, the most important means to social, psychological and spiritual healthiness, combines fervency and deliberation, passion and reason but is at no time reducible to fixed rules.[10]

It will also be noticed that Butler's social conservatism is a biographically contingent, not a theoretically necessary, fact. The practical role of the judgement tends to render passive the impoverished objects of charity, as charity is the practical activity of individuals, whose individuality emerges through their social activity. The existence of an unequal society is not a theoretical prerequisite but only the contingent occasion for the praxis of charitable conduct, which is a complex of in-born affections, conscience and judgement. We saw this emerge when Butler observed to Wesley, when discussing 'justifying faith', that 'I believe some good men have this, but not all'[11] – that, in other words, an inner conviction of grace is a temper of mind not intrinsically more important than a consistent practice of charity. The charitable person is constantly engaged in bringing together the affections of self-love ('private' affections, in the passage just quoted) and benevolence ('social' affections), uniting both in a praxis of Christian good. *Infirmary 1748* (pp. 9–12) suggests a process of constantly bringing a case-by-case consideration of the need to discourage improvidence among the poor into a creative dynamic with the need to 'be sure not to expect more from them than can be expected, in a moderate Way of considering Things' (p. 12). In other words, the offer of charitable benevolence may be rejected by the recipient, deliberately or by incapability.

This dialectical praxis of charity benefits giver and receiver. We can easily see why Butler came to think Methodist practices self-indulgent and anti-social: his concern is for a network of social relations which is valid in spite of, not because of, social inequalities. In such circumstances the existence of religious dissent is unwelcome, as it fragments the programme of social charity which alone can provide a healthy population. Thus, as early in his episcopate as *SPG 1739*, Butler calls for non-denominational missionary activity, based on respect for 'our particular Form of Christianity, the confessed Standard of Christian Religion, the Scripture' (*SPG 1739*, p. 18) and urges organizational unity, observing that '[some] well-disposed Persons ... discountenance what is good, because it is not better ... [and separate themselves from rectifying] what they think capable of Amendment, ... unless they will join in the Designs themselves; which they must acknowledge to be good and necessary ones' (*SPG 1739*, p. 21).[12] This acute diagnosis of a political perennial – the call for

---

10 As we saw in Chapter 4, with the 'Letter to a Lady' (p. 141).
11 Chapter 4, pp. 135–6.
12 This argument for unity was repeated in Thomas Secker's Charity Schools sermon [Romans 14:16] of 1743, *Fourteen Sermons Preached on Several Occasions* (*ed. cit.*), p. 186, and presumably marks a point of discussion between them about practical charity.

unity, but only on one's own terms – was to gain sharpness of relevance half a century later, when the SPG was formally challenged from within the Church by the emergence of the Church Missionary Society. It is identical to Butler's discussion of political liberty in his 1741 sermon before the House of Lords (*Martyrdom 1741*, pp. 7–13 and *passim*).

We have several times noted Butler's principled ethical democracy and his opposition to Shaftesbury's aristocratic ethics. He is the first moral philosopher in English to consider the ethical problems of the stratification of society by socio-economic class. While he sees that such classes and their membership are in a state of flux he does not think it a function of the state, the church or organized charity to encourage movement between them: moral goodness is desirable in all classes (*Infirmary 1748*, p. 24). He was acutely aware of the social responsibilities, as employers and heads of extended households, of the period's relatively small middle class; of the sharp divide between rich and poor; and the culture, embodied in legislation, of regulating labour while not restraining the employer. He did not envisage the poor taking a lead in their own moral improvement, because of their economic instability and vulnerability. Thus, for example, in *Spital 1740* he says that to fulfil their class function the rich need to be morally good and in charity exercise responsibility for the poor (p. 12). This includes setting an example to the poor; the rich are more blameworthy for their moral and social failures than the poor (p. 14), having had fewer pressures on them, just as the children of the rich, being less in contact with other children, are less open to moral corruption. Powerful people exercise authority which ultimately 'is of divine Appointment' (*Accession 1747*, p. 8) and the 'Oppression, Injustice, Cruelty' which human political authority breeds is 'necessary Discipline, and just Punishment' (*Accession 1747*, p. 8) because it is an imperfect expression of the divine in an imperfect world. A frugal and industrious conduct of one's life and affairs 'is itself charity' as it potentially releases money for charitable redistribution (*Infirmary 1748*, p. 24), 'more particularly still in Persons in Trade and Commerce', such as the leading lights of his audience.[13] The doctrine of the moral duty of the commercial and industrial middle class, the owners of the instruments of wealth creation, is thus definitively formulated by Butler a century before its political apogee. Moreover, in a society such as Butler has diagnosed, the concept and practice of charity – an extroverted love of one's fellows in society and a definer and motor of social inclusion – was inevitably involved with giving money and with forms of regulation of wealth and power.

---

[13] Listening to the sermon with the trustees and governors were as many of the five thousand charity school children as could be accommodated (see Josiah Tucker's Charity School sermon, p. 6 n) – sometimes referred to by the preachers but never addressed. This presence/absence is the subject of work in progress. Later, from 1782, when Beilby Porteus preached the sermon, the event was moved to St Paul's Cathedral, which was fitted with special temporary accommodation for ten thousand children, apparently provoking William Blake's 'Holy Thursday', although the event had not been held at Eastertime since the 1730s.

Masters and servants

Religious and political liberty aside – and every organization for which Butler preached was devoted to a Whig conception of liberty – the most notable liberty was economic: the right to work, trade and possess, fettered only by the over-arching liberties which guaranteed stable and civilized life. Butler has a great deal to say about this. Indeed, virtually all of the non-political matter, considered narrowly, of the six sermons may be drawn into a discussion of the application of charity to economic activity. His account of economics, as given to the Court of Aldermen in *Spital 1740*, is traditional (pp. 3–5): historically, a subsistence economy has produced surpluses which are appropriated by the rich and rein-vested in the production and trading of luxury goods, and thence to a banking of the surplus values through a money system (value made 'portable', p. 5), thus 'enlarg[ing] the middle Rank of People' (p. 6), creating an ever-widening distinction of rich from poor, and thence (p. 7) the creation of 'one Society' in which rich and poor have a 'mutual Want' which 'still unites them insepa-rably' (p. 7), entailing a system of social obligations of the rich to the expropri-ated poor. Butler does not consider the system of credit and debt which was then enabling Britain to defeat France, which on paper looked enormously the bigger and richer country,[14] although since debt is fundamentally the borrowing of credit against the future production of the workforce, his ethical diagnosis, which we will describe, could readily have been applied to a capitalist system which was, historically and mechanically, an extrapolation of mercantilism. Butler's interest is entirely about charity, the socially benevolent and respon-sibly conducted relationship between rich and poor.

Butler lived in the period immediately preceding the origin of the modern contract of employment,[15] which did not come to full flower until the later nine-teenth century[16] and is a development of the law governing the pre-existing master–servant relationship. Masters had – and modern British employers have inherited – a range of responsibilities for their employees: their 'duty of care'. Butler discusses this general point at some length in *Infirmary 1748*, advising an audience of London merchants, that 'seamen in merchant-service' and 'manu-facturers' (that is, industrial craftsmen) are the merchants' 'servants' in the same sense as those in their direct domestic service and thus subject to the same duty of care. Employees were to be classified as 'servants' in Blackstone's *Commen-*

14 See James Macdonald, *A Free Nation Deep in Debt: The Financial Roots of Democracy*, New York, 2003, *passim* but especially Chapter 6. Clive Wilkinson, *The British Navy and the State in the Eighteenth Century*, Woodbridge, 2004, pp. 57–65, describes how the contemporary Royal Navy managed its debt.
15 The following remarks are largely based on the standard work: Simon Deakin and Frank Wilkinson, *The Law of the Labour Market*, Oxford, 2005, especially Chapter 2, 'The Origins of the Contract of Employment'.
16 Deakin and Wilkinson, p. 42; Otto Kahn-Freund, 'Blackstone's Neglected Child: The Contract of Employment', *Law Quarterly Review*, vol. 93 (1978), pp. 508–28.

taries of 1765.[17] Deakin and Wilkinson (p. 50) note that 'household' did not by this time imply an economically self-sufficient unit, so that practices within its terms were already acquiring a colouring of ethical obligation and (pp. 61–2) that the master–servant relationship was not a quaint survival from a feudal past but a newly revitalized concept. In terms of their mode of engagement, seafarers fell within the 'servant' category because they were hired by the voyage; even the round trip from London to the Newcastle coal wharves took several weeks and the crews of merchantmen, often sailing with the owner living on board as captain, were as stable as those of warships were in constant flux.

By noting the inclusion of 'manufacturers' (paid on piece-work)[18] and seafarers in the servant category, by arguing for its extension to include charity school children and slaves and by defining the master–servant relationship as fundamentally charitable in the specifically religious sense, Butler is attempting to draw the most oppressed and marginal groups into what, as a legislator, he saw as an economically and morally virtuous circle: the process in which servants of the employer's 'household' could become day-labourers, able to save money and become upwardly mobile property owners.[19] As Tucker was to put it, 'the Poor ought [not] to be kept in a State of Slavery of the most abject Kind, without a Possibility of emerging from it'.[20] Thus, parliament attempted to regulate the labour market by enforcing maximum wages and extending the quasi-familial duties and rights of employers and employees (typically, apprentices). In the event, state control of labour relations failed, as in practice, if not in theory, only the employers, and not the employed, had access to parliament.

In *Accession 1747*, using the first-person plural to which he was entitled as a member of the legislature which had just passed the law, Butler notes that, 'we have ... emancipated our northern Provinces from most of their *legal* Remains of Slavery: for *voluntary* Slavery cannot be abolished, at least not directly, by Law' (pp. 11–12). This refers to the first of the Master and Servant Acts (1747).[21] The 1747 Act extended the application of the Statute of Artificers (1562), which was still substantially intact and in force, although the incidence of setting and

---

[17] This was not an anachronism in Butler's time. John Rule (*The Labouring Classes in Early Industrial England 1750–1850*, London, 1988, p. 18) observed that '[the numbers] of the labouring people who depend[ed] on selling their labour power [had increased] a long way by 1750'. Employment law, however, had not yet changed to accommodate the growth of this industrial proletariat. Deakin and Wilkinson report that two-thirds of workers were already dependent on selling their labour by the early seventeenth century.

[18] An important point, because 'servants' are usually understood to be paid not by results but by virtue of their subordinate status.

[19] Deakin and Wilkinson note (p. 45) the traditional rural phenomenon of unmarried servants becoming married wage-labourers and thence (through savings) potentially entering the propertied classes.

[20] Josiah Tucker, *Charity Schools* sermon [Proverbs 22.6], 1766, p. 20. Plantation slaves, of course, could (but need not) suffer simultaneously from both domestic and political slavery.

[21] Deakin and Wilkinson, p. 63. Subsequent Acts were passed in 1758, 1766 and 1823. Initially relatively even-handed in regulating the master–servant relationship, they were increasingly hostile to tolerating the workers' ability to vary or terminate contracts.

applying wage rates declined steeply after 1700.[22] The new Act extended to industrial workers, whether or not their rates had been fixed by magistrates, and gave the latter wide powers to enforce the payment of wages and to enforce or void contracts. The Act also applied to workers on all fixed-term contracts, not, as before, only the annual ones which, in the course of nature, were a feature of agricultural work. Piece-workers and seafarers possessed *de facto* contracts and fell within the scope of the legislation.

A number of things may be noted. The first is Butler's concentration on the Act's effects on the 'northern Provinces', by which he means principally the province of York and specifically the diocese of Durham, with its long-established coalfields. This shows that he is still mindful of the former and future locale of his ministry.[23] The second is that the recent Act reinforced the right of the state, so that Butler is in effect supporting local government brakes on the wages system (in the absence of trade union organization, wage rates thus fixed were in effect maxima rather than minima)[24] and was thereby encouraging the continuance of a culture of the quasi-familial system of non-wage payments in kind. The third thing to note is the remark that '*voluntary* Slavery cannot be abolished'. As a moral point this does not need pressing on the modern reader, brought up on sentiments like '[They] died as men before their bodies died'.[25] It is, however, also a legal one. In a substantially informal economy, legal constraints were only enforceable by mutual agreement: a maximum wage could be circumvented by secret payments in kind, just as a minimum wage could be (and still is) undermined by the imposition of unpaid tasks. Workers' failure to assert and defend rights granted by parliament was their failure to accept agreed safeguards and to become morally despicable.[26]

Butler uses the fact of one's responsibility in law for one's household, in this newly extended sense, to rule that the ethics of charity covers the same ground (*Infirmary 1748*, pp. 26–7). He remarks in *Charity Schools 1745* (p. 10) that the Elizabethan laws which remained the basis of English parochial charity had been extended by the developing sense of children's needs – '[the poor

[22] Deakin and Wilkinson, p. 53.

[23] The Act specifies 'artificers, handicraftmen, miners, colliers, keelmen, pitmen, glassmen, potters and other labourers', indicating the predominance in the skilled industrial workforce of the coal trade between the north of England and London. Keelmen were crew on coastal barges, many involved in shipping coal down the east coast. Handicraftsmen were carpenters' mates and caulkers in shipbuilding. Artificers were skilled craftsmen such as nailers, joiners and cartwrights, again active in building ships and road vehicular transport.

[24] The success (quickly reversed) of the Gloucestershire weaving craftsmen in obtaining a minimum wage law in 1756 was sufficiently unusual to merit special notice by Deakin and Wilkinson (p. 53).

[25] W. H. Auden, 'The Shield of Achilles' (1952).

[26] D. J. Ibbetson, *A Historical Introduction to the Law of Obligations*, Oxford, 1999, Chapter 12, discusses the influence on the English common law of theories of natural law and the rise of theories about the will. Although he does not discuss Butler, he contrasts will theory with the law of contract (Chapter 11, instancing Hobbes), and discusses the question of damages, and thus by implication, that of responsibility and diminished responsibility. His instance (pp. 229–30) is an industrial case: an invitation to further research in the context of the present analysis.

children's] Case always requires more than mere Maintenance; it requires that they be educated in some proper Manner' (p. 10), something which Elizabethan philanthropy had not recognized. He had also gone past the seventeenth-century 'body politic' metaphor and seen that while the rich and poor need each other, they '*meet* upon a Foot of great Inequality ...' (*Spital 1740*, p. 7), an inequality which increases as society becomes richer, 'and the Evil [goes] on increasing' (*Charity Schools 1745*, p. 11). Thus for Butler, with his narrative of the growth of production and trade in luxuries, the concept of the social family changes over time as society changes.

The charity schools unavoidably brought together the care of children and the legal concept of the extended household. Child labour was endemic in eighteenth-century England (and, although softened by modern sensibilities, it remains so in agricultural areas) and orphan children could hardly expect to be exempted, especially in the light of the Elizabethan laws to which Butler refers. Habituating orphan children to the forms of adult life accorded with Butler's fundamental principle that 'Tempers of Mind' are strengthened by practice and repetition and in this, as in other ways, his doctrine extended past the merely epistemological environment of Locke's doctrine of ideas. Butler, demonstrating his readiness to go where his basic principles lead, draws on practices in some English and, he says, all Irish ('a neighbouring Kingdom', *Spital 1740*, p. 20) charity schools to formulate a proposal which was to become notorious for its inhumanity: the updating and rationalizing on a philosophical basis of the Elizabethan poor laws workhouse.

Butler proposes that all charity schools institute a regime of 'easy Labour, suitable to [the children's] Age' (*Spital 1740*, p. 20).[27] Inevitably, once implemented this led to charities funding the teachers' pay out of the profits, so that, unchecked, the culture arose of intensifying work even at the expense of the duty of care. This was fully in line with the practice in the eighteenth and previous centuries of farming public offices, in the absence of anything more than a rudimentary civil service.[28] However, since most charity school children were destitute and orphaned or illegitimate the incidence of crime and antisocial behaviour among recruits was high. Butler treats them accordingly. His doctrine of resentment made illegitimate any policy of societal revenge on criminals.[29] Laying down the radical principle that 'the only Purposes of Punishments less than capital, are to reform the Offenders themselves' (p. 20), he considers that a course of disciplined behaviour is essential:

---

[27] Work on Secker's and Tucker's development of Butler's ideas is in progress.
[28] Farming the Royal Navy's support services has been well treated by N. A. M. Rodger, *The Command of the Ocean*, London, 2004, Chapters 7, 12 and 19, and is familiar to the general reader from the diaries of Samuel Pepys. See also Clive Wilkinson, *The British Navy and the State in the Eighteenth Century*, *passim*, but especially Chapter 3.
[29] Chapter 2, p. 56.

[To] exclude utterly all sorts of Revel-mirth from Places where Offenders are confined, to separate the Young from the Old, and force them Both, in Solitude, with Labour and low Diet, to make the Experiment, how far their natural Strength of Mind can support them under Guilt and Shame and Poverty; this may deserve Consideration. (pp. 20–1)

What Butler did not anticipate is that such a regime inevitably implies a cultural seepage into the institutions' overall strategy. The charity schools movement applied the reform without exhaustive examination of its implications and came to make exaggerated claims about the virtually total effectiveness of this system in eliminating youth crime.[30] The result cut both ways: slaves on the West Indian plantations and charity school children in London were seen equally as proba-tioners, of legally similar status and with the same route into citizenship. Butler accentuates the rigour of his application of principles by prioritizing the deploy-ment of scarce pastoral resources to these subjects, if necessary at the expense of ministering to those adults condemned to death:

[It] must be acknowledged of greater Consequence, in a religious, as well as civil Respect, how Persons live, than how they die; it cannot but be even more incumbent on us, to endeavour, in all Ways, to reclaim those Offenders, who are to return again into the World, than those who are to be removed out of it: and the only effectual Means of reclaiming them, is to instil into them a Principle of Religion. (p. 21)

The reader, looking back across Victorian sentimentality, inevitably finds this observation shockingly brutal, but Butler is consistent in seeing benevolence as needing to find reciprocation in its object, by the child's accepting the freedoms and duties of a society morally bound only to eliminate ethical inequality, all in the context of a chronic lack of human and financial resources and a target group almost entirely lacking acculturation.[31] His giving priority to social rehabilitation over spiritual ease in death is not literally consonant with the Prayer Book (as he was to expound it in his 1749 Bristol charge) and points to a feature we will discuss later – the need for the individual to acquire legal and, above all, moral rights of citizenship. While noting the Church's lack of ministerial resources he fails to see that to propose a new system which required an intensified use of such resources was likely to be counter-productive. While he was careful to say that his suggestions merely deserved 'consideration' he forgot how persuasive might be the speculative thoughts of people in high public office, and of high intellectual authority, voiced on a great formal occasion to an elite audience.

---

30 This extended to the colonies and the slave converts. Preaching in 1828, J. C. Barker, a protégé of Beilby Porteus, chaplain to the bishop of Barbados and introducer of Porteus's monitor system of educa-tion, noted claims that even a week's attendance at a National School was effective (*The Education of the poor, a religious duty [Matt. 25.40]*, Grenada, 1828, p. 9).
31 The SPG Board meetings which Butler attended provide several examples of decisions which were forced by the need to prioritize the allocation of scarce resources. Discussions sometimes descended to refusals to provide a new Bible to a missionary.

However, the sermon extended further into society the emancipatory proposals of *SPG 1739* and prepared the way for *Charity Schools 1745*. Thus it was a powerful tool in creating British public policy. Whether the undoubted benefit to the slaves in calling forth a campaign of emancipation outweighed the oppressive effect on the nation's poor children might be debated.

Butler is possibly the first Briton to consider the question of resources philosophically. He repeats it in his last published sermon, *Infirmary 1748*. Noting that the demand for provision outstrips supply he expresses approval of the:

> settled Rules of the House for *Admission of Patients* ... that *none who are judged to be in an asthmatick, consumptive, or dying Condition be admitted on any Account whatsoever*. Harsh as these Words sound, they proceed out of the Mouth of Charity herself ... [that such applicants] be denied [care] ..., if their Case does not admit of Recovery, rather than that Others, whose Case does admit of it, be left to perish. (pp. 21–2)

While this principle may disturb squeamish modern opinion, it remains, in the last extremity, the standard practice of any organization under stress, such as emergency services in crises or armed forces in action, while the rationing of public service provision is a fact tacitly admitted but publicly concealed. We should also bear in mind the individual 'case conference' system which, as we will see, he advocated in tandem with it in *Charity Schools 1745*. He was entitled to expect that the general level of charitable culture would rise in future decades, as, indeed, in some ways it did. In giving an account of human relations structured on 'master–servant' lines Butler's version of the social contract is less obviously democratic than Locke's but it at least has the strengths of being founded on actually existing common and statute law rather than on a foundation myth and containing within it established routes towards socio-economic betterment, through mutual benevolence.

Charity and education

The main locus of Butler's doctrine about charity and education is *Charity Schools 1745*. More explicitly than *Fifteen Sermons* and *The Analogy* it describes laws and customs as effective because constitutional objectifications of human nature and subject to strengthening through habituation: there exists 'a Law of Reputation [which] enforces those civil Laws' (*Martyrdom 1741*, p. 6), and determines that self-love leads us to seek others' approval, so that we may even conceal our vices and profess virtues which we do not yet possess.

Charity Schools 1745 has two main themes. The first is the care of charity school children. It is notable that, in contrast to *SPG 1739*, he gives an account of child development which reverts to Aristotle as his main authority, in addition to his Proverbs text and Locke's doctrine of ideas and impressions (*Charity Schools 1745*, p. 3 ff), thus suggesting that it is only in politics and legal doctrines that he dissents from Aristotle. What is unique to humanity is child education, going beyond animals' nurturing their offspring's instinctual equipment and enabling each generation to build upon the legacy of its predecessors.

> Children have as much Right to some proper Education, as to have their Lives preserved; and that when this is not given them by their Parents, the Care of it devolves upon all Persons, it becomes the Duty of all, who are capable of contributing to it, and whose Help is wanted.
>
> (*Charity Schools 1745*, p. 5)

Why does Butler believe that there is such a right? First of all, it is sanctioned, at least implicitly, by his Proverbs 22.6 text: 'Train up a child in the way he should go: and when he is old he will not depart from it.' Another reason – entailing charitable institutions – is the typically Butlerian argument, whose context we have seen developed in *The Analogy*, that an educational curriculum based on 'the Judgment of the Publick, and the Determination of the Publick' is *ipso facto* secure. This is a challenge to a common deist argument whose source is in Locke:[32] that education may turn out to be a matter of instilling parental prejudices.[33] Locke had also argued (*Essay* I. iii. 23) that moral precepts based on crude doctrine expose young people to demoralizing disillusionment. For Butler, charitable institutions were a benevolent and less tainted base.

A third reason connects directly with Butler's conception of religion: 'Our Religion being thus practical, [consists] in a Frame of Mind and [a] Course of Behaviour, suitable to the Dispensation we are under, and which will bring us to our final Good' (*Charity Schools 1745*, p. 8). Without the enforcement of a course of behaviour, '[children, born in sin,] will grow up in a direct contrary Behaviour, and be hardened in direct contrary Habits. They will more and more corrupt themselves, and spoil their proper Nature' (p. 8). This is both orthodox and congruent with the distinction between the inner (the affection of self-love) and the outer (the affection of benevolence) and the mediating role of the conscience and religiously educated will in habituating morally good behaviour. Thus society has a duty to nurture and support its members: no single person's will could be sufficiently strong and consistent to lead a good life in a society which was in a vicious circle of moral degeneracy. Butler points out that Elizabethan legislation had long established this principle in general for the poor (p. 10), but he also proposes that local charity schools are not an adequate contribution to society's duty to the juvenile poor. 'And whenever there began to be Need of *legal* Provision for the *Maintenance* of the Poor, there must immediately have been Need also of some *particular* legal Provision in Behalf of poor Children for their Education; this not being included in what we call their Maintenance' (p. 10). Thus, there is a deficiency in the present legislation, which

---

[32] *Essay concerning Human Understanding* I. iii. 22.

[33] It is unnecessary for present purposes to exemplify the deist argument but relevant to note that the Christian rebuttal, in an account of wholesome parental influence, is always distinctively Butlerian, most intensively, in the SPCK annual sermons, from William Dodwell (1758) to Butler's editor, Samuel Hallifax (1779).

was eventually to be met by the National Schools movement, a development of the SPCK itself. Having gone so far, Butler then tactfully retreats, praising the relatively recent incorporation of the SPCK as a body with a national mission.[34]

For Butler the education of orphans was both a moral and legal duty of fitting children for useful lives from which their destitution would otherwise exclude them (p. 12).[35] This necessarily included not only education 'in the Principles of Religion, as well as civil Life' and domestic placement but also clothing, which should be 'in a Manner which cannot but be a Restraint upon the Children ... [because] if this ... gives them any little Vanity, as has been poorly objected, whilst they are Children, it is scarce possible but that it will have even quite a contrary Effect when they are grown up ...' (p. 12). Thus he is led to theorize the institutional provision of uniform clothing as a social signifier.[36] Uniforms, distinctively designed and coloured (in Britain at least, school jackets are still called 'blazers', after the Victorian medieval-cum-heraldic fashion), did indeed become a standard for British children, as symbols of the corporate will of the communities. It was Butler who here gave them their philosophical under-pinning.

The second theme of Butler's *Charity Schools 1745* is the proper adminis-tration of charitable enterprises. As an extension of his proposal for in-house work training Butler wished 'particularly in greater Endeavours [i.e. sectors of the manufacturing economy] to introduce Manufactures into these Schools; and in more particular Care [i.e. cases] to place the Children out to Employments in which they are most wanted, and may be most serviceable, and which are most suitable to their Ranks' (p. 23). But it should be noticed that he hedges his proposal with operational limitations. Instruction must be in 'easy Labour', through placing-out individuals, and 'must be approved by every one', which suggests a system, in modern terminology, of individual case conferences, with care taken to place those of 'a very weakly Constitution, or of a very distin-guished Capacity ... in Employments adapted to their particular Cases' (p. 16). Where there is disagreement in the management of a charity, he suggests:

> ... these Things must be referr'd to the Judgment of the Publick, and
> the Determination of the Publick complied with. Such Compliance is
> an essential Principle of all charitable Associations; for without it they

---

[34] Gladstone (*Butler's Works*, vol. II, p. 292) calls this 'a remarkable example of Butler's sagacious forethought', not seeing that it proceeds logically from his definition of charity. What is remarkable is not Butler's power of prophecy but his steadiness in following through to conclusions in social policy.

[35] Under the sixteenth-century Acts 'orphanage' meant the duty of guardianship exercised by the Mayor and Aldermen over the city's orphans under the age of twenty-one (OED, orphanage 2). Twenty-one being the age of majority, the City was legally obliged to seek to place orphans in apprenticeships or service, inevitably in the households of craftsmen and merchants.

[36] It should be remembered that eighteenth-century Britain, its aristocratic households no longer possessing posses of 'footmen', was a society largely without uniforms for the lower classes, apart from the coloured coats of the Army, which were essential for identification amid the mêlée of the battlefield. Even the Royal Navy, when first adopting uniforms in 1787, did so only for its officers (N. A. M. Rodger, *The Command of the Ocean*, London, 2004, p. 393).

> could not subsist at all ... Now he who refuses to help forward the good
> Work before us, because it is not conducted exactly in his own Way,
> breaks in upon that general Principle of Union [in this good cause] ...
>
> (p. 23)

The term 'publick' must include at least the more respectable stratum of the working population, the more so because, in the last analysis, charity schools depended on placing orphans in workshops and domestic service and on fund-raising through parochial collections. Perhaps because of both his own origins and the political tendency of the Bristol merchant class Butler remains acutely aware of the culture of Dissent, repeating his *SPG 1739* warning about the need for unity. The Church of England is positioned to lead society's united charitable work, and to do so in a non-sectarian way.

There is, however, a radical defect in Established Christianity: a lack of care for the spiritual well-being of the poor, arising from:

> [the] Discontinuance of that religious Intercourse between Pastors and People in private, which remains in Protestant Churches abroad, as well as in the Church of *Rome*; and from our small publick Care and Provision for keeping up a Sense of Religion in the lower Rank, except by distributing religious Books. (p. 15)[37]

Since without the SPCK there would have been no religious books to distribute, this suggestion of an unspecified range of pastoral neglect constitutes fairly direct criticism of the shallowness of support for the parochial clergy. However, he considers that the parochial charity schools benefited the local population, both rich and poor, working an effect on community morale (pp. 20–1). He notes that some people of rank fear the literacy of the poor:

> [By] what odd Reverse of Things has it happened, that such as pretend to be distinguished for the Love of Liberty, should be the only Persons who plead for keeping down the Poor[?] ... For till within a Century or two, all Ranks were nearly upon a Level as to the Learning in question ... [The] Character of the common People, with whom these Children are to live ... may more or less defeat the good Effects of their Education. And so likewise may the Character of Men of Rank under whose Influence they are to live. (pp. 13, 20)

Thence Butler restates in economic terms John Foxe's purely religious diagnosis: the creation of the reformed Church of England on the back of the mass production of vernacular bibles after the invention of printing. In Butler's account, before the printing press 'all ranks were nearly upon a level as to ... learning' – equally deprived, that is. The Reformation, he supposes, plausibly enough, was driven by the better classes in the name of liberty, the invention of printing being 'providentially reserved until these latter Ages ... to be instru-

---

[37] As we saw in Chapter 4, this was a point which would be returned to in the Durham Charge.

mental for the future in carrying on the appointed Course of Things' (p. 13).[38] From his observation about the effects of print technology he continues, 'And if this be a Blessing, we ought to let the Poor, in their Degree, share it with us. The present State of Things and Course of Providence plainly leads us to do so' (p. 13). This is because:

> ... if we do not, it is certain ... that they will be upon a greater Disadvantage, on many Accounts, especially in populous Places, than they were in the dark Ages: for they will be more ignorant, comparatively with the People about them, than they were then; and the ordinary Affairs of the World are now put in a Way which requires, that they should have some Knowledge of Letters, which was not the Case then. And therefore, to bring up the Poor in their former Ignorance ... would be, not to keep them in the same, but to put them into a lower Condition of Life than what they were formerly ... [Unless] Superiors of the present Age are greater Examples of Decency, Virtue and Religion, than those of former Times; ... their Example should have this greater Influence over the Poor ... (pp. 13–15)

Thus, the Protestant reformed religion of personal redemption drove the need for a consensual social policy of redistributing wealth and knowledge. Butler's is a very early and elegant diagnosis of this. We can see, more easily than his contemporaries, how the acceleration of technological development plunges the poor into new depths of deprivation, whether financial (deskilling, pressure on pay), social (the destruction of local cultures by monopolistic forces) or intellectual (information poverty) – a concept of exponential decline reminiscent of *The Analogy*'s theorizing.[39] Butler thinks that if 'Superiors' are to retain their eminence – his analysis could accommodate but does not require an equalitarian revolution – public ethical standards need to rise: upwardly redistributed wealth and knowledge, the product of capital-intensive technological innovation, must be accompanied by voluntary charitable social policy. He therefore addresses the question to the City's aldermen, leaders of the expanding middle class. We have seen that a permanent policy of ceding advantage to the disadvantaged would, in Butlerian terms, be contrary to the unmediated affection of self-love in the advantaged, while the affection of benevolence by itself when applied to individuals is, as Butler argues plausibly, insufficient to resist the tendency towards inequality built into the technological and capitalist structures of contemporary society. Thus, organized charity becomes a necessity if the healthy dynamic between self-love and benevolence is to continue to define

---

[38] 'The Lord began to work for his church ... with printing, writing, and reading ... [so that] either the pope must abolish printing, or he must seek a new world to reign over: for else, as this world standeth, printing doubtless will abolish him' (John Foxe, *Acts and Monuments*, ed. Josiah Pratt, 4th edn, London, [1877?], volume III, pp. 719–20).

[39] From a generally optimistic perspective Manuel Castells is the modern originator of this analysis. See his seminal work, *The Information Age: Economy, Society, and Culture*, 1996–2000, and especially *The Rise of the Network Society* (1996).

what is truly human. The ethical becomes the economic, as it does with Adam Smith, who knew Butler, possibly directly and certainly through Reid.

It is likely that Butler was the first British thinker to formulate these problems. Consequently, he might be seen as a political thinker as profoundly insightful as even Hobbes. Earlier accounts, whether of ethics (Shaftesbury), politics (Hobbes) or epistemology (Locke), have essentially static conceptions of the State. For Butler the mind was a bifurcated dynamic structure, as was the extrusion of the mass of minds, civil society. Mental and moral health was the product of the engagement of conscience and will. Stability was provided by good theology and charitable practice. Behind Butler is Hobbes's fear of an anarchic nature. In Butler's case social stability is threatened by the theoretical inadequacies of natural religion, as diagnosed in *The Analogy*.

Missions and slavery

The above account reveals Butler's extrovert view of a Church venturing into a new phase of shaping society through engagement with economic and social policy. He seems suddenly to become a very modern, post-Enlightenment, thinker. The primacy of the role of the will requires cohesion among both the general population and the leadership, and hence requires revisiting the concept of the Church's 'mission'. We will approach this through a discussion of *SPG 1739*.

Butler's SPG sermon was preceded by Herring's (1738) and may also be seen in the context of Maddox's (1734). Maddox was born a Presbyterian – the first of three preachers in nine years who became bishops from Presbyterian origins – and was currently Dean of Wells and Clerk of the Closet to Queen Caroline (in which post he was succeeded by Butler); the month after preaching his SPG sermon he was appointed Bishop of St. Asaph.

Theologically Maddox is interesting because he emphasizes the fears which humankind feels as consequences of the sense of sin.[40] Universally, religion includes 'expiatory Rites and Ceremonies … [to] pacify an offended Deity' (p. 6) and recognize 'moral Obligations, which certainly arise from the State and Constitution of Things appointed by the great Creator' (p. 8). Christianity differs from merely cultic religion in its possession of prophecies, martyr testimony and apostolic doctrine (p. 14). The perception of Christianity as bearing a cultic dimension (and consequently as separable from conceptions of natural justice)[41] is to be noted; Butler makes the same point in *The Analogy*.[42] When discussing the slave population Maddox had quoted Bosman's *Description of the Coast*

---

[40] Isaac Maddox, *Sermon … before the [SPG] [Titus 2:11–13]*, London, J. Downing, 1734, p. 5.
[41] This is a point congruent to that about the 'Ultimate Good' raised in relation to Butlerian ethics by Henry Sidgwick, *The Methods of Ethics*, 1907 edn, pp. 3–4.
[42] See Chapter 3, p. 120.

of Guinea[43] as an authority and suggested that there be 'a *constant Direction* to every *Minister* employed Abroad, to *instruct* the Negroes that belong to the Inhabitants allotted to his Care' (p. 28) because 'The harder State of Bondage these poor Creatures, engaged in Labour for our Pleasure and Advantage, must now endure: the more reasonable it is, to alleviate their Minds with good Principles ... ' (p. 29). Maddox certainly thinks slavery is a bad thing, but the slave trade, because it did not bring slaves into British ports, was neither illegal nor contrary to national security, which alone, by precedent, could be used to restrain trade. At this point the legality of slavery in Britain was not well-tested in the courts. Whig doctrine was that legality and morality were virtually coextensive,[44] but in this case they seemed not to be. In 1729, contrary to Chief Justice Holt's 1706 ruling on the common law in *Smith v. Brown and Cooper*, attorney-general Sir Philip Yorke and solicitor-general Charles Talbot, Butler's own patron, had given their opinion that a slave was not automatically free in England.[45] Colonial slavery was certainly not illegal, because it was not certain that English common and statute law applied and in any case governors-general could not enforce them against the wishes of the local population.

In 1738 Herring tried to tackle this.[46] He allocated the non-white population of the American colonies to the category of the 'poor', by which he meant lacking manufactured goods (p. 8), 'placed out of the Opportunity and Temptations to Luxury, ignorant indeed of the true Religion, but not Enemies to it' (p. 14). The slaves' (and Indians') poverty would aid their reception of religion, while their natural intellectual faculties needed only to be diverted from false cultic gods ('Rites and Services', p. 20). 'Christianity is more the Religion of the Heart, than of the Head, and the Excellence and Majesty of it consists in the Reasonableness and Simplicity of its Doctrines, productive of an innocent and useful, and pious Life' (p. 29). This simplicity made for universal appeal.

Butler's *SPG 1739* takes as its text Matthew 24.14: 'And this gospel of the kingdom shall be preached in all the world, for a witness unto all nations.' It begins with a powerfully synthetic passage:

> The general Doctrine of Religion ... having been established by repeated Revelations in the first Ages of the World ... to be honestly preserved pure and intire ... And though Reason, almost intuitively, bare witness to the Truth of this moral System of Nature, yet it soon appeared, that *they did not like to retain God in their knowledge* [Romans 1.28], as to any Purposes of real Piety. (p. 3)

---

[43] Willem Bosman, *A New and Accurate Description of the Coast of Guinea*, London, J. Knapton & D. Midwinter, 1705.
[44] This doctrine found expression in the Constitution of the USA and continues, possibly with unfortunate results, in modern American moral philosophy (see Chapter 6, pp. 207–10).
[45] Hugh Thomas, *The Slave Trade*, New York, 1997, p. 474.
[46] Thomas Herring, *A Sermon preached before the [SPG] [Matthew 11.5]*, London, J. & J. Pemberton, 1738.

We previously noted exegetical patches and strategies in *Fifteen Sermons*, but the present case is of equal power. It anchors an application[47] of the Matthew 24.14 text in a combination of epiphanies from the Pentateuch (of which Christ's ministry was the historically decisive and sufficient republication), a Lockean definition of reason and Paul's diagnosis of the wilful and systematic perversion which is the failure of conscience to mediate the affections. These are the three fixed points – exegetical, epistemological and ethical – on which Butler builds his account of the mission of charity to all within the Church of England's sphere of influence.

Butler's position is typically economical and powerful. In the Old Testament, God had appeared to Jewish prophets, and reason – in Locke's terms, the combination of ideas, working 'almost intuitively' – is a sure guide to the essential and necessary principles of piety, virtue and salvation. As we have seen, the phrase 'almost intuitively' is Butler's 'fuzzy' alternative to Locke, and exhibits a degree of remoteness from the Cartesian account: the mind, grounded in the affections, has been reassessed as a dynamic and soulful thing rather than the autonomic clearing-house of sense impressions which was the legacy of Locke's *Essay*. In such a context, Matthew Tindal's account of *Christianity as* [being as] *Old as the Creation,* and *the Gospel* [as] *a Republication of the Religion of Nature*, published as recently as 1730 and currently in the full spate of controversy, was a powerful factor and it is notable that Butler follows his own tactic from *The Analogy* of avoiding a head-on confrontation.[48] Indeed, he goes on to mention 'this general Doctrine of Religion' – that is, 'that all things are under the Direction of One righteous Governor' (*SPG 1739*, p. 3) – as 'authoritatively republished in its Purity' by the 'particular Dispensation of Providence ... manifested to all Men [by the Christian revelation]' (p. 4). Elsewhere he characterizes this republication in psychological terms: Old Testament religion is the 'fear of God', New Testament 'faith in Christ' (*Charity Schools 1745*, pp. 7–8). The power of revelation comes from the fact that it is 'a distinguished Favour to us, and naturally strikes us with the greatest Awe' (*SPG 1739*, p. 11). And, indeed, insofar as the deists advanced attractive arguments, based in contemporary natural science, Butler co-opts them for his own purposes. The three-part formula with which *SPG 1739* begins, however, is completed by one of Paul's most strenuous passages: his account of the slide into sin which is framed as an attack on male and female sexual perversion, an attack on the *mores* of the contemporary Graeco-Roman aristocracy and intelligentsia. This does not seem a synthesis from which would emerge naturally an announcement by Butler that the political ruling class should be co-opted into the SPG's missionary project. As so often with a thinker somewhat at an angle to his contemporaries, it is interesting to see how he gets there.

---

[47] In the technical sense that the sermon 'applies' exegesis to its subject.
[48] We noted in Chapter 4 his advice, in the Durham Charge, about the inappropriateness of controversy in the pulpit.

First of all there is an unusually sustained effort at demonstrating that the Bible teaches that 'the Salvation of every man cannot but depend upon his Behaviour ... and is necessarily his own Concern, in a Sense, in which it cannot be another's' (pp. 9–10).[49] This involves quotations from Ezekiel, Luke, Job, Proverbs, 1 Corinthians, John, Revelation and Ecclesiasticus, for Butler an ostentatiously wide selection of authorities.

He proceeds to a statement about the visible Church and its role in spreading the Gospel and maintaining affiliations, asserting that it is each actual church building which bears the Church's value and mission. In a figure which was to be repeated and elaborated by several SPG and CMS preachers in the early nineteenth century, the stones of the church are its fabric as much as the communicants are.[50]

> [By] an Institution of external Religion fitted for all Men ... it pleased God to unite Christians in Communities or visible Churches ... over a great Part of the World; and thus perpetuate a general Publication of the Gospel ... [Even] such of these Communities, as ... have corrupted Christianity the most, have yet continually carried, together with their Corruptions, the Confutation of them ... [Any] particular Church, in whatever Place established, is like *a City that is set on an hill, which cannot be hid*, inviting all who pass by, to enter into it ... They are reminded of that Religion, which natural Conscience attests the Truth of: and they may ... obtain eternal Life ... And *Lastly*, Out of these Churches have all along gone forth Persons, who have preached the Gospel in remote Places, with greater or less good Effect: For the Establishment of any Profession of Christianity, however corrupt, I call a good Effect ... notwithstanding it may for some Time lie quite neglected. (*SPG 1739*, pp. 5–7)

It is immediately obvious that there are several unusual elements in this passage. Thus, the practice of revealed Christianity is described as a matter of the institution of 'external religion': instruction and discipline, in visible churches. Butler merely assumes, tacitly, the existence of apprehensions of the Holy Spirit. The Christian community has a range of experiences and beliefs and it is not essential for everyone to have these experiences but only for everyone to participate in the whole community. The term 'Church' holds in a synthesis all manifestations of religion: the Church as local community, as global organization, as exclusive gathering, as physical building in which the Bible is displayed for the passer-by, as the physical home base for the American missionary. Access to the Gospels, as effected for the English by Tyndale, guarantees the validity of the communion and its mission, because such communions carry the seeds

---

[49] As edited by Gladstone, this passage provides an example of his editorial mangling of the flow of the text by imposing subdivisions contrary to its sense.
[50] A classic example is Henry Venn's sermon, *Academical Studies Subservient to the Edification of the Church [1 Corinthians 14.12]*, Cambridge, 1828, with its play on the double meaning of the root word 'edify'.

of their purification within their own resources. Thus, 'the bare establishment of Christianity in any place, even the external form and profession of it, is a very important and valuable effect. It is a serious call upon men to attend to the natural and the revealed doctrine of religion ...' (*SPG 1739*, p. 15). Thus literal church-building and the charitable donation of private capital, and even parliamentary taxation, for that purpose, are key: the Church of England had no centralized income.

It is possible to suggest reasons why Butler should take this position on 'external Religion'. For *Accession 1747* he was to choose as his text 1 Timothy 2.1–2:

> I exhort, that first of all, supplications, prayers, intercessions, and giving of thanks be made for all men: for kings, and for all that are in authority; that we may lead a quiet and peaceable life in all godliness and honesty.
>
> (p. 5)

This may be borne in mind when, in *SPG 1739*, Butler preaches that '[private worship] will by no means excuse the Neglect of [one's] appointed Part in keeping up the Profession of Christianity amongst Mankind' and that such neglect 'must prevent those good Purposes, which were intended to be answered [by Christian communities] ... over the World'. Adding that public worship is a direct injunction from God (p. 8) and that 'The visible Constitution and Course of Nature, the moral Law written in our Hearts, the positive Institutions of Religion ... are all Witnesses ... in behalf of God, to Mankind' (pp. 8–9), he draws on Ezekiel and Luke (p. 9) to conclude his argument that the importance of evangelizing is principally the bearing of witness (pp. 8–9) enabling people to:

> unite in religious Communities ... Christianity is very particularly to be considered as a Trust, deposited with us in Behalf of Others, in Behalf of Mankind, as well as for our own Instruction ... No one has a Right to be called a Christian, who doth not do somewhat in his Station ... [to] assist in keeping up the Profession of Christianity where he lives ... [and to] assist in doing it in our Factories abroad; and in the Colonies to which we are related, by their being peopled from our own Mother-country ... and nearer yet is the Obligation upon such Persons in particular, as have the Intercourse of an advantageous Commerce with them. (p. 12)

The connection between the missionary bearing of witness and the ministration to the overseas subjects of the Crown is, as we have seen in earlier chapters, linguistic and cultural rather than nationalist and politically expedient. It leads naturally to the thought which increasingly shaped Anglican thinking about the overseas missions as the Royal Navy and the British merchant marine came to dominate global communications: that 'Navigation and Commerce should be consecrated to the Service of Religion' (p. 14). This thought is in no way original to Butler – it is found even in Gilbert Burnet's founding SPG sermon – but his theological approach to it is distinctive and powerful: the disciplining of the natural conscience by regular worship, the subjective-objective nature of godliness, the crucial importance of 'external Religion'.

It is here that the anti-deist strand in Butler's ministry engages with the charitable element. We have already seen that moral conduct is impossible without the reception and practice of revealed religion, because natural philosophy and natural religion are inadequate, even though they are a sound basis for receiving 'republished' Christianity. This issue, of course, was thoroughly discussed in the seventeenth century and in taking it up Butler in one sense reaches back past the contemporary deists and the school of sentiment and sensibility. In the fourth chapter of her study of eighteenth-century evangelism in the American colonies, *The Poor Indians: British Missionaries, Native Americans, and Colonial Sensibility*, Laura Stevens develops an account of the connection between the Church of England's theological campaign against deism domestically and some characteristics of its approaches to the rhetoric and methods of its missionary movement, specifically of the SPG. She describes the tension between, on the one hand, the proto-'Sentimental' compassion for the 'poor Indians' expressed from within the deist sphere of intellectual influence and, on the other, from within the orthodox Christian sphere of influence, what she denotes as the more 'callous' belief that the unconverted were damned (Stevens, p. 117). While one would not concede the full force of this dichotomy – the belief that the great pagan Greek philosophers would be saved featured in the early, pre-patristic, Church and the damnation of those to whom the gospel had not been made available was never mainstream doctrine – she is surely correct in thinking that charity rather than sentiment was the basis of the Anglican strategy. She also (p. 134) identifies Butler's explanation of the phenomenon of Christianity's spread through evangelizing rather than simultaneous universal publication: quoting Butler to the effect that '[God] has appointed, that Men should be instructed by the Assistance of their Fellow-Creatures' she points out that this is 'because [God] wanted to link humans more closely together'. This describes well the society-building nature of Butler's concept of benevolence and hints at what we have called his church-building theology.

As Stevens observes, the SPG was widely criticized in the early eighteenth century for its lack of missionary dynamism. However, membership of the Church of England was, constitutionally, restricted to natives of explicitly identified realms, except for those dissenters exempted by Act of Parliament,[51] and it did not aspire to be a catholic communion, but only that part of the catholic Church which comprised the English nation and, above all, was administered

---

[51] '(§1) [No] manner of obedience, or subjection, within his Majesty's realms and dominions, is due to any … foreign power, but that the King's power, within his realms of England, Scotland, and Ireland, and all other his dominions and countries, is the highest power under God … [The] Church of England, by law established under the King's Majesty, is … a true and Apostolical Church … (§11) Whoever shall hereafter affirm or maintain, That there are within this realm other meetings, assemblies, or congregations of this King's born subjects, than such as by the laws of this land are held and allowed … let him be excommunicated …' (*Constitutions and Canons Ecclesiastical … of the Church of England*, §§1, 11).

by an authorized clergy. Whether in Ireland or North America the Church of England was never sure that its mission extended beyond this limitation.[52] There would appear to be no claimed legal right to attempt to encompass within the Church of England people not born subjects of the British crown, while active relationships with foreign (and domiciled) Protestant communions and the Orthodox Churches continued to express the vision of a catholic Reformed Church.[53] Thus, the Church of England was more inhibited than the Roman Catholic Church in evangelizing the world's population and when it finally accepted the legitimacy of undertaking a worldwide mission it was in the light of secular events: time and again in the late eighteenth and early nineteenth centuries preachers of the SPG, SPCK and CMS were to argue that the success of the Royal Navy in establishing global hegemony and of the British merchant marine in dominating inter-continental trade was proof of a new divine dispensation and the working through of Old and New Testament prophecies – that a missionary duty had been imposed, willy-nilly, on the English nation. However, in the period before the Peace of Paris (1763), which effectively created this situation, this was not an evident duty of the Church of England and a sustainable Anglican communion overseas barely existed.[54] Given the existence of the legally established Presbyterian Church of Scotland it is difficult, indeed, to see how the very term 'Anglican communion' could have been used without Clause 1 of the Constitution being rewritten.[55]

It is typical of Butler that his approach to the problem caused by this confluence of the pastoral, legal and constitutional was to apply the governing principles of his philosophy. Before discussing this, however, it is interesting to note his later involvement in an attempt at a reform which would attack the problem at its constitutional root. Successive Bishops of London, notionally responsible for the members of the Church of England overseas but not permitted suffragans, had appointed commissaries to supervise the colonial clergy, but their remoteness from the home base had severely undermined their local authority. Numerous preachers of the SPG anniversary sermon had called for reform in the 1730s and 1740s, most notably Thomas Secker, who had renewed the call for the appointment of suffragan bishops. When Bishop Edmund Gibson's patent

---

[52] See the discussions in Nigel Yates, *The Religious Condition of Ireland 1770–1850*, Oxford, 2006, Chapter 1 and Rowan Strong, *Anglicanism and the British Empire*, Oxford, 2007, Chapter 2.

[53] Contemporary unease at the presence of protestant Moravian bishops in American colonies bereft of Anglican bishops was caused more by doubts about their political loyalty and by a sense of discriminatory unfairness, than by their ecclesiastical affiliation. See pp. 337 and 343 in Stephen Taylor, 'Whigs, Bishops and America: The Politics of Church Reform in Mid-eighteenth-century England', *The Historical Journal*, vol. 36, no. 2 (1993), pp. 331–56. The SPG supported German protestant congregations in America – both in the future USA and later in Canada – and was to hold funds for European protestant groups (for example, the Vaudois and Debritzen trusts). See Bob Tennant, *Corporate Holiness*, Chapter 2.

[54] Before the creation of the Bishopric of Nova Scotia in 1787 the only ecclesiastical structure overseas was the radically flawed system of commissaries of the Bishop of London, described below.

[55] The Constitution was amended in 1865 without this point being met.

to appoint commissaries had expired with his death in 1748 his successor in the London see, Thomas Sherlock, did not seek its renewal but instead put a paper to the king, the government and the SPG proposing the creation of American bishops with strictly limited powers. This paper became known, and in 1765 was published as, Butler's, although there is no direct evidence that he wrote it.[56] The paper proposed that:

> no coercive power is desired over the laity ... but only a power to regulate the behaviour of the clergy who are in episcopal orders ... That nothing is desired for such bishops, that may in the least interfere with the dignity, or authority, or interest of the governor, or any other office of state ... [That the] maintenance of such bishops not to be at the charge of the colonies [i.e. the colonial authorities; and that] no bishops are intended to be settled [*sic*] in places where the government is left in the hands of Dissenters ... But authority to be given, only to ordain clergy for such church of England congregations as are among them, and to inspect into the manners and behaviour of the said clergy, and to confirm the members thereof.

These proposals adroitly avoid the difficulties implicit in attempting the exportation of the English ecclesiastical constitution to the colonies and, despite being frustrated by domestic as well as colonial complications,[57] in effect were to form the basis of the Episcopal Church of the USA. The whole controversy belongs to the history of Church, Union and Empire rather than to Butler but the discussions emphasized the Church's modesty in asserting any legal claim to religious supervision of the colonial populations and, consequently, an even greater hesitation about the legitimacy of proselytizing among non-English peoples beyond the 'households' of the colonial populations.

To focus more narrowly to Butler's approach, it should be remembered that Whig attitudes were governed by the concepts of political liberty and property rights. In the case of subject peoples these could conflict. For Aristotle men (women were somewhat at a tangent to this subject) could involuntarily lose their rights, that is, their status as a person, in such cases as debt, or military defeat, when capture inevitably resulted in slavery. Such doctrines were reinforced by the Old Testament, in which forced conversions and buying and selling into slavery are too common to require illustration. Butler's approach to the enslaved peoples, and those on the fringes of the English sphere of influence

---

[56] Near-contemporary opinion was that he was the author: see East Apthorp's *Review of Dr. Mayhew's Remarks on the Answer to his Observations on the Charter and conduct of the [SPG]*, London, John Rivington, 1765, p. 55; the *Annual Register*, London, J. Dodsley, 1765, p. 108; and Beilby Porteus, *Life of Archbishop Secker*, p. 63. The attribution was not challenged at the time but has been denied by Stephen Taylor ('Whigs, Bishops and America', see his note 58) and Ingram, *Religion, Reform and Modernity in the Eighteenth Century*, Chapter 7. The question is complex, but the present author thinks it likeliest that Butler produced at least a draft for Sherlock's consideration. This is the subject of work in progress.

[57] Stephen Taylor, 'Whigs, Bishops and America', gives a convincing account of the difficulties.

is of a piece with the American bishops paper and, indeed, to avoid the murky waters of constitutionalism, he resorts, unusually, to the deployment of irony.

The passage Butler gives to consideration of African slaves in the British possessions is short enough to quote entire:

> Of these our Colonies, the Slaves ought to be considered as inferior Members, and therefore to be treated as Members of them; and not merely as Cattle or Goods, the Property of their Masters. Nor can the highest Property, possible to be acquired in these Servants, cancel the Obligation to take care of their religious Instruction. Despicable as they may appear in our Eyes, they are the Creatures of God, and of the Race of Mankind, for whom Christ died: and it is inexcusable to keep them in Ignorance of the End, for which they were made; and the Means, whereby they may become Partakers of the general Redemption. On the contrary, if the Necessity of the Case requires, that they be treated with the very utmost Rigour, that Humanity will at all permit, as they certainly are; and, for our Advantage, made as miserable as they well can be in the present World; this surely heightens our Obligation to put them into as advantageous a Situation as we are able, with regard to Another. (*SPG 1739*, p. 13)

When Butler says that slaves are not the 'Property' of their masters he is relying on a narrow legal definition: it was never proposed that slave-owners had property rights in the full sense of unrestricted use and disposal of assets, such as the right of life and death. This is revealed by the technical use of the term 'Property' in the second sentence quoted above ('Nor can the highest Property ...'). Butler proceeds to apply the term 'Servant' to slaves and it becomes obvious that the term cannot be taken as an anachronistic euphemism.[58]

By including slaves in the class of servants Butler is in essence treating the purchase price as a sort of transfer fee between discrete legal systems and setting aside the fact, probably contrary to the common law, of the individual becoming subject to sale and contractual bondage. Moreover, and again contrary to Aristotle and his contemporary followers, slaves are for Butler full human beings ('for whom Christ died')[59] who, if drawn into the British and Anglican family would become culturally English.[60] The modern reader feels discomfort at the suggestion that the slaves may be 'despicable' in 'our' eyes, but we may remember that Butler would also describe as despicable English miners who failed to uphold their own rights. However, he proceeds to observe that

---

[58] Among the multitude of frustrations for Butler's biographers is the loss of his correspondence with a Mr Vassall of Cornwall, inheritor of a slave plantation in Jamaica, about 'the lawfulness of retaining a possession which was to be cultivated by slave labour' (Bartlett, p. 308).

[59] This point still needed emphasizing later in the century. When Josiah Tucker, in his 1766 Charity Schools sermon dropped the remark, 'the Offspring of *Hottentots* become *Hottentots* themselves' (p. 4), the very casualness of his implication that, suitably educated, they might become English instead was itself calculated to be rhetorically striking.

[60] Again, this is made explicit by Tucker (*Charity School* sermon, p. 5) and was to be taken up by Beilby Porteus in his own SPG sermon.

they are 'certainly' treated with 'the very utmost Rigour' – conduct which is not required towards a servant and fellow-human although it might be legitimized by 'Necessity' – and, 'for our Advantage' are made 'as miserable as they well can be'. This third fact goes beyond what was legally, let alone ethically, permissible and we cannot avoid concluding that Butler was speaking with an irony originating in 'despicable' (which denotes something subjective in 'us'), moving through 'Rigour' (a condition of interaction between 'us' and 'them'), and reaching the height of the crescendo with 'miserable' (something subjective in 'them' and culpable in 'us', its cause). The word 'despicable' is then seen in its full meaning. The northern miners were slaves voluntarily, but the plantation slaves were not willing parties to their status. Their moral health depends crucially on parliament and its laws – and Butler has just announced ('... we ...') that he had been a party in the creation of just such a law. Thus, Butler employs Swiftian irony for a strategic purpose, something without precedent in the series of SPG sermons and with very few successors in that series until late in the century. Butler was undermining the SPG's collective satisfaction with its probity, and doing so from a basis in English common law.[61]

Butler moves discussion of slavery away from questions about whether a human individual could be another's property (which, if put thus baldly, could under English common law be settled only one way) and towards acceptance that slaves enjoyed the same legal employment rights as free servants and the same claims on charitable behaviour, that is, within the scope of the state's regulation of class relationships and charitable organizations' provision for the 'poor'. In doing so Butler heads off the Sentimental treatment of the slave as a victim and lays the foundation of practical public policy. Thus Beilby Porteus, in his tract *An Essay towards a Plan for the more effectual Civilization and Conversion of the Negroe Slaves, on the [SPG] Trust Estate in Barbadoes* (1783, and subsequently much reworked and reprinted) was to provide routes both to conversion and to legal and economic emancipation which while Sentimental in imagery were described in micro-management terms. Unlike Butler, however, Porteus sees such charitable endeavours as an *imitatio Christi* and in several sermons provides a Sentimental iconography and psychology of Christ in life.[62] Closer to Butler is Yorick Smithies in his *Cooperation of Human Benevolence with the Divine [1 Corinthians 3:9]* (30 June 1789), preached for the benefit of the Colchester Sunday schools and an early example of the genre, only five years after Robert Raikes's pioneering venture in Gloucester.[63] Sturdily anti-Christological, Smithies sees his benevolent fellow-citizens in a voluntary

---

[61] Should the reader suppose that Butler was conservative, reactionary or nostalgic by the lights of his own times, it is well to note that Deakin and Wilkinson (p. 51) record that the legal framework created by the 1562 Act started to be dismantled only in 1813 – sixty years after Butler's death.

[62] Bob Tennant, 'Sentiment, Politics, and Empire: A Study of Beilby Porteus's Anti-Slavery Sermon', in *Discourses of Slavery and Abolition*, ed. B. Carey, M. Ellis and S. Salih, London, 2004, pp. 166–9.

[63] Yorick Smithies, *Cooperation of Human Benevolence with the Divine [1 Corinthians 3:9]*, Colchester, W Keymer, [1789]. Raikes himself seems heavily influenced by Butler.

relationship with God, their charity being analogical to the divine love. The 'uniform, and active, and mutual cooperation' (p. 12) in a course of collective benevolence creates a 'common cause' as part of the Church as the body of Christ. Thus at national and local levels voluntary societies were increasingly united in adopting Butler's voice. Superficially, the biggest difference between Butler and Smithies is the latter's deployment of statistics, in this case the two hundred-thousand children accommodated by Sunday schools after the first five years' development ('The present state of your schools is in *full* proof of your merits', he puns, p. 16, italics supplied).[64] This was an inevitable consequence of the charity sermons being in the nature of annual reports and therefore giving accounts of work done and progress made. It was the interplay of theology and statistics which was to give the charity and missionary society sermon genres their distinctive character from the late eighteenth century.

Thus, Butler called to missionary arms not a religious elite but those who were operatively nearest the work. His view of society was that it constituted a field of, as it were, overlapping circles: family, friends, neighbours, countrymen, Christians of all nations, humankind generally.[65] It is easier and more natural to see family and friends as neighbours, but the example of the Good Samaritan shows that this ease is habitual not categorical. Indeed, this suggestion is rein-forced in *SPG 1739*. Moving to consider the 'Natives' of colonized territo-ries (pp. 13–14), Butler says that they are 'in all Respects, of one Family with ourselves, the Family of Mankind ... [with a] *common Salvation* [Jude 3] ... [and capable] of moral Improvements' (pp. 13–14). This forces the conclusion that it is charity which underpins not only attitudes and policy towards slaves but also towards the servant class as just defined. 'For incidental Circumstances ... appropriate all the general Obligations of Charity to particular Persons; and make such and such Instances of it, the Duty of One Man rather than Another' (p. 13).

As late as 1780, when the American Revolution had temporarily disturbed the SPG's agenda for the Americas, John Thomas (bishop of Rochester) signalled unease:

> ... [ministrations were supplied] to many native Indians, and negro-slaves; who, after due instruction, were solemnly admitted to Christian baptism; which although it did not entitle them to civil freedom, yet, in a

64 Smithies borrowed this statistic from a sermon preached by Raikes's friend Samuel Glasse in Pain-swick, Gloucestershire, in 1786 (*The Piety, Wisdom, and Policy, of Promoting Sunday-Schools [Deuter-onomy 31.12–3]*, London, Rivingtons, 1786, p. 5n). Glasse dedicated his sermon to Raikes, 'an instructor of the ignorant, and a father to the poor'. Apart from in the annual SPG reports, reliable statistics in every area of socially charitable Christianity were rare and examples abound of their use even when genera-tions out of date. 'Facts' relating to the SPG's Codrington slave plantation in Barbados over more than a century are a particularly flagrant example, while, lacking an administrative infrastructure, the SPCK's statistics about the non-metropolitan English, Scottish and Welsh charity schools went unrevised for decades at a time. See Bob Tennant, *Corporate Holiness*, Chapter 4.
65 We saw in Chapter 4 that in his will Butler, a childless bachelor, wrote of having taken William Emm into his 'family', as a servant.

religious sense, they were *no more strangers and foreigners, but fellow-citizens with the Saints, and of the household of God* ...[66]

Thomas's phrase, 'the household of God', bringing Pauline doctrine (Ephesians 2.19) into the contemporary missionary praxis, recalls the analogy Butler has drawn between the spiritually well-regulated life and the terms and conditions of service defined by English law.

In concluding we will note how colleagues applied Butler's doctrine of charitable duty to the role of the priesthood. In *The Needfulness of a Revelation, shewn from the Imperfection of the Law of Nature considered as a Rule of Duty [Luke 1.78–9]*, Butler's successor at Bristol, John Conybeare,[67] presented his account in a critique of Tindal's *Christianity as Old as the Creation*: 'The Law of Nature signifies such a Collection of moral Rules as are discoverable by us in the proper Use of those Faculties which we enjoy. By discovering how far these will carry us, we shall learn the proper Extent of this Law.' The moral law is discoverable by, and therefore different for, each person, 'so that we ought to distinguish between *a Rule of Fitness*, and *a Law of Duty*. The former will be the same to all Mankind; but the latter must vary in proportion to each particular Man's Attainments or Opportunities.' This easily enables him to argue that revelation is necessary, to supply each person's shortcomings, and that the Church, whose role is teaching and preaching, exists as the body which makes the Christian revelation available to individual need.[68] This is a variant, adapted to pastoral work, of Butler's description of the infinitely variable mix of affections between individuals. The Church thus comprises a laity, in need of instruction and with individually varying duties of charity and moral endeavour, and a priesthood, a body of 'watchmen', 'pastors' and 'ambassadors' – Conybeare's paraphrase of the 'Messengers, Watchmen, and Stewards of the Lord' which is the ordination service's description of the clergy.[69] The Church is an association of morally active individuals. Another variant is seen in Secker's *Instructions given to Candidates for Orders*. Secker has this to say about the clergy's duty:

> Candidates ... are asked: *Do you trust that you are inwardly moved by the Holy Ghost to take upon you this Office and Ministration?* ... Observe then: it is not said, *Do you feel*; have you an immediate Perception of such an Impulse from the Holy Ghost, as you can distinguish from all other inward Movements by its Manner of impressing upon you: but, *Do you trust*; are you on good Grounds persuaded? ... Will

---

[66] John Thomas, *Sermon Preached before the [SPG] [Matthew 7:24]*, London, T. Harrison & S. Brooke, 1780, pp. 19–20.

[67] John Conybeare, *Sermons*, London, 1757, vol. 1, pp. 155–90. Conybeare too was a protégé of the Talbot family.

[68] *Sermons*, volume 2, pp. 159, 160–1, 183. Tindal is dealt with explicitly on p. 182 ff.

[69] *Charge to his Clergy, Delivered at his Primary Visitation [at Bristol], in the Month of JULY, 1752, Sermons*, volume 2, p. 501 ff.

you reverently obey your Ordinary, and them to whom the Government over you is committed?[70]

Like Butler, and Conybeare, Secker requires not feelings or experiences but trust and an acceptance of duty. As the Durham charge shows, Butler saw the parish priest as holding a special position of social and ethical authority, but needing to work hard at upholding the moral right to do so: 'it [is] an awful thing to appear before the Moral Governor of the world'.[71]

There is no evidence to suggest that Butler ever envisaged expanding the *Six Sermons* into a larger work of social policy. Indeed, he appears to have lost intellectual vitality towards the end of his time in Bristol. The six were not included in the twentieth-century narratives of eighteenth- and nineteenth-century social reform, whose authors, often for politically or religiously sectarian reasons, over-emphasized the contribution of Dissent, which was supposed to be driven by the middle class which Marx identified as the progressive socio-economic element in the capitalist phase. Research into the work of the organizations to which Butler preached would undoubtedly reveal their long-term influence. The present work, in its final chapter, will present a number of analyses as correctives, from the period when Butler was among the best-selling and most authoritative figures in British intellectual history. It will also make a start to an evaluation of Butler's contribution to the ideology and policy of the SPG in the half-century after his death.

[70] Thomas Secker, *Eight Charges Delivered to the Clergy of the Dioceses of Oxford and Canterbury*, 3rd edn, London, John, Francis & Charles Rivington, 1780, pp. 330, 331, 336. In explaining this last clause Secker omits to mention the prescribed response ('I will endeavour myself, the Lord being my helper'), presumably because it allows some sanction for a priest's inability in conscience to obey bishop and government.
[71] Butler's deathbed saying, as recorded in Bartlett, p. 225.

6

The Long Nineteenth Century

The civil union, ... and positive laws, create a certain amount of practical morality. Certain principles of moral philosophy, through this organisation, cease to be merely speculative, and become powerfully operative.[1]

Introduction

Since their first publication Butler's major works, *Fifteen Sermons* and *The Analogy*, have probably never been out of print somewhere in the anglophone world. In Butler's lifetime *The Analogy* was printed, with his own emendations, in 1736 (twice in London, once in Dublin), 1740 and 1750. *Fifteen Sermons* was printed in 1726, 1729, 1736 and 1749, all in London.

In the second half of the eighteenth century *The Analogy* was published in London, Glasgow, Aberdeen and Boston (USA) and *Fifteen Sermons* in London and Glasgow. In the nineteenth century there was a spectacular increase in editions, probably exceeding the reissues of all other eighteenth-century British divines put together. Throughout the nineteenth century the two books were variously set texts in the universities and theological colleges of the three kingdoms and influential in the established Episcopalian and Presbyterian Churches, as well as in the USA and the colleges of the British colonies. They were also stocked by the working-class reading rooms and night-schools and, whether actually read or not, must consequently have been accepted as authorities in the co-operatives and trade unions. Thus, Butler was inescapable for virtually anyone who attended a British university (and increasingly an American theology, divinity or philosophy school), who was ordained in the worldwide Anglican communion, who was trained in the Protestant ministry of virtually any denomination, who did philosophy or was an educationalist, activist or simply a well-educated person. He attracted a number of biographies, usually prefixed to his works, notably by Hallifax, Andrew Kippis[2] and, above all, Thomas Bartlett.

---

[1] Sir J. R. Seeley, *Ecce Homo* (1865), preface to the fifth edition, London [n.d. (1866)], p. 10.
[2] Andrew Kippis, 'The Life of Dr. Butler', in *The Works of Joseph Butler*, Edinburgh, 1804 and in the *Biographia Britannia*, [S.l.], 1846.

He was also translated into Welsh, Hindustani, Tamil and French.[3] For the use of teachers, and possibly of students too, there were some thirty 'cribs' published – volumes which gave a more or less detailed précis, analysis or index of *The Analogy*, sometimes with the addition of specimen examination questions. The following table, which is almost certainly incomplete, gives some idea of his printing history up to 1900, but including only the two major volumes and recording only '[British] + [American]' editions.

Table 1: Butler's publishing history, 1726–1900

Dates	Analogy	Fifteen Sermons	Collected Works	Cribs etc.	Totals
To 1752	6 + 0	4 + 0	0 + 0	0 + 0	10
1753–75	6 + 0	5 + 0	0 + 0	0 + 0	11
1776–1800	7 + 1	1 + 0	0 + 0	0 + 0	9
1801–25	11 + 3	1 + 0	3 + 1	1 + 0	20
1826–50	15 + 11	8 + 3	9 + 2	9 + 1	58
1851–75	18 + 11	6 + 3	2 + 1	12 + 2	55
1876–1900	12 + 5	3 + 0	3 + 0	8 + 2	33

Some saw him as that most interesting type of intellectual: the projector of a systematic philosophy which was left for others to complete. Thus, S. T. Coleridge, Renn Dickson Hampden in Oxford and William Whewell in Cambridge inaugurated a century of engagement of his work with the stream of critical German philosophy and theology which flowed from Kant and also with the new stream of Biblical criticism. As late as 1914 we find the Scottish scholar George Galloway taking bearings from Butler, particularly on the limitations of human knowledge, in his heavily Germanic account of the *Philosophy of Religion*.[4] While it is scarcely to Butler's credit, Henry Drummond's once-famous *Natural Law in the Spiritual World* (1883), a curious confection of pulpit piety, lecture-hall rhetoric, Darwinian science and Romantic imagery, occupies space created by *The Analogy*.

This mass of editions, and their influence on several generations of clergy, academics and leaders of both middle- and working-class culture, means that to map Butler's influence would require an intellectual history of the nineteenth-century anglophone world and could not be adequately done without a discussion of his impact on the Presbyterian Church of Scotland and the various communions of Irish Christianity – he is so frequently spoken of as a guide and inspiration that it seems unsafe to omit him from accounts of those traditions.[5] He had

[3] As with other standard and basic devotional works, French versions were for use in the colonial territories rather than metropolitan France.
[4] Published by the Edinburgh firm of T. & T. Clark.
[5] Numbers of editions in Ireland, in addition to cribs and expositions, were comparatively large. Yet modern historians (Toby Barnard, *A New Anatomy of Ireland: The Irish Protestants, 1649–1770*, New Haven, CT, 2003; Andrew Holmes, *The Shaping of Ulster Presbyterian Belief and Practice 1770–1840*,

a seminal influence on sharply contrary currents and conflicting parties. Most strikingly his works were a foundation for the Oxford Movement[6] and a practical support for the evangelicals, for the politically conservative High Church on the one hand and the co-operators and socialists on the other.[7] His contribution to ethics and the study of human nature was seriously, and frequently, compared with that of Newton's to physics and mathematics and it may be said plausibly that one reason why Charles Darwin's theories found so ready a welcome in the Church of England was their broad compatibility with Butler's ethics.[8] Indeed, Butler seems closer in approach to the nineteenth-century Darwin[9] than to the seventeenth-century physico-theologians: their demonstrative route to certainty is always the shortest possible distance, whereas Darwin's own method was to accumulate huge amounts of evidence and subject it to a scrutiny of Butlerian caution. Darwin placed at the head of the second edition of *The Origin of Species* a passage from *The Analogy* which identified divine immanence as the factor which creates stability in a world in flux. As Gillian Beer in effect pointed out, if he had merely wanted to put Butler (together with William Whewell and Bacon) on his frontispiece as a sop to contemporary religious sensitivities, he could have selected a passage identifying the phenomenon of chance as a construct of a humanity in a state of ignorance about natural laws as yet undiscovered.[10] Butler remains one of the few classic moralists cited by modern neo-Darwinians.

On the other hand, after the long period of his predominance, the inclusion of Mark Pattison's vitriolic 'Tendencies of Religious Thought in England, 1688–1750' in the 1860 volume *Essays and Reviews* and Matthew Arnold's essay 'Bishop Butler and the Zeit-Geist'[11] put Butler under challenge in the universities, other educational institutions and in society generally: the long

Oxford, 2006; Nigel Yates, *The Religious Condition of Ireland 1770–1850*, Oxford, 2006) do not mention Butler. Nor did Claude Welch in *Protestant Thought in the Nineteenth Century 1799–1870*, New Haven, CT, 1972.

6   The scholarly literature is so vast that it seems unnecessary, and even unfeasible, to give it any consideration in the present work. It is sufficient here to refer the reader to the first chapter of Newman's *Apologia*; his *University Sermons*, ed. James David Earnest and Gerard Tracey, Oxford, 2006; and Jane Garnett's essay, 'Bishop Butler and the Zeitgeist' in *Tercentenary Essays*.

7   There does not appear to be a study of Butler's influence on the ethics of the atheist Robert Owen.

8   My impression, in the present lack of a comprehensive sermons catalogue, is that, contrary to the belief of modern campaigners for atheism and creationism, positive, even enthusiastic, references to Darwin and Lyell in contemporary Anglican and Nonconformist sermons hugely outnumbered negative ones. See Keith Francis, 'Nineteenth-Century British Sermons on Evolution and *The Origin Of Species*: The Dog That Didn't Bark?', in *A New History of the Nineteenth-Century Sermon*, ed. Robert E. Ellison, New York, 2010.

9   As a modern evolutionist puts it, 'Natural selection tends to work underground, by shaping human feelings, not by making humans conscious of its logic' (Robert Wright, *The Moral Animal*, London, 1995, p. 173).

10   Gillian Beer, *Darwin's Plots*, pp. 84–5. Beer set the two passages side by side but is not responsible for this point. From her perspective as an interpreter of the nineteenth century Beer is especially aware of the 'magical' nature of analogy.

11   Matthew Arnold, *Last Essays on Church and Religion*, London, 1877.

retreat of Christianity from the hub of academic life is also involved with the narrowing of Butler studies.

Thus, his posthumous reputation and use are difficult to assess, for reasons, the combination of which makes him unique in anglophone cultural history. One is the pervasiveness we have indicated. The other is the perennial difficulty in accommodating to his followers' needs Butler's angle on things – to use a deliberately fuzzy expression. Time and again we encounter quotations from Butler, calls on his authority, attributions of authors' thoughts to his influence. The most advanced thinkers and the most reactionary alike appeal to him with confidence. Yet when we return to Butler's own works they often seem to survive this appropriation rather than invite it.

An imperial nation needs a narrative of its imperial pre-history as self-justification and after Waterloo, Britain entered a period of post-Enlightenment tradition-building.[12] The anti-tradition, probabilistic Butler, his metaphysical and mathematical axioms ignored, was seen to have produced an empirical account of the human condition which, in a conservative way, was congruent with and supported by the Christian revelation. Since he was also a native theologian, broadly compatible with Kant and the German school of theology, it is not surprising that his works became key components of this process and that the ambition quickly emerged of remaking *The Analogy* as systematic theology and moral philosophy, however contrary this was to his own motives and method. It may be that Britain was fortunate in having available to do duty as its great native moral philosopher a writer who lacked a nationalist or even factional edge and for whom the exploration of intellectual and religious doubt was a central personal experience.

It seems necessary, therefore, to supply a discussion of a few manifestations of Butler's posthumous influence. Given the ambition of the present work to present a refreshed reading, the task of engaging in a single chapter with figures who have large current critical and historical literatures is impossible; thus Reid, Adam Smith, Coleridge, Newman and the Tractarians,[13] Mill and the Utilitarians are set aside, as are the developing sciences of educational theory, sociology and psychology,[14] as well as Gladstone, the politicians and Victorian charity. Figures

---

[12] The strange death and revival of the term 'tradition' in Whig and Enlightenment Britain is discussed in Stephen Prickett's recent essay in the historiography of nineteenth-century tradition-building, in *Modernity and the Reinvention of Tradition*, Cambridge, 2009.

[13] James Pereiro, *'Ethos' and the Oxford Movement: At the Heart of Tractarianism*, Oxford, 2008, especially Chapter 5, justifies the present omission by giving a most interesting and closely-read account of Butler's influence on Keble and Newman. If Pereiro is correct (as he surely is) in contrasting their differing debts to Butler – Keble emphasizing probability and Newman 'ethos' (pp. 222–5 and Chapter 5 *passim*) – he has identified imbalances in the Tractarians' readings of Butler which are congruent with the non-Tractarian case studies in the present chapter.

[14] Butler was completely neglected, however, by Graham Richards, *Mental Machinery: The Origins and Consequences of Psychological Ideas, Part 1: 1600–1850*, London, 1992, and Suzanne R. Kirschner, *The Religious and Romantic Origins of Psychoanalysis*, Cambridge, 1996. Practising psychologists, from the present as far back as Joan Wynn Reeves (*Body and Mind in Western Thought*, Harmondsworth, 1958) seem more mindful. Reeves's assessment was noted in Chapter 3.

like Thomas Chalmers, the leading Scottish churchman, theologian and social thinker of the nineteenth century, Reginald Heber, the first Anglican bishop in India, Renn Dickson Hampden, Oxford's equivalent of Whewell, Samuel Wilberforce, bishop of Oxford, and several others have also been set aside, as having developed readings of Butler less amenable to criticism in compressed form. In none of these cases, except perhaps Newman's, has Butler's influence been assessed critically and definitively by modern scholars. Further, a discussion of the principles behind the various Butler editions of the long nineteenth century – notably those of Hallifax (nominally), Gladstone and Bernard – would best be left to a new edition.

This chapter, therefore, attempts only three things. First, it analyses Butler's intellectual legacy to the SPG, which, for all the good work of the SPCK and the CMS, was statistically the most important extrovert organization in creating the worldwide Anglican communion.

Second, it provides four brief case studies of figures who, while certainly not of minor importance, do not have scholarly industries around them: the Scottish Episcopalian minister and poet Robert Morehead, who may serve as a vehicle for exploring the connection of Butler with Romanticism; one of his editors, Daniel Wilson, the long-serving evangelical Bishop of Calcutta, who more than anyone else established Anglicanism in India and had a practical rather than theoretical interest; William Whewell, the great Cambridge administrator, scientist and theologian; and the mutually uncomprehending H. L. Mansel and F. D. Maurice, the latter one of those who put the Anglican missionary praxis to the service of the domestic mission.

The third thing attempted is a discussion of Henry Sidgwick's reading of Butler in his work towards a systematic moral philosophy. As the person who, historically, interred Butler in an obsolete orthodoxy, he is allowed the last word.

Butler's legacy to the SPG

In the century and a half after Butler's death hundreds of sermons preached on behalf of the foreign and domestic missionary and charitable societies show clear, and often acknowledged, debts to his doctrine of benevolence. The Bath District Society of the SPCK heard that:

> [As] we are all made by the same Creator, originally bearing his image, we are so far connected together by one common link, and therefore all have one common title to the exercise of our benevolence. Although, however, this principle applies to all, yet it is not universally applicable in the same extent; because some have a right to a greater share of our benevolence than others.[15]

[15] C. M. Mount, *The Apostolic Labour of a Church-of-England Association [Galatians 6.10]*, Bath, 1822, p. 5.

His concept of charitable organization as 'the cement of society' lay behind the creation of Charles Kingsley's heroes and Dickens's merciless satire of *Bleak House*'s Mrs Jellyby, campaigning for reform legislation while her own children run wild in domestic squalor, applying her duty of benevolence to remote objects and improperly neglecting those closer to home. The first instinct when a social issue was identified was to preach a sermon, form a committee, raise funds and draft legislation. As this praxis was increasingly applied in the later eighteenth century it drove a development which was unforeseen by Butler and directly contrary to his cast of thought: a revival of Christological theology and of the concept of the Hero as analogy of Christ. This was inevitable: the phenomenon of moral development and self-examination intrinsic to Butler's doctrine led naturally to morally exemplary conduct offering its practitioners as teachers and exemplars, whether these were human or the incarnate Christ. Hence emerged the Butlerian Hero, the moral man[16] who administered a spreading complex of organizations, undertaking the global export of the Anglican 'way' and exhibiting a continuous process of moral engagement with situations and peoples as they were encountered. The Hero's benevolence became a quasi-ceremonial duty and hence entailed a degree of anxiety about the status and authenticity of his morale. The Butlerian Hero, as portrayed in missionary reports, biographies, poetry and fiction, may be seen as a large sub-category of the Romantic Hero.[17] He eventually took his place in SPG (and especially CMS and non-conformist) sermons in the early nineteenth century, helping at once to transform and reintegrate British culture. Butler himself was to become a Butlerian Hero.

His posthumous influence in public affairs is seen first in the existing Church Societies. We saw in Chapter 5 that his SPG sermon contained historically important theoretical innovations about the status of slaves and their potential spiritual and civic development. We will therefore examine policy discussions in the eighteenth-century SPG, the biggest institution in the Church.[18]

The SPG, of which Butler was a Vice-President,[19] was the only organization to which he bequeathed a legacy – £500: generous but not ostentatious.[20] In his life he had maintained membership and frequent attendance[21] and supported the

---

[16] Because portrayed, whether in fiction, poetry or actual biography, as active in the public sphere the hero is overwhelmingly male. Real-life female Butlerian heroes abounded in the overseas and domestic mission fields and eventually emerged in the propaganda. At least half of the 'missionary community' overseas was female.

[17] The present author has sketched Conrad, the hero of Byron's *Corsair*, as a Butlerian Hero in 'On the Good Name of the Dead: Peace, Liberty and Empire in Robert Morehead's Waterloo Sermon', in *Religion in the Age of the Enlightenment*, vol. 1, ed. Brett McInelly, New York, 2009, pp. 249–75.

[18] See Rowan Strong, *Anglicanism and the British Empire c. 1700–1850*, especially Chapter 2.

[19] Together with Richard Smalbroke (Bishop of Coventry and Lichfield) Butler was 'sworn Vice-President' at the Board meeting of 20 March 1740/41.

[20] Butler's will is available in Bernard's edition of the *Works*. The original is in the British Library (Add Mss 9815); a contemporary copy, presumably for diocesan use in settling his affairs, is in the Durham University Library.

[21] The Board minutes identify the more prominent attendees, the corporate (*ex officio*) and associate (elected) members.

paper about American bishops discussed in Chapter 5. The SPG engaged in three sorts of activity: it managed the Codrington estate in Barbados;[22] it supplied and resourced missionaries, parochial clergy and teachers in the colonies; and it convened domestic support for an extrovert ecclesiastical policy and its practical manifestations. Butler's posthumous influence can best be assessed through an examination of the anniversary sermons.[23] There are several strongly Butlerian sermons by individual preachers (all of whom were bishops after 1749). Most notable is Beilby Porteus's 1783 effort, which combines Butlerian ethics with Sentimentalism but is so eccentric in the context of the whole series that special allowance must be for it in any survey. Butler's general influence was, however, pervasive, although not hegemonic.[24]

As Butler's own SPG sermon showed, his model of social thinking comprised three related categories: concerning ethics (and the associated account of the mind), the law (society's expression of its ethics) and something which approximates to what the modern reader understands by 'human rights'. An examination of the corpus of anniversary sermons, decade by decade, from the 1740s, when Butler became a dominant intellectual force in the Church, to the 1790s (after which the cause of abolishing the slave trade changed the nature of public rhetoric – as it happens, towards Butler's ideas) shows interesting results when these three categories are borne in mind. This examination is supported by a reading of the corpus and, further, by the tabulation of electronic word searches, which are displayed and discussed in the Appendix.[25]

The distinctively Butlerian moral concepts are affections, benevolence, charity and conscience. They occur frequently in the series, at a rate of 5.0 page-hits per sermon, in other words, they are found on five out of about twenty pages

---

[22] The century-long mismanagement was not due to ignorance or complacency but to two failures: the first, to make a slave estate function both humanely and efficiently; and the second, to devise a robust system of managerial accountability. Missions-minded Britons envied the Spanish success in establishing the pueblo-model missions while not appreciating that their shortcomings – and, notably, their brutality – were intrinsic to the model's theology.

[23] There was an early start to his influence overseas. John Rotheram, of the Codrington College in Barbados, acknowledged the influence of *The Analogy* in his *Sketch of the One Great Argument, Formed from the Several Concurring Evidences, for the Truth of Christianity*, Oxford, Richard Clement, 1754, Preface, p. iv.

[24] In 1740 the veteran bishop of Sodor and Man, Thomas Wilson, published his *Essay towards an Instruction for the Indians*, London, J. Osborn & W. Thorn. Butler and Wilson were acquainted: Wilson examined Butler for the Bristol consecration (see Chapter 4, p. 128). It is notable that Wilson's *Essay* misses all the Butlerian criteria applied in this chapter. His policy towards the Indians is neither 'charitable' nor 'benevolent' and vigorously represents the doctrine that non-acculturated contact with the Scriptures and natural religion would be a sufficient basis for conversion. This doctrine survived into the nineteenth century and proved a symptom of a lack of a developed missionary praxis in emerging missionary societies. See the present author's 'Missions, Slavery, and the Anglican Pulpit, 1780–1850', in *A New History of the Nineteenth-Century Sermon*, ed. Robert E. Ellison, New York, p. 2. My thanks to Laura Stevens for urging consideration of the *Essay*.

[25] Three methods are used. 'Word searches' are a mechanical and judgement-free process. 'Examination' means an assessment of a document: its physical state, provenance, and contents. 'Reading' means a values-laden, contemplative engagement with a literary text.

in the average sermon,[26] a rate fairly constant across the six decades. There is, however, a shift during the period. In the 1740s the preachers put great emphasis on characterizing the SPG's mission as charitable, while only committed Butlerians like Secker insinuated benevolence into their preaching. This gradually changed, and the generation after Butler's, absorbing his doctrine, came to associate the two concepts, so that in the last three decades they appear with about equal frequency and are usually associated closely with each other. Readings suggest that the SPG's mission of charity (a unidirectional duty of care for one's neighbour) became more closely involved with that of benevolence, a psychological and ethical bonding process: the affection of benevolence cannot, in Butler's theory, survive its rejection by its object and this rejection also undermines the validity of charitable works. Readings show a progressive absorption of Butler's doctrine.

Use of the concepts of conscience and the affections (the mechanisms of response to external factors) is much less frequent but also shows increases, as the proportion of Butlerian bishops increases. 'Affection' is almost always used in the Butlerian rather than the restricted modern sense, which was also current throughout the eighteenth century in which use it was promoted by the Sentimental movement. Few of the preachers match their sense of duty in encouraging missionary activity with a sense of emotions-driven compulsion.

We have seen that with his synthesis of the law, property and the circles of family and friends, Butler gave his ethics an environment of emancipation and reform when applied to relations with the economically oppressed or marginal. Here the results of readings and analysis are striking.[27] The anniversary sermons never discussed practicalities (again, with the exception of Porteus). Where the words property, family, household and law are found they always suggest elements of God's relationship with missionary activity, its social target and its combinative role among worshippers. Not unnaturally, the decade of the American Revolution witnessed a surge in references to 'law', while the following decade, when defeated loyalists were being exiled or their property expropriated, used 'property' with exceptional frequency. But apart from a few isolated cases, the familial aspect of Butler's thinking was not integrated into the SPG's theology, despite the intimate involvement of the missionaries' domestic lives with those of their target populations. It was to be rediscovered in the early nineteenth century, when missions were established in the culturally alien and densely populated environments of India and in the often physically dangerous, non-coastal settlements of West Africa. Reports from the field suggested to preachers the relevance of Butler's concept of the household.

Finally, there is the question of slavery. Butler's own sermon formulated both a policy environment and a policy and this was broadly welcomed. Its influence on the SPG's institutional culture is perceptible in the sermons of

---

[26] See Appendix Table 1 ('ethics' column).
[27] See Appendix Tables 1 and 3.

the first seven years of the 1740s, when the presence of black slaves in the colonies commanded as much attention as that of the colonists and (as the prevalence of the term 'Negroes' indicates) a definite body of people was being discussed, not merely a concept.[28] Thereafter the statistics as presented are somewhat misleading: the question subsides to a low level. In the period 1747–1800 a mere seven of the 54 sermons account for 70 percent of all references to slavery, and Porteus by himself for 32 percent. Many of the other six occur in the 'Revolutionary' decade (1771–80), when 'slavery' hits achieve an eighteenth-century high[29] and readings confirm that preachers expressed anger that Independence might isolate the American slaves from sympathetic policy in the English home base. This may to some extent be discounted as a reaction to military defeat, as aside from these seven, the remaining forty-seven sermons average a mere 0.9 page-hits, which suggests an absence of clear policy towards the slave population outside the context of the War. As readings confirm, there is a corresponding emphasis on congregation-building among the colonial population – a corollary of the lack of support commanded by Butler's familial policy, which would inevitably draw attention to the (slave) servants of the extended households. Apart from Porteus and Philip Bearcroft, the Society's Secretary (a junior cleric whose 1745 sermon is essentially a redaction of the annual report), only two preachers so much as mentioned the Society's own Barbados estate, despite its being the subject of very frank annual reports.[30] Berkeley's suggestions about this estate had been obviously utopian and local institutions were as yet lacking to implement and sustain Butler's. As we have seen, Butler's theory could not accommodate evil as an *institutional* component in a stable and healthy society and there was real unease about slavery as an existing social institution. Whereas SPG preachers' theology was compatible with ignoring its existence before Butler's sermon, after it the debate, when raised, was about theology and operational means: essentially, whether attempts at conversion should precede or follow legal emancipation. Not until Porteus's 1783 SPG sermon was the Butlerian conscience- and affections-centred argument fully developed, that slavery caused as much spiritual damage to owner as to slave and that the Anglican communion should be a family comprising and uniting both. In 1790, when Britain was, according to French and American propagandists, fighting against the rights of man, Lewis Bagot, in rhetoric whose low-key urbanity is the expression of a moral victory already won,[31] could talk of slaves, with the same strategy of irony which Butler had used, as:

---

[28] See Appendix Table 1. In 1748–50 there is only a single page-hit in the 'slavery' category.

[29] *Porteus 1783* always excepted.

[30] The two were Hallifax (1789) and Douglas (1793), both clearly Butlerian in their language and doctrine.

[31] Lewis Bagot, *Sermon preached before the [SPG] [Daniel 12:3]*, London, S. Brooke, 1790. Bagot's confidence was bolstered by the creation of the first bishop in Canada (Nova Scotia, 1787), with Quebec (1793) pending (p. 18).

... those over whose persons some of us individually claim an absolute right of property, and exact the utmost that their strength can perform, for our own advantage. Whether such a system be morally wrong in itself or not, this at least is certain, where so much is demanded some-thing must be equitably due in return. They are men as well as ourselves. However a claim on their part to civil immunities may be resisted, it cannot be denied they have an interest in the blood of Him who died for all: they have a right to know from us what He hath done for them, ... we, as Christians, have no right to with-hold such knowledge from them. (pp. 17–18)

The rhetoric is emphatically inclusive and as big an advance towards Butler's moral ascendancy as Porteus's Sentimental and Christological arguments.

Even more interesting is the period of transition. A single example must suffice. The 1764 anniversary sermon was given by Richard Terrick,[32] a successor of Butler at the Rolls Chapel. His contribution was timely, as he was about to be translated from Peterborough to London (June 1764), thus becoming nominally the diocesan of all Anglican clergy beyond the home territories. He starts (pp. 3–8) by describing the hopes of the early Church for the universal propaga-tion of true religion and the foundation of the SPG, under 'Royal Patronage and Protection', to revive those hopes. He then discusses his Isaiah text as a prophecy of the Society's endeavours, in what develops into a disguised paean for success in the Seven Years War (this appears explicitly only late in the sermon). As eightccnth-ccntury Britain emerged definitively from home waters into a global presence, resort to the Old Testament prophecies for moral sanction of such extroversion was frequent; we recall the evangelical and patriotic poet Christopher Smart writing of a contemporary admiral's expedition to the West Indies, that he sailed 'With prophecies of sure success'.[33] In an analogy, Terrick then argues that the British nation has acquired the ancient Jewish nation's ability actually to interpret and export such prophecies (pp. 9–13). The sermon proceeds with a complex of Butlerian concepts about the relationship between God, human psychology, ethics and political conduct. Religion provides 'rules ... for the Government of the heart and affections. They are adapted to the nature of man, as a reasonable and social Creature. ... Every affection ... was cultivated and improved by the benevolent Spirit of the Gospel ...' (p. 13) and contrary ones disciplined (p. 14). '[This] Guard ... upon the heart and affections ... [is not] suited only to one Nation' (p. 14); the 'Christian Law' applies to all nations (p. 15), to 'the Conscience and affections of every Man, leading him to a conduct, which his own heart must approve, directing him to that happiness, which is the natural desire of all' (p. 17). From this account of the affections

---

[32] Richard Terrick, *Sermon preached before the [SPG] [Isaiah 11:9]*, London, E. Owen & T. Harrison, 1764.
[33] Christopher Smart, 'Ode to Admiral Sir George Pocock (1762)', in *The Poetical Works of Christo-pher Smart*, ed. Karina Williamson, vol. IV, Oxford, 1987, pp. 339–41.

and conscience Terrick continues with consideration of benevolence and charity (pp. 19–23) and the formation of a 'Christian temper ... [which will] steal upon the affections, and gain Converts to a Religion, in itself lovely and amiable, and whose genuine fruits are peace and love' (p. 19). In Terrick's account (e.g. p. 22 ff) the English Christian's joy at his fortunate situation – a 'disposition to attend to every design of humanity and compassion' (p. 22) – will be affectively transferred to the target population, tending to convert it. Thus emerges, out of Butlerian ethics and psychology, the exemplary English Christian Hero, whose affections and conscience have produced benevolence and charitable behaviour in a virtuous circle.

The sermon ends with a long passage of patriotic celebration, deviating sufficiently from Butlerian orthodoxy to promise the world protection against 'the Toleration of the free exercise of the Popish Religion in the conquered Countries ... [and its] zeal and bigotry' (p. 28). In the peroration Terrick pulls back to a repetition of his charity- and conscience-based civil ethics (pp. 34–6), buttressed, Butler-fashion, by 'the regular Administration of [the] offices [of the Anglican liturgy, which] as, we are in Conscience persuaded, will most effectually answer [the] purposes of Religion and Virtue' (p. 35). In a phrase borrowed from *Fifteen Sermons*, the Church's enemies will, 'in their cooler thoughts ... return to a better temper' (pp. 35–6).

Terrick's sermon is an indication that the Church would emerge from British naval successes with a strengthened command not of only of short-term triumphalist rhetoric but of long-term Butlerian policy.

The Butlerian nineteenth century: case studies

Robert Morehead: Romantic churchman

Many of the great Romantics drew on Butler – S. T. Coleridge, Wordsworth, Southey, Hazlitt; we may add Jane Austen. In the case of Coleridge the influence is widely recognized to have gone deep. Although his first recorded reference to Butler (via Priestley) is that one of his teachings was 'nonsense',[34] the young Coleridge quickly came to admire him, and contemplated producing an edition of *The Analogy* as a means of fighting infidelity (*loc. cit.*). He called Butler, Hartley and Berkeley '[the] three *great* Metaphysicians which this Country *has* produced' (p. 151n). In a footnote to *A Lay Sermon*[35] Coleridge points to Butler as having 'detected' the fallacy in Paley's teachings on prudential obedience to God. Accounts of Coleridge's intellectual debt to Butler have proliferated since Stephen Prickett's *Religion and Romanticism*,[36] although it is yet to be explored systematically.

[34] S. T. Coleridge, *Lectures 1795 on Politics and Religion*, Lecture 5, ed. Lewis Patton and Peter Mann, London, 1971, p. 204.
[35] S. T. Coleridge, *A Lay Sermon*, ed. R. J. White, London, 1972, pp. 186–7 and editors' note, p. 187.
[36] Cambridge, 1976.

A lesser, but more accessible, Romantic poet is Robert Morehead (1777–1842).[37] He was a prominent, and even fashionable, preacher and a theologian of a self-confessed popularizing bent,[38] as well as the composer of verse epistles and almost a hundred and fifty sonnets of good quality. No culturally marginal figure, his publishers were among the most prestigious available: Constable in Edinburgh and Longman in London. He was a Scottish Episcopalian, an associate of Thomas Chalmers, the great Presbyterian (and ultimately 'Wee Free' secessionist), and for many years served Edinburgh's socially prestigious Cowgate Chapel as the junior of Archibald Alison, whose *Essays on the Nature and Principles of Taste*[39] remains familiar even to undergraduate students of aesthetics and Romanticism. For present purposes we will entirely set aside his poetry, as, naturally, it provides less direct evidence.

There are many examples, both acknowledged and implicit, of Butler's influence on Morehead: '[Such] reflections … tend to cultivate those dispositions which lay the foundations of religious belief, not only in our understanding, but our affections,'[40] 'affections' here bearing in context the full scope of the Butlerian technical term. Like Butler, Morehead sees religion partly in terms of cult and acculturation in the way of Anglican Christianity, 'way' being a pointer to a fairly literal account of the journey of sensibility described in various poetical epistles where journeys through landscapes become, in Wordsworthian fashion, expressive of spiritual journey.[41] As we saw with Butler himself,[42] knowledge is not set against belief, as with Descartes and Malebranche, but is a category of it, standing in a relationship with truth, which exists objectively but is not fully accessible. This is a necessary consequence of the form which Morehead adopts of the theory that the Christian revelation was supplied by the actually living Jesus Christ: that humankind accepts the teachings because of the obvious personal authority of the teacher. Thus:

> … our Saviour *"shewed the Father,"* by exhibiting in human nature a model of divine perfection. It is here, probably, that natural religion is most obviously defective. Man feels that he is unworthy of his Maker; and cannot form to himself any distinct or satisfactory ideas of the Being

---

[37] Robert Morehead is not featured in the DNB or ODNB, although his sons, who were major figures in colonial India, are. One of them, Charles Morehead, produced a biography, *Memorials of the Life and Writings of the Rev. Robert Morehead, DD*, Edinburgh, 1875. The only modern study of Morehead appears to be the present author's 'On the Good Name of the Dead: Peace, Liberty and Empire in Robert Morehead's Waterloo Sermon'.

[38] Robert Morehead, *A Series of Discourses, on the Principles of Religious Belief, as Connected with Human Happiness and Improvement*, Edinburgh, 1809, Preface, p. vii.

[39] Archibald Alison, *Essays on the Nature and Principles of Taste*, London, J. J. G. & G. Robinson, 1790.

[40] Robert Morehead, *Series of Discourses*, Edinburgh, 1809, Preface, p. ix.

[41] His 1813 volume of poems was dedicated to the poet Thomas Campbell, a friend from college, and the 1814 edition to Wordsworth, 'the poet and priest of nature, [to whom] these translations from ancient poets, (however unworthy his notice,) are inscribed, with the truest sentiments of veneration and gratitude'.

[42] Chapter 3, pp. 102–3.

to whom he is eager to approach … Unable to resist the impulse which calls upon him to bend before invisible power, yet incapable, from his own imperfections, of forming any just conception of the God whom it becomes him to adore, [natural] man at all times, instead of exhibiting in himself the image of his Maker, has represented the divine nature under the infinite variety of images suggested by his own weakness, ignorance, and vices.[43]

This suggests that natural religion, like all bodies of knowledge produced by human endeavour, produces superstition because the knowledge available is intrinsically deficient, relying on a narrower base than one supported by divine authority. Indeed, with an explicit reference to Butler, to whom he attributes the thought, Morehead writes of the screen that we place 'between us and the Deity' and the:

supposition of a Divine Intelligence involved in Nature … labouring in the brain of every human being, but only … very seldom [having] strength to come quite to birth. This notion is no novelty of mine, but is to be found expressly stated by Bishop Butler, though he does not see, I think, how much may be made of it.[44]

Thus Morehead, in common with probably all other readers of Butler, experienced his power of suggestiveness, in his doctrine of what we have previously called the 'God in us' nature of the affections. It immediately became the core of Morehead's mode of expression of his Romantic imagination and doctrine – it emerges again in his sermon *Of Christ's Knowledge of the Heart of Man [John 2.25]*,[45] where the incarnate Christ corrects moral imbalances in human nature by his doctrine and example. Only by recognizing Christ's loving affection for created humanity can humanity reciprocally love God. Thus, Morehead presents Christ as a hero, albeit a somewhat feminized one, a teacher who encourages not bullies, anticipating the iconography and doctrine of the Sunday School movement as it developed towards the end of the nineteenth century.

[Christ] saw that in this wonderful creature [i.e. human nature] virtues and vices, wisdom and prejudices, are unaccountably mixed together; and who while he was most zealous to elevate the one and to remove the other, yet touched both with that delicacy and tenderness, that even the very pride of the heart which He corrected could scarcely take offence at his gentle hand.[46]

[43] *Series of Discourses*, Sermon VI: *On Revealed Religion [John 14:9]*, pp. 85–7.
[44] Robert Morehead, *Dialogues on Natural and Revealed Religion*, Edinburgh, 1830, pp. xxii–xxiii.
[45] In *Dialogues on Natural and Revealed Religion*, 1830.
[46] *Of Christ's Knowledge of the Heart of Man*, p. 120. The late nineteenth-century Sunday School image of Christ as a feminized teacher was to culminate in the phenomenal international success of the London Missionary Society-commissioned painting *The Hope of the World* by Harold Copping (1915). Late imperial concern about the need to reassert Christ's masculinity is associated with the LMS's commission of Tom Curr's image *Follow Me* (1935). See David Morgan, *Protestants and Pictures: Religion, Visual Culture, and the Age of American Mass Production*, Oxford, 1999, Chapter 9 and Sandy Brewer, 'From

The Romantic Morehead is prepared to state more emphatically the transformative effect on human nature of the Christian gospel but it cannot be said that he misreads or distorts Butler's sermons *Upon the Love of God*, where Butler writes thus of the way that the gospel allows a refocusing and development of the personality:

> [You cannot] alter [your] real Nature. Therefore no Exercise of the Mind can be recommended, but only the Exercise of those Faculties you are conscious of. Religion does not demand new Affections, but only claims the Direction of those you already have, those Affections you daily feel.
> (Sermon XIII, *1729*, pp. 275–6)

Like Butler, Morehead preaches frequently about personal development but is notably little interested in the theology of redemption.

A striking example of Morehead's dependence on Butler is seen in the episode where he played a public and ecumenical role of unusual prominence for an Episcopalian in Scotland. On 6 November 1828 Chalmers was inaugurated as Professor of Divinity in the University of Edinburgh.[47] It was customary, and indeed necessary, to raise funds publicly to supplement the stipend and Morehead was selected to present the proceeds – a very unusual privilege for someone who was not a member of the established Presbyterian Church of Scotland. This presentation, on 13 April 1829, was accompanied by a letter which from its style is obviously a transcript of his public speech on that occasion.

> Among those for whom I speak there are churchmen of different denominations; clergymen of the national [Presbyterian] establishment, who return again to listen with zealous edification to the arguments and fervour with which you maintain the awful but venerable tenets of their Calvinistic creed; clergymen, too, of the sister [Episcopalian] Church, who have equal delight to meet once more in the text-books which you have so liberally introduced, the milder lights of their own eminent divines, reflected back upon them with the mingled comment of a no less powerful and original mind. We have thus been taught to give and take in turn; we pass mutually and amicably into the separate schools of Edwards and of Butler; and ... we feel as if we were of one heart and of one mind, while, like the primitive Christians of old, the same great truths are announced to each of us in his own customary language and dialect.

The heavy rhetorical redundancies, untypical of his style, show Morehead being over-emphatic in his ecumenical triumphalism; it is a political but not statesmanlike speech. Whether it contributed to the fact that he ended his days as a

---

Darkest England to the Hope of the World'. My thanks are due to Dr Brewer for private information about her work in progress on this subject.
[47] This account is sourced from William Hanna, *Memoirs of the Life and Writings of Thomas Chalmers*, Edinburgh, 1850, vol. III, p. 224 ff.

rector in Yorkshire cannot be said; a published poet and reviewer was, in any case, not a likely candidate for even an English, let alone a Scottish, see.[48]

Most notable, however, is Morehead's identification of the Church of Scotland by the theology of John Edwards (1637–1716 – not the eighteenth-century American Jonathan Edwards) and the Church of England by that of Butler. Edwards, a Calvinist who was English (a fact unlikely to be overlooked by either Morehead or Chalmers, Scots traditionally priding themselves on their influence on English intellectual and technological culture) is named in preference to the more obvious choice of John Knox. Three reasons suggest themselves. First, in addition to his general prominence as a Calvinist theologian, Edwards, like Butler, was the author of a famous controversial work, in his case *The Socinian Creed* (1697), which the recent resurgence of Socinianism had given renewed topicality. Second, he had published several works against Locke's theology, philosophy and theory of education. To advance Edwards and Butler as representatives of the best of the Calvinist and Anglican traditions was to suggest, subliminally, that Locke was to be opposed within the academy, something which was also being said around this time in Cambridge by William Whewell, to whom we will turn in due course. This was also Chalmers's own position, one on which he had already published. Third, the pairing was a reference to Chalmers's own interests: he lectured and published on *Fifteen Sermons* and, especially, *The Analogy*.[49] The implication seems inescapable: Butler defined not only English but British reformed Christianity. In Morehead's younger years the emperor Napoleon was the icon of aggressive infidel politics and ethics[50] and thus he, several times, especially during the wars, restated Butler's account of Britain as a Christian society held together by mutual charity, both private and institutional, under the protection of the common and statute law and the policy of toleration.

Even when the external threat had receded, his sermons tended to express this position, as titles such as *Protestantism its own Protection [Ephesians 6.10]* indicate.[51] Writing as a minister of the minority and permanently embattled Scottish Episcopal Church, this sermon positively welcomes political marginality as a spur to a unity of purpose among the Protestant communions and sects:

---

[48] Morehead was to serve as a chaplain to Charlotte, Princess of Wales, minister in St Paul's Episcopal Chapel, Edinburgh, and as Dean of Edinburgh before becoming Rector of Easington in Yorkshire.
[49] For example, Thomas Chalmers, *Prelections on Butler's Analogy*, published posthumously by William Hanna, *Posthumous Works of Thomas Chalmers*, vol. 9, Edinburgh, 1849. Chalmers has been discussed in this context by David Nicholls in *God and Government in an 'Age of Reason'*, e.g. p. 17.
[50] Largely suppressed during the Wars, except in sermons given to Volunteer regiments, this assessment of Napoleon was given freer rein in the corpus of Waterloo sermons in 1815–6 (work in progress).
[51] This sermon, published singly (Edinburgh, 1829), was preached on 17 June 1829, at one of Bishop Daniel Sandford's visitations, and dedicated to Mountstuart Elphinstone. Preached on the occasion of the government's disestablishing ten Anglican Irish sees, it is Morehead's equivalent of Keble's Assize sermon.

Removed from all the conflicts of the world's policy, we have the advantage of being more entirely surrounded with professional objects, than the Clergy of high and splendid Establishments [i.e. the Presbyterian Church of Scotland], and in the retirement of lives which have little of worldly ambition to solicit them, we can, perhaps, obtain a more distinct version of the spiritual course of events, and of the duties to which the contemplation of Churchmen ought, in these days, more especially to be opened ... (pp. 37–8)

While this constitutes a retreat from his more youthful ambition for the Episcopalians to take the leading role in Scotland it parallels Butler's own simultaneous upholding of constitutional prerogatives and reluctance to participate beyond the limits of duty.[52]

In several early works, notably his *Series of Discourses, on the Principles of Religious Belief, as Connected with Human Happiness*, Morehead shows himself less interested in theology than in explorations of the minister as the analogue of Christ as pastor and hero, arising from a use of Butler's account of the relationship between the divine and human minds. For Morehead, undoubtedly influenced by Alison, the contemplation of spiritual and ethically motivated behaviour arouses aesthetic feelings, but he is emphatic that such feelings do not constitute the good. Thus, writing of improper concepts and practices of charity, he says, 'It may be merely an epicurean species of liberality, which avoids giving trouble, that others may give no trouble in return, but which has no foundation in the love of truth and holiness.'[53] The tension implicit in this caveat seems to underlie the central relationship of Christ, the hero and teacher, with humankind, the taught. Morehead here emphasizes to his fellow clergy his affiliation to the Stoics and Butler. Moreover, he is preaching a 'visitation' sermon, to his colleagues in the presence of their bishop (in this case Sandford, the leader of the Scottish Episcopalians), as a pre-agreed part of the diocesan strategy. His reading has a naturalness and accuracy which, in the present work, we will find hereafter only in William Whewell, a man similarly interested more in philosophical and cultural reform than in preferment.

Daniel Wilson: Bishop of Bombay
Morehead was not only the father of colonial administrators but also the exporter of religious literature to India.[54] A contemporary was Daniel Wilson (1778–1858), who after long years as a prominent evangelical preacher and vicar left

---

52 In his 1832 farewell sermon to his Edinburgh congregation Morehead was to reinforce this view of its social placing. *A Farewell Sermon, preached in St Paul's Chapel, York Place, Edinburgh, On the 11th Day of November 1832 [1 John 2:13]*, Edinburgh and London, 1832, pp. 9–10 and *passim*.
53 *Protestantism its own Protection*, p. 30.
54 Mountstuart Elphinstone, writing from Poona in May 1814, reported that Morehead's sermons were already circulating in India. *Memorials of the Life and Writings of the Rev. Robert Morehead, D.D.*, ed. Charles Morehead, Edinburgh, 1875, p. 379. Morehead seems to have undertaken the shipping of religious and secular literature to Elphinstone, for distribution.

England in 1832 to become the fifth bishop of Calcutta but actually only the second (after the inaugural bishop, T. F. Middleton) to survive long enough to establish his ministry and leadership. In the event he served from 1832 to 1858. A man of enormous personal force, he quickly established himself as the semi-official metropolitan for the Church of England in the East, overseeing the growth of dioceses,[55] and criss-crossing the sub-continent in a series of arduous visitations, which were meticulously prepared and expedited and whose associated charges reported in great detail to the clergy and officials of each diocese. The vigour of his views as expressed in his sermons and charges, whose Butlerian approach coexists seamlessly with vehement anti-Tractarianism, reminds us both that the colonial churches were not isolated from the domestic mainstream and that Butler was not monopolized theologically by the Newman circle.

In December 1824, when Wilson, then the evangelical vicar of St Mary's, Islington, signed off the introduction to his own edition, *The Analogy* had already been printed in Britain at least thirteen times in the preceding quarter-century. His edition, nevertheless, was published not only in London but also in Glasgow (1829). In his long *Introductory Essay* (pp. v–clxi) he did not mention *Fifteen Sermons* at all and presented the 'negative' Butler – the Butler whose method was not actively to promote Christianity but to undermine opposition to it. Wilson's edition was an evangelical primer, the first half (to p. lxxxv) providing a rather crude summary of *The Analogy*'s argument.

Wilson's central interest finds expression in the long set of 'Observations on the connection of this argument with the other branches of the Christian evidence, and on its peculiar use and importance; and also on our author's view of practical Christianity, and on the adaptation of his argument to the Christian religion in all its extent' (p. lxxxv ff). In this way Wilson keeps the 'negative' and 'positive' parts of his essay distinct. He sees 'negative' analogical evidence as particularly useful in public debate (p. xcvi), undermining the non-believer's or doubter's pride: 'his proud reasonings sink – faith resumes her sway – humility acknowledges the ignorance and littleness of man … and the incomprehensibility of God' (pp. c–ci).

Wilson's 'positive' application of Butler makes it clear that *The Analogy* constitutes a critique and a programme of action going far beyond the question of evidence. Thus, he claims that, for all of Butler's abundant shortcomings (pp. cxvi–cxxxv are largely given over to them), *The Analogy* provides grounding for a systematic evangelical theology. He recapitulates the standard Protestant historiography of theology (pp. cxxxvii–cxxxix), with the usual thousand-year gap of 'thick darkness' between Augustine and Luther (lightened only by the

---

[55] Calcutta (founded 1814) was the first Anglican diocese outside the old Atlantic territories. During the course of Wilson's episcopate it developed into a province comprising Calcutta itself, Madras (1835), Bombay (1837), Jerusalem (1841), Colombo (1845), Victoria, Hong Kong (1849), and Singapore, Labuan and Sarawak (1855). See H. W. Tucker, *The Classified Digest of the Records of the [SPG] 1701–1892*, p. 766.

Albigenses and Waldenses) and presents Butler's arguments as an apologetic and a logical underpinning of a proposed refreshment of the Reformation's doctrines of original sin, justification, salvation, regeneration and 'communion with God by the Holy Spirit' (p. cxxxviii).

On the question of evidence (p. lxxxvi) Wilson makes explicit what Butler had hinted at: the necessity of developing rigorous textual criticism of the Scriptures, as a critical basis for an unreserved acceptance of the 'divine credentials' of the messenger. The entire legitimacy of theology is in critical work:

> We have no right at all to examine the nature of the discoveries, or doctrines, or precepts of Christianity, with the view of determining whether they seem to us becoming the wisdom of God, and agreeable to the reason of man ... Let it be fairly made out to come from God, and it is enough. More than this is injurious ... We have no right to call the Almighty Creator to the bar of our feeble reason. (pp. lxxxvi, lxxxviii)

It is here that Wilson amplifies what we have noted in Morehead: the emergence of Christ as a Romantic hero, approached through iconic imagery. Christ's miracles give us 'the pledge of ... the character of Christ, of his condescension – the accompanying influence, of his grace and goodness – the fulfilment of the promises, of his veracity. Thus the evidences of Christianity have an impression of the divine glory irradiating them' (pp. ci–cii). This is a fairly accurate application of Butler's synthesis of testimony and evidence, the latter, deployed by Butler in a 'negative' and analogical manner, clearing the surrounding controversies to allow a full display of the testimony of the personal God.

Wilson's understanding of Butler on natural religion is acute. For Butler, he says, natural religion is:

> that service ... which men owe to [God] ... and which arise out of the relations in which they stand to Him, as the rational and accountable beings whom he formed for his glory, and governs by his law. These primitive obligations of religion may plainly be distinguished from Christianity, which is an additional dispensation ... Indeed, Natural Religion is, properly speaking, distinct from those anticipations of the Christian redemption, which the early revelations to our first parents, to the patriarchs and to the Jewish people, comprised. (pp. cvi–cvii)

For a future colonial bishop this is a very important point, as it lays down the principle, contrary to earlier missionary theorists like Claudius Buchanan,[56] that an uncorrupted natural religion is valid, if dangerously incomplete. This is applied to the non-Christian religions of Britain's new empire in the East, which need no longer to be seen as devil-worshipping cults. The universal existence

---

[56] For example, in his epoch-making volume of sermons (and its long appendix) to the CMS and Cambridge University, *Two Discourses preached before the University of Cambridge, on Commencement Sunday, July 1st, 1810 [Gen. 1:3], and a Sermon preached before the [CMS] ..., June 12, 1810 [Matt. 5:14]. To which are added, Christian researches in Asia*, London, 1812, *passim*.

of natural religion is a fact of psychology and anthropology. The imposition on top of it of revealed religion (bringing with it the exercise of the will to good, the education of the conscience and the ethics-saturated consciousness) creates a 'new man' in the sense set out in Paul's epistles, which he cites in support of this view (p. cviii). It is possible that all nineteenth-century English expressions of the partial validity of non-Christian religions derive from Butler, who was, in any case, certainly the first British theologian to advance the proposition.

When Wilson died, such was his standing that an elaborate, all-day, memorial event was organized in his old parish of Islington, with three preachers, including Charles Sumner, the long-serving bishop of Winchester, and Henry Venn, Honorary Secretary of the CMS. It is notable that Sumner's tribute laid great emphasis on this *Introductory Essay*, which was then thirty-four years old: 'the preliminary remarks and analysis of the argument, prefixed to the volume, are in themselves masterly performances, and may not improperly be instanced as the finest proof he has left of his mental power'.[57]

William Whewell: Butler in Cambridge
The series of four sermons preached before the University of Cambridge in 1837 by William Whewell, administrator, polymath and educationalist, constitutes perhaps the single most transformative event in Butler's posthumous reception. Whewell, a close friend of the geologist Lyell, was at this time the professor of mineralogy. He had just published his *Principles of an English University Education* and was shortly to be elected Knightsbridge professor of moral philosophy. He was subsequently to found the moral and physical sciences triposes. A student of Kant, and wishing to introduce an anti-Lockean philosophy, he did not originate the nineteenth-century academy's perception of a link between Kant and Butler but certainly strengthened it.

Whewell's four sermons were published at the end of 1839 under the title *On the Foundations of Morals*,[58] and incidentally demonstrated the continuing power of the pulpit and the university sermon sub-genre. Whewell set himself, successfully, to displace Paley's *Moral Philosophy* as a Cambridge set book.

> I do not think it can be doubted that the general currency which Paley's Moral Philosophy has acquired ... has had a very large share in producing the confusion and vacillation of thought respecting the grounds of morals, which is at present so generally prevalent in England, even among persons of cultivated minds. (Preface, p. vii)

---

[57] Charles Richard Sumner, *Sermon on the Death of Daniel Wilson [2 Kings 2:11–2]*, London, 1858, pp. 30–1.
[58] William Whewell, *On the Foundations of Morals*, Cambridge, 1839. References are to the 1839 second Cambridge edition.

Whewell argued for Butler's replacement of Paley, not as the author of a ready-made systematic moral philosophy but because of his achievements 'mainly in the discussion of the fundamental principle of his subject' (p. vii).

> [A] system of Ethics should ... point out the rational grounds of the good institutions which prevail in organized societies, with regard to the objects of men's desires and affections; and thus invest those institutions with the sanction of morality as well as law. Butler does not attempt any such application of his principles, and therefore his writings are very defective as an ethical system. (p. x)

It is, of course, possible that Whewell had not read the *Six Sermons*, but he has put Butler in place as provider of the prolegomena of a projected school of philosophy. Indeed, in the preface to the second edition (dated 3 March 1839), where Whewell feels compelled to deny that he has asserted 'that virtue consists in obeying the impulses of a certain *instinct* which God has placed within us to direct our conduct, without any regard to the good or evil tendency of such conduct' (p. xiii) – a misreading of Butler by his critics – he announces the post-ponement of an edition of Butler's sermons, because Butler's admirers would not welcome the alterations necessary to systematize them: a statement of revo-lutionary intent.[59]

Whewell's first sermon, *Conscience is the evidence of God's righteous-ness [Romans 1.20]*, establishes that Butler, the Christian empiricist, unites the science of nature and the science of man as grounds for the science of God. Starting with a discussion of conscience as defined in Romans 2 and 3 he proceeds to use metaphors of nature and science in the Romantic fashion, suggesting that Paley cannot express, or even conceive, the moral values which, he implies, Butler has displayed:

> [God] sits enthroned, not only among the clouds and lightnings, stars and planets; but also in the wider and deeper world of thought and will, of passion and action, his government is felt, his strength and wisdom.... The Author of man is the author of his moral constitution [and conscience], as well as of his corporeal frame.... We now see our Maker and Judge, as through a glass, darkly. We see but the remote beams of his radiance, the outskirts of his glory; but we believe that these scattered rays and broken reflexions proceed from a central orb of unutterable brightness.... But while we are in our present condition [on earth], we may not omit to look into our hearts and into our consciences for a distinct and significant evidence of God's nature and purposes.
>
> (pp. 8, 14, 15, 16)

---

59 Whewell's project had some success in America, where Joseph C. Passmore published an edition of *Bishop Butler's Ethical Discourses; to which are Added some Remains, hitherto Unpublished. Prepared as a Text Book in Moral Philosophy; with a Syllabus, by Dr. Whewell. Edited, with an Introductory Essay on the Author's Life and Writings*, Philadelphia, PA, 1855.

The divine thoughts are the 'perfect archetype of all which conscience approves and admires' (p. 14). Whewell's thinking is coarser than Butler's – he describes man as 'a creature born to think as well as to feel' (p. 2), which for Butler would be inelegant and redundant – but, a hundred years on, with twenty-eight Anglican bishops on thrones in the USA and the Empire, with an accelerating rate of creation of dioceses and with many hundreds of missionary staff in the field, he has a wider view of geography and history. Thus, 'The prevalent opinions concerning the first principles of religion and morality, tinge, through innumerable channels, the remotest streams of religious and moral teaching; and thus affect the spiritual welfare of millions of our fellow-christians' (p. 2). Whewell's thought is expressed in scientific, in fact mineralogical, metaphors, popular opinion colouring the pure water of religion just as iron ore stains the streams of the uplands. When Whewell borrows from *The Analogy* the metaphor of the ravening beasts he transmogrifies them into more homely lions and adds images of flowers and quiet lakes (emblems of a tranquil conscience), thus arriving at a place to which Butler pointed but did not seek to occupy: '*if there be any virtue*, there is also an accompanying *praise*' (p. 8).[60] Thus, the academic scientist and philosopher use the same language with regard to Butler's role as the evangelical poet Smart and the Romantics Coleridge and Morehead.

Oddly, for Whewell can hardly have known Smart's poem, his second sermon, *Conscience requires cultivation [Acts 24.16]*, adopts the Acts text of its first line: 'conscience void of offence'. Substituting 'steady' for Butler's 'cool', he writes:

> [When] we see principles [i.e. mental components like passion and reason] thus embodied and impersonated; – when we are thus assisted by our practical judgments and sympathies; – we *can* contemplate steadily, and often, it may be, profitably, the workings and struggles, the impelling and regulating movements, of man's heart and mind. (p. 20)

This sermon is of exceptional interest because it shows Whewell simultaneously at his most and least Butlerian. Thus, he continues by discussing the acculturative aspect of the conscience, through social intercourse, literature and the seepage into public opinion of the 'meditations of the most profound and acute thinkers' (p. 21). He also follows Butler in his care to maintain that terms like 'mental faculty' ('a faculty distinct from the other impelling and guiding principles of his actions', as he puts it in Sermon I, p. 21) are verbal counters, pointing to things which cannot finally be analysed. 'For who shall undertake thus to parcel man's soul into different portions? Who shall say, – Here memory ends; – Here imagination begins; – This is reason's exclusive domain?' (p. 21). This cautiously nominalist approach is, however, somewhat confused by his attempt to force a distinction between the conscience and 'prudential or long-

---

[60] Again one recalls Smart's poem 'Conscience', which extrapolates from Butler to make exactly the same point.

sighted love of gain or of pleasure or of power, which some [people] point at as her nearest kindred ... [although] they meet without recognising each other's language; ... and though they may travel in company, they look on each other with a constant mutual suspicion' (p. 22).[61] This was presumably in reaction to Paley and the early Utilitarians, who are designated as 'men who have in their own imagination, reduced the course of the world to a chain of inevitable consequences of which they care only to number the links' (pp. 31–2). Whewell's distinction between conscience and love of gain is not, of course, found in Butler, who asserts their general coincidence and the common nature of the affections and conscience as analogues of aspects of the divine nature and its creation and sustention of the world. Butler's own nominalism is based on a refusal to systematize upon the few axioms he adopts from Clarke, a method accentuated, and concealed from Whewell, by Butler's reticence about his sources.

Sermon III, *Conscience is in accordance with God's government [Job 36.2–3]*, is an essay in separating moral acts from the self-interest which predominates in the Scriptures, and particularly the Old Testament. Whewell asserts that conscience 'is the reflexion of Divine holiness in man' (p. 46), thus attempting to follow Butler in his analogical analysis of the human nature in relation to the divine: 'the power of God which surrounds us corresponds to the moral power which is within us. The moral law written upon the heart is God's writing' (p. 46). In the concluding sermon, *Moral good is superior in kind to pleasure [Romans 6.12–13]*, this point is elaborated. While, as we have seen, Whewell does not argue for the existence of an absolutely discrete moral faculty, he follows Butler in thinking that one may be nurtured in the individual by the development of a praxis, although, unlike Butler, he does not extend this into a social doctrine. The sermons' centrepiece (p. 66 ff) is his call for a programme of research into a system of ethics based on the supremacy of the conscience and the sense of duty, starting from *Fifteen Sermons*. Paley has misrepresented human nature and thus helped actually to warp it in his disciples and their circle of influence (Sermon II, p. 33). His moral philosophy, based on 'expediency' (p. 67), is thus a force for evil (p. 61) and academic philosophers, who have been complicit by teaching it, can make amends by developing good doctrine (p. 63).

In effect, by calling for a programme of research Whewell is continuing Butler's own use of support from the empirical sciences and mathematics as a base for an account of the moral nature of the human individual in relation to God and society. We have noted that Whewell founded the Cambridge human and natural science triposes. Butler's theoretical grounding in the law, sciences and probability theory, his social concerns and his general suggestiveness now made him a central feature on the nineteenth-century intellectual map. The hints we gather about Whewell's conception of 'duty' are noteworthy, however. On

---

[61] In Chapter 3 we noted that the mathematician and moralist Thomas Bayes sketched an efficiently conceived model of utilitarian 'universal hedonism' on probabilistic grounds, an achievement which was historically a dead end.

the one hand, he certainly aligns with Butler against Locke insofar as 'duty' is conceived in an ethical not political context. On the other hand, and despite Whewell's High Church affiliation, Butler's conception of duty as quasi-litur-gical and ceremonial behaviour is absent; the perpetuation and elaboration of this aspect of Butlerian duty must be sought elsewhere. Even with Whewell, preaching a sermon, Butler is seen as a philosopher rather than a priest.

> [This] better teacher calls upon man to discern and remember that there *is* a higher and nobler part of his nature; – that his principles of action *do* differ in right and office; – that appetite stands rightfully beneath prudence, and that both are under the authority of conscience [Butler's Sermons]. (p. 65; Whewell's footnote interpolated)

Whewell, whose career was to divert somewhat from research into administra-tion, made a start to following this programme through with his *Elements of Morality* (1846), although J. S. Mill's devastatingly Utilitarian essay, 'Whewell and Moral Philosophy' (1852)[62] checked him. The next generation – notably Wilberforce, Maurice and Sidgwick, in their different ways – was to do consid-erably more.

H. L. Mansel and F. D. Maurice

The mid-century Church was preoccupied by a number of political and theo-logical problems, the most prominent being the Crimean War (started 1854), the Indian Mutiny (1857),[63] the controversy over H. L. Mansel's Bampton lectures (1858), the publication of *The Origin of Species* (1859) and of *Essays and Reviews* (1860) and the Colenso controversy (*Commentary on the Pentateuch*, from 1862). In all of these, Butler was used as a resource and authority by leading clergy and theologians, as he was, indeed, by Darwin.

The nature of F. D. Maurice's debt to Butler may be seen most economically by examining some works in a narrow time frame, contrasting him with Mansel, another follower of Butler, and by discussing briefly his *Letters to a Missionary* and *Indian Mutiny* sermons.

Mansel was a follower of Sir William Hamilton, who himself had absorbed much Butler, and the titles alone of works like *The Limits of Demonstrative Science Considered. In a Letter to Dr. Whewell* (1853) and his inaugural lecture, *Psychology the Test of Metaphysical Philosophy* (1855) suffice to suggest his place in the present narrative. In his Bampton lectures, which he begins with a motto from Berkeley and praise of *The Analogy* ('an example of a profound and searching philosophical spirit, combined with a just perception of the bounds within which all human philosophy must be confined, to which, in the whole

---

[62] Reprinted in John Stuart Mill and Jeremy Bentham, *Utilitarianism and Other Essays*, ed. Alan Ryan, London, 1987.

[63] The contemporary name of this episode is preferred in the Anglocentric context of the present work, as it did indeed involve a mutiny and was presented as such to the British people by the authorities.

range of similar investigations, it would be difficult, if not impossible, to find a parallel')[64] he set himself the question,

> Does there exist in the human mind any direct faculty of religious knowledge, by which we are enabled to decide, independently of all external Revelation, what is the true nature of God, and the manner in which He must manifest Himself to [p. viii] the world; and by which we are entitled authoritatively to decide for or against the claims of any professed Revelation of the Divine Nature and Attributes?
>
> (Preface, first edition, pp. vii–viii)

The Analogy, he observes, 'only clears the ground for the production of proper evidence' (Preface, third edition, p. ii). He accurately restates Butler:

> So far as certain difficulties are inherent in the constitution of the human mind itself, they must of necessity occupy the same position with respect to all religions, the false no less than the true. It is sufficient if it can be shewn that they have not, as is too often supposed, any peculiar force against Christianity alone. (Preface, third edition, p. iii)

His account of the strength of the eclectic method of gathering and assessing evidence (p. ix) and his note that 'a *conception of the Absolute* implies a self-contradiction at the outset' (p. xxi) are also indebted to Butler. Indeed, bringing evidence against the charge that he was influenced by Newman, he proves his chronological priority, throwing additional emphasis on his debt to Butler. But whereas Butler, progressively underplaying the axiomatic and metaphysical basis of his account of created humanity's inherent affections but still reserving his apologetic position, puts the weight of its proof upon consensus and the 'cement of society', Mansel, through his critical engagement with Kant and German metaphysics, argues that 'Consciousness [is] a Relation between the human mind and its object; and [that] this conclusion, once established, is fatal to the very conception of a Philosophy of the Absolute' (Lecture VII, p. 201). Seeking to correct Kant he concludes that 'The Moral Law, and the ideas which it carries with it, are ... merely facts of human consciousness' (p. 201) and attempts to identify a special religious consciousness which humankind possesses. Thus he arrives at a metaphysically somewhat flabby but not perverse version of Butler's own position and goes some way towards carrying on what we have called the 'Whewell project'. For Mansel, a system of ethics obtains its persuasiveness from a study of the psychological, and consequently biological, nature of the human being.

All this seemed to Maurice to avoid the personal relationship with God through revelation, throwing ethics back into the sphere of natural religion, and put him in a rage which was unique in his intellectual life, while Mansel's contributions to the ensuing controversy reveal his puzzlement at what seemed to him a

---

[64] Henry Longueville Mansel, *The Limits of Religious Thought*, Oxford, 1858, Preface to first edition, p. ix.

misunderstanding. Maurice's published responses are all the more revealing for being off-balance. His initial riposte, a series of 'anti-Bampton' sermons, *What is Revelation?* (1859), is headed by a motto from Butler – significantly, from *Fifteen Sermons* not *The Analogy*, hitherto, as we see with Mansel, the more favoured work. In these sermons is found the prototype of the thoughts further developed in his later work, *The Conflict of Good and Evil in our Day. Twelve Letters to a Missionary* (1865), into something like the ideological basis for the proposal to reform the Church of England as a mass missionary organization, both overseas and domestically.

The core of Maurice's complaint against Mansel is this:

> There is a Constitution belonging to us as men, a different Constitution from that which is to be seen in Nature, but not a less real one. There is an Analogy between it and the Constitution and Course of Nature. Does not our Lord say so? ... Is there still something in these words, 'Religion, Natural or [*sic*] Revealed,' which grates upon your ear.... Well, ... I think Butler adopted his [terminology] from the custom of his age. If it strikes you that the word 'Religion' is better limited to the internal life ... I shall not complain ...[65]

Throughout he treats Butler as a person, a Butlerian Hero, indeed, whose character needs to be understood for the force of his teaching to be appreciated (e.g. p. 171n). While he sees that the core of Butler's preaching, in *Fifteen Sermons*, is to '[drive] us to seek a real not an artificial ground for a society of men – a Church of men – to rest upon' (p. 185), he fails to acknowledge the fact that Butler went on to secure his ethical doctrine by a strategy which was elaborately controversial. While (Letter VII) he is good at exposing the merely verbal nature of Mansel's Schleiermacher-derived distinction of 'consciousness' and 'religious consciousness', in Letter X he states that 'What we have been taught in our Creed is, that because Absolute Morality could not have been fixed in a human conception, it came forth in the life of a Person, in His acts, His suffering' (p. 402). This is not irreconcilable with Butler, but is not found in his works. In the end, Maurice finds intolerable Mansel's proposition that 'God did create the human manifestation of Morality'.[66] Maurice retorts, 'What, is Christ not the human manifestation of Morality? Or does Mr. Mansel mean to set aside the words of the Creed, "Not created, but begotten?"' (p. 402). The disagreement is based on a difference of meaning in the word 'manifestation', where Mansel means (in accordance with natural usage) 'moral behaviour as exhibited in people' and Maurice means 'the example of moral behaviour as exhibited in people'.

The Mansel–Maurice controversy was less about any shortcomings of Mansel, who provides useful critiques of Kant and Schleiermacher, than about

---

[65] *What is Revelation?* (1859), 'Letter III: Mr. Mansel's Preface. – Butler', pp. 181–2.
[66] Quoted in *What is Revelation?*, p. 402.

Maurice's sense of urgency in transforming the Church of England's strategy of engagement with the populations of both the home base and the Empire. 'It is not that the church of God has lost the great towns; it has never had them' – a brilliance typical of the Maurice tradition.[67] The controversy coincides with the start of the career of *Fifteen Sermons* as the senior partner in Butler's oeuvre and anticipated the 'settlement missions' in the East End of London, the Church's equivalent of the Salvation Army missions and Czarist Russia's largely secular Narodnik movement. Since these settlements were the roots the quasi-revolutionary Labour borough councils of the East End of London, Clement Attlee's political education and the great reforming Labour government of 1945, it may be thought that Maurice had the better of the exchange. We have seen that, in Morehead, Christ was reinterpreted as a Butlerian Hero. The missionary movement, and in particular the CMS, transferred this heroic quality to the ministry and evangelical clerisy. The end-product was late Victorian Christian militants like General Charles Gordon (of Khartoum), one of many hundreds of evangelical army officers throughout the Empire, and the cricketer-turned-missionary C. T. Studd, who, rejecting celebrity, joined the China Inland Mission and later in life journeyed deep into Central Africa, not on a river-boat or wagon but on that most democratic and accessible of machines, a bicycle.

Henry Sidgwick

Both as practitioner and critical historian Henry Sidgwick has served as an entry point to moral philosophy for many generations of students in the anglophone world, so that his use of Butler and his differences from him are worth discussing in some detail. For reasons of space and because of its intrinsic importance to both Butler and Sidgwick we will focus on a single question, that of happiness, and examine Sidgwick's account of Butler's doctrine.

Sidgwick's aim is to produce a synthetic ethics from a confluence of the German and British schools and despite his great intellectual integrity this leads to some distortions. He presents Butler's treatment of Shaftesbury's doctrine as a revision, albeit a fundamental one, rather than a critique and thinks that Butler describes a psychological system 'in which some springs of action are naturally governing and regulative, while others are naturally submissive to regulation'.[68] But we have already seen that for Butler the affections struggle with each other to such an extent that special attention was paid to anger and the violent emotions and he for some time hesitated to decide whether self-love and benevolence occupy a discrete and higher categorical level. Sidgwick does admit that 'It is … difficult to ascertain Butler's view of the naturally regulative

---

[67] Arthur Winnington-Ingram, future bishop of London (1896). Quoted in Nigel Scotland's *Squires in the Slums: Settlements and Missions in Late Victorian London*, London, 2007, p. 1, a work which identifies Maurice's (but not Butler's) contribution to the movement's theology.
[68] *Outlines of the History of Ethics* (1886), 3rd edn, London, 1892, pp. 193–4.

principles' (*Outlines*, p. 194) but he underestimates the importance to Butler of the dynamic between public and private and the intimacy of their relationship: hence his ludicrous claim that Butler disbelieved in 'the existence of public benevolence', in which he is supposed to prefigure Hume (*Outlines*, p. 195). It is possible that Sidgwick had not read the *Six Sermons*, but this is an indefensible reading even of *Fifteen Sermons*. It also misses the point about Butler's account of politics as a mass process of co-operation between individuals and colliding circles of communities small and large. Perhaps for Sidgwick this would imply a definite political programme, as indeed is displayed in *Six Sermons*, which would escape the proper boundaries of philosophy: he notes that Butler was closer to Hobbes's political experience[69] than to that of the mid-Victorians.

Sidgwick himself believes that happiness is the object of human actions and practical ethics: 'happiness is made up of feelings that result from the satisfaction of impulses other than self-love ...' (*Outlines*, p. 193), although it is not clear why he thinks that self-love too cannot produce happiness. Since its absence certainly brings unhappiness it seems that he is using the term in a special sense. As we have noted previously, happiness for Butler is a symptom of well-being, and to be valued as such, rather than as an end in itself. In *Of Personal Identity* Butler had made the point that consciousness of one's identity could not itself constitute that identity. He was content to believe, with Clarke, that the person was an immaterial substance of which people were aware by empirical experiences and epistemological mechanisms, the latter broadly such as those described by Locke. The religious, legal, social and ethical institutions existed as consequences of the kind of consciousness which people had of their own identity and hence served definite purposes. The affective mechanisms which constituted the material from which consciousness arose gave, as it were, a unique colouring to each individual personality, some aspects of which were inevitably emotional. Sidgwick himself quotes Butler: 'interest, one's own happiness, is a manifest *obligation*' (*Methods*, p. 7, italics supplied), which is rather different from saying that happiness is important in itself, or that the term 'happiness' is to be understood in a purely emotional sense, rather than with the colouring of 'prosperity' and 'felicity'[70] which is intrinsic to Butler's account of it as the affective state of recognizing that something has happened which is of benefit to the individual or the community. For Butler, to say that we seek happiness is an elision, which requires caution when thinking ethically in practical situations or philosophically about ethics. Ultimately, of course, for Butler as for any Christian, redemption and salvation are more important than 'happiness' and, as he observed, the good life has only an uncertain correspondence with the happy life.[71]

---

[69] Henry Sidgwick, *Philosophy, its Scope and Relations*, London, 1902, Lecture II, §2.
[70] OED, 'happiness' 1 and 3, respectively. Only twentieth-century totalitarians dared the attempt actually to enforce their subjects' *duty* to feel happy.
[71] See Chapter 2, pp. 66–7.

Thus, Sidgwick claims that for 'rational Egoists' the 'ruling impulse' is Butler's and Hutcheson's '"calm" or "cool" self-love' but for people with a different philosophy it may be impersonal authority or personal (religious) authority,[72] or self-respect, or freedom, or admiration.[73] 'Other phases of emotion might be mentioned, all [being] ... inseparable from an apparent cognition ... of *rightness* in the conduct which they prompt'.[74] Note the force of 'apparent': these various philosophies are built on various degrees of self-deception, beneath which lies the deep structure of a scientific ethics, accessible only to the researches of contemporary professional philosophers.[75] All these 'impulses', like, indeed, Sidgwick's own 'happiness', might be subsumed under the Aristotelian term 'eudaimonia', since the definition of happiness which we supplied in an earlier chapter to elucidate Butler's own thinking ('the well-being which consists in engaging in morally right actions')[76] could be applied to them, thereby bringing them within a philosophical psychology.

Sidgwick develops his views in *The Methods of Ethics*, Book I, Chapter IV, in which, unusually, he writes in the first person. His attempt to prepare the way for devising a firmer basis for a Utilitarian ethics starts from the argument (pp. 40–1) that the sort of views held by Butler require the inference that if we wish to do something because we are driven thus by the attraction of pleasure (or repellence of pain) there cannot be a different course of action to which we are driven by reason. He proceeds to a treatment of the pleasure principle.

However interesting and useful Sidgwick's work may be, he seems to read Butler as a version of Hutcheson. His argument starts from a direct contradiction of Butler himself, who developed an analysis of the mind becoming consciously active in creating ethical mediation of the naturally occurring and coexisting affections, an ethics which put in the centre of attention the cooperative society, not the aristocratic or competitive individual. In Butler's view, which he illustrated in his treatment of resentment, if people were unable to act contrary to instinctual or emotional drives (typically of Butler, a speculative account of the mechanisms was avoided) they would be incapable of functioning in complex social situations. This accords with common experience: all readers will have seen people failing to protect their vital interests, or acting in functionally reckless ways, when under high levels of stress. We have seen Butler (following

---

[72] Albert Barnes, author of the *Popular Family Commentary on the New Testament* (published from 1832 and frequently reprinted), made Butler's point, which escaped Sidgwick, that the scientific 'knowledge' of the population is based on trust in the authority of Newton and the other great scientists (*Butler's Analogy: A Review*, London, n.d., p. 32). In his opinion, 'Butler ... seems to stand alone [in the] department of investigation ... [into] the moral government of the world' (*Butler's Analogy*, p. 6).

[73] In this Sidgwick is repeating Aristotle's preliminary comment in the *Nicomachean Ethics*, Book 1, Chapter 4 (1095ª 21).

[74] *The Methods of Ethics* (1874), 7th edn, London, 1907, pp. 39–40. This edition was reprinted (Indianapolis, IN, 1981) with an introduction by John Rawls.

[75] A position characteristic of a century which graced its successor with the application, often at gunpoint, of deterministic and 'scientific' accounts of economic history and 'race'.

[76] See pp. 70–1.

Hobbes) exempt people in such situations from the sanctions of morality. In fact, and anticipating Hume's critique of causality, Butler avoids the concept of determination and is content to observe events and actions as contingencies, to be discussed probabilistically within a system whose totality is unknowable but which is familiar and therefore to a degree predictable. It appears, indeed, that it is Sidgwick's lack of interest in physical science, social dynamics and psychological stress which leads him away from Butler, which is a pity, given that insights into these are Butler's main contribution to moral philosophy.

Another aspect of the doctrine of happiness where Sidgwick conceives a disagreement with Butler concerns the latter's account of the relation between the will and the affections. He quotes (*Methods*, p. 44) Butler's point that the particular passions are '*necessarily presupposed by the very idea* of an interested pursuit; since the very idea of interest or happiness consists in this, that an appetite or affection enjoys its object'. Sidgwick agrees that 'We could not pursue pleasure at all, unless we had desires for something else than pleasure; for pleasure consists in the satisfaction of just these "disinterested" impulses' (p. 44). He continues, however, to assert that there are many 'desires of which the object is something other than my own pleasure' (p. 45) and proceeds to give examples. All these examples are of behaviour which might be categorized as non-ethical, or animal, or concerning physical well-being. They are connected to the ethical, as Hume (who, Sidgwick admits, shares Butler's view) says, only by '[becoming] the object of another species of inclination that is secondary and interested' (*Methods*, p. 44 n2). Thus, Butler and Hume see self-love and benevolence as within the scope of ethics and the necessary, animal, appetites as not,[77] although, at least in Butler's case, a process of moral development or acculturation could bring ever more of human life into the ethical, by means of the voluntary – even liturgical – forming of habits of thought and conduct.

Sidgwick thinks that Butler 'does not distinctly recognise a calm regard for general happiness as a normal governing principle', parallel to the calm regard for private happiness which he calls self-love (*Outlines*, p. 195). His substitution of 'calm' for Butler's obsolescent (and nowadays misleading) 'cool' is editorially tactful, even if it constitutes a rather loaded borrowing from Hutcheson, whose doctrine bearing on happiness – the proto-Utilitarian 'greatest happiness of the greatest number' – Sidgwick describes as 'more guarded and ... unexceptional [in] form' (*Methods*, p. 44). But in thinking that Butler assigns any sort of higher ethical priority to the personal than to the public Sidgwick is wrong. Neither, considered separately, constitutes an ethical analysis of a situation. He is also wrong in supposing that Butler saw happiness as an end rather than as a very welcome and natural symptom; and he is wrong, therefore, to see Butler's 'self-love' as a regard for happiness. His being right that Butler

---

[77] Stephen Darwall points out that 'Berkeley thinks that ['nonmoral good'] is identical with pleasure'. ('Berkeley's Moral and Political Philosophy', in *Cambridge Companion to Berkeley*, p. 318). This is also true of Butler.

'does not distinctly recognise a calm regard for general happiness as a normal governing principle' is therefore fortuitous and without value.

It is interesting that in his *Outlines* (p. 233) Sidgwick identifies in Whewell's *Elements of Morality* (1846) an account of happiness which, although distinctly different from Butler's, nevertheless has areas of contact:

> ... a point where we may trace the influence of Kant – viz., in his rejection of self-love as an independent rational and governing principle, and his consequent refusal to admit happiness, apart from duty, as a reasonable end for the individual.

Butler was never as decided as that about the special status of self-love and benevolence and would not call them either 'rational', except in a wide sense, or 'governing', since they must contend with the conscience. But he certainly did not believe that happiness was the 'end' of practical ethics.

Sidgwick read Butler in an entirely secular spirit, congruous with his historically more justified readings of Hutcheson, Hume, Bentham and Mill, and used the results to underpin Utilitarianism at what he saw as some of its weaker points. As his *Methods* progresses, in its laborious and systematic fashion, the reader becomes ever more aware that discussions of putative faculties and categories are attempts less at definition than at the proposal of structures which are the least offensive to protests that there is no evidence for structures, a strategy of causing the least offence to the greatest number. 'So, again,' he says, 'moralists diverge widely in estimating the ethical value of Self-love' (p. 366). Butler's understanding of self-love may have been based on a borrowing from Clarke about the analogy between divine and human nature, and philosophers might well wish to examine the analogy's implications and sufficiency, but at least the number of his metaphysical axioms appears very small and the observations about human nature as it is actually perceived and experienced are acute and persuasive. Sidgwick places the moralists in a pattern of mutual relationships, influences and priorities but presents them as system-builders, and therefore as failures, rather than as explorers. 'We ought ... – with Butler – to regard resentment as a salutary "balance to the weakness of pity" ...' (*Methods*, p. 371). Butler did indeed say this, but the context is forgotten. Butler recognized, acutely and painfully, the existence of anger and resentment but his observation is not theological (about design) or philosophical (about categories or imperatives) but behavioural: he seeks to explain how the full extent of human nature produces an ethics which is not wholly natural but is an aspect of the historical and developmental acculturation of the Christian gospel. In actual day-to-day living, feelings of resentment, pity and so on have a way of discharging themselves. Butler knows this to be a truism, because everything is what it is (and not another thing) and if things did not balance out we would not be around to talk about them – Hobbesian resentment would have eaten up pity long ago and then eaten up itself, a point he made in *The Analogy* with his parables of the wild beasts.

Sidgwick's tutor, Whewell, had announced his Butler-based research programme from St Mary's pulpit, in a series of discourses in the traditional 'university sermon' genre. Sidgwick reacted strongly against Whewell, whom he includes among the 'Intuitional moralists [who were] ... hopelessly loose (as compared to mathematicians) in their definitions and axioms' (*Methods*, Preface, p. xvii). Now the breach between academic moral philosophy and theology had become definite, at the cost of making Butler, as well as many other writers on ethics, appear to be profound, even brilliant, but also rather odd and curiously deficient. In effect, Sidgwick has denied public space to Christian ethics, but at the cost of his own work expressing an unexplored, and even unacknowledged, secular metaphysics or meta-history.

This bred new misreadings of Butler, as generations of undergraduates were introduced to moral philosophy through Sidgwick's writings and anthologies. This was the case especially in America, where the *Methods* may still be described as 'the most philosophically profound of the strictly classical works'[78] and where several monographs were produced, in the 1920s and 1930s, presenting exceptionally etiolated readings of Butler's thought.

After Sidgwick

Sidgwick's final edition of the *Methods* was issued posthumously, in 1907, five years after G. E. Moore adopted Butler as a prototype of the modern language-oriented and analytical thinker. Sidgwickian Butler is still current, however: John Rawls, who placed ethics at the centre of his account of political society, not only introduced Sidgwick's work but to an extent absorbed it.

There seem, however, to remain difficulties not dissimilar to those which we saw in Sidgwick. Take, as an example, the 'problem of envy' as identified by Rawls himself.[79] 'A rational individual is not subject to envy, at least when the differences between himself and others are not thought to be the result of injustice and do not exceed certain limits' (p. 530). This dictum reads awkwardly. There are hints of an elitist and anti-empirical disgust with human nature as it really is ('rational individual ... not subject ...') and an appeal to the authority and judgement of a putative Supreme Court ('... injustice ...') which presumably could alone decide the scope of the 'certain limits'; this could hardly be left to individuals or interested pressure groups. An injustice is such only when the legislature decides that it be recognized as an issue. Clearly, Rawls's formulations, however interesting and powerful, lack a Butlerian simplicity and persuasiveness and require extensive restatement or exegesis. From Butler's point of view, as described in the present work and insofar as Rawls's society were actually instituted in reality, morality, the conscience and individual consciousness are not obviously allowed scope for their full development.

---

[78] John Rawls, Foreword to Sidgwick's *Methods*, Indianapolis, IN, 1982, p. v.
[79] John Rawls, *A Theory of Justice*, Oxford, 1972, §80, pp. 530–4.

By contrast, as we have seen, for Butler there are existential facts – envy exists (his own example is 'resentment') and may be tagged as problematic by the conscience – but not an existential problem, or even one of 'certain limits'. Envy will certainly be engaged by other affections in situations as they really occur and may be addressed by a course of habit-forming corrective action based on a thoughtful mediation of self-love and benevolence. Envy is thus managed but remains a welcome part of our diverse human nature, something to be used in our moral growth. The difference between Rawls and Butler probably does 'exceed certain limits': while both would agree that a nation's laws are coextensive with the broad outlines of its civic ethics, Rawls's ultimate ethical authority seems to be a judiciary, whereas, for Butler, authority lies in the consensus (the 'Cement of Society', in his brilliantly improvised phrase) emerging from the dynamic relations between the persons who constitute society, not rulings by institutions with delegated powers.[80] Rawls and Butler are akin in that each implies that the good person has, as it were, an ethical algorithm running continuously in the mind and that contemplating one's reactions to the socio-political environment can transform moral, or emotional, states. It does not appear that Rawls considered the merits of Butler's less formal and socially more dynamic model. Perhaps he would not have disagreed with Butler's proposition that humankind is fundamentally nothing but a moral animal, but, in *A Theory of Justice*, he is restricted to quoting Butler only from Selby-Bigge's secularized nineteenth-century anthology of *British Moralists*.[81]

Rawls transfers authority from the high street[82] to the court-room. This is also seen in Michael Sandel, who seeks to supersede Rawls.[83] Sandel's thesis is that ethics is embedded in the constitutional forms of the state, producing a norm of public discourse – he attaches the term 'neutral' to it, implying that there is a pale within which the status quo, of State (or Federal) ethics, struggles continuously to maintain its sufficiency. Beyond the pale there are moral dissidents, whose voices have a different (non-'neutral') quality in public spaces. This seems essentially factional. Butler, by contrast, locates the core of ethics not in the myths and coercive administration of the State but in the tangled networks of the individuals who comprise, and actively create, society.[84] We have seen

---

[80] The Whigs' refusal to convene Convocation probably helped Butler avoid constitutionalism.

[81] This practice extends to scholars of the eighteenth century. In a footnote in his *The Party of Humanity: Writing Moral Psychology in Eighteenth-Century Britain*, Baltimore, MD, 2000 (p. 120), Blakey Vermeule cites Butler from Selby-Bigge's 1897 anthology of *British Moralists* as the source of the century's key definitions of prudence and self-interest while, in the same sentence, resorting to the OED for a definition of compassion, rather than to Butler, who dealt with it extensively. There are no references to Butler in Vermeule's main text. Thus, Butler is simultaneously confined to footnotes and misrepresented.

[82] In American parlance, main street.

[83] Michael Sandel, *Liberalism and the Limits of Justice*, Cambridge, 1982; *Democracy's Discontent: America in Search of a Public Philosophy*, Cambridge, MA, 1996.

[84] It must be admitted that in practice he avoided meeting David Hume and Henry Home, on the grounds of his ineptness in and distaste for oral debate.

Butler express his disgust with factional behaviour in parliament, and we do not suppose the court and the robing-room to be very much better. To locate moral authority in a central legislature or judiciary seems to etiolate moral activity and exalt fallible individuals. For Butler the forensic is heuristic not judgemental.

Christine M. Korsgaard's 1992 Tanner lectures[85] are based more obviously in the discipline's historiography than the work of Rawls and Sandel. She is explicit in finding Butler useful, emphasizing his likeness with Hume and approaching him by way of the insight that Hobbes's account of human moral nature requires the sanction of an external authority.[86] Butler's critique of Hobbes was largely shaped by his wish to establish the ethical relations of terms like self-love and benevolence, pity and compassion, but Korsgaard points out that he also thinks that, while moral authority is a formally different thing from obligation enforced by (political) power, the mechanism of conscience reintroduces the mechanism of authority (pp. 30, 104; the formulation is the present author's). She also draws attention to Butler's proof that benevolent, 'disinterested', actions are theoretically as morally compelling and satisfying as those arising from self-love (p. 56). She thus seems to avoid the legalism implicit in Rawls's and Sandel's theories. However, the 'norms' she discusses are ethical, and consequently the conscience, which Butler experiences as giving liberation and fulfilment, is for her a constraint.[87] By contrast, Butler's equivalent of Korsgaard's 'norms', that which anchors ethical judgements so as to make them intelligible to others, is found in natural affective mechanisms and his ethics arises from the dynamic relationship between them, which is reassessed situation by situation. Certainly, the conscience requires the conscious mediation of the relationship between situation, (fallen) human nature and the Christian revelation but, as we have seen, the conscience and, consequently, the consciousness are always developing. Thus, the Butlerian person contributes, in every ethical transaction, to the building of society, the City on the Hill. Korsgaard's person, like Rawls's and Sandel's, is a citizen who submits, in every ethical transaction, to a State which builds itself on a constitution and the myth of a social contract. Butler is closer to the 'bioethics' of the neo-Darwinians – he believes in God's creativity in humankind as they believe in genetics. His 'Cement of Society' is a more robust concept than 'norms' and he appears philosophically less constricted by local political culture. Surprisingly, Korsgaard, like Rawls and Sandel, does not

---

[85] *The Sources of Normativity*, Cambridge, 1996. Russell Hardin (*David Hume: Moral and Political Theorist*, Oxford, 2007) has recently criticized the concept of the normative but not, I think, in a way which detracts from Korsgaard's core theses.

[86] She links Hobbes with Pufendorf. Unfortunately, however likely it is that Butler read Pufendorf he does not explicitly cite him – another frustrating reticence.

[87] When Butler denied that one should obey the moral authority of one's father if ordered to commit an unchristian act he referred not to the repressive authority of one's own conscience (which would merely signal the existence of a problem) but to an intelligent, critical *reception* of the gospel (Henri Talon, *Selections from the Journals and Papers of John Byrom*, pp. 169–72).

claim or advocate a reading of Butler beyond an anthologized selection from *Fifteen Sermons*.

The Butlerian person could survive in a 'post-Christian' society as well as in his own, of whose religious and moral deficiencies Butler was in any case acutely aware; could, theoretically, be pushed back into a social circle of only 'two or three' persons (Matthew 18.20) and yet just about maintain moral sanity and work towards creating a good society. Perhaps it is ironical, but salutary, that Butler, a member of the legislature, looked at society- and morale-building as a bottom-up process. With a Book and a 'way' (an 'ethos', in Newman's vocabulary) Butler is challenged unremittingly by conscience and moral choice but not by the existential anxiety of the secular liberal.

Conclusion

Butler was a major, even at times a dominant, figure in the Enlightenment, Romantic and Victorian periods, so that the case for a refreshed reading of his works scarcely needs arguing. We have reviewed, and in some instances criticized, the enormous range of thinkers who drew on him and noted the multitude of seemingly incompatible narratives to which he was acknowledged, or claimed, to have contributed. An exploration of this proliferation of Butlers, and Butler's contribution to anglophone intellectual and social history, cannot be done unless we also agree to investigate what he actually said. Regrettably, we have noted instances – and passed over many more – of philosophers and scholars unashamedly deriving their readings from anthologies or third-party accounts. Moreover, the situation is complicated by the absence of reliable texts. All posthumous editions are, to varying extents, inaccurate and misleading: in particular, *Fifteen Sermons* needs a variorum edition. The minor works and manuscript fragments have not yet been transcribed and edited accurately. With some of Butler's writings, therefore, the present book produced attempts at publishing the first developed readings (notably Chapters 4 and 5), while with the Clarke letters and *Fifteen Sermons* it required in effect the preparation of new editions. The twentieth-century Anglo-American approach to Butler was set aside; it tended to offer a stimulating but secularized figure, deficient in terminological rigour, playing anachronistically to weaknesses some of which he would have denied were such. The fairly small body of recent good work about him has not succeeded in setting Butler studies on a scholarly basis or reassessing his legacy. The starting point for the present book has therefore been one fact of fundamental importance: that his work was pastoral and apologetic, motivated and defined by his ministerial vocation.

For Butler the human reason was primarily a survival mechanism, poorly fitted for speculation and systematic thought: the ethical person must struggle unremittingly to become human. Locke had proposed that the mind was a *tabula rasa* but, in conscious opposition to this, Butler denied that it was solely a processor and store of information. He set the reception and construction of knowledge within psychological affective mechanisms, which produced mental states in which knowledge and emotions were formally inseparable and to be described in ethical terms.[1] Edmund Wilson's phrase, 'the shock of recognition',

---

[1] Steven Pinker, in *The Language Instinct*, New York, 1994, and subsequent works, notably *The Stuff of Thought: Language as a Window into Human Nature*, New York, 2007, has innocently applied similar approaches to Butler's, although of course vastly more developed and not oriented towards ethics.

could have been invented for him.[2] Humankind was thus not the *homo sapiens* of Butler's contemporary Linnaeus,[3] or the *homo faber* of Henri Bergson[4] or the *homo ludens* of Johan Huizinga,[5] but *homo moralis*, a being defined not by capability, activity or even biological species but by awareness of self and of physical and spiritual context, a being not of contemplation or activity but of complex praxis: sapient, constructive or playful, perhaps, but first of all spiritually and socially dutiful. For Butler knowledge and reasoning were probabilistic syntheses of data themselves received probabilistically; types of knowledge which were apparently different were in essence one (in the mind of God, by whom everything was known simultaneously and immediately). The society which accumulated and negotiated them consisted of multitudes of concentric, overlapping and colliding circles. He thence urged the duty of social solidarity and consensus-building. He threw belief, in a sense wider than the narrowly religious, onto trust in God. His ethics was based on analysis of specific situations but was supported by an acceptance of the metaphorical and fuzzy nature of language and by recognition of the need for more advanced textual criticism of the Scriptures than was currently available. He thought English, reformed Christian, society sufficiently viable, and apparently more so than past and present alternatives, but he did not advocate a theocratic, constitutional ethics: the Butlerian good person could, theoretically, function in any sort of society, even if the tendency was towards collective charity and, in Warburton's phrase, corporate holiness.[6]

Thus, in all his clerical appointments Butler attended scrupulously to his duties. As a parish priest he resided for many years in Stanhope, despite maintaining a curate, so that, with two priests in residence there must have been, in his large rural-cum-industrial parish, an anticipation of that typically nineteenth-century urban development, the team ministry. His social maladroitness, of which we see traces in his evidently deficient handling of parish committee and building contractors, was very likely a greater problem than later, when he was bolstered by the dignity of fame and episcopal status. Unlike some of the clergy and laity with whom he worked – Samuel Clarke and the Talbots, Sherlock and Secker – Butler did not exercise patronage strategically and left little mark on the Church of England in terms of clients who rose to prominence. He lacked the political skills to build networks which could have made him a force in this sort of way. There is no evidence that he desired them.

2   Edmund Wilson, *The Shock of Recognition*, New York, 1943.
3   Carolus Linnaeus, *Systema naturae*, Magdebourg, 1735.
4   Henri Bergson, *L'Evolution créatrice*, Paris, 1907.
5   Johan Huizinga, *Homo Ludens: A Study of the Play Element in Culture*, Haarlem, 1938; English edition, London, 1949.
6   William Warburton, *The Character and Office of the Messiah [1 Corinthians 1.30]*, in *The Principles of Natural and Revealed Religion*, London, J. & P. Knapton, 1753, vol. 1, p. 154.

While he loyally paid the minimum due attention to the Church's political environment (although, by later standards, a great deal), the heart of Butler's ministry was more personal. Indeed, his conception of the State was a projection of his conception of personal ethical relationships. He believed that a Christian society was a broader and safer base than a more narrowly personal one, however fundamentally important family and friends were in his philosophy. Thus, his ordination in the Church of England was delayed, but not prevented, by parental opposition: he was intended by his father for the Presbyterian ministry and, when he rejected that and conformed to the Church of England, for the law. His ordination did not proceed until a compromise became available: a ministry to the legal profession. The letters to Clarke suggest that ordination was also delayed by his felt need for a submissive and disciplined acceptance of an authority more sufficient than that of a parent. He meditated for many years on Clarke's metaphysics, applying to it doubt so strenuous and so acutely formulated that commentators have congratulated him on producing definitive critiques of Clarke's position. Nevertheless, his acceptance of Clarke's doctrine became the basis of both his ethics and his epistemology. Next, the *Fifteen Sermons*, the fruit of his duty to a congregation of lawyers and administrators, was recast, in its second edition, to serve as blueprint for a more general parochial purpose: it is distinctly more oriented towards the love of God. Whether or not the components of the second edition of *Fifteen Sermons* were preached in the Stanhope pulpit – and some slight evidence from minor textual changes has been advanced to suggest that for Butler they remained texts for oral delivery – they certainly provided a reconsidered framework for the development of his ministry. Similarly, although the strategy of *The Analogy* considered as a whole had a breadth of scope unnecessary for a parochial ministry, and a negativity of method inappropriate to it, its strategic inclusiveness was most certainly appropriate to a bishop and intellectual leader of a Church attacked on the one side by deism – an aggressive rejection of the revelation of the Second Person – and on the other by Methodism, which at that stage laid the greatest emphasis on moments of individual redemption. Moreover, it was a massive attempt at building social cohesion on the foundations of a tolerant Christian engagement with a world which, Butler postulated, could only be conceived empirically and probabilistically. Standing on the shoulders of these achievements – Newton's saying, about his own work's debt to his predecessors, is adapted to suggest the comparative loneliness of Butler's endeavours – the *Six Sermons* set out social policies which anticipate, and in at least some respects guided, the events of the next hundred years. The nation took half a century to absorb his work, through thinkers like Hartley, Reid, Adam Smith, Paley, Coleridge, Newman and Daniel Wilson and ultimately a group as mutually incompatible as Maurice, Sidgwick and even Charles Darwin. Nevertheless, a theologian addresses the people and the Church as they are found, not as they should be. It is therefore significant that beyond what we might loosely call the extended Talbot circle those most wholly welcoming of his works as they appeared successively in the 1730s and

1740s were evangelicals like Whitefield, Heylyn, Romaine, even Wesley,[7] and the poets Christopher Smart and John Byrom, together with those associated with the SPCK and the SPG. The latter organization increasingly recognized its need of an extrovert and socializing theology and a philosophy which, while, in Enlightenment style, not cloaking itself in technical virtuosity, was nevertheless equipped to give a multi-layered, Christian account of the human species and its cultural diversity.

All his major publications were sermons or, in the case of *The Analogy*, to a large extent assembled and edited from sermons. The personal tone of the letters to Clarke may have given way to a more formal style, but the convoluted syntax and density of thought often give the impression that he was thinking aloud, not only defending his propositions, even from attacks which might never be launched, but also putting painfully private thoughts into a public place in the guise of the administration of doctrine. His ministerial vocation seems very intimately connected with his private strategy of bringing doubt into play as a corrective to spiritual and intellectual arrogance. One of the most fundamental of his contributions to ethics and psychology – his account of 'resentment' (anger) – deliberately recovers ground from Hobbes but tests the proportions of his work to such an extent that it must have been written from a personal need. His account of the dynamics of benevolence and self-love was presented not as a scheme of fixed points but as the creation of human nature from a seething congeries of the darker emotions and from religious hope and duty. The insecure and embattled Hobbes felt fear and one can imagine the urbane and aristocratic Shaftesbury feeling disdain, but they could hardly acknowledge the boiling 'resentment' which Butler managed, in an act of originality and even genius, to secure among the fundamentals of his account of the balanced and ethically good person.

The minor publications (the Durham Charge, its associated *Articles of Visitation and Enquiry*), letters and fragments of his later years illustrate the clumsiness but deliberateness of his professional relations as a minister of religion. Whether the correspondents were philosophers, like Lord Kames, reluctant slave owners or the possessors of lands and rents which might more properly belong to the Church, their problems received a pastoral analysis of a peculiarly definitive kind, holding firmly to Butler's philosophical first principles. Thus, the Durham Charge, written by a self-confessed social maladroit, advises clergy on their conduct at dinner parties when faced with atheistic raillery, and gives Butler's reasons for the advice. The private fragments reveal constant anxiety but also a continuous process of orienting faith and doctrine to circumstance. No other English philosopher, except perhaps Hobbes, so obviously developed their philosophy as a practical support to their life or vocation.

Butler was sufficiently an intellectual phenomenon to exert an immediate and

---

7 '[A] strong and well-wrote treatise; but, I am afraid, far too deep for their understanding to whom it is primarily addressed,' John Wesley, *Journal*, 21 January 1746.

profound influence on his fellow clergy and intellectuals. His works' admission, in his lifetime, to the lecture halls of Oxford, and soon thereafter their circulation in Cambridge, Glasgow and Dublin, meant that the generation of clergy after his own was educated in them. By the end of the century the theology and ethics of most of the bishops were deeply in his debt, yet his period of greatest influence was still to come. We have seen, in the example of the SPG anniversary preachers, how his technical terminology and ethical concepts – the characteristic meanings assigned to 'conscience', 'consciousness', 'charity', 'analogy', 'probability', 'family', 'household' and so on – coloured their work and effected strategic changes in the Church's theological extroversion and inclusiveness. When the deistic, anti-revelation strain re-emerged in English public life in the early nineteenth century, *The Analogy* remained of sufficient intellectual power and scope to be available to present again an Anglican Christianity welcoming of rigorous empiricism and the new German Biblical criticism, while securing revelation and orthodoxy for a doubting and messy humankind.

This analysis leads unavoidably to the observation that modern accounts of the nineteenth century, in which Butler often features in the footnotes while being absent from the narratives, drastically rewrite history by underestimating or even concealing his influence. We have even suggested that the fissure in Anglo-American culture might helpfully be explored through an account of the differing receptions of Butler in the Empire and the Union. Modern America continues to use his work as a source and authority and it is arguable that the constitutionalism in which he engaged in the controversy about American bishops and his influence on political theory continue to affect American moral philosophy. On the other hand, Britain's moral philosophers in the second half of the twentieth century perhaps perversely turned away from a thinker who, by engaging with common sense, doubt, probability and the metaphorical and improvisatory nature of language, might have seemed a role model.

The present book has sought to extend the scope of and integrate the various disciplines active in current Butler studies, introducing discussions of employment law, justice, economics, probability theory and the application of the concept of exponential functions to moral philosophy and social analysis. With regard to the latter point, current Western, and indeed global, economies depend on exponential growth for their viability. This was not foreseen in the early eighteenth century, when the predominant economic theories were still painfully detaching themselves from a secular application of the injunction (Matthew 6.20) to 'lay up for yourselves treasures in heaven',[8] an expression of theories of arbitrarily accretional growth. We should recall that as late as 1798 Thomas Malthus, in his *Essay on the Principle of Population*, feared exponential population growth because he could not conceive of the possibility of corresponding exponential

---

[8]   The anonymous *Considerations of the East-India Trade*, London, J. Roberts, 1701 (perhaps by Henry Martin), is an early critique of the orthodox doctrine that the prime aim of trade was to accumulate bullion.

growth in the industrialized production of food. It may be considered that Butler laid the theoretical groundwork for this broader understanding; certainly, his social application of the relevant concepts from *The Analogy* required exponential growth in the social development and application of personal benevolence and in its corollary, the institutional development of Christian culture. Historically, his philosophy drove the development of the immense range of voluntary associations and their expression of an ever-increasing stock of public benevolence and its associated sense of personal well-being.

Butler's unashamedly putting his faith and ministry in the centre of his work is something which modern academics have tended to find either quaint or intolerable and it has been written out of accounts of his philosophy. However, we ended Chapter 6 with the question, whether he might stimulate an ethics which could flourish in a secular society, and we might have added that wanton secularizing of his philosophy has underpinned the extremes of twentieth-century liberal individualism. For that matter, his unexpurgated philosophy might diagnose the effective malignity – the anti-benevolence, as it were – of forces and institutions in modern society which psychologically cripple so large a proportion of the population in the name of caring for it. We owe to Butler our appreciation that ethics explores the dynamic relationship between people's inner and outer space – their morale (a word, if not a concept, unavailable to him). It is suggested that, compared with these liberal philosophies, his method – using mathematical and scientific as well as philosophical and theological tools to explore the human condition and embracing doubt, solidarity and the infinitely varied contingencies of experience – remains suggestive of an ethical, political and social philosophy relatively short on coercion and long on responsibility.

We have noted Butler's move towards a relativistic, 'multicultural', view of society, towards what postmodern thinkers described as 'narratives', competing, conflicting and coexisting.[9] His was a relatively narrow world compared with ours: his toleration of other cultures was hardly tested in practice, for the Dissenting community into which he was born and the evangelical movement which was rising around him were hardly alien to the Church and State of contemporary England. Nevertheless, it does seem that Butler thought in such terms. His was a religion of both the Book – we have seen his nods towards the Biblical textual criticism which was beginning to emerge – and the Way – we have explored his deliberate application of his philosophy to problems of social and intellectual conduct posed to him by laity as well as clergy. We have noted Newman's debt to him in this respect. His growing interest in ceremony and ritual confirms this wish to establish a defined, although both practically and theoretically elastic, boundary for Christian faith and culture. In his meetings with Wesley he emphasized the law, secular and ecclesiastical. A decade

---

[9]   A critique of this postmodernist concept has been provided by Stephen Prickett in his *Narrative, Religion and Science: Fundamentalism versus Irony, 1700–1999*, Cambridge, 2002.

later, in the Durham Charge, the doctrine is the same but the emphasis is on the liturgical.

This is of a piece with his unitary account of knowledge, in which there can be no hierarchy of authority, except on grounds of expedience. The concepts of consensus – a predominating climate of opinion from which dissent is possible only by self-exclusion from society[10] – and solidarity[11] were not available to Butler, and his own solution – 'cements of society' – turns from knowledge to collective conduct, demonstrating that he did not theorize exclusion or dissent. He believed that the fact that a society was cohesive and open to charitable benevolence was solid grounds for trusting its effective sufficiency. This would be a circular argument, of course, but for the special, transcendent, nature of the act of trust. This is one of his very few axioms and was a late reassertion of his Clarkean metaphysics. The doctrine of trust in the cements of society, its networks of benevolent and charitable institutions and personal relationships, was buttressed by a consciously unstructured collection of empirical data and forensic arguments, which are displayed in the *Six Sermons*. For example, contemporary Britain was plausibly a freer society than others. While not yet distinctively wealthier it was demonstrably experiencing greater economic growth and had entered a successfully expansionary phase, or even mode. British domestic society seemed to have a wholesome dynamic, as instanced by State regulation of labour exploitation and the charitable provision of mass education. Such factors had within them the need for progress and growth, and Butler had edged towards a formulation and application of the concept 'exponential', whose effectiveness would guarantee the sustainability of institutions which were constitutionally healthy (by contrast, of course, merely accretional growth would not test so severely the integrity of the original structure). Butler's own rather dark nature usefully counterbalanced this optimism and his account of the consciousness as fundamentally a device of ethical heuristics put the requirement of continuous struggle in the place where nationalist triumphalism might otherwise flourish.

These observations perhaps suggest why Butler's occupancy of the ideological space he created may increase his value for the engagement of modern philosophy with the metaphysical and moral speculations of present-day biologists, geneticists, mathematicians, physicists, astronomers, information technologists, climatologists, sociologists, and so on. The development or rejuvenation of these disciplines has generated an exuberant conviction in some practitioners that their new tools are intellectually and empirically all-sufficient. Although some of these authors advertise their religious faith, this flood of literature, a convergence of the scholarly and the journalistic, often displays urgency and

---

[10] The OED's first citation (as a scientific term) is dated 1854 and its first in the predominant modern sense 1861 – significantly, in relation to the Colenso controversy's disrupting a community of missionaries.

[11] The OED's first citation (1841) bears the Butlerian meaning 'collective responsibility'.

passion in seeking to persuade, and even to convert, the general reader to a scientific atheism or a sort of New Age godless piety, riddled with unacknowledged metaphysical speculation. In this their authors appear as true successors to the deists of the Enlightenment, and just as likely as the deists to attain only temporary fame or notoriety because of the imbalance of their narratives, which are, however, yet to be critically engaged by scholars with a different range of interests. As we have noted, Butler did not attack the deists; his method enabled him to draw them willy-nilly into the pale of orthodox society, offering big concessions in exchange for his big ideas. Thus, while he reassured the contemporary Church by being reasonably orthodox theologically and loyal politically, some of his thinking was and continues to be challenging. His position of accepting capital punishment but holding that otherwise the law should seek to reform not punish is awkward for all sides. His thinking about citizenship, slavery and education was notably realistic and unsentimental, combining caution with boldness. It merits close consideration, as the issues remain practically urgent for our societies, and, indeed, for the United Nations. His exploration of the ethical relationship of inner and outer fairly obviously adumbrates twentieth-century individualism and identity politics, while his doctrine of benevolence has been recognized since the mid-nineteenth century as entailing the concession of animal rights. The consequent suggestion of lowered barriers between species and the definition of humanity as something other than merely the narrowly biological suggests entry points into an analysis of his influence on Charles Darwin and his possible usefulness in engaging with modern neo-Darwinians. The question appears not yet to have been posed, whether a more precise understanding of Butler's 'negative' methodology might contribute to moral philosophy in relation to the mathematical and natural sciences.

In distinction from Hobbes and Locke, Butler held that society is consensual but non-contractual, the product of the mass of individuals trying to get along together, in a mess of anger, fear and love. His central thesis was that the conscience begets the consciousness, so that the human mind cannot but interpret and negotiate everything ethically. Introvert self-love cannot protect the individual, let alone build society, without extrovert benevolence. Charity is a dutiful extrusion from their dynamic relationship and necessarily becomes institutionalized. Here he offers an analysis of the stratification of rich and poor: neither the proponents of private charity nor those of state provision should find his thinking comfortable. Social policy is undeniably ethical in origin and Butler is worth renewed engagement as a theoretician of human nature, epistemology and moral philosophy and, perhaps, even as a theologian of the Church he served so doggedly.

Appendix
Some lexical features of SPG annual sermons,
1741–1800 (see Chapter 6)

To support the discussion of Butler's influence on the series of SPG annual sermons up to the abolition of the slave trade (1807) the entire corpus was examined, the majority of the items were read, and the following searches were performed on page images; the results were tabulated by decade, up to 1800 (after which the culture of the series was disturbed by the campaign for abolition). This appendix gives details of the aims, method and results.

It was hypothesized that a lexical search of the corpus for some of Butler's key words would provide material for a discussion of the influence of Butler's own sermon, and his moral philosophy in general. These were grouped in three categories. After each word the search string is given in parentheses:

- Moral philosophy: of the large core vocabulary of the subject, words especially distinctive to Butler were: benevolence (benevolen*); charity (charit*); conscience (conscience); affection (affection*);
- Slavery: slavery (slave*); Negro (negro*); Barbados (barbad*);
- Law in regard to the master–servant relationship: property (property); family (family); household (household); law (law).

In the last category plurals were excluded from the searches because they would indicate discussion of particulars, not principles.

The word searches were performed on the items held on Gale Publishing's ECCO, using its search engine as it performed on 12–13 October 2009, set to 'low fuzziness'.

In two cases (Yorke, 1779 and Warren, 1787) ECCO did not hold the sermon and in two others (Harcourt, 1798 and Courtenay, 1800) the images could not be accessed on those days. These four sermons were examined manually at the Bodleian Library, using the same parameters put to Gale's search engine.

The search results were hits on page images; hence two occurrences of 'conscience' on one page would result in one hit. The results therefore tabulate not the density of the lexical features but the frequency (per sermon) of pages containing those features. Hence a score of 1.0 indicates that the average sermon used 'conscience' on one page. Many hits therefore indicate not greater local density but a more extended consideration of a concept. Variations in purely local density (on a single page, roughly equivalent to an episode in an argument) is an indication of rhetorical style, rather than variations in intensity of concentration on a given concept.

Optical character recognition software, especially when applied to images of pre-twentieth-century material, remains unreliable, and in the present case certainly failed to identify all possible hits. Hence the results were used to test hypotheses arising from examinations and readings, not to direct the examination of the corpus.

The absence of electronic plain text versions generated to scholarly standards is the greatest single barrier to advances in the critical reading of printed literature, as it prevents the support of normally sensitive readings by statistical analyses at grammatical and syntactical levels as well as preventing the development of word search techniques: all too many studies by corpus linguists are based on unrepresentative samples and texts of unscholarly provenance.

In Appendix Table 1, for the decade 1781–90 the figures exclude 1783, the year of Porteus's highly atypical sermon; (the figures in brackets include *Porteus 1783*). *Porteus 1783* claims 72 percent of all references to slavery in the decade. The figure would be even higher if word counts were used.

Table 1: SPG sermons, 1741–1800: average page-hits per sermon, by decade

	Ethics	Slavery	Property/law
1741–50	6.1	3.3	3.5
1751–60	5.0	3.2	3.2
1761–70	5.1	1.5	3.2
1771–80	4.2	5.4	4.1
1781–90	5.4 (5.4)	2.1 (6.2)	2.9 (3.3)
1791–1800	4.0	2.6	2.7
1741–1800	5.0	3.1 (3.8)	3.3

Table 2: SPG sermons, 1741–1800: ethical terminology: average page-hits per sermon, by decade

	Benevolence	Charity	Conscience	Affections
1741–50	0.4	4.8	0.7	0.2
1751–60	1.0	3.0	0.3	0.4
1761–70	0.9	2.7	1.0	0.5
1771–80	1.6	2.6	0.3	0.1
1781–90	1.9	1.6	1.3	0.4
1791–1800	1.8	1.5	0.3	0.4
1741–1800	1.3	2.7	0.7	0.3

Table 3: SPG sermons, 1741–1800: social terminology:
average page-hits per sermon, by decade

	Property	Family	Household	Law
1741–50	0.7	0.3	0	2.5
1751–60	0.8	0.4	0.1	1.9
1761–70	1.1	0.2	0.1	1.8
1771–80	1.1	0.2	0.2	2.6
1781–90	1.8	0.3	0	1.3
1791–1800	0.6	0.5	0	1.6
1741–1800	1.0	0.3	0.1	2.0

Bibliography

Included are all editions of Butler's works published in his lifetime (arranged in the order in which their first editions appeared), and those posthumous editions actually cited (arranged in order of publication). The names of publishers are given for items printed in the eighteenth-century because such information is frequently important in discussing their ideological environment. The 'nineteenth-century digests ...' list, few of whose items are actually cited, aspires to be comprehensive but is very much work in progress. It is included to demonstrate Butler's importance as a textbook.

Locations of MSS material consulted

Bodleian Library
British Library
Durham Cathedral Library
Durham University Library
Lambeth Palace Library
Oriel College, Oxford

Seventeenth- and eighteenth-century works

Annual Register, London, J. Dodsley, 1765 etc.
Anon. (Henry Martin?), *Considerations of the East-India Trade*, London, J. Roberts, 1701
Apthorp, East, *Review of Dr. Mayhew's Remarks on the Answer to his Observations on the Charter and conduct of the [SPG]*, London, John Rivington, 1765
Atkey, Anthony, *The Rectitude of Providence under the Severest Dispensations [Jeremiah 12.1]*, London, J. Roberts, 1733
Bagot, Lewis, *Sermon preached before the [SPG] [Daniel 12:3]*, London, S. Brooke, 1790
Balguy, John, *Letter to a Deist, Concerning the Beauty and Excellency of Moral Virtue*, London, John Pemberton, 1726
Balguy, John, *The Foundation of Moral Goodness*, London, John Pemberton, 1728 and 1729
Balguy, John, *Divine Rectitude*, London, John Pemberton, 1733
Bayes, Thomas, *Divine Benevolence*, London, John Noon, 1731
Bayes, Thomas, *An Introduction to the Doctrine of Fluxions*, London, J. Noon, 1736
Bentham, Edward, *An Index to the Analogy of Bishop Butler*, rev. and ed. Thomas Bartlett, London, 1842
Bentley, Richard, *Proposals for Printing a New Edition of the Greek Testament and St. Hierom's Latin Version*, London, J. Knapton, 1721

Bentley, Richard, *Works*, three volumes, ed. A. Dyce, London, 1836–8

Berkeley, George, *The Analyst; or, a Discourse Addressed to an Infidel Mathematician*, London, J. Tonson, 1734

Berkeley, George, *Works*, ed. A. A. Luce and T. E. Jessop, London, 1948–51

Blackstone, William, *Commentaries on the Laws of England*, London, Clarendon Press, 1765

Bosman, Willem, *A New and Accurate Description of the Coast of Guinea*, London, J. Knapton, D. Midwinter, 1705

Bott, Thomas (Philanthropus), *Remarks upon Dr. Butler's Sixth Chapter of the Analogy of Religion, &c. Concerning Necessity; And also upon the Dissertation of the Nature of Virtue*, London, J. Noon, 1737

Boyle, Robert, *Some Motives and Incentives to the Love of God* (1659), 4th edn, London, Henry Herringman, 1665

Browne, Isaac Hawkins, *Poems upon Various Subject, Latin and English*, London, J. Nourse, 1768

Browne, Peter, *The Procedure, Extent, and Limits of Human Understanding*, London, William Innys, 1728

Browne, Peter, *Things Divine and Supernatural Conceived by Analogy with Things Natural and Human*, London, William Innys & Richard Manby, 1733

Burnet, Thomas, *The Demonstration of True Religion*, two volumes, London, A. Bettesworth, 1726

Butler, Joseph, *Several Letters ... Relating to the First Volume of the Sermons Preached at Mr Boyle's Lecture*: See below, Samuel Clarke, *A Demonstration of the Being and Attributes of God ... The Fourth Edition, Corrected*, London, James Knapton, 1716

Butler, Joseph, *Fifteen Sermons Preached at the Rolls Chapel*, London, James & John Knapton, 1726

Butler, Joseph, *Fifteen Sermons Preached at the Rolls Chapel. The Second Edition, corrected: To which is added a Preface*, London, James & John Knapton, 1729

Butler, Joseph, *Fifteen Sermons*, 3rd edn, London, James, John & Paul Knapton, 1736

Butler, Joseph, *Fifteen Sermons*, 4th edition, London, James, John & Paul Knapton, 1749

Butler, Joseph, *The Analogy of Religion, Natural and Revealed, to the Constitution and Course of Nature. To which are added Two brief Dissertations ...*, London, James, John & Paul Knapton, 1736

Butler, Joseph, *The Analogy of Religion, Natural and Revealed, to the Constitution and Course of Nature. To which are added Two brief Dissertations ...*, Dublin, George Ewing, 1736

Butler, Joseph, *The Analogy of Religion*, 2nd edn, London, James, John & Paul Knapton, 1736

Butler, Joseph, *The Analogy of Religion*, 3rd edn, London, John & James Knapton, 1740

Butler, Joseph, *The Analogy of Religion*, 4th edn, London, John & James Knapton, 1750

Butler, Joseph, *A Sermon Preached before the Incorporated Society for the Prop-

agation of the Gospel in Foreign Parts; ... on Friday, February 16, 1738–9, London, J. & P. Knapton, 1739

Butler, Joseph, *A Sermon Preached before the Right Honourable the Lord-Mayor ... on Monday in Easter-Week, 1740*, London, John & Paul Knapton, 1740

Butler, Joseph, *A Sermon Preached before the House of Lords ... Jan. 30, 1740–41*, London, J. & P. Knapton, 1741

Butler, Joseph, *A Sermon Preached ... on Thursday May the 9th, 1745*, London, B. Dod, 1745

Butler, Joseph, *A Sermon Preached before the House of Lords ... on Thursday, June 11, 1747*, London, John & Paul Knapton, 1747

Butler, Joseph, *A Sermon Preached ... for the Relief of Sick and Diseased Persons ... on Thursday, March 31*, London, H. Woodfall, 1748

[Butler, Joseph & John Dolben], *The Reverend Sir John Dolben's Speech to the Right Reverend Father in GOD Joseph ... On his Lordship's First Arrival in his Diocese, on Friday June 28, 1751. With his Lordship's Answer*, Newcastle, J. White, n.d. [1751]

Butler, Joseph, *A Charge Deliver'd to the Clergy, at the Primary Visitation of the Diocese of Durham*, Durham, J. Richardson, 1751

Butler, Joseph, *Articles of Visitation and Enquiry, Concerning Matters Ecclesiastical Exhibited to the Ministers, Church-Wardens, and Sidesmen, of Every Parish with the Diocese of Durham, at the Primary Visitation of the Right Reverend Father in GOD, Joseph ... In the Year 1751*, Durham, Isaac Lane, n.d. [1751]

Butler, Joseph, *The Works ... To which is prefixed, a Life of the Author, by Dr. Kippis; with a Preface, giving some Account of his Character and Writings by Samuel Hallifax*, two volumes, Edinburgh, 1804

Butler, Joseph, *The Analogy of Religion*, introduction by Daniel Wilson (1825), 3rd edn, Glasgow, 1829

Butler, Joseph, *The Works*, ed. Samuel Hallifax, 2nd edn, London, 1841

Butler, Joseph, *Some Remains, hitherto unpublished, of Joseph Butler*, ed. Edward Steere, London, 1853

Butler, Joseph, *The Analogy of Religion ... With Analytical Index by Edward Steere*, London, 1857

Butler, Joseph, *The Sermons and Remains of Joseph Butler*, ed. Edward Steere, London, 1862

Butler, Joseph, *The Works*, ed. W. E. Gladstone, two volumes, Oxford, 1897

Butler, Joseph, *The Works*, ed. J. R. Bernard, two volumes, London, 1900

Butler, Joseph, *Fifteen Sermons Preached at the Rolls Chapel & A Dissertation on the Nature of Virtue*, ed. W. R. Matthews, London, 1914

Butler, Joseph, *The Works*, ed. David E. White, Rochester, NY and Woodbridge, 2006

Byrom, John, *The Private Journal and Literary Remains*, ed. R. Parkinson, Manchester, 1856

Cardano, Gerolamo, *Liber de ludo aleae. 'The Book on Games of Chance'* (1663), trans. Sydney Henry Gould, in Oystein Ore, *Cardano, the Gambling Scholar*, Princeton, NJ, 1953

Charleton, Walter, *The Darknes of Atheism Dispelled by the Light of Nature. A Physico-Theologicall Treatise*, London, William Lee, 1652

Clagett, Nicholas, *A Sermon preached before the [SPG]*, London, J. & J. Pemberton, 1737

Clarke, John, trans., *Rohault's System of Natural Philosophy*, London, James Knapton, 1723

Clarke, Samuel, *A Demonstration of the Being and Attributes of God: more particularly in answer to Mr. Hobbs, Spinoza, and their Followers. Wherein the Notion of Liberty is Stated, and the Possibility and Certainty of it Proved, in Opposition to Necessity and Fate. Being the Substance of Eight Sermons Preach'd ... in the Year 1704, at the Lecture Founded by the Honourable Robert Boyle*, London, J. Knapton, 1705

Clarke, Samuel, *A Discourse concerning the Unchangeable Obligations of Natural Religion, and the Truth and Certainty of the Christian Revelation. Being Eight Sermons Preach'd ... in the Year 1705, at the Lecture Founded by the Honourable Robert Boyle, Esq.*, London, J. Knapton, 1706

Clarke, Samuel, *A Demonstration of the Being and Attributes of God ... The Fourth Edition, Corrected*, London, James Knapton, 1716

Clarke, Samuel and Gottfried Wilhelm Leibniz, *A Collection of Papers, which Passed between the Late Learned Mr. Leibnitz, and Dr. Clarke, in the Years 1715 and 1716. Relating to the Principles of Natural Philosophy and Religion*, London, James Knapton, 1717

Conybeare, J., *Sermons*, two volumes, London, Samuel Richardson, 1757

Coxe, William, *Memoirs of the Life and Administration of Sir Robert Walpole*, London, T. Cadell, jun. & W. Davies, 1798

Derham, William, *Physico-Theology: Or, a Demonstration of the Being and Attributes of God, from his Works of Creation*, London, W. Innys, 1713

Derham, William, *Astro-Theology: Or, a Demonstration of the Being and Attributes of God, from a Survey of the Heavens*, London, W. Innys, 1715

Descartes, René, *Œuvres philosophiques et morales*, Paris, 1948

Dodwell, William, *A [Charity Schools] Sermon [Psalm 34.11]*, London, B. Dod, 1758

Edwards, John, *The Socinian Creed*, London, J. Robinson & J. Wyat, 1697

Epictetus, *The Discourses of Epictetus*, trans. Elizabeth Carter (1758), reprinted London, 1910

Glasse, Samuel, *The Piety, Wisdom, and Policy, of Promoting Sunday-Schools [Deuteronomy 31.12–3]*, London, Mess. Rivingtons & Gardner, 1786

Gyll, Thomas, *The Diary of Thomas Gyll, The Publications of the Surtees Society, vol. CXVIII*, Durham, 1910

Hallifax, Samuel, *A [Charity Schools] Sermon [Proverbs 29.15]*, London, J. F. & C. Rivington, 1789

Hare, Francis, *Sermon preached before the [SPG] [Romans 10:13–15]*, London, S. Buckley, 1735

Hartley, David, *Observations on Man, his Frame, his Duty, and his Expectations*, two volumes, London, James Leake and Wm Frederick, 1749

Herring, Thomas, *A Sermon preached before the [SPG] [Matthew 11.5]*, London, J. & J. Pemberton, 1738

Heylyn, John, *A Sermon Preached to the Societies for the Reformation of Manners, at St. Mary-le-Bow, on Wednesday January the 18th, 1728 [Romans 13.4]*, London, Joseph Downing, 1729

Heylyn, John, *A Sermon Preached at St. Sepulchre's Church; April the 25th, 1734 [Luke 16.19–20]*, London, Joseph Downing, 1734

Heylyn, John, *A Sermon Preached ... [at] the Consecration of ... Joseph, Lord Bishop of Bristol [2 Timothy 2.15–16]*, London, C. Rivington, 1738

Heylyn, John, *Theological Lectures at Westminster-Abbey*, London, J. & R. Tonson & S. Draper, 1749

Hoadly, Benjamin, *Preservative against the Principles and Practices of the Nonjurors both in Church and State*, London, James Knapton, 1716

Hobbes, Thomas, *The Elements of Law*, ed. J. C. A. Gaskin, Oxford, 1994

Hobbes, Thomas, *Leviathan*, ed. G. A. J. Rogers and Karl Schuhmann, two volumes, London, 2003

Hooper, George, *A Fair and Methodical Discussion of the First and Great Controversy between the Church of England and Church of Rome, Concerning the Infallible Guide*, London, R. Chiswell & R. Bentley, 1689

Hooper, George, 'A Calculation of the Credibility of Human Testimony', *Philosophical Transactions*, London, October 1699

Hooper, George, *Works*, Oxford, James Fletcher, 1757

Hume, David, *Enquiries Concerning Human Understanding and Concerning the Principles of Morals*, ed. P. H. Nidditch, 3rd edn, Oxford, 1975

Hume, David, *A Treatise of Human Nature*, ed. L. A. Selby-Bigge, Oxford, 1896

Hutcheson, Francis, *Essay on the Nature and Conduct of the Passions and Affections*, London, John Smith & William Bruce, 1728

Hutchinson, William, *The History and Antiquities of the County Palatinate of Durham*, Newcastle, S. Hodgson & Robinson, 1785

Jones, Jeremiah, *A New and Full Method of Settling the Canonical Authority of the New Testament*, London, J. Clark & R. Hett, 1726

Jurin, James (pseud: Philalethes Cantabrigiensis), *Geometry No Friend to Infidelity: or, a Defence of Sir Isaac Newton and the British Mathematicians, in a Letter to the Author of the Analyst*, London, T. Cooper, 1734

Locke, John, *An Essay concerning Human Understanding*, ed. John W. Yolton, rev. edn, two volumes, London, 1965

Lowth, Robert, *De sacra poesi Hebraeorum*, Oxford, Clarendon Press, 1753

Maddox, Isaac, *Vindication of the Government, Doctrine, and Worship of the Church of England, established in the Reign of Queen Elizabeth*, London, A. Bettesworth & C. Hitch, 1733

Maddox, Isaac, *Sermon preached ... before the [SPG] [Titus 2:11–13]*, London, J. Downing, 1734

Malebranche, Nicholas, *De la recherche de la vérité*, three volumes, Paris, André Pralard, 1674–5

Malebranche, Nicholas, *Treatise on Nature and Grace*, trans. Patrick Riley, Oxford, 1992

Malthus, Thomas, *Essay on the Principle of Population*, London, J. Johnson, 1798

Monboddo, James Burnet, Lord, *Of the Origin and Progress of Language*, Edinburgh, A. Kincaid & W. Creech, 1773–92

More, Henry, *The Complete Poems*, ed. Alexander B. Grosart (1878), reprinted Hildesheim, 1969

Newton, Isaac, *Philosophia naturalis principia mathematica*, Londoni, Jussu Societas Regiae, 1687

Newton, Isaac, *Optice: ... Latine reddidit S.Clarke*, Londoni, Sam. Smith & Benj. Walford, 1706

Newton, Thomas, *Dissertations on the Prophecies*, London, J. & R. Tonson, 1754

Norris, John, *A Collection of Miscellanies* (1687), 2nd edn, London, J. Crosley & S. Manship, 1692

Perronet, Vincent, *A Vindication of Mr. Locke*, London, James, John & Paul Knapton, 1736

Perronet, Vincent, *A Second Vindication of Mr. Locke*, London, Fletcher Gyles, 1738

Pope, Alexander, *Poetical Works*, ed. Herbert Davis, London, 1966

Porteus, Beilby, *An Essay towards a Plan for the more Effectual Civilization and Conversion of the Negroe Slaves, on the Trust Estate in Barbadoes* (1783), *Tracts on Various Subjects*, London, T. Cadell & W. Davies, 1807

Porteus, Beilby, *A Review of the Life and Character of the Right Rev. Dr. Thomas Secker*, 5th edn, London, 1797

Price, Richard, *Review of the Principal Questions and Difficulties in Morals*, London, A. Millar, 1758

Price, Richard, *Four Dissertations* (1758), 2nd edn, London, A. Millar & T. Cadell, 1768 (reprinted Bristol, 1990, Introduction by John Stephens)

Reid, Thomas, *An Inquiry into the Human Mind, on the Principles of Common Sense*, Edinburgh, A. Millar, 1764

Reid, Thomas, *Essays on the Intellectual Powers of Man*, Edinburgh, J. Bell, 1785

Romaine, William, *The Whole Works*, eight volumes, London, 1821

Rotheram, John, *A Sketch of the One Great Argument, Formed from the Several Concurring Evidences, for the Truth of Christianity*, Oxford, Richard Clement, 1754

Scott, Daniel, *An Essay towards a Demonstration of the Scripture-Trinity*, London, J. Noon, 1725

Scott, Daniel, *Appendix ad Thesaurum Graecae linguae ab Hen. Stephano constructum; et ad Lexica Constantini & Scapulae*, Londoni, Joh. Noon, 1745, 1746

Secker, Thomas, *Fourteen Sermons Preached on Several Occasions*, 2nd edn, London, J. & F. Rivington, 1771

Secker, Thomas, *Eight Charges Delivered to the Clergy of the Dioceses of Oxford and Canterbury*, 3rd edn, London, John, Francis & Charles Rivington, 1780

Secker, Thomas, *The Autobiography of Thomas Secker, Archbishop of Canterbury*, ed. J. S. Macauley & R. W. Greaves, Lawrence, KS, 1988

Shaftesbury, Anthony Ashley Cooper, Third Earl of, *Characteristics of Men, Manners, Opinions, Times, etc*, introduction by David McNaughton, Bristol, 1999

Shaftesbury, Anthony Ashley Cooper, Third Earl of, *The Life, Unpublished Letters, and Philosophical Regimen*, ed. Benjamin Rand, London and New York, 1900, reprinted Bristol, 1999

Sherlock, Thomas, *The Tryal of the Witnesses of the Resurrection of Jesus*, London, J. Roberts, 1729

Sherlock, Thomas, *Several Discourses Preached at the Temple Church* (1753), four volumes, 6th edn, London, J. Whiston & B. White *et al.*, 1772

Smart, Christopher, *Hymns for the Amusement of Children* (1770), Dublin, W. Sleator & J. Williams, 1772, reprinted London, 1973

Smart, Christopher, *The Poetical Works of Christopher Smart*, ed. Karina Williamson, Oxford, 1980–96

Smithies, Yorick, *Cooperation of Human Benevolence with the Divine [1 Corinthians 3:9]*, Colchester, W. Keymer, [1789]

Stow, William, *Remarks on London*, London, T. Norris & H. Tracy, 1722

Terrick, Richard, *Sermon preached before the [SPG] [Isaiah 11.9]*, London, E. Owen & T. Harrison, 1764

Thomas, John, *Sermon Preached before the [SPG] [Matthew 7.24]*, London, T. Harrison & S. Brooke, 1780

Tillotson, John, *Sermons on Several Subjects and Occasions, by the most Reverend Dr. John Tillotson*, 12 volumes, London, C. Hitch & L. Hawes, 1757

Tindal, Matthew, *Christianity as Old as the Creation, or the Gospel a Republication of the Religion of Nature*, London, [s.n.], 1730

Trimnell, Charles, *A sermon preach'd before the Honourable House of Commons (Proverbs 21.30-31)*, London, Thomas Chapman, 1708

Tucker, Josiah, *The Life and Particular Proceedings of the Rev. Mr. George Whitefield*, London, J. Roberts, 1739

Tucker, Josiah, *A Brief History of the Principles of Methodism*, Oxford, James Fletcher, 1742

Tucker, Josiah, *Charity Schools Sermon [Proverbs 22.6]*, London, SPCK, 1766

Tucker, Josiah, *An Humble Address, and Earnest Appeal*, Gloucester, [for] T. Cadell, 1775

Tucker, Josiah, *Four Tracts, together with Two Sermons, on Political and Commercial Subjects*, Gloucester, [for] J. Rivington, 1774

Voltaire, *The Philosophical Dictionary for the Pocket*, trans. Anon, London, Thomas Brown, 1765

Warburton, William, *The Principles of Natural and Revealed Religion*, London, J. & P. Knapton, 1753

Wesley, John, *Works*, ed. Thomas Jackson, 3rd edn, London, 1831 (also available as *The Works of John Wesley on Compact Disc*, Franklin, TN, Providence House Publishers, 1995)

White, Joseph, *On the duty of attempting the propagation of the Gospel [Mark 16.15]*, London, G. G. J. Robinson, 1785

White, Joseph, *Sermons preached before the University of Oxford ... at the Lecture Founded by the Rev. J. Bampton* (1784), London, G. G. J. & J. Robinson, 1789

Whitefield, George, *Journals*, Edinburgh, 1960

Whitefield, George, *Letters of George Whitefield for the Period 1734–1742*, Edinburgh, 1976

Whitefield, George, *A Continuation [of the Journal]*, London, James Hatton, 1739

Wilkins, John, *The Principles and Duties of Natural Religion*, London, T. Basset, H. Brome, R. Chiswell, 1675

Wilson, Thomas, *An Essay towards an Instruction for the Indians*, London, J. Osborn & W. Thorn, 1740

Wollaston, William, *The Religion of Nature Delineated* (1722), London, J. Knapton, 1724

Wood, James, *Readiness to good Works, and Largeness of Mind in them [1 Timothy 6.17–19]*, London, R. Hett, 1732

Nineteenth-century digests, primers and cribs for students

(in order of publication)

1820: Wrangham, Francis, *The Principal Parts of Bishop Butler's Analogy ... Abridged*, London

1821: Leigh, Chandos, *A Short Discourse ... abstracted from Butler's Analogy*, Warwick

1823: [Anon], *Hints to Medical Students upon the Subject of a Future Life*, York

1826: Sleater, Charles, *A Succinct Analysis of the Analogy of Butler*, Dublin

1834: Hobart, Richard, *An Analysis of Bishop Butler's Analogy*, Dublin

1836: Smith, John Bainbridge, *A Compendium of Rudiments in Theology, containing a Digest of Bishop Butler's Analogy ... For the Use of Students*, London

1837: Wilson, John Posthumous, *An Analysis of Bishop Butler's Analogy*, Oxford

1841: Allen, M., *Four Hundred Questions on Butler's Analogy*, Dublin

1842: Bentham, Edward, *An Index to Analogy of Butler*, London [compiled 1736]

1847: Duke, Henry Hinxman, *A Systematic Analysis of Bishop Butler's Analogy*, London

1847: Wilkinson, John, *A Systematic Analysis of Bishop Butler's Analogy*, Oxford

1847: McKee, Joseph, *The Analogy of Religion ... with an Introductory Preface by Bishop Hallifax; to which are Added, Copious Analytical Questions for the Examination of Students by Joseph McKee*, New York

1850: Wilson, John Posthumous, *An Analysis of Bishop Butler's Analogy*, London (rpt of Oxford, 1837)

1854: Hulton, Campbell Grey, *A Catechistical Help to Bishop Butler's Analogy*, London

1855: Gorle, James, *An Analysis of Butler's Analogy*, Cambridge (with examination questions)

1856: Swainson, C.A., *Hand-book to Butler's Analogy*, Cambridge

1857: [Anon], Joseph Butler, *Principles of Moral Science*, Madras (in Tamil)

1859: Champlin, J.T., *Bishop Butler's Ethical Discourses*, Boston

1859: Hulton, Campbell Grey, *A Catechistical Help to Bishop Butler's Analogy*, second edition, London

1859: Hobart, Richard, *An Analysis of Bishop Butler's Analogy*, New York (rpt of Dublin, 1834)

1864: Napier, Joseph, *Lectures on Butler's Analogy of Religion to the Constitution and Course of Nature. Delivered before the members of the Dublin Young Men's Christian Association in connection with the United Church of England and Ireland*, Dublin

1872: Poyntz, Newdigate, *The Truth of Christianity*, London (excerpts from Butler)
1873: Huckin, Henry Robert, *Analogy of Religion Founded upon Butler*, London
1875: Smith, Leonidas L, *Questions on Butler's Analogy*, New York
1879: D., E.V., *A Catechistical Epitome of Bishop Butler's Analogy*, Dublin
1881: Collins, W. Lucas, *Butler*, Edinburgh
1881: Thomas, Robert Owen, *A Synopsis of Butler's Analogy*, London
1882: Angus, Joseph, *An Analysis of Butler's Analogy*, London
1883: Cooper, VK, *The Gist of Butler: sermons I., II., III. ... To which is Appended an Epitome of the Analogy: Chap. III.*, Durham
1886: Norris, J.P., *Lectures on Butler's Analogy*, London
1888: Hughes, W, *A Catechistical Analysis of Butler's Analogy*, Dublin
1889: Pynchon, Thomas Ruggles, *Bishop Butler ... A Sketch of his Life. With an Examination of the "Analogy"*, New York
1890: Anon, *Analytical Commentary on Butler's Analogy*, Guildford
1891: Cady, P.K., Butler's Analogy: *Notes and Lectures* [for seminary students], New York
1898: Hughes, Henry, *A Critical Examination of Butler's Analogy*, London
1903: Whyte, Alexander, *Bishop Butler: an Appreciation with the Best Passages of his Writings selected and arranged*, Edinburgh

Other printed material

Ahlstrom, Sydney E., *A Religious History of the American People*, New Haven, CT, 1972
Anscombe, G. E. M., 'Modern Moral Philosophy', in *Ethics, Politics and Religion*, Oxford, 1981
Aquinas, Thomas, *Selected Writings*, trans. Robert P. Goodwin, Indianapolis, IN, 1965
Aristotle, *The Complete Works*, ed. Jonathan Barnes, two volumes, Princeton, NJ, 1984
Arnold, Matthew, 'Bishop Butler and the *Zeit-Geist*', in *Last Essays on Church and Religion*, London, 1877
Audi, Robert, *The Good in the Right: A Theory of Intuition and Intrinsic Value*, Princeton, NJ, 2004
Austin-Jones, *Butler's Moral Philosophy*, Harmondsworth, 1951
Baker, Frank, 'John Wesley and Bishop Joseph Butler: A Fragment of John Wesley's Manuscript Journal 16th to 24th August 1739', *Proceedings of the Wesley Historical Society*, vol. XLII (May 1980), pp. 93–100
Baker, Frank, *John Wesley and the Church of England*, 2nd edn, London, 2000
Bamborough, Renford, *Moral Scepticism and Moral Knowledge*, London, 1979
Barker, J. C., *The Education of the poor, a religious duty [Matt. 25.40]*, Grenada, 1828
Barnard, Toby, *A New Anatomy of Ireland: The Irish Protestants, 1649–1770*, New Haven, CT, 2003
Barnes, Albert, *Butler's Analogy: A Review*, London, [1860]

Bartlett, Thomas, *Memoirs of the life, character and writings of Joseph Butler*, London, 1839

Baum, Eric B., *What Is Thought?*, Cambridge, MA, 2004

Baxter, Donald L. M., 'Identity in the Loose and Popular Sense', *Mind*, NS, vol. 97, no. 388 (October 1988), pp. 575–82

Beddard, Robert, ed., *The Revolutions of 1688*, Oxford, 1991

Beer, Gillian, *Darwin's Plots: Evolutionary Narrative in Darwin, George Eliot and Nineteenth-century Fiction*, London, 1983

Benson, Christopher, *The first and second verses of the Book of Genesis examined*, London, 1861

Biographia Britannia, ed. Thomas Wright, London, 1846

Bosworth, F., *England and Missions: Being the Sermon preached before the Baptist Missionary Society ... April 25, 1860*, London, 1860

Branch, Lori, *Rituals of Spontaneity: Sentiment and Secularism from Free Prayer to Wordsworth*, Waco, TX, 2006

Branch, Lori, 'Bishop Butler', in *Oxford Handbook of English Literature and Theology*, ed. Andrew Hass, David Jasper and Elisabeth Jay, Oxford, 2007, pp. 590–606

Bray, Gerald, ed., *The Anglican Canons 1529–1947*, Woodbridge, 1998

Brewer, Sandy, 'From Darkest England to *The Hope of the World*: Protestant Pedagogy and the Visual Culture of the London Missionary Society', *Material Religion*, vol. 1, no. 1 (2005), pp. 98–124

Brinton, Alan, '"Following Nature" in Butler's Sermons', *Philosophical Quarterly*, vol. 41, no. 164 (July 1991), pp. 325–32

Broad, C. D., *Five Types of Ethical Theory*, London, 1930

Broughton, Janet, *Descartes's Method of Doubt*, Princeton, NJ, 2002

Buchanan, Claudius, *Two Discourses preached before the University of Cambridge, on Commencement Sunday, July 1st, 1810 [Gen. 1.3], and a Sermon preached before the [CMS] ..., June 12, 1810 [Matt. 5.14]. To which are added, Christian researches in Asia*, London, 1812

Campbell, Archibald, *Harmony of Revelation and the Sciences. Address delivered to the Members of the Edinburgh Philosophical Institution, November 4, 1864*, Edinburgh, 1864

Cambridge Prize Poems ... 1750–1806, 2 volumes, Cambridge, 1817

Caplan, Harry and Henry H. King, 'Pulpit Eloquence: A List of Doctrinal and Historical Studies in English', *Speech Monographs*, vol. XXII, no. 4 (Special Issue, 1955)

Carlsson, P. Allan, *Butler's Ethics*, The Hague, 1964

Castells, Manuel, *The Information Age: Economy, Society, and Culture*, Oxford, 1996–2000

Certain Sermons or Homilies [and] The Constitutions and Canons Ecclesiastical, to which are added the Thirty-nine Articles of the Church of England, London, SPCK, 1890

Chalmers, Thomas, *Prelections on Butler's Analogy, Posthumous Works*, ed. William Hanna, volume 9, Edinburgh, 1849

Chambers's Miscellany of Useful and Entertaining Tracts, four volumes, Edinburgh, 1845

Choisy, F. T. de, *Journal du voyage de Siam fait en M.DC.LXXXV. et M.DC.XXXVI*, Paris, S. Mabre-Cramoisy, 1687

The Christian Examiner, and Church of Ireland Magazine, Dublin, October 1837

Cicero, Marcus Tullius, *De natura deorum: Academica*, trans. H. Rackham, London, 1933

Claydon, Tony, 'The Sermon, the "Public Sphere" and the Political Culture of Late Seventeenth-century England', in *The English Sermon Revised*, ed. Lori Anne Ferrell and Peter McCullough, Manchester, 2000

The Clergyman's Assistant; or, a Collection of Acts of Parliament, Forms and Ordinances, relative to Certain Duties and Rights of the Parochial Clergy, Oxford, 1806

Coleridge, S. T., *Lectures 1795 on Politics and Religion*, ed. Lewis Patton and Peter Mann, London, 1971

Coleridge, S. T., *A Lay Sermon*, ed. R. J. White, London, 1972

Collingwood, R. G., *Philosophical Method* (1933), reprint Oxford, 2005

Collis, Jeffrey R., *The Allegiance of Thomas Hobbes*, Oxford, 2005

Cuneo, Terence and René van Woudenberg, *The Cambridge Companion to Thomas Reid*, Cambridge, 2004

Cunliffe, Christopher, ed., *Joseph Butler's Moral and Religious Thought: Tercentenary Essays*, Oxford, 1992

Cunliffe, Christopher, 'Joseph Butler', *ODNB*, Oxford, 2004

Dallimore, Arnold A., *George Whitefield*, two volumes, London, 1970

Damasio, Antonio R., *Descartes' Error: Emotion, Reason, and the Human Brain*, New York, 1994

Darwall, Stephen, *The British Moralists and the Internal 'Ought', 1640–1740*, Cambridge, 1995

Darwall, Stephen, 'Sympathetic Liberalism: Recent Work on Adam Smith', *Philosophy and Public Affairs*, vol. 28, no. 2 (spring 1999), pp. 139–64

Darwin, Charles, *The Origin of Species* (1859), 2nd edn, London, 1860

Dawkins, Richard, *The Selfish Gene*, Oxford, 1976

Day, J. P., 'Compensatory Discrimination', *Philosophy*, vol. 56, no. 215 (January 1981), pp. 55–72

Deakin, Simon and Frank Wilkinson, *The Law of the Labour Market: Industrialization, Employment and Legal Evolution*, Oxford, 2005

Deane-Drummond, Celia E., *Creation Through Wisdom: Theology and the New Biology*, Edinburgh, 2000

Des Chene, Dennis, *Physiologia: Natural Philosophy in Late Aristotelian and Cartesian Thought* (1996), reprint Ithaca, NY, 2000

Dillon, Robin S., 'Self-Forgiveness and Self-Respect', *Ethics*, vol. 112, no. 1. (October 2001), pp. 53–83

Downey, James, *The Eighteenth Century Pulpit*, Oxford, 1969

Drew, Philip, 'Jane Austen and Bishop Butler', *Nineteenth-Century Fiction*, vol. 35, no. 2 (September 1980), pp. 127–49

Drummond, Henry, *Natural Law in the Spiritual World*, London, 1883

Duncan-Jones, Austin, *Butler's Moral Philosophy*, Harmondsworth, 1951

Eckardt, Bettina von, *Ethik der Selbstliebe: Joseph Butlers Theorie der menschliche Natur*, Heidelberg, 1980

Egglestone, William Morris, *Stanhope Memorials of Bishop Butler*, London, 1878

Elliott-Binns, L. E., *English Thought 1860–1900: The Theological Aspect*, London, 1956

Estlund, David M., 'Mutual Benevolence and the Theory of Happiness', *The Journal of Philosophy*, vol. 87, no. 4 (April 1990), pp. 187–204

European Magazine, volume 41, London, J. Sewell, 1802

Fischer, Steven Roger, *A History of Reading*, London, 2003

Francis, Keith, 'Nineteenth-Century British Sermons on Evolution and *The Origin Of Species*: The Dog That Didn't Bark?', in *A New History of the Nineteenth-Century Sermon*, ed. Robert E. Ellison, New York, 2010

Galloway, George, *The Philosophy of Religion*, Edinburgh, 1914

Gibson, William, *The Church of England 1688–1832: Unity and Accord*, London, 2001

Gibson, William, *Enlightenment Prelate: Benjamin Hoadly 1676–1761*, Cambridge, 2004

Gibson, William, 'William Talbot and Church Parties', *Journal of Ecclesiastical History*, vol. 58, no. 1 (January 2007), pp. 26–48

Gibson, William, *James II and the Trial of the Seven Bishops*, London, 2009

Gladstone, William Ewart, *Studies Subsidiary to the Works of Bishop Butler*, Oxford, 1896

Golinski, Jan, *Science and Public Culture: Chemistry and Enlightenment in Britain, 1760–1820*, Cambridge, 1992

Goodpaster, Kenneth E., 'Kohlbergian Theory: A Philosophical Counterinvitation', *Ethics*, vol. 92, no. 3 (April 1982), pp. 491–8

Gould, Stephen Jay, *Rocks of Ages: Science and Religion in the Fullness of Life*, London, 2001

Grattan-Guinness, I., ed., *Companion Encyclopedia of the History and Philosophy of the Mathematical Sciences*, 2 volumes, Baltimore, MD, 1994

Grinfield, E. W., *The Force of Contrast [between BFBS & SPCK] [1 Thessalonians 5.21]*, Bath, 1812

Gullberg, Jan, *Mathematics: From the Birth of Numbers*, New York, 1997

Habgood, John, *Being a Person: Where Faith and Science Meet*, London, 1998

Habgood, John, *Varieties of Unbelief*, London, 2000

Hallesby, O., *Conscience*, trans. C. J. Carlsen, London, 1950

Hampden, Renn Dickson, *The Scholastic Philosophy considered in its relation to Christian theology, in a course of lectures delivered before the University of Oxford, in the year MDCCCXXXII. At the lecture founded by John Bampton*, Oxford, 1833

Hanna, William, *Memoirs of the Life and Writings of Thomas Chalmers*, Edinburgh, 1850

Happel, Stephen, *Metaphors for God's Time in Science and Religion*, London, 2002

Hardin, Russell, *David Hume: Moral and Political Theorist*, Oxford, 2007

Harris, James A., *Of Liberty and Necessity: The Free Will Debate in Eighteenth-Century British Philosophy*, Oxford, 2005

Haugen, Einar, *The Ecology of Language*, Stanford, CA, 1972

Hazlitt, William, *My First Acquaintance with Poets*, ed. Jonathan Wordsworth, Oxford, 1993

Henson, Richard G., 'Butler on Selfishness and Self-Love', *Philosophy and Phenomenological Research*, vol. 49, no. 1 (September 1988), pp. 31–57

Holmes, Andrew, *The Shaping of Ulster Presbyterian Belief and Practice 1770–1840*, Oxford, 2006

Horsley, Samuel, *The Charges of Samuel Horsley*, London, 1830

Howe, Daniel Walter, 'The Cambridge Platonists of Old England and the Cambridge Platonists of New England', *Church History*, vol. 57, no. 4 (December 1988), pp. 470–85

Hylson-Smith, Kenneth, *The Churches in England from Elizabeth I to Elizabeth II*, three volumes, London, 1997

Ibbetson, D. J., *A Historical Introduction to the Law of Obligations*, Oxford, 1999

Ingram, Robert G., *Religion, Reform and Modernity in the Eighteenth Century: Thomas Secker and the Church of England*, Woodbridge, 2007

Jacob, W. M., *The Clerical Profession in the Long Eighteenth Century*, Oxford, 2007

Jeffner, Anders, *Butler and Hume on Religion: A Comparative Analysis*, trans. Keith Bradfiel, Stockholm, 1966

Kahn-Freund, Otto, 'Blackstone's Neglected Child: The Contract of Employment', *Law Quarterly Review*, vol. 93 (1978), pp. 508–28

Kenny, Anthony, ed., *Aquinas: A Collection of Critical Essays*, London, 1969

Kenny, Anthony, *The Unknown God* (2004), London, 2005

Kiernan-Lewis, J. D., 'Review of *Divine Hiddenness and Human Reason* by J.L. Schellenberg', *The Journal of Religion*, vol. 75, no. 2 (April 1995), pp. 295–6

Kirschner, Suzanne R., *The Religious and Romantic Origins of Psychoanalysis*, Cambridge, 1996

Kohlberg, Lawrence, *The Philosophy of Moral Development: Moral Stages and the Idea of Justice*, San Francisco, CA, 1981

Korsgaard, Christine M., *The Sources of Normativity*, Cambridge, 1996

Leighton, C. D. A., 'William Law, Behmenism, and Counter Enlightenment', *Harvard Theological Review*, vol. 91, no. 3 (July 1998), pp. 301–20

Lightfoot, Joseph Barber, *Leaders in the Northern Church: sermons preached in the diocese of Durham*, London, 1890

Lloyd, G. E. R., *Polarity and Analogy: Two Types of Argumentation in Early Greek Thought* (1966), reprint Bristol, 1987

Lucas, J. R., *Butler's Philosophy of Religion Vindicated*, Durham, 1978

Macdonald, James, *A Free Nation Deep in Debt: The Financial Roots of Democracy*, New York, 2003

Macgregor, G. H. C., *The Gospel of John* (in the *Moffat New Testament Commentary*), London, 1928

Mackie, J. L., *Ethics: Inventing Right and Wrong* (1977), reprint London, 1990

Macmurray, John, *The Self as Agent*, London, 1957

Macquarrie, John, *Christian Hope*, London, 1978

Mansel, Henry Longueville, *The Limits of Demonstrative Science Considered. In a Letter to Dr. Whewell*, Oxford, 1853

Mansel, Henry Longueville, *Psychology the Test of Moral and Metaphysical Philosophy*, Oxford, 1855

Mansel, Henry Longueville, *The Limits of Religious Thought Examined*, Oxford, 1858

Marshall, William M., *George Hooper 1640–1727 Bishop of Bath and Wells*, Sherborne, 1976

Maurice, F. D., *The Conflict of Good and Evil in Our Day: Twelve Letters to a Missionary*, London, 1865

Maurice, F. D., *What is Revelation?*, Cambridge, 1859

Maurice, F. D., *Modern Philosophy*, London, 1862

McLaverty, James, 'Warburton's False Comma: Reason and Virtue in Pope's "Essay on Man"', *Modern Philology*, vol. 99, no. 3 (February 2002), pp. 379–92

Mill, John Stuart, *A System of Logic, Ratiocinative and Inductive*, ed. J. M. Robson and R. F. McRae (1973), Indianapolis, IN, 2006

Mill, John Stuart, *On Liberty and Other Essays*, ed. John Gray, Oxford, 1991

Mill, John Stuart, 'Whewell on Moral Philosophy', in John Stuart Mill and Jeremy Bentham, *Utilitarianism and Other Essays*, ed. Alan Ryan, London, 1987

Millar, Alan, 'Following Nature', *Philosophical Quarterly*, vol. 38, no. 151 (April 1988), pp. 165–85

Millar, Alan, 'Reply to Brinton', *Philosophical Quarterly*, vol. 42, no. 169 (October 1992), pp. 486–91

Miller, John, *James II: A Study in Kingship*, London, 1978

Money, D. K., *The English Horace*, Oxford, 1998

Moore, G. E., *Principia Ethica*, Cambridge, 1903

Morehead, Charles, ed., *Memoirs of the Life and Writings of the Rev. Robert Morehead*, Edinburgh, 1875

Morehead, Robert, *A Series of Discourses, on the Principles of Religious Belief, as Connected with Human Happiness and Improvement*, Edinburgh, first volume 1809, second volume ('third edition') 1816

Morehead, Robert, *Protestantism its own Protection [Ephesians 6.10]*, Edinburgh, 1829

Morehead, Robert, *Dialogues on Natural and Revealed Religion*, Edinburgh, 1830

Morehead, Robert, *A Farewell Sermon, preached in St Paul's Chapel, York Place, Edinburgh, On the 11th Day of November 1832 [1 John 2.13]*, Edinburgh and London, 1832

Morgan, David, *Protestants and Pictures: Religion, Visual Culture, and the Age of American Mass Production*, Oxford, 1999

Morton, Bradley, ed., *Images of Empiricism*, Oxford, 2007

Mossner, Ernest Campbell, 'Coleridge and Bishop Butler', *The Philosophical Review*, vol. 45, no. 2 (March 1936), pp. 206–08

Mossner, Ernest Campbell, *Bishop Butler and the Age of Reason*, New York, 1936

Mount, C. M., *The Apostolic Labour of a Church-of-England Association [Galatians 6.10]*, Bath, J. Upham, 1822

Muehlmann, Robert G., *Berkeley's Ontology*, Indianapolis, IN, 1992

Nadler, Steven, ed., *The Cambridge Companion to Malebranche*, Cambridge, 2000

Nelson, William N., 'Mutual Benevolence and Happiness', *Journal of Philosophy*, vol. 91, no. 1 (January 1994), pp. 50–1

Newberry, Paul A., 'Joseph Butler on Forgiveness: A Presupposed Theory of Emotion', *Journal of the History of Ideas*, vol. 62, no. 2. (April 2001), pp. 233–44

Newman, J. H., *Fifteen Sermons Preached before the University of Oxford*, ed. James David Earnest and Gerard Tracey, Oxford, 2006

Newman, J. H., *An Essay in Aid of a Grammar of Assent* (1870), London, 1903

Nicholls, David, *God and Government in an 'Age of Reason'*, London, 1995

Novitz, David, 'Forgiveness and Self-Respect', *Philosophy and Phenomenological Research*, vol. 58, no. 2. (June 1998), pp. 299–315

Nuovo, Victor, *John Locke and Christianity: Contemporary Responses to the Reasonableness of Christianity*, Bristol, 1997

Overton, J. H., *The Church in England*, London, 1897

Padgett, Alan G., *Science and the Study of God: A Mutuality Model for Theology and Science*, Grand Rapids, MO, 2003

Pappas, George S., *Berkeley's Thought*, Ithaca, NY, 2000

Passmore, Joseph C., *Bishop Butler's Ethical Discourses; to which are Added some Remains, hitherto Unpublished. Prepared as a Text Book in Moral Philosophy; with a Syllabus, by Dr. Whewell. Edited, with an Introductory Essay on the Author's Life and Writings*, Philadelphia, PA, 1855

Pattison, Mark, 'Tendencies of Religious Thought in England, 1688–1750', in *Essays and Reviews*, London, 1860

Pattison, Robert, *The Great Dissent: John Henry Newman and the Liberal Heresy*, New York, 1991

Penelhum, Terence, *Butler*, London, 1985

Penelhum, Terence, 'Butler and Hume', *Hume Studies*, vol. 14 (1988), pp. 251–76

Pereiro, James, *'Ethos' and the Oxford Movement: At the Heart of Tractarianism*, Oxford, 2008

Pfizenmaier, Thomas C., *The Trinitarian Theology of Dr. Samuel Clarke (1675–1729): Context, Sources, and Controversy*, Leiden, 1997

Pfizenmaier, Thomas C., 'Why the Third Fell Out: Trinitarian Dissent', in *Religion, Politics and Dissent, 1660–1832*, ed. Robert D. Cornwall and William Gibson, London, 2009

Phillips, David, 'Butler and the Nature of Self-Interest', *Philosophy and Phenomenological Research*, vol. 60, no. 2 (March 2000), pp. 421–38

Pincus, Steven, *1688: The First Modern Revolution*, New Haven, CT, 2009

Pinker, Steven, *The Language Instinct*, New York, 1994

Pinker, Steven, *The Stuff of Thought: Language as a Window into Human Nature*, New York, 2007

Plato, *The Dialogues*, ed. and trans. B. Jowett, five volumes, 3rd edn, Oxford, 1892

Prickett, Stephen, *Religion and Romanticism*, Cambridge, 1976

Prickett, Stephen, *Narrative, Religion and Science: Fundamentalism versus Irony, 1700–1999*, Cambridge, 2002

Prickett, Stephen, *Modernity and the Reinvention of Tradition*, Cambridge, 2009

Ramsey, Ian, *Religious Language*, London, 1957

Ramsey, Ian, *Joseph Butler ... Some Features of his Life and Thought*, London, 1969

Randall, Ian, *What a Friend We Have in Jesus: The Evangelical Tradition*, London, 2005

Rattenbury, J. E., *Wesley's Legacy to the World*, Epworth, 1928

Rawls, John, *A Theory of Justice*, Oxford, 1972

Reeves, Joan Wynn, *Body and Mind in Western Thought*, Harmondsworth, 1958

Richards, Graham, *Mental Machinery: The Origins and Consequences of Psychological Ideas. Part 1 1600–1850*, London, 1992

Rivers, Isabel, *Reason, Grace, and Sentiment*, two volumes, Cambridge, 1991, 2000

Roberts, T. A., *The Concept of Benevolence: Aspects of Eighteenth-Century Moral Philosophy*, London, 1973

Rodes, Robert E., Jr, *Law and Modernization in the Church of England: Charles II to the Welfare State*, Notre Dame, IN, 1991

Rodger, N. A. M., *The Command of the Ocean*, London, 2004

Rosenberg, Jay F., *Accessing Kant*, Oxford, 2005

Rule, John, *The Labouring Classes in Early Industrial England 1750–1850*, London, 1988

Ryle, Gilbert, *Dilemmas: The Tarner Lectures 1953*, London, 1954

Sandel, Michael, *Liberalism and the Limits of Justice*, Cambridge, 1982

Sandel, Michael, *Democracy's Discontent: America in Search of a Public Philosophy*, Cambridge, MA, 1996

Schellenberg, J. L., *Divine Hiddenness and Human Reason*, Ithaca, NY, 1993

Schilder, Florian von and Neil Tennant, *Philosophy, Evolution and Human Nature*, London, 1984

Schilpp, Paul Arthur, ed., *The Philosophy of C. D. Broad*, New York, 1959

Schmaltz, Tad M., *Malebranche's Theory of the Soul*, New York, 1996

Schramm, Jan-Melissa, *Testimony and Advocacy in Victorian Law*, Cambridge, 2000

Scotland, Nigel, *Squires in the Slums: Settlements and Missions in Late Victorian London*, London, 2007

Seeley, Sir J. R., *Ecce Homo*, 5th edn, London, [1866]

Seneca, *Letters from a Stoic*, trans. Robin Campbell, Harmondsworth, 1974

Shadwell, Charles Lancelot, *Registrum Orielense: An Account of the Members of Oriel College, Oxford*, two volumes, Oxford, 1902

Shoemaker, Sydney, 'Self and Substance', *Noûs*, vol. 31, Supplement: Philosophical Perspectives, 11, Mind, Causation, and World (1997), pp. 283–304

Shuler, Jon Christopher, 'The Pastoral and Ecclesiastical Administration of the Diocese of Durham 1721–1771; with Particular Reference to the Archdeaconry of Northumberland', unpublished PhD thesis, University of Durham, 1976

Sidgwick, Henry, *The Methods of Ethics* (1874), 7th edn, London, 1907 (reprint with introduction by John Rawls, Indianapolis, IN, 1981)

Sidgwick, Henry, *Outlines of the History of Ethics* (1886), 3rd edn, London, 1892

Sidgwick, Henry, *Philosophy: Its Scope and Relations*, London, 1902

Sober, Elliott, 'Hedonism and Butler's Stone', *Ethics*, vol. 103, no. 1 (October 1992), pp. 97–103

Spaulding, J. Gordon, *Pulpit Publications 1660–1783*, six volumes, New York, 1995

Spooner, W. A., *Bishop Butler*, London, Methuen, 1901

Steere, Edward, *An Essay on the Existence and Attributes of God*, London, 1856

Stevens, Laura, *The Poor Indians: British Missionaries, Native Americans, and Colonial Sensibility*, Philadelphia, PA, 2004

Stewart, M. A. and John P. Wright, ed., *Hume and Hume's Connexions*, University Park, PA, 1995

Strong, Rowan, *Anglicanism and the British Empire*, Oxford, 2007

Sumner, Charles Richard, *Sermon on the Death of Daniel Wilson [2 Kings 2.11–2]*, London, 1858

Sykes, Norman, 'Bishop Butler and the Church of his Age', *Durham University Journal*, NS, vol. XXI, no. I (December 1950), pp. 5–6

Talon, Henri, *Selections from the Journals and Papers of John Byrom*, London, 1950

Taylor, Charles, *The Sources of the Self: The Making of the Modern Identity*, Cambridge, MA, 1989

Taylor, Stephen, 'Whigs, Bishops and America: The Politics of Church Reform in Mid-eighteenth-century England', *The Historical Journal*, vol. 36, no. 2 (1993), pp. 331–56

Taylor, Stephen, Richard Connors and Clyve Jones, ed., *Hanoverian Britain and Empire: Essays in Memory of Philip Lawson*, Woodbridge, 1998

Tennant, Bob, 'Christopher Smart and *The Whole Duty of Man*', *Eighteenth-Century Studies*, vol. 13, no. 1 (1979), pp. 63–78

Tennant, Bob, 'The Anglican Response to Locke's Theory of Personal Identity', *Journal of the History of Ideas*, vol. 43, no. 1 (1982), pp. 73–90

Tennant, Bob, 'Sentiment, Politics, and Empire: A Study of Beilby Porteus's Anti-Slavery Sermon', in *Discourses of Slavery and Abolition*, ed. B. Carey, M. Ellis and S. Salih, London, 2004, pp. 158–74

Tennant, Bob, 'John Tillotson and the Voice of Anglicanism', in *Religion in the Age of Reason*, ed. Kathryn Duncan, New York, 2009, pp. 97–119

Tennant, Bob, 'On the Good Name of the Dead: Peace, Liberty and Empire in Robert Morehead's Waterloo Sermon', in *Religion in the Age of the Enlightenment*, Vol. 1, ed. Brett McInelly, New York, 2010, pp. 249–75

Tennant, Bob, 'Missions, Slavery, and the Anglican Pulpit, 1780–1850', in *A New History of the Nineteenth-Century Sermon*, ed. Robert E. Ellison, New York, 2010

Thomas, Hugh, *The Slave Trade*, New York, 1997

Toulmin, Stephen, *Reason in Ethics*, Cambridge, 1950

Toulmin, Stephen, *The Uses of Argument*, Cambridge, 1958

Tucker, H. W., *The Classified Digest of the Records of the Society for the Propagation of the Gospel in Foreign Parts 1701–1892*, London, 1893

Tyerman, Luke, *The Life of the Rev. George Whitefield*, London, 1876

Unger, Peter, *Consciousness and Value*, New York, 1990

van Fraassen, Bas C., *The Scientific Image*, Oxford, 1980

Venn, Henry, *Academical Studies Subservient to the Edification of the Church [1 Cor. 14:12]*, Cambridge, 1828

Wadell, P.J., 'Growing Together in the Divine Love: The Role of Charity in the Moral Theology of Thomas Aquinas', in *Aquinas and Empowerment*, ed. G. S. Harak, Washington, DC, 1996, pp. 148–63

Waismann, F., 'Language Strata', in *Language and Logic*, second series, ed. A. Flew, Oxford, 1966, pp. 11–31

Walker, William, *Locke, Literary Criticism, and Philosophy*, Cambridge, 1994

Weinreb, Ben, Christopher Hibbert *et al.*, *The London Encyclopaedia*, London, 2008

Welsh, Alexander, 'The Evidence of Things Not Seen: Justice Stephen and Bishop Butler', *Representations*, no. 22 (spring 1988), pp. 60–88

Welsh, Alexander, 'Burke and Bentham on the Narrative Potential of Circumstantial Evidence', *New Literary History*, vol. 21, no. 3 (spring 1990), pp. 607–27

Welsh, Alexander, *Strong Representations: Narrative and Circumstantial Evidence in England*, Baltimore, MD, 1992

Whewell, William, *Principles of an English University Education*, London, 1837

Whewell, William, *On the Foundations of Morals* (1837), 2nd edn, Cambridge, 1839

Whewell, William, *Elements of Morality*, London, 1846

White, Alan, 'Conscience and Self-Love in Butler's Sermons', *Philosophy*, vol. 27 no. 103 (October 1952), pp. 329–44

Wilkinson, Clive, *The British Navy and the State in the Eighteenth Century*, Woodbridge, 2004

Wilks, S. G., *Christian Missions an Enlightened Species of Charity*, London, 1819

Williams, Howard, *Kant's Critique of Hobbes: Sovereignty and Cosmopolitanism*, Cardiff, 2003

Winkler, Kenneth P., ed., *The Cambridge Companion to Berkeley*, Cambridge, 2005

Winnett, A. R., *Peter Browne: Provost, Bishop, Metaphysician*, London, 1974

Wright, Robert, *The Moral Animal* (1994), London, 1995

Yates, Nigel, *The Religious Condition of Ireland 1770–1850*, Oxford, 2006

Index

STUDIES IN MODERN BRITISH RELIGIOUS HISTORY

Previously published volumes in this series